dBASE III PLUS™

Programmer's Library

Related Titles

dBASE III PLUS™ Programmer's Reference Guide
Ed Jones

Managing with dBASE III®
Michael J. Clifford

Best Book of: dBASE II®/III®
Ken Knecht

Best Book of: Lotus® 1-2-3®, Second Edition
Alan Simpson

Best Book of: WordPerfect®
Vincent Alfieri

Macro Programming for 1-2-3®
Daniel N. Shaffer

Mastering WordStar®
Vincent Alfieri

Working with Microsoft® Works
John Campbell

Discovering MS-DOS®
Kate O'Day, The Waite Group

MS-DOS® Bible
Steven Simrin, The Waite Group

MS-DOS® Developer's Guide
John Angermeyer and Kevin Jaeger, The Waite Group

Tricks of the MS-DOS® Masters
John Angermeyer, Kevin Jaeger, Rich Fahringer, and Dan Shafer, The Waite Group

Microsoft® C Programming on the IBM®
Robert Lafore, The Waite Group

C Programmer's Guide to Serial Communications
Joe Campbell

C Primer Plus, Revised Edition
Mitchell Waite, Stephen Prata, and Donald Martin, The Waite Group

Advanced C Primer ++
Stephen Prata, The Waite Group

For the retailer nearest you, or to order directly from the publisher, call 800-428-SAMS. In Indiana, Alaska, and Hawaii call 317-298-5699.

dBASE III PLUS™ Programmer's Library

Joseph-David Carrabis

HOWARD W. SAMS & COMPANY
A Division of Macmillan, Inc.
4300 West 62nd Street
Indianapolis, Indiana 46268 USA

Companion diskettes containing all the code in this book are available from the author. An order form follows the index.

FIRST EDITION
SECOND PRINTING — 1987

International Standard Book Number: 0-672-22579-4
Library of Congress Catalog Card Number: 87-60536

Acquisitions Editor: *Greg Michael*
Copy and Production Editors: *Brown Editorial Service*
Interior Designer: *T. R. Emrick*
Cover Graphic: *Celeste Design*
Compositor: *Impressions, Inc.*

Printed in the United States of America

To Sandra, my sister, who took me for long rides
and listened to my dreams.

CONTENTS

PREFACE

I should start this preface by telling you what this book gives you:

A better understanding of how to code in dBASE III PLUS

A thorough set of dBASE III PLUS tools

Code that you can use in a variety of applications, not just those listed in this book

Code specific to applications

Explanations of how to code efficiently, with examples

This book is a code library. There isn't much text in it. I did that on purpose. The *raison d'être* for this book is to provide you, the reader/programmer/coder with something to make your life easier. I have given you a cornucopia of dBASE III PLUS code that you can use in just about any application you have. I do include four fully developed applications in the last four chapters of this book, but those are more instructive than informative.

The real meat of this book is in Chapters 3 and 5. The code that I give in those two chapters can be used in virtually any application without changes. That's right, you can use the code in virtually *any* application—medical and/or dental records keeping, fundraising work, sports records systems, small business management, inventory management, newspaper and/or magazine subscription systems, service and/or client systems, the list goes on—with few or no modifications.

How can code be used in so many applications?

Quite simple. I've played with the dBASEs and consulted for several years and have discovered a pattern. Your client tracking needs may be different from a trucking firm's, but the way an inventory system works is essentially the same, no matter what your individual needs are. This means the core of the work is always identical, only the reporting and displaying of that work is different. This holds true for every application.

That said, you'll notice a lot of repetition in the last four chapters of this book. The repetition comes from using the same kernels of code—what I show you in Chapters 3 and 5—to perform all the background tasks necessary for each application. As in the old "Dragnet" series, only the names have been changed to protect the innocent.

I also realize that I'm giving you a tremendous amount of code in this book. You may not want to run the risk of copying the code yourself. The Howard W. Sams people have provided an order card in the back of the book that you can use to purchase a two-disk set of all the code in this book.

I'd like to hear your comments about the book. Contact me through Sams, or leave messages for me on CompuServe at #76137,1300, Delphi for JESURAN, or on The Source at BEM948.

ACKNOWLEDGMENTS

No book is the effort of one person. Any editor will tell you so. In this case much appreciation to:

Scott Darling and Centronics Corporation for the PS 220 printer and ribbons.

Peter Robertson of The Shootists, Nashua, NH, for his patience, laughter, and back corner shot.

Michael Kaltschnee and Wendy of APG, Ltd. for the INSET software that produced the screen dumps used in this book.

Steve and Dan of White Mountain Computer, Nashua, NH for their help and consideration.

Madelyn Theodore, who gave me many moments of laughter.

The editorial crew at Sams, who were patient when deadlines got tight.

Lynn Brown and Michael Burditt of Brown Editorial Service for their endless typesetting codes in the program listings.

And, of course, my wife, Susan, who puts up with the child inside the man.

Joseph-David Carrabis

TRADEMARKS

COSMOS and Federal Express are registered trademarks of Federal Express Corporation.

DATA BASED FORUM is a trademark of Data Base Solutions.

dBASE II and dBASE III are registered trademarks, and dBASE III PLUS, dBASE PROGRAMMER'S UTILITIES, Developers' Release, and Framework II are trademarks of Ashton-Tate.

GURU and Knowledgman are trademarks of mdbs.

KeyWorks is a trademark of Alpha Software.

Lotus, Lotus 1-2-3, and Symphony are registered trademarks of Lotus Development Corp.

LSEARCH is a trademark of Thinker's Apprentice.

Multiplan is a registered trademark of Microsoft Corporation.

ProKey is a registered trademark of RoseSoft Corp.

Q&A is a registered trademark of Symantec Software.

REFLEX and SuperKey are registered trademarks of Borland International.

WordStar is a registered trademark of MicroPro Corporation.

P A R T

1

The Kernels

The first part of this book, composed of Chapters 1 to 5, is actually the more important of the two parts, although you probably purchased this book for Part 2. Part 2 is working code you can use in your application. Chapters 1 through 5 contain code you can use to build your applications.

People who are familiar with my other dBASE III and III PLUS books know I stress modular, kernel-oriented coding. *Kernels* are the smallest blocks of code necessary to get a specific task done. *Modular coding* means you break each programming project—whether it's keeping track of your household finances, handling a mailing list, or managing the accounting of a good sized office—into its component parts and code those parts first, then code the larger project using the pieces you coded separately. It's also an example of kernel style coding.

This part provides you with what I believe are all the kernels you'll need to develop some powerful application software. The second part shows you the code necessary to handle those applications, and how kernels and modular programming help you realize those applications.

CHAPTER

1

WHO CAN BENEFIT MOST FROM THIS BOOK?

There are basically three types of people who probably will buy this book. The first is new to the various versions of dBASE and feels the best way to learn the language is to see how someone else uses it. The second has been using III PLUS for a while and wants to learn more about its use and perhaps expand his or her programming ability. The third type has already been developing dBASE III PLUS applications and wants to build a code library. This chapter explains how this book might best be used by each type of reader.

THIS BOOK AND THE NEW USER

You are new to dBASE III PLUS and are interested in quickly developing code that you can use in your business. Welcome. We were all there at some point.

What can this book do for you? First, this book can get you working with III PLUS faster than most others. Why is that? You bought III PLUS to get a particular job done. Maybe you've been using it for a while and want to use its programming ability to automate what you've been doing by hand. You need code. Chances are you know that you can write a short program to mimic, step by step, what you've been doing interactively.

All well and good. But do you know the Law of Programming Inertia? Allow me to summarize: The more you program, the more you'll find that needs to be programmed. That is actually a corollary. The Law of Programming Inertia is "The more you program, the more you'll need to program."

This means you'll find other aspects of your business that need to be or can be handled better by software once you start programming your first project. In short, you'll go wild with the power of good software. It's easy to do. There is a certain visceral satisfaction that goes with getting these little electronic marvels to do exactly what we want when we want it done. Go ahead. Go wild.

But in that wildness, recognize some patterns. That is what I've done. This book provides you with the patterns around which you can build your applications. Much of this book emphasizes coding in kernels. Each kernel can be used to do one specific task. Each task can be applied to a wide variety of jobs.

This book emphasizes the efficient use of dBASE III PLUS and shows you how to minimize your coding time and maximize your code's usability. You'll learn why certain techniques are used in place of others and how/why/when certain applications demand unique solutions. All in all, you'll gain experience in your own III PLUS coding while developing an extensive library of working, transportable III PLUS code.

THIS BOOK AND LEARNING TO PROGRAM IN dBASE III PLUS

You are an experienced dBASE II or dBASE III programmer and are making the leap to III PLUS. Congratulations. That is how most III PLUS programmers started.

Is there a preference among the three products? Many programmers still get requests for 8-bit work; therefore, they still use dBASE II. (In all fairness, there are a number of other, more powerful 8-bit database management systems available. Most programmers let the application's objectives guide their selection.) But when allowed to run MS/PC-DOS machines, and when the environment allows, many programmers still go with III PLUS.

The reason is simple. III PLUS has a very C-like structure and has more power and capabilities than dBASE III. Always opt for the more powerful package—dBASE III plus—when you have the chance. III PLUS also allows programmers to include hooks for network use without jumping through hoops.

How will this book help you to rethink your applications in III PLUS? If you code like I do, you'll take with you a lot of dBASE II and dBASE III prejudices into your III PLUS work. There is nothing wrong with that. The theory and development of kernel programming started because dBASE II didn't allow much room in 64K CP/M and MP/M machines.

Much of what this book does in III PLUS will be recognizable to dBASE II and dBASE III programmers and can trace its roots to the time when the only computers available had 4K of memory. Programmers on those machines learned to pack a lot into a little, because they didn't have much room to begin with. Most of the III PLUS work in this book is similar to what you can do in dBASE II and dBASE III, but it makes use of the new features of dBASE III PLUS. You might want to think of the transition from II to III to III PLUS as expanding your vocabulary. You've become more literate as a programmer. Just as your vernacular matured with you, so have the versions of dBASE.

This book will show you how to code easily in III PLUS. Much of the code you'll need for your applications is here and ready for you to use without modification. You should be able to use this book's code and techniques to clean up your own code problems and develop applications. Once that's done you can begin applying these coding techniques to other aspects of your system. How so?

The Acknowledgments mention Madelyn Theodore. I came into her office one fine day, long before I started writing this book, and noticed a dBASE III screen display on her PC. I asked to play with it and immediately looked at the code. To start with, the original applications programmer had written some 93 files to handle the system's needs. That didn't include databases, index files, and so on. Those 93 files were program, format, and such. Whoosh!

I asked Madelyn whether I could borrow the system's files and recode them. "Please, do so!" The result, shown later in this book, is some 19 files that handle all the same functions as the original programmer's 93! The core PRG file is EDIT.PRG. That file handles 90 percent of all DBMS needs. All other files are for screen generation, reporting of one kind or another, or housekeeping.

How do you go from 93 files to 19? What's more, how do you do it in a day and a half? In this case, I had the other programmer's logic to guide me. That helped. The other programmer's logic was incredibly simple (not simplistic—there's a difference) and easy to follow. That's always a help. The other reason the coding only took a day and a half is because I had coded highly transportable kernels previously. These reusable packets of code have been dropped into every package or application I've worked on. Coding in this manner allows the developer to generate applications in far less time than it takes most people from scratch.

Now, some readers are saying, "Right, and you end up like a run-time library. You've got every little code packet in the world in your application even when you don't need it."

Au contraire. That would be a bit of a waste, wouldn't it? Chapter 3 emphasizes minimalism in coding. Never carry excess baggage with you; only take what you need. Granted, sometimes you can't be sure what you'll need. But you won't take an arctic parka on a trip to the Sahara.

THIS BOOK AND THE dBASE III PLUS APPLICATIONS PROGRAMMER

You are the person that's been programming for some time, either with some version of dBASE or some other high-level language. Chances are you program for a company or are an independent consultant. Both of you generate lots of code, but your needs are actually different.

My heart is with the independent consultant. You are the hired gun, the Pro from Dover, and the bane of every in-house system developer. Why? Because you come in and solve the problems that have been giving them headaches. Have you ever wondered why you can do that? Probably it's because you have seen such a wide variety of applications and problems that experience gives you the edge. I doubt there are any particularly gifted or brilliant programmers—I'm the exception, of course—but there are programmers with incredible experience. Your experience allows you to use code you developed for a biotechnology firm and apply it to a private cable company.

The shade under the rock: One of the problems with experienced consultants is that they're not always malleable about how to do things. They will often say or think, "This has worked a thousand times before so I'll use it again and it will work here." Right?

Wrong. You are too comfortable in your abilities and don't remember the time when you survived eating cream of catsup soup. Face each new programming task with a tool kit of kernels. Like a carpenter, use these tools to build your application from the lumber around you. Now, how many of you have done carpentry? Remember making your first miter box? Remember needing to make your first miter box?

So, like a good carpenter, use the tools in your kit to make new tools as they're needed. A similar example is using the same basic genetic code to make an incredible variety of life as seen on the planet.

This book will give you the same cachet of tools that I use. It will also give you a good look at how those tools are managed, mixed, matched, and—most important—improvised and modified for each application.

It is true that you can use the kernels developed here in any application unchanged. However, each application may use several different databases. Each different database might have some unique features that are best addressed by changes in the kernel. That either means you have a lot of kernels that overlap each other or a single block of code based on a kernel, but that now handles several different tasks for the same job.

Remember, survival is based on adaptability. Those who can't adapt, can't survive. Don't get so comfortable in your abilities that you can't see an innovation when inspiration strikes.

What about the in-house programmer? You've been developing dBASE applications for your company for some time and need to improve your efficiency. Can this book help you?

Most definitely. I mentioned analyzing an existing system and recoding it in less than two days. The secret to that speed is what you'll learn in this book. You can code fast and be sloppy. You can also code fast and be impressive, provided you use previously proven code. As an in-house developer, you see a variety of small applications each week. The garage needs an inventory system for vehicle parts, the mechanics need something for vehicle maintenance, shipping needs a loryman program—and we haven't touched on the more generic accounting needs.

The company's program needs grow as the company does. Not only do you have more applications to write, you need to make sure each application can talk to each other application.

Actually, this doesn't present as much of a coding problem as you might think. The solution is to code as is demonstrated in this book. Start with several small, reusable packages of code. Don't code each new application from scratch. Look through your tool kit and see what tools you can use just as they are, what tools need slight modifications, and so on. Eventually you'll see what new tools have to be designed and can then add those to your tool kit, ready for the next application.

This method of coding naturally speeds up development. It also has the advantage of making each application transportable to several environments. Because the code for all of them is so similar, you can make sure each application can communicate with the other applications with minimal effort.

CHAPTER

2

WHAT IS A LIBRARY?

Throughout this book emphasis will be on two basic principles in writing code and developing applications. Those two principles are coding in kernels and keeping those kernels in libraries. Kernels are introduced and discussed in Chapter 3 and again in Chapter 5. This chapter serves as an introduction to maintaining code libraries.

The best example of a library can be seen in a TREE listing of a disk directory, shown in Figure 2–1.

Most people create directories and subdirectories along some logical scheme. Figure 2–1 shows a DB3 (dBASE III PLUS) directory with subdirectories for CTOOLS, BIN, PROGRAMM, and UTILITY. Each of these subdirectories holds a group of files that each fall into one of the four categories given by the name of the individual subdirectory. This same logic holds with the FW and CLIPPER directories. In other words, each subdirectory is a library of files corresponding to and related to the name of the different subdirectories.

Now consider the TREE hierarchy in Figure 2–2, which displays dBASE directories and subdirectories. This TREE listing was made from a disk that holds my III PLUS libraries. Note that it follows a certain logic in creating directories, subdirectories, and so on. You want to create directories of major DBMS needs with this DOS command. Some of those directories have subdirectories that hold III PLUS files necessary for specific types of DBMS work. The ACCOUNTING directory holds subdirectories for all accounting needs. One of those subdirectories is the INVENTORY directory. This subdirectory holds III PLUS files for all types of inventory system work you've encountered while consulting. The directory itself is broken down into files used for single warehouse systems, multiple warehouse systems, shipping, and receiving.

Each of these disk areas holds files. These files are ones written before but used repeatedly. They form a reference shelf of reusable, transportable code. The reference shelf is your library. When you need some code for an inventory system with a single warehouse you can get files from the \ACCOUNTI\INVENTOR\1HOUSE directory. When you need a system for a company with several warehouses—some of which act as customer warehouses and others as company warehouses—you can get III PLUS files from all the INVENTORY subdirectories

```
Path: \CLIPPER

Subdirectories:  DBPC
                 OBJ


Path: \CLIPPER\DBPC

Subdirectories:  None


Path: \CLIPPER\OBJ

Subdirectories:  None


Path: \DB3

Subdirectories:  BIN
                 CTOOLS
                 PROGRAMM
                 UTILITY


Path: \DB3\BIN

Subdirectories:  None


Path: \DB3\CTOOLS

Subdirectories:  AZTEC
                 DBDIR
                 LATTICE


Path: \DB3\CTOOLS\AZTEC

Subdirectories:  None


Path: \DB3\CTOOLS\DBDIR

Subdirectories:  None
```

Figure 2-1 This TREE listing of a disk directory is an example of a library.

```
Path: \DB3\CTOOLS\LATTICE

Subdirectories:  None


Path: \DB3\PROGRAMM

Subdirectories:  None


Path: \DB3\UTILITY

Subdirectories:  None


Path: \EDIT

Subdirectories:  None


Path: \FW

Subdirectories:  CORRESPO
                 FICTION
                 PROGRAMM
                 SEARCH


Path: \FW\CORRESPO

Subdirectories:  None


Path: \FW\FICTION

Subdirectories:  None


Path: \FW\PROGRAMM

Subdirectories:  None
```

Figure 2–1 (cont.)

```
Path: \FW\SEARCH

Subdirectories:  None


Path: \LIBRARY

Subdirectories:  None


Path: \NORTON

Subdirectories:  None


Path: \UTILITY

Subdirectories:  None


Path: \WFAL

Subdirectories:  None
```

Figure 2–1 (cont.)

and match and modify them as necessary. Modified files go back into the library, complete with documentation, should you need them for some other project down the road.

There's one point you should know before getting into the chapter. It might be unethical to sell an application written specifically for one group to another group unless you retain copyright and marketing privileges rather than assigning them to the client. There is no copyright infringement if you use code and coding *techniques* repeatedly, but not fully developed applications.

FLOWCHARTING AND SYSTEM DESIGN

Creating Flowcharts

Whether your next application is your first attempt at coding or your millionth, you'll use a flowchart before you begin writing any code. You may flowchart in your head. You may use a ream of paper to write down your flowchart. Why is a flowchart so important?

```
B:\>TREE

DIRECTORY PATH LISTING

Path: \EDIT

Subdirectories:  MULTIDBF
                 MULTINDX
                 MULTIFMT


Path: \EDIT\MULTIDBF

Subdirectories:  None


Path: \EDIT\MULTINDX

Subdirectories:  None


Path: \EDIT\MULTIFMT

Subdirectories:  None


Path: \SUBSCRIB

Subdirectories:  None


Path: \REPORTS

Subdirectories:  None


Path: \SCHEDULI

Subdirectories:  None
```

Figure 2–2 This TREE hierarchy shows libraries of dBASE code in the directories and subdirectories.

```
Path: \SERVICE

Subdirectories:  JOBCOST


Path: \SERVICE\JOBCOST

Subdirectories:  None


Path: \ACCOUNTI

Subdirectories:  INVENTOR
                 PAYROLL
                 AR
                 AP
                 GENJOUR
                 GENLEDG
                 JOBCOST
                 ORDERTRA


Path: \ACCOUNTI\INVENTOR

Subdirectories:  1HOUSE
                 MANYHOUS
                 SHIPPING
                 RECEIVIN


Path: \ACCOUNTI\INVENTOR\1HOUSE

Subdirectories:  None


Path: \ACCOUNTI\INVENTOR\MANYHOUS

Subdirectories:  None


Path: \ACCOUNTI\INVENTOR\SHIPPING

Subdirectories:  None
```

Figure 2–2 (cont.)

```
Path: \ACCOUNTI\INVENTOR\RECEIVIN

Subdirectories:  None


Path: \ACCOUNTI\PAYROLL

Subdirectories:  None


Path: \ACCOUNTI\AR

Subdirectories:  PRFTCNTR
                 LATE


Path: \ACCOUNTI\AR\PRFTCNTR

Subdirectories:  None


Path: \ACCOUNTI\AR\LATE

Subdirectories:  None


Path: \ACCOUNTI\AP

Subdirectories:  1BUSINES
                 MANYBUS


Path: \ACCOUNTI\AP\1BUSINES

Subdirectories:  None


Path: \ACCOUNTI\AP\MANYBUS

Subdirectories:  None
```

Figure 2–2 (cont.)

```
Path: \ACCOUNTI\GENJOUR

Subdirectories:  None


Path: \ACCOUNTI\GENLEDG

Subdirectories:  None


Path: \ACCOUNTI\JOBCOST

Subdirectories:  None


Path: \ACCOUNTI\ORDERTRA

Subdirectories:  None


Path: \CLIENT

Subdirectories:  PROSPECT


Path: \CLIENT\PROSPECT

Subdirectories:  None


Path: \MAILING

Subdirectories:  LETTERGE
                 LABELGEN


Path: \MAILING\LETTERGE

Subdirectories:  None


Path: \MAILING\LABELGEN

Subdirectories:  None
```

Figure 2–2 (cont.)

A *flowchart* is the roadmap of the application, telling you where you have to go and how you must get there. For an analogy of why flowcharts are useful, imagine driving to someplace you've never been. It may be a party at a friend's house, a new client's office, or a vacation spot. If you've never been there before you'll need a roadmap to find your way, even if that roadmap is nothing more than hazily remembered instructions heard on the phone.

The map shows you how to achieve your goal, and there is a chance you'll get lost without it. I take lots of drives, and traveling partners have asked me more than once if we were lost. My standard reply has been: "No, I was lost once and this place doesn't look anything like it."

The flowchart is the roadmap of an application. You may encounter a side road with some interesting or intriguing scenery, but, if you're being paid by the hour or have a deadline to meet, you shouldn't let yourself get sidetracked. You can always note where and how you got to that interesting spot and investigate it later when the pressure is off.

How do we design flowcharts? Begin at the top and work down. Let's use a magazine subscription company as an example. Its primary concern is managing subscriber lists. A close second concern is making sure each subscriber has a payment record and is paying. This company's managers haven't mentioned any accounting needs, any mailing needs, and so on, for development. These other concerns may come later, and usually they do. Right now we are concerned with their two major concerns: managing the subscriber and payment records.

What does this company want to do with subscribers?

1. Add/edit/view the subscriber records.
2. Generate reports based on subscriber activity.
3. Generate mailing labels for subscribers.
4. Make sure that there is a payment record for each subscriber.

What does the company want to do with payment records?

1. Add/edit/view the payment records.
2. Generate reports based on the payment records.
3. Generate late payment letters based on the payment records.

That's it. That is the most concise listing of their desires. Note the fourth payment record item of the first list. This need is an extremely important one. (Anecdote: One particular client didn't specify this need when I was contracted to write the system. However, experience told me it was a useful feature, and I'd previously developed the kernels to do it, so I included the option. I demonstrated this part of the application and floored the client with the results: nearly 5 percent of subscribers had no payment record. Some of those clients had been receiving service for a year, without making one payment! It is nice to prove your worth with little things like that.)

The flowchart's contents are growing. You can break down payment records option 2 by reporting on late payments and on-time payments. You can further break down all reporting options by listing reports for each area of service (this could be street, city, state, and so on. It depends on the geographical or demographic size of a company's service area.)

So, this flowchart is really a list of what needs to be done. Some people create flowcharts that have little geometric shapes and arrows. Those are useful, but some programmers prefer to create flowcharts that resemble outlines. Another advantage to the outline style flowchart is that most people learned how to make outlines in school, but few people know how to make a proper flowchart. (What is a proper flowchart? It is one that works for you, of course. Yours can't be good because it doesn't follow the standard rules everybody else's follows? Have you ever heard of Feynman Diagrams? 'Nuff said.)

Make your flowcharts so that you can follow them. The heck with whether anyone else can follow them. This book shares with you how I flowchart and explains why this method was chosen over others. You can feel free to use this method or develop your own.

The subscription company's wants list becomes the following outline style flowchart shown in Figure 2–3.

The outline form is useful because it gives a good handle on the levels you'll have to code and allows you to see each separate task as it relates to each separate job. For example, Job 1 is the subscriber system. That system has four separate tasks involved. Each separate task is a job with its own tasks. Breaking the project down this way also allows you to see any duplication of effort. Both top-level jobs need an editing system. It is easier to use a single editing system and switch databases than it is to switch between two complete editing systems. Notice that we look for *conditions* on the data when we generate reports. It is easier to get a condition and apply it to all reports than to get the same condition repeatedly for several reports.

The outline method of flowcharting also gives you a better idea of how steps are linked together. The subscriber system flowchart tells you that to get from reporting by condition on all the subscriber records to editing the payment records involves moving through four levels of the program:

I.B.1.a. → I.B.1. → [I.B. → (I. → II.)] → II.A.

Looking at the flowchart as an outline gives you the flexibility to easily design an alternative. Figure 2–4 is a much simpler flowchart because items are grouped by task. This outline cuts down on the levels necessary to code and can be used for the system design.

System Design from Flowcharts

System design is the process of going from the flowchart to the finished product. Just as you take the roadmap when you go on a trip because you may encounter detours, system design follows flowcharting and completes the process of combining the kernels to arrive at the application. In that sense, you can think of the kernels as building blocks and the application as a finished building. The system design is the architect's rendition of the blueprint the construction supervisor

I. Subscriber System
  A. Edit Subscriber Records
  B. Report Generator
    1. Report for all Records
      a. Report by Condition
    2. Report by Area
      a. Report by Condition
  C. Label Generator
    1. Labels for all Records
      a. Labels by Condition
    2. Labels by Area
      a. Labels by Condition
  D. Match Subscribers to Payments
II. Payment System
  A. Edit Payment Records
  B. Report Generator
    1. All Records
      a. All Late Records
        i. All Late Records by Condition
      b. All Records by Condition
    2. Records by Area
      a. Late Records by Area
        i. Late Records by Area and Condition
      b. Records by Area and Condition
  C. Late Payment Letter Generator
    1. All Late Records
      a. All Late Records by Condition
    2. Late Records by Area
      a. Late Records by Area and Condition

Figure 2–3 This outline style flowchart maps how to develop a subscriber system.

used to construct the building. Sometimes both the flowchart and the system design fall short, but most times they don't.

The key to creating serviceable flowcharts and systems is getting all the information from the user at the start of the project and then keeping close ties with the client while the project is being developed.

RECOGNIZING TASKS

A central element to developing transportable code is recognizing tasks when you code. A *task* is a piece of work that is repeated, either within a given application or among several applications. An example from the preceding flowchart would

- I. Editing System
    - A. Subscriber Records
    - B. Payment Records
- II. Subscriber System
    - A. Report Generator
        1. Get Condition for Reports
        2. Report for all Areas
        3. Report by Area
    - B. Label Generator
        1. Get Condition for Labels
        2. Labels for all Areas
        3. Labels by Area
    - C. Match Payments to Subscribers
- III. Payment System
    - A. Report/Letter Generator
        1. Get Condition (Part of which can be Late Payments)
        2. All Records
        3. Records by Area

Figure 2–4 This flowchart groups items by task.

be placing conditions on reports. The need to conditionally perform a process is used several times in the flowchart.

That tells us that placing conditions on output is a transportable task. It is true that the actual code for placing conditions on reports and letters and whatever else is different, but it can't be *that* different from database to database. After all, we are always trying to do the same thing—place a condition on output.

Another task is editing a database. This is much more transportable, because you can use the editing kernel in many applications. You may only be able to use code that places conditions on processes in this one application, but you almost always need a process for editing databases in applications.

So, what coding procedures are required to prepare a task? A task is any repeating action in an application. Any repeating action, even if that action is repeated on several databases, can usually be handled by a single piece of code. Sometimes the code can be so generic that you can drop it into any application without making a single change. Other times the code needs to be modified slightly for differences in each database it will work with.

An example of the former is a bit of code to make a duplicate record of a database in the same database, shown in Listing 2–1:

Listing 2–1

```
** CODE TO COPY A SINGLE RECORD INTO THE SAME DATABASE
*
COPY NEXT 1 TO TANK
```

Listing 2–1 (cont.)

```
APPE FROM TANK
*
** EOF
```

Readers familiar with dBASE might wonder why I didn't write:

Listing 2–2

```
** NOT THE BEST CODE FOR DUPLICATING RECORDS IN A DATABASE
*
SET CARRY ON
APPEND
SET CARRY OFF
*
** EOF
```

as code to duplicate a record in a database. What is wrong with the second listing? The second listing forces the user to edit each record as it is appended. If nothing else, the user has to press CTRL-W (the dBASE key combination to tell dBASE III PLUS to save the record currently being edited) for each record as it is appended to the database. This is a lot to ask from the user and is unnecessary. We don't even know if the user *wants* to edit the duplicated records. All we know is the user wants to duplicate some records.

CODING FOR A TASK

Now that we can recognize tasks as independent of applications, how do we code for them? Part of coding has to do with knowing the language you're coding in. I've written several books on dBASE III and III PLUS, but I'm not so vain as to think I'm an expert on those languages. (Bertrand Russell said an expert is anyone that can spit over a boxcar. I won't tell you how wet the front of my shirt is.)

What I do know is how to code tasks and take those tasks with me where ever I go. Both of the databases in our editing flowchart require the ability to be edited. Part of editing is adding records to the database. A basic kernel to add data to a database is:

Listing 2–3

```
** CODE TO ADD RECORDS TO AN EXISTING DATABASE
*
COPY STRUC TO TANK
SELE 2
USE TANK
REPEATER = FIELD(1)
```

Listing 2–3 (cont.)

```
*
DO WHILE LEN(TRIM(&REPEATER)) <> 0
   APPE BLAN
   DO &GETTER
ENDD
*
DELE
USE
SELE 1
SET DELE ON
APPE FROM TANK
SET DELE OFF
DO &GETTER
CLEA GETS
*
** EOF
```

A full explanation for this code is given later in this book, but to summarize:

1. We copy the database's structure to a temporary file to ensure the integrity of the original file should anything happen.
2. Next we add new data to the temporary file.
3. When we're through adding new data, we copy the new records into the original database.

You can perform the same task with slightly less code, but this listing keeps a clean house. This code is serviceable for both the SUBSCRIBER and PAYMENTS databases shown in the previous flowchart. But you may remember the need to make sure each subscriber has a payment record. Is there something that can be done to this code so that a payment record can be added when a subscriber record is added? Yes, of course there is. And this brings us to the subject of libraries.

TASKS AND LIBRARIES

The code shown in Listing 2–3 can be called an Add kernel. It can be used in any application where data needs to be added to a single database at a time.

Any application.

Add can be used in so many applications that it should be placed in a special place—someplace where we can go get it whenever we need code to add data to a database. Do you remember the TREE directory of a dBASE library shown earlier? One part of that figure was a subdirectory called EDIT. What are the contents of that subdirectory? They're shown in Figure 2–5.

```
B:\EDIT>DIR

 Volume in drive B has no label
 Directory of  B:\EDIT

.            <DIR>       5-03-86   7:26
..           <DIR>       5-03-86   7:26
MULTIDBF     <DIR>       5-03-86   7:26
MULTINDX     <DIR>       5-03-86   7:27
MULTIFMT     <DIR>       5-03-86   7:27
EDIT     KNL       940   5-03-86   9:38
BACK     KNL       523   5-03-86   9:56
SKIP     KNL       523   5-03-86   9:56
GOTO     KNL       128  11-11-86  11:20
KILL     KNL       128  16-07-86   7:46
RSTR     KNL       128  27-06-86  10:05
QUIT     KNL       128   2-07-86  22:57
FIND     KNL       384  11-11-86  11:20
LOCA     KNL       142  11-06-85   6:45
CONT     KNL       128  27-06-86  10:05
DISP     KNL       369  21-01-85  15:00
COPY     KNL       940   5-03-86   9:38
ADD      KNL      1462  14-11-86   8:35
UPDA     KNL       523   5-03-86   9:56
EDIT     PRG      4992  30-05-86  20:57
        20 File(s)    309248 bytes free
```

Figure 2–5 This directory lists the editing kernels in the EDIT subdirectory.

Surprise, surprise. The directory is full of kernels of code (files with KNL extensions). All the tasks that have anything to do with editing a database are in that directory. That directory is a library of all the code to perform the megatask of editing.

The point here is that logically grouped tasks can be used to make libraries of code. These libraries can be constantly referenced as new applications arise. Previously coded kernels can then be modified for new situations. That is how the EDIT subdirectories—MULTIDBF, MULTINDX, and MULTIFMT—came about.

The previous section ended with the situation of an Add kernel that could handle two databases simultaneously. Specifically, we needed to add a record to a second database due to a record being added to one particular database.

We take our original Add kernel and modify it to the following:

Listing 2–4

```
** Add KERNEL FOR TWO MATCHED DATABASE SYSTEM
*
```

Listing 2–4 (cont.)

```
COPY STRUC TO TANK
SELE 6
USE TANK
REPEATER = FIELD(1)
*
IF db1$DBFILE
   SELE 2
   USE db2 INDE db2ndx1, db2ndx2
   COPY STRUC TO TANK2
   SELE 7
   USE TANK2
   SELE 6
ENDI
*
TRUTH = .T.
*
DO WHIL .T.
   APPE BLAN
   DO &GETTER
   READ
*
   IF LEN(TRIM(&REPEATER)) = 0
      DELE
      EXIT
   ENDI
*
   IF db1$DBFILE
      SELE 7
      CLEA
      APPE BLANK
      REPL common fields in db2 WITH fields in db1
      DO &SAYER2
      DO &GETTER2
      READ
      SELE 6
      CLEA
      DO &SAYER
   ENDI
*
ENDD
*
IF db1$DBFILE
   SELE 7
   USE
   SELE 2
```

Listing 2-4 (cont.)

```
   APPE FROM TANK2
   ERAS TANK2.DBF
ENDI
*
SELE 6
USE
SELE 1
SET DELE ON
APPE FROM TANK
SET DELE OFF
DO &GETTER
CLEA GETS
ERAS TANK.DBF
*
** EOF
```

You'll notice that our original Add kernel serves as the outer shell for this listing. The difference lies in making sure information can get into two databases in a single pass. Also note that the code only allows adding to two databases in a single pass when db1 is the primary database being used. There is no need to add a SUBSCRIBER record each time a PAYMENT record is added, but there is a definite need to ensure that a PAYMENT record is added each time a SUBSCRIBER record is added. Note further that the code, as written, can be transported to any similar two matched database editing systems.

HOW ARE LIBRARIES DESIGNED?

Good question, that. Libraries are designed according to needs, just as anything else is designed according to needs. You don't add an extra room to a house unless you have a need that can't be addressed by shuffling the existing rooms around.

This holds for designing libraries. Again, consider the EDIT directory. Remember that much of this code was originated in dBASE II and upgraded as the versions of dBASE matured. Because I don't like to keep too many databases open at a given time, I never designed systems that juggled several databases. Somewhere down the line, however, an application came along that was best solved using the SET LINKAGE ON/OFF command (a dBASE II command that you might consider the precursor to the dBASE III and III PLUS SET RELATION TO command). Suddenly there was a need for editing kernels that handled more than one open database at a time.

The wonderful files for single database use already existed. Was there much work involved in adding the necessary code for handling two databases simultaneously? No, hardly any. Ashton-Tate then introduced dBASE III and many programmers, myself included, wondered what to do.

The dBASE III package came with dCONVERT, a utility that translated dBASE II files into dBASE III files. dCONVERT was nice, but didn't produce code that was as workable as what experienced programmers could produce. Again, need forced me to design editing kernels. dBASE III also allowed one to feel safe keeping more than one database open at a time. The multiple file kernels were recoded and placed in the subdirectories MULTIDBF, MULTINDX, and MULTIFMT.

Many programmers realize they work more in certain areas than in others. For example, I seem to specialize in text management systems rather than number management systems. This specialization has produced some unique seek and seizure algorithms, shown later in this book.

The point is that libraries design themselves around the programmer's specialties. This book will provide you with a good number of kernels to start your library. A strong recommendation is to modify these kernels and keep your modifications handy. You'll use them again and again, and there is certainly no point in recoding them each time the need arises.

HOW ARE LIBRARIES USED?

You know now about tasks and libraries. This chapter concludes with a discussion of how libraries are put into service.

Earlier it was mentioned that a certain system was developed in less than two days. Part of that speed was due to having the previous programmer's logic as a trail guide. That similar logic can show what the original designer wanted to do with each database, how the databases were linked, what kinds of things the developer looked for in each database, and so on. That leads to creating a flowchart that the new programmer can use to get an idea of how the system is supposed to be designed.

Next, the new programmer can compare the flowchart and with his or her code libraries. Does any existing code fit the needs? The example mentioned earlier and shown in Figure 2–4 produced the matches shown in Figure 2–6.

No, I didn't pop kernels (oh, I'm sorry, I couldn't help myself) into a PRG file and run databases through it. How is this code-to-task matching done?

1. Look at each kernel that you feel will do the job.
2. Evaluate it.
3. Use it as is if that was all that was necessary.
4. Modify it accordingly, if that's necessary.
5. Run test databases through the finished PRG files.
6. Debug the code and add new code (which then goes into the appropriate libraries).
7. Take the product to the client. The client will have some changes, which are usually cosmetic and easily accommodated.

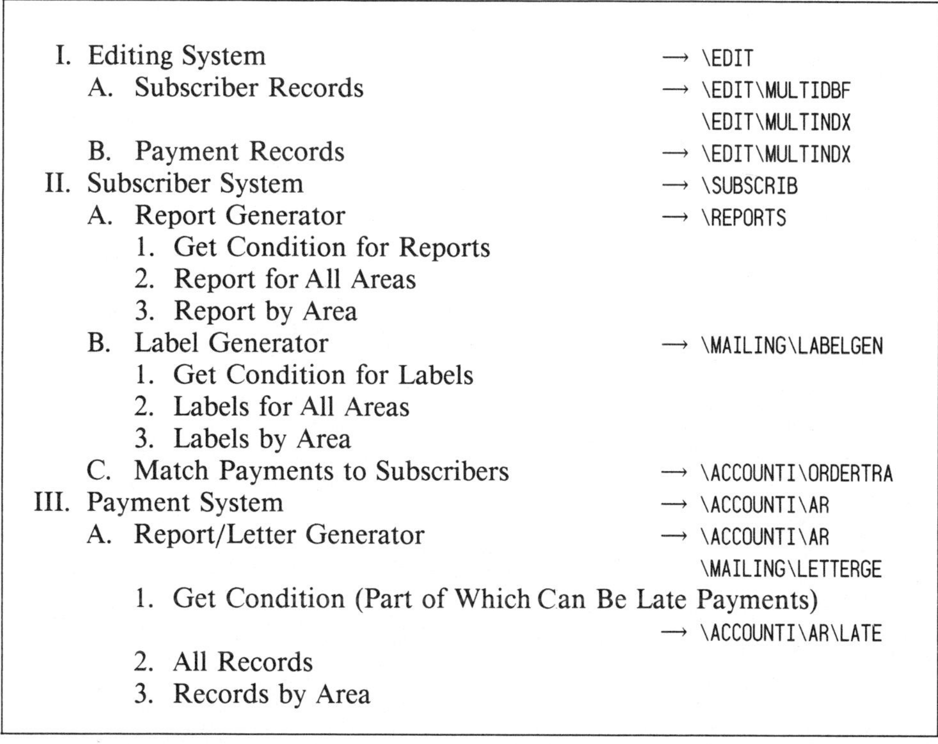

I. Editing System → \EDIT
  A. Subscriber Records → \EDIT\MULTIDBF
    \EDIT\MULTINDX
  B. Payment Records → \EDIT\MULTINDX
II. Subscriber System → \SUBSCRIB
  A. Report Generator → \REPORTS
    1. Get Condition for Reports
    2. Report for All Areas
    3. Report by Area
  B. Label Generator → \MAILING\LABELGEN
    1. Get Condition for Labels
    2. Labels for All Areas
    3. Labels by Area
  C. Match Payments to Subscribers → \ACCOUNTI\ORDERTRA
III. Payment System → \ACCOUNTI\AR
  A. Report/Letter Generator → \ACCOUNTI\AR
    \MAILING\LETTERGE
    1. Get Condition (Part of Which Can Be Late Payments)
      → \ACCOUNTI\AR\LATE
    2. All Records
    3. Records by Area

Figure 2–6 Using your flowchart to track the structure of the database system you're creating, match kernels of code stored in your library to those needed to build the new system.

The moral to this? Be a good carpenter. You don't need a crow's-foot when a flathead hammer will do the job of pulling most nails. Likewise, you don't need a flathead hammer if all you have is a ballpeen and you want to drive a few nails.

You could generate new code for each new application as it arises. That is time inefficient. If nothing else, you should learn from this book that you can code faster and better by following a few commonsense rules of coding in kernels and keeping those kernels in logical libraries.

CHAPTER

3

BASIC KERNELS

Chapter 2 described the benefits and attributes of code libraries. *Kernels* of code form the backbone of the libraries; a kernel is the minimum amount of code needed to do one specific task.

This chapter begins with a discussion of kernels as minimized code. From there, it develops the kernels that are necessary for the basic tasks of database management. Finally, this chapter shows how to link those kernels into a working menu system.

MINIMALISM AND EXPANSION IN CODING

There are two prerequisites to writing good, tight code. The first is knowing the minimum amount of code needed to do a task (minimalism). Second, the programmer needs to know how to expand the minimal kernels of code for each application (expansion). This section describes minimalism and expansion using data entry as an example.

Minimalism in Coding

The task of data entry is to get information from the user to the database. How much code does it take to do this?

dBASE III PLUS offers two basic methods. We can use:

Listing 3–1

```
@ row,column GET field name
READ
```

or:

Listing 3–2

```
SET FORM TO format file
APPE
```

We have to determine which of these commands will lend itself to general applications.

Each command has strengths and weaknesses. The @ GET READ method is fine if there are only a few fields that have to be input. Note, however, that each field adds one line of code. A database that has only four fields requires a @ GET READ combination as follows:

Listing 3–3

```
@ X1,Y1 GET FIELD1
@ X2,Y2 GET FIELD2
@ X3,Y3 GET FIELD3
@ X4,Y4 GET FIELD4
READ
```

A database of 20 fields requires 16 more lines of code. A similar construction using the SET FORM TO and APPEND method, again using a database with 4 fields, is:

Listing 3–4

```
SET FORM TO format file
APPE
```

This construction, used for a database of 20 fields, is identical to what is shown in Listing 3–4. There are literally no changes in the code whether you use a database with 1 field or 200 fields.

Those not familiar with dBASE III PLUS might think I've made a mistake. The beauty of the FMT file is that the command SET FORMAT TO format file allows input to any size database. The method doesn't change from the original code. Your first guess as to which one is better is probably the SET FORMAT TO method. But which method lends itself to our goal of reusable code that doesn't waste memory or disk space? We must know how dBASE III PLUS works to answer this.

The SET FORMAT TO and APPEND command pair recalls the format file and rewrites the screen with each APPEND. This chews up memory and machine time needlessly when we are working with a small database and a single input screen. The SET FORMAT TO and APPEND method is very useful when there is a large database in USE and several associated input screens. The programmer can create up to 32 simultaneous input screens, give the user the PG UP and PG DN keys to shuttle between screens, and use the READ command to indicate a change of screen. This use of the SET FORMAT TO and APPEND pair is ideal, as you are rewriting the screen with each READ command. The record? If a single database requires more than one input screen, use the SET FORMAT TO, APPEND combination.

We have to know what a FMT file looks like to understand why these commands work as they do. A FMT file for our four-field database might be:

Listing 3–5

```
* FOUR-FIELD FORMAT FILE
@ 10,0 SAY"Field 1"
@ 10,12 GET FIELD1
@ 11,0 SAY"Field 2"
@ 11,12 GET FIELD2
@ 12,0 SAY"Field 3"
@ 12,12 GET FIELD3
@ 13,0 SAY"Field 4"
@ 13,12 GET FIELD4
* EOF
```

When dBASE III PLUS gets a SET FORMAT TO format file command it loads the FMT file into memory and keeps it there until it gets a SET FORMAT TO, CLOSE FORMAT, CLOSE ALL, or a SET FORMAT TO (another) format file command. The SET FORMAT TO format file command uses memory space when there may be no need to. Also, each APPEND operation rewrites the screen. III PLUS is doing SAY operations when all it really needs to do is GET commands.

So, from top to bottom, the SET FORMAT TO and APPEND construct is two lines of code that call several other lines of code, chew up memory, and cause dBASE III PLUS to do extra work for each APPEND.

Return now to the minimum amount of code necessary to get data from the user to the database. For our immediate discussion, it is:

Listing 3–6

```
@ X1,Y1 GET FIELD1
@ X2,Y2 GET FIELD2
. . . .
. . . .
@ Xn,Yn GET FIELDn
READ
```

This barest minimum is a kernel of code—the smallest amount of code necessary to get data from the user to the database *once.* This kernel and other such small modules can be expanded to perform similar tasks in diverse applications. The key to creating kernels is to only write the code to do the specific task at hand.

Expansion in Coding

Now that we've seen what the least amount of code necessary to do the task of data entry is, we need to learn how to expand code to flesh out the bones of our applications. The application used as an example in the rest of this chapter is based on the service and subscription system mentioned earlier in this book. The database for this application is seen in Figure 3–1.

My eventual goal in developing an application for this chapter is to show you how to add, edit, search through, analyze, and so on, the SUBS database.

We need a custom screen form for this application, but we don't want an FMT file.

With dBASE III PLUS, you can automate the process of custom screen generation with the MODIFY SCREEN command. This tool is best used to create our necessary screen forms, which we can expand for several parts of our application. Figure 3–2 shows the menu displaced by MODIFY SCREEN, while Figure 3–3 illustrates how a *palette* helps you move fields and data to an I/O form.

```
Structure for database: D:SUBS.dbf
Number of data records:        0
Date of last update   : 11/06/86
Field  Field Name  Type       Width    Dec
    1  ACCT        Character      7
    2  LNAME       Character     15
    3  FNAME       Character     15
    4  ADDRESS     Character     25
    5  ADDRESS1    Character     25
    6  BLDG        Character      2
    7  APT         Character      2
    8  LOT         Character      3
    9  CITY        Character     15
   10  STATE       Character      2
   11  ZIP         Character      5
   12  HTEL        Character     12
   13  WTEL        Character     12
   14  TIER1       Logical        1
   15  TIER2       Logical        1
   16  TIER3       Logical        1
   17  TIER4       Logical        1
   18  TIER5       Logical        1
   19  TIER6       Logical        1
   20  TIER7       Logical        1
   21  TIER8       Logical        1
   22  TIER9       Logical        1
   23  TIER10      Logical        1
   24  TIER11      Logical        1
   25  TIER12      Logical        1
   26  RATE        Numeric        5      2
   27  CONVERTER   Character      8
   28  HOOKED_UP   Date           8
** Total **                     174
```

Figure 3–1 These are the structures for the SUBSCRIBER and PAYMENTS databases.

```
Structure for database: D:PAYMENTS.dbf
Number of data records:       0
Date of last update   : 11/15/86
Field  Field Name  Type       Width    Dec
    1  ACCT        Character      7
    2  LNAME       Character     15
    3  FNAME       Character     15
    4  JAN         Numeric        6      2
    5  CK1         Character      6
    6  N1          Character     30
    7  FEB         Numeric        6      2
    8  CK2         Character      6
    9  N2          Character     30
   10  MAR         Numeric        6      2
   11  CK3         Character      6
   12  N3          Character     30
   13  APR         Numeric        6      2
   14  CK4         Character      6
   15  N4          Character     30
   16  MAY         Numeric        6      2
   17  CK5         Character      6
   18  N5          Character     30
   19  JUN         Numeric        6      2
   20  CK6         Character      6
   21  N6          Character     30
   22  JUL         Numeric        6      2
   23  CK7         Character      6
   24  N7          Character     30
   25  AUG         Numeric        6      2
   26  CK8         Character      6
   27  N8          Character     30
   28  SEP         Numeric        6      2
   29  CK9         Character      6
   30  N9          Character     30
   31  OCT         Numeric        6      2
   32  CK10        Character      6
   33  N10         Character     30
   34  NOV         Numeric        6      2
   35  CK11        Character      6
   36  N11         Character     30
   37  DEC         Numeric        6      2
   38  CK12        Character      6
   39  N12         Character     30
   40  DISC        Logical        1
   41  FIRST_PAY   Date           8
   42  NEW         Numeric        6      2
   43  NEWCK       Character      6
   44  INFO        Character     30
** Total **                     593
```

Figure 3–1 (cont.)

Figure 3–2 The MODIFY SCREEN command opens with a menu system that you use to select or create a database, then to create custom screen forms.

An example of going from a defined database to a FMT file can be seen in the progression from Figures 3–1 through 3–3 and Listing 3–7.

Looking at Listing 3–7, note that the MODIFY SCREEN command has generated more code than needed for the specific task of getting information from

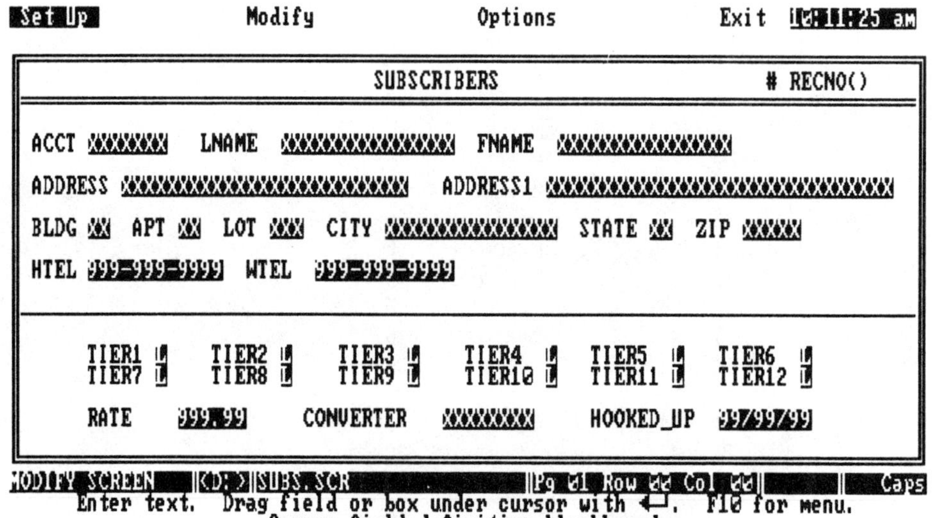

Figure 3–3 With the MODIFY SCREEN command you can move database field names and fields across a palette, *plus add single and double lines and boxes, graphics characters, and other changes to an I/O form.*

the user to the database. All we really need are the GET phrases grouped together. We also need a way of telling the user what information goes in what blank. We can accomplish this by grouping the SAY statements together. Expanding the FMT file into separate files of just GET and just SAY commands, we can create our custom screen, get data from the user to the database and vice versa, and save memory space.

Listing 3–7

```
@  2, 32  SAY "SUBSCRIBERS                        # RECNO()"
@  5,  2  SAY "ACCT"
@  5,  7  GET  SUBS->ACCT
@  5, 17  SAY "LNAME"
@  5, 24  GET  SUBS->LNAME
@  5, 41  SAY "FNAME"
@  5, 48  GET  SUBS->FNAME
@  7,  2  SAY "ADDRESS"
@  7, 10  GET  SUBS->ADDRESS
@  7, 38  SAY "ADDRESS1"
@  7, 47  GET  SUBS->ADDRESS1  PICTURE       "XXXXXXXXXXXXXXXXXXXXXXXXXXXXXX"
@  9,  2  SAY "BLDG"
@  9,  7  GET  SUBS->BLDG
@  9, 11  SAY "APT"
@  9, 15  GET  SUBS->APT
@  9, 19  SAY "LOT"
@  9, 23  GET  SUBS->LOT
@  9, 28  SAY "CITY"
@  9, 33  GET  SUBS->CITY
@  9, 50  SAY "STATE"
@  9, 56  GET  SUBS->STATE
@  9, 60  SAY "ZIP"
@  9, 64  GET  SUBS->ZIP
@ 11,  2  SAY "HTEL"
@ 11,  7  GET  SUBS->HTEL  PICTURE "999-999-9999"
@ 11, 21  SAY "WTEL"
@ 11, 27  GET  SUBS->WTEL  PICTURE "999-999-9999"
@ 13, 32  SAY "SERVICES"
@ 15,  7  SAY "TIER1"
@ 15, 13  GET  SUBS->TIER1
@ 15, 18  SAY "TIER2"
@ 15, 24  GET  SUBS->TIER2
@ 15, 29  SAY "TIER3"
@ 15, 35  GET  SUBS->TIER3
@ 15, 40  SAY "TIER4"
@ 15, 47  GET  SUBS->TIER4
@ 15, 51  SAY "TIER5"
@ 15, 58  GET  SUBS->TIER5
```

Listing 3–7 (cont.)

```
@ 15, 62  SAY "TIER6"
@ 15, 69  GET  SUBS->TIER6
@ 16,  7  SAY "TIER7"
@ 16, 13  GET  SUBS->TIER7
@ 16, 18  SAY "TIER8"
@ 16, 24  GET  SUBS->TIER8
@ 16, 29  SAY "TIER9"
@ 16, 35  GET  SUBS->TIER9
@ 16, 40  SAY "TIER10"
@ 16, 47  GET  SUBS->TIER10
@ 16, 51  SAY "TIER11"
@ 16, 58  GET  SUBS->TIER11
@ 16, 62  SAY "TIER12"
@ 16, 69  GET  SUBS->TIER12
@ 18,  7  SAY "RATE"
@ 18, 15  GET  SUBS->RATE  PICTURE "999.99"
@ 18, 26  SAY "CONVERTER"
@ 18, 38  GET  SUBS->CONVERTER
@ 18, 51  SAY "HOOKED_UP"
@ 18, 62  GET  SUBS->HOOKED_UP
@  1,  0  TO 20, 79    DOUBLE
@  3,  1  TO  3, 78    DOUBLE
@ 13,  1  TO 13, 15
@ 13,  1  TO 13, 78
```

CONCLUSIONS ABOUT MINIMIZING AND EXPANDING CODE

What is minimalism? It's coding from the most specific tasks up to the least specific tasks. This allows you to make use of previously coded modules in new applications. Minimalism teaches us not to code the entire system from top to bottom.

What is expansion? It's altering the previously written modules only as necessary for the immediate application. Expansion teaches us to expand the kernels only for the immediate goal. Don't write what the user doesn't need. Remember the programmer's adage: KISS (Keep It Simple, Stupid!)

THE FILES NECESSARY FOR CUSTOM SCREENS

The GET and SAY files created as we minimized and expanded code provide the necessary files for our sample application's custom screen. These files are discussed more fully here.

->

Figure 3–4 This screen can be used to input data in the subscriber database, but it is doubtful that the user will know what data goes in what blank.

The SAY File

No DBMS is very useful unless the user knows what data is going where. The screen in Figure 3–4 is generated by a GET file and could be used for data input, but such an operation would be playing pin the tail on the donkey.

Another PRG file should be called first, ahead of the one that generated the screen in Figure 3–4, which gives the user some idea of what goes where and why. We need the SAY commands from the MODIFY SCREEN written FMT file.

Listing 3–8

```
@  5,  2  SAY "ACCT"
@  5, 17  SAY "LNAME"
@  5, 41  SAY "FNAME"
@  7,  2  SAY "ADDRESS"
@  7, 38  SAY "ADDRESS1"
@  9,  2  SAY "BLDG"
@  9, 11  SAY "APT"
@  9, 19  SAY "LOT"
@  9, 28  SAY "CITY"
@  9, 50  SAY "STATE"
@  9, 60  SAY "ZIP"
@ 11,  2  SAY "HTEL"
@ 11, 21  SAY "WTEL"
@ 13, 32  SAY "SERVICES"
@ 15,  7  SAY "TIER1"
```

Listing 3–8 (cont.)

```
@ 15, 18  SAY "TIER2"
@ 15, 29  SAY "TIER3"
@ 15, 40  SAY "TIER4"
@ 15, 51  SAY "TIER5"
@ 15, 62  SAY "TIER6"
@ 16,  7  SAY "TIER7"
@ 16, 18  SAY "TIER8"
@ 16, 29  SAY "TIER9"
@ 16, 40  SAY "TIER10"
@ 16, 51  SAY "TIER11"
@ 16, 62  SAY "TIER12"
@ 18,  7  SAY "RATE"
@ 18, 26  SAY "CONVERTER"
@ 18, 51  SAY "HOOKED_UP"
```

Do you remember that the SET FORMAT TO and APPEND commands rewrote the screen with each APPEND? That method refreshed the screen by repeating the list of commands shown in this listing for each APPEND.

Why? Is it necessary to refresh the SAYS on the screen for each record we APPEND? No. You're merely providing a backdrop for the user. Listing 3–8 shows the user what data is supposed to go in what blank. The only time the commands should be repeated is when the screen has been used for something else. Reading the SAY file once frees memory for other tasks.

Are there any other things that should be included in this command list? It might be nice to make sure the screen is clear of everything else. Include the CLEAR command when the SAY file is called. It's also nice to know what database we're working with. In this case, we already know we're working with a subscriber database, but that could be broken down into smaller databases. We might have subscriber databases broken down by state, city, type of service, and so on. Together, all these libraries make up a master database (a *masterbase*) of all the subscribers. How do we let the user know which database is in use? By including the code:

```
@  2, PLACE SAY DBFILE
```

This line assumes the PLACE and DBFILE variables have been defined in a calling program. With the two variables, PLACE and DEFILE, this part of the SAY file can be used by any other SAY file.

It might be helpful to know which record we're using when we're going through the database. That is solved with two commands. The first command goes in the SAY file, and the second command goes in the GET file described next. The first command is:

```
2,65 SAY "#"
```

Aesthetics can be important, so we add a little luster to our screen with:

Listing 3–9

```
@  1,  0  TO 19, 79    DOUBLE
@  3,  1  TO  3, 78    DOUBLE
```

I've mentioned the fact that this list of SAYS and other commands are going into a file. Good housekeeping practices require us to put some remarks at the beginning and end of our files. The information in the remarks should be kept to a minimum, as they are not going to be used by III PLUS.

Listing 3–10

```
** SUB.SAY FILE
*
*
** EOF
```

The completed SAY file becomes:

Listing 3–11

```
** SUB.SAY FILE
*
CLEAR
@  1,  0  TO 19, 79    DOUBLE
@  3,  1  TO  3, 78    DOUBLE
@ 13,  1  TO 13, 15
@ 13,  1  TO 13, 78
@  2, PLACE SAY DBFILE
@  2,65 SAY "# "
@  5,  2  SAY "ACCT"
@  5, 17  SAY "LNAME"
@  5, 41  SAY "FNAME"
@  7,  2  SAY "ADDRESS"
@  7, 38  SAY "ADDRESS1"
@  9,  2  SAY "BLDG"
@  9, 11  SAY "APT"
@  9, 19  SAY "LOT"
@  9, 28  SAY "CITY"
@  9, 50  SAY "STATE"
@  9, 60  SAY "ZIP"
@ 11,  2  SAY "HTEL"
@ 11, 21  SAY "WTEL"
@ 13, 32  SAY "SERVICES"
@ 15,  7  SAY "TIER1"
@ 15, 18  SAY "TIER2"
@ 15, 29  SAY "TIER3"
@ 15, 40  SAY "TIER4"
@ 15, 51  SAY "TIER5"
```

Listing 3–11 (cont.)

```
@ 15, 62  SAY "TIER6"
@ 16,  7  SAY "TIER7"
@ 16, 18  SAY "TIER8"
@ 16, 29  SAY "TIER9"
@ 16, 40  SAY "TIER10"
@ 16, 51  SAY "TIER11"
@ 16, 62  SAY "TIER12"
@ 18,  7  SAY "RATE"
@ 18, 26  SAY "CONVERTER"
@ 18, 51  SAY "HOOKED_UP"
*
** EOF
```

What has been presented here is a SAY file. The premise of the SAY file is:

1. The file is accessed only to SAY the screen.
2. The file lets the user know what data goes in which field.

This SAY file concept is valid in all applications, not just the subscription system shown here.

Before leaving this section, realize that we have expanded a kernel of code. What kernel?

Listing 3–12

```
CLEA
@  2, PLACE SAY DBFILE
* SAY COMMANDS
@   3,  1  TO  3, 78    DOUBLE
@   1,  0  TO 19, 79    DOUBLE
@  2, 65 SAY "# "
```

The group of commands in Listing 3–12 is the kernel of every SAY file used in this book. The asterisk (*) is where you expand the SAY kernel with your particular application's SAY commands. Figure 3–5 shows the screen created with the SAY file.

The GET File

Now that you've created a file to let the user know what goes where and why, we need to get that information. We've used all the SAY commands from the MODIFY SCREEN written FMT file. It would be a good guess that we're going to use the GET commands here.

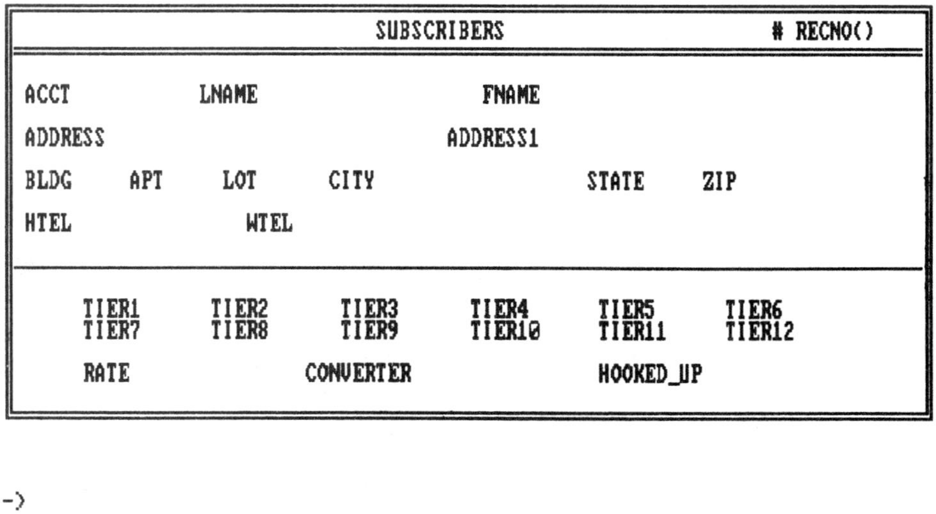

```
                              SUBSCRIBERS                       # RECNO()

ACCT          LNAME                  FNAME
ADDRESS                           ADDRESS1
BLDG     APT      LOT      CITY                  STATE     ZIP
HTEL               WTEL

     TIER1      TIER2      TIER3      TIER4      TIER5      TIER6
     TIER7      TIER8      TIER9      TIER10     TIER11     TIER12
     RATE                CONVERTER               HOOKED_UP

->
```

Figure 3–5 The completed SAY file creates a screen image that is written once during an add, edit, or review session.

Those commands, taken from the FMT file, are:

Listing 3–13

```
@  5,  7  GET  SUBS->ACCT
@  5, 24  GET  SUBS->LNAME
@  5, 48  GET  SUBS->FNAME
@  7, 10  GET  SUBS->ADDRESS
@  7, 47  GET  SUBS->ADDRESS1  PICTURE "XXXXXXXXXXXXXXXXXXXXXXXXXXXXXX"
@  9,  7  GET  SUBS->BLDG
@  9, 15  GET  SUBS->APT
@  9, 23  GET  SUBS->LOT
@  9, 33  GET  SUBS->CITY
@  9, 56  GET  SUBS->STATE
@  9, 64  GET  SUBS->ZIP
@ 11,  7  GET  SUBS->HTEL  PICTURE "999-999-9999"
@ 11, 27  GET  SUBS->WTEL  PICTURE "999-999-9999"
@ 15, 13  GET  SUBS->TIER1
@ 15, 24  GET  SUBS->TIER2
@ 15, 35  GET  SUBS->TIER3
@ 15, 47  GET  SUBS->TIER4
@ 15, 58  GET  SUBS->TIER5
@ 15, 69  GET  SUBS->TIER6
@ 16, 13  GET  SUBS->TIER7
@ 16, 24  GET  SUBS->TIER8
@ 16, 35  GET  SUBS->TIER9
```

Listing 3–13 (cont.)

```
@ 16, 47  GET  SUBS->TIER10
@ 16, 58  GET  SUBS->TIER11
@ 16, 69  GET  SUBS->TIER12
@ 18, 15  GET  SUBS->RATE  PICTURE "999.99"
@ 18, 38  GET  SUBS->CONVERTER
@ 18, 62  GET  SUBS->HOOKED_UP
```

We already know that this code will be used to actually get information from the user to a particular database record and vice versa. The transfer of data from the user to the database with a READ command is not enough. Remember that this screen is going to be used for adding, editing, and reviewing data in the database. That assumes there will be data in the database record to be read. That isn't always the case. We have to add something to the READ statement to make sure the system doesn't blow up if there is nothing in the database to READ.

dBASE III PLUS can't GET or READ anything from a record that is out of the range of the database. In other words, if there are only 100 records in the database in USE, you can't GET or READ from record 101. Trying to GET or READ from a record beyond the beginning or end of the database produces an error. In particular, it produces ERROR(5) (a list of dBASE III PLUS's error messages can be found in Ashton-Tate's *Learning and Using dBASE III PLUS*). We know that trying to READ or GET a record beyond the scope of the database produces an error, and we can make use of the dBASE II PLUS error trapping command, ERROR(N) to do something based on that error. In this case, we include an error trap.

Listing 3–14

```
IF ERROR() <> 5
   READ
ELSE
   WAIT "I can't get that record. Press any "+;
   "key to continue."
ENDI
```

Letting the user know what record is in use involves the second command mentioned in the SAY section. The SAY file's command was:

```
2,65 SAY '#'
```

That record number marker doesn't need to be repeated. But we do need to update the actual record number each time the GET file is accessed. The GET file's command is:

```
2,70 SAY(),4,0
```

We also include our usual beginning and end of file markers to make the completed GET file.

Listing 3–15

```
** SUBS.GET
*
@ 2,70 SAY STR(RECNO(),4,0)
@  5,  7  GET  SUBS->ACCT
@  5, 24  GET  SUBS->LNAME
@  5, 48  GET  SUBS->FNAME
@  7, 10  GET  SUBS->ADDRESS
@  7, 47  GET  SUBS->ADDRESS1  PICTURE "XXXXXXXXXXXXXXXXXXXXXXXXXXXXXX"
@  9,  7  GET  SUBS->BLDG
@  9, 15  GET  SUBS->APT
@  9, 23  GET  SUBS->LOT
@  9, 33  GET  SUBS->CITY
@  9, 56  GET  SUBS->STATE
@  9, 64  GET  SUBS->ZIP
@ 11,  7  GET  SUBS->HTEL  PICTURE "999-999-9999"
@ 11, 27  GET  SUBS->WTEL  PICTURE "999-999-9999"
@ 15, 13  GET  SUBS->TIER1
@ 15, 24  GET  SUBS->TIER2
@ 15, 35  GET  SUBS->TIER3
@ 15, 47  GET  SUBS->TIER4
@ 15, 58  GET  SUBS->TIER5
@ 15, 69  GET  SUBS->TIER6
@ 16, 13  GET  SUBS->TIER7
@ 16, 24  GET  SUBS->TIER8
@ 16, 35  GET  SUBS->TIER9
@ 16, 47  GET  SUBS->TIER10
@ 16, 58  GET  SUBS->TIER11
@ 16, 69  GET  SUBS->TIER12
@ 18, 15  GET  SUBS->RATE  PICTURE "999.99"
@ 18, 38  GET  SUBS->CONVERTER
@ 18, 62  GET  SUBS->HOOKED_UP
*
IF ERROR() <> 5
   READ
ELSE
   WAIT "I can't get that record. Press any "+;
   "key to continue."
ENDI
*
** EOF
```

This file, run by itself to produce Figure 3–2, can be used with the previous section's SAY file to produce Figure 3–6.

The beauty of the GET file is that is the part of the MODIFY SCREEN written FMT file required to add, edit, or review data repeatedly. Each time you

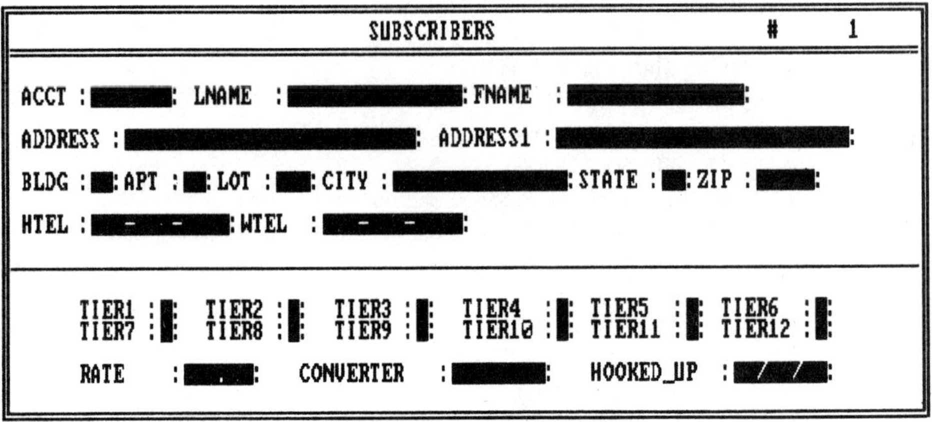

Figure 3-6 The combination of the SAY and GET files produces a custom screen that can be used for adding, editing, and reviewing data.

query the database, you are interested in GETting information from the fields. What is the kernel of code for the GET file?

Listing 3-16

```
@ 2,70 SAY STR(RECNO(),4,0)
* GET COMMANDS
IF ERROR() <> 5
   READ
ELSE
   WAIT "I can't get that record. Press any "+;
   "key to continue."
ENDI
```

The asterisk (*) here is where you place the GET statements that are specific to your application.

THE EDIT KERNEL

Editing a database record is the act of changing existing data. You may want to change information in every field in the record, or you may only wish to change data in one field. The important features of editing to know are that the record already contains data and that you want to change some of the data in that record.

What is essential to editing existing data?

1. We must get the data to the screen in a form that is recognizable by the user.
2. We must allow the user to see the changes as they are made.
3. We must save the changes once they are made.
4. We assume that the database pointer is already at the record we want to edit.
5. We assume a SAY file has already been executed, as editing only involves GETting new information.
6. We assume that the editing will be noncontiguous. That means that you don't want to edit records 1, 2, 3, 4, and so on in that order to the end of the database. Usually you want to edit records 2, 10, 11, 37, or some such random order. We begin with the last assumption, writing our Edit kernel to be a one-pass operation.

Listing 3–17

```
* Edit KERNEL
@ 20,0 CLEAR
@ 22,0 SAY "Press CTRL-W to save edit, CTRL-Q to"+;
   " quit without saving edit."
* DO GETS
* END OF Edit KERNEL
```

Remember that I inferred the bottom of the screen would be used for messages and such? Notice here that the kernel CLEARs everything beneath the SAY file. Once that area is CLEARed, the kernel places a message there (the CTRL-W and CTRL-Q functions are part of dBASE III PLUS and don't need to be programmed into your system). After positioning the message, the kernel GETs the necessary information. Last the code exits the Edit kernel.

That's it. There is nothing else to do. But that short piece of code contains everything necessary to edit existing data. It doesn't find the record to edit, nor does it allow for multiple editing (as written, it is not recursive). It is the minimum amount of code necessary to do the task of editing a database record.

THE ADD KERNEL

An empty database is not likely to stay empty for long (at least that's your hope) and so the system should include a means of adding data. What are our assumptions when we code to add data to an existing database?

1. The database is already open.
2. We must get the data from the screen to the database.
3. We assume that more than one record will be added at a time (adding data is usually not a one-pass operation).

4. We assume a SAY file has already been executed as adding data only involves GETting information.
5. It is assumed that we want to preserve the integrity of the database during the adding session (we don't want someone to get frustrated and turn the computer off without properly exiting, thus destroying the database).
6. We assume that the database is indexed on one or more fields.
7. We'd like to make the data entry as effortless as possible.

The sparsest Add kernel is:

Listing 3–18

```
* Add KERNEL
COPY STRU TO TANK
SELE 2
USE TANK
@ 20,0 CLEA
@ 22,0 SAY "Press CTRL-W to save and continue,"+;
    " CTRL-W at an empty screen exits this mode."
REPEATER = FIELD(1)
*
DO WHIL .T.
   APPE BLAN
   * DO GETS
*
   IF LEN(TRIM(&REPEATER)) = 0
      DELE
      EXIT
   ENDI
*
ENDD
*
SET DELE ON
USE
SELE 1
APPE FROM TANK
SET DELE OFF

ERAS TANK.DBF
* DO GETS
CLEA GETS
* END OF Add KERNEL
```

The first line, COPY STRUCTURE TO TANK, ensures the integrity of our masterbase. We don't want to directly APPEND to the masterbase, as opening the masterbase subjects it to the possibility of being lost due to power shortage, power surge, inadvertently (or advertently) quitting III PLUS, shutting off the machine, and so on. The masterbase is kept intact by COPYing the STRUCTURE of the masterbase to a temporary, storage TANK database.

We SELECT 2 and USE TANK in lines two and three. Why don't we just USE TANK? That would close all the NDX files associated with our masterbase, which means we'd have to reopen them later. Reopening a database and its associated NDX files takes far more time than if we SELECT 2 and USE TANK.

I include the @ 20,0 CLEA and @ 22,0 SAY "(message)" lines for the same reason they appear in the Edit kernel. There is going to be something at the bottom of the screen, underneath the SAY file. These two lines CLEAR whatever is there and give the user a prompt.

REPEATER = FIELD(1) makes this code a kernel. This command tells III PLUS to create a variable named REPEATER and assign that variable the name of the first field in the database in USE. With the FIELD() function, we can use this code in any number of applications. I chose the first field in the database because I create my databases with the most important field at the top (every record will have an entry in the first field; see Chapter 4 for more on this subject). It is not necessary to use the first field, however.

The DO WHILE . . . ENDDO loop is what actually gets data from the user to the TANK database. As long as the first field in the APPENDed record has information, III PLUS will continue through the loop. The second line in the loop is where you enter the GET file for your specific application.

Inside the DO WHILE . . . ENDDO loop is an IF . . . ENDIF statement. This provides the EXIT condition for the DO WHILE . . . ENDDO loop. IF the LENgth of the TRIMmed first field in the APPENDed record is 0 (if there is no information in that field), then DELETE the empty record and EXIT the DO WHILE . . . ENDDO loop.

The SET DELE ON following the DO WHILE . . . ENDDO loop tells III PLUS to ignore DELETEd records in the following commands. This is necessary because we need to transfer the new records in the TANK database to our masterbase, but we don't want to include the DELETEd record we create each time we exit the add session.

The USE command closes the TANK database. That is necessary because we SELE 1 and APPE FROM TANK. dBASE III PLUS won't APPEND from an open database.

Now that we've transferred the new records from the TANK to the masterbase, we can SET DELE OFF, as we may want to work with some previously DELETEd records in our masterbase. Leaving SET DELETED ON prevents us from working with the masterbase's DELETEd records. Last, we free up disk space with ERAS TANK.DBF.

At this point our user is back to the masterbase. However, he or she will be sitting in front of a blank SAY and GET screen unless we fill the blanks using our GET file. The CLEA GETS doesn't allow the user to enter or edit data in the masterbase, it merely shows the last record entered.

Listing 3–18 is the minimum amount of code necessary to have a reusable Add kernel. The only thing not addressed is making the adding of repetitive data as effortless as possible. The problem with entering repetitive data is that the process is tedious, boring, dull, and entails more colorful adjectives. The tedium can be somewhat alleviated by programming the function keys with data from the last record added. Repetitive data can then be entered in new records by pressing one of the function keys. New data can be added by typing, as usual. Listing 3–19 can be used to capture the most repeated fields in the database and ease data entry.

Listing 3–19

```
FIELD1 = FIELD(1)
FIELD2 = FIELD(2)
FIELD3 = FIELD(3)
FIELD4 = FIELD(4)
FIELD5 = FIELD(5)
FIELD6 = FIELD(6)
FIELD7 = FIELD(7)
FIELD8 = FIELD(8)
FIELD9 = FIELD(9)
****
**** OTHER CODE
****
SET FUNC 2 TO TRIM(&FIELD1)+";"
SET FUNC 3 TO TRIM(&FIELD2)+";"
SET FUNC 4 TO TRIM(&FIELD3)+";"
SET FUNC 5 TO TRIM(&FIELD4)+";"
SET FUNC 6 TO TRIM(&FIELD5)+";"
SET FUNC 7 TO TRIM(&FIELD6)+";"
SET FUNC 8 TO TRIM(&FIELD7)+";"
SET FUNC 9 TO TRIM(&FIELD8)+";"
SET FUNC 10 TO TRIM(&FIELD9)+";"
****
**** OTHER CODE
****
```

The equivalencies tell III PLUS that some variables will be used to hold the names of some database fields. I chose the first nine fields in the database, but any fields can be used. The SET commands are placed in the Add kernel's DO WHILE . . . ENDDO loop, after the IF . . . ENDIF command. The SET commands assign function keys 2 through 9 the information in each of the first nine fields in the current record (F1 is reserved by dBASE III PLUS). Those assignments stay in place until a new record is accepted into TANK. Before that new record is accepted, and while data is being entered into it, the function keys will "copy" the data from the last record to the current record.

Using these commands, the Add kernel becomes:

Listing 3–20

```
* Add KERNEL
COPY STRU TO TANK
```

Listing 3–20 (cont.)

```
SELE 2
USE TANK
FIELD1 = FIELD(1)
FIELD2 = FIELD(2)
FIELD3 = FIELD(3)
FIELD4 = FIELD(4)
FIELD5 = FIELD(5)
FIELD6 = FIELD(6)
FIELD7 = FIELD(7)
FIELD8 = FIELD(8)
FIELD9 = FIELD(9)
@ 20,0 CLEA
@ 22,0 SAY "Press CTRL-W to save and continue,"+;
 " CTRL-W at an empty screen exits this mode."
REPEATER = FIELD(1)
*
DO WHIL .T.
   APPE BLAN
   * DO GETS
*
   IF LEN(TRIM(&REPEATER)) = 0
      DELE
      EXIT
   ENDI
*
   SET FUNC 2 TO TRIM(&FIELD1)+";"
   SET FUNC 3 TO TRIM(&FIELD2)+";"
   SET FUNC 4 TO TRIM(&FIELD3)+";"
   SET FUNC 5 TO TRIM(&FIELD4)+";"
   SET FUNC 6 TO TRIM(&FIELD5)+";"
   SET FUNC 7 TO TRIM(&FIELD6)+";"
   SET FUNC 8 TO TRIM(&FIELD7)+";"
   SET FUNC 9 TO TRIM(&FIELD8)+";"
   SET FUNC 10 TO TRIM(&FIELD9)+";"
ENDD
*
SET DELE ON
USE
SELE 1
APPE FROM TANK
SET DELE OFF
ERAS TANK.DBF
* DO GETS
CLEA GETS
* END OF Add KERNEL
```

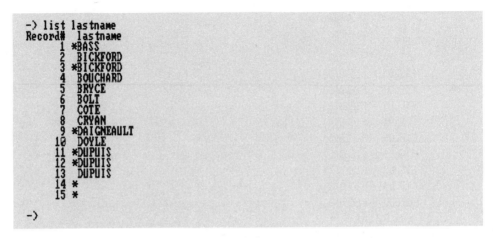

Figure 3–7 DELETEd records are not removed from a database by the act of using DELETE on them. They are merely marked to be DELETEd.

Experienced programmers may wonder why I didn't use the SET CARRY ON and APPEND commands as a means of filling repeated fields in a database. First, some editing must be done in an APPENDed record for that record to be added. My method assumed each new record will have new information and gave the user the option of adding data from the previous record or new data. The user doesn't have to edit through existing data. In this kernel I can also decide, based on the application, which fields the data entry people will have to enter and which they can slough through.

THE DELETE KERNEL

The Delete kernel is more than just a piece of code for removing unwanted records from a database. Previously I mentioned that we might want to delete records from a database for different reasons. Not all of those reasons involve physically *removing* the records from a database. Sometimes we want to delete a record only to *mask* it from some other operations that will follow later in the program. Likewise, when considering physically removing the records from the database, we have to ask if we're going to wipe out all the records, or only certain ones. dBASE III PLUS uses the DELETE, SET DELETED ON, PACK, and ZAP commands and the DELETED() function to do most of this.

You can DELETE a record from a database, but that doesn't physically remove the DELETEd record from the database. In fact, it doesn't do anything other than mark the record. If you DISPLAY a database with DELETEd records, those records will still show up. Figures 3–7 and 3–8 illustrate how DELETE works.

You can "hide" DELETEd records from certain commands using the SET DELETED ON command. This command tells dBASE III PLUS to behave as if the DELETEd records didn't exist in the database. You have, in effect, filtered

```
-> SET DELE ON
-> DISPLAY ALL LASTNAME
Record#  LASTNAME
      2  BICKFORD
      4  BOUCHARD
      5  BRYCE
      6  BOLT
      7  COTE
      8  CRYAN
     10  DOYLE
     13  DUPUIS

->
```

Figure 3–8 The SET DELETED ON command tells dBASE III PLUS to "hide" DELETEd records from certain commands, such as DISPLAY. This doesn't mean the records have been removed from the database—they are simply transparent to certain commands.

the database, which is similar to filtering with the SET FILTER TO command. The SET DELETED ON command is a specialized filter in the sense that the filtering mechanism is built into the dBASE III PLUS program.

DELETED() is a logical function that tells the user if a particular record has been DELETEd. It can be used as a reverse filter to SET DELETED ON, as shown in Figure 3–9.

There will be times that you want to physically remove the DELETEd records from the database. You do so with the PACK command. PACK is a destructive, nonreversible command that physically changes the size of the database by removing all records marked as DELETEd. All records that aren't DELETEd are preserved during a PACK.

An additional way to eliminate records from a database is the ZAP command. This is a destructive, nonreversible command that physically removes *all* records from a database, *regardless if they are marked for deletion or not!* So, III PLUS offers several methods of clobbering the database with this group of com-

```
-> SET DELE OFF
-> DISP LASTNAME FOR DELETED()
Record#  LASTNAME
      1 *BASS
      3 *BICKFORD
      9 *DAIGNEAULT
     11 *DUPUIS
     12 *DUPUIS
     14 *
     15 *

->
```

Figure 3–9 The DELETED() function can be used with dBASE III PLUS commands, such as DISPLAY, as a reverse filter. The example here uses DISP FOR DELETED() to list all the records marked to be DELETEd. Notice that the DISPLAYed records are those not DISPLAYed in Figure 3–8.

```
                                                        Bytes remaining:   3826

    Field Name  Type       Width  Dec         Field Name  Type       Width  Dec

 1  ACCT        Character    7            16  TIER3       Logical      1
 2  LNAME       Character   15            17  TIER4       Logical      1
 3  FNAME       Character   15            18  TIER5       Logical      1
 4  ADDRESS     Character   25            19  TIER6       Logical      1
 5  ADDRESS1    Character   25            20  TIER7       Logical      1
 6  BLDG        Character    2            21  TIER8       Logical      1
 7  APT         Character    2            22  TIER9       Logical      1
 8  LOT         Character    3            23  TIER10      Logical      1
 9  CITY        Character   15            24  TIER11      Logical      1
10  STATE       Character    2            25  TIER12      Logical      1
11  ZIP         Character    5            26  RATE        Numeric      5    2
12  HTEL        Character   12            27  CONVERTER   Character    8
13  WTEL        Character   12            28  HOOKED_UP   Date         8
14  TIER1       Logical      1            29  PERM        Logical      1
15  TIER2       Logical      1            30              Character

MODIFY STRUCTURE ||<D:>||SUBS                ||Field: 30/30      ||Ins  ||   Caps
                              Enter the field name.
Field names begin with a letter and may contain letters, digits and underscores
```

Figure 3–10 This is the same database as was used previously in this chapter. The only change is the addition of the logical PERM field at the bottom of the structure.

mands and functions. Our task in designing a kernel to DELETE records from a database is to recognize that the user:

1. may want to "hide" records for a while, but not DELETE them permanently.
2. may want to hide records, but not DELETE all the hidden records.
3. may want to DELETE records permanently.
4. may want to DELETE all the records permanently.
5. will be allowed to DELETE only one record at a time.
6. will know whether the record is going to DELETEd temporarily or permanently. In other words, the user will know if the record can be physically removed from the database or only hidden temporarily.
7. *will make no physical removal of records at this time.*
8. that we have used SAY and GET for the screen as necessary to ensure that the user is using DELETE on the correct record.

Including code for item 7 is vital. It provides us with a safety measure lest our user be trigger happy, change his or her mind, or misunderstand the system's documentation.

We start by adding a new field at the very end of our database structure. Using the database structure for the SUBS.DBF file in the subscriber system, we add the logical field PERM. The result is shown in Figure 3–10.

What does our kernel look like?

Listing 3–21

```
* Delete KERNEL
DELE
@ 20,0 CLEA
@ 22,0 SAY "Is this a PERMANENT deletion? ";
   GET PERM PICTURE "N"
READ
DELFLAG = .T.
* END OF Delete KERNEL
```

There it is—a simple, elegant tool that we can use us to consider several options for the user. How does the user know which records are marked and what they are marked for? The only time a user needs to know that a record is marked is when he or she is GETting the screen. We can add two lines to our calling program that handle that situation. The two lines are executed before the GET file is called.

Listing 3–22

```
@ 2,60 SAY IIF(DELETED(),"DELETED ",SPACE(8)) +;
              IIF(PERM,"PERMANENT",SPACE(9))
```

These two lines tell the user whether the record is marked with DELETE and if the record will be eliminated PERManently. We haven't explained the DELFLAG = .T. command in our kernel yet. Item 7 in our list implies that records aren't DELETEd permanently at this time. True. At the end of a work session, the calling program can check the DELFLAG variable to prompt the user to DELETE the records permanently with the code:

Listing 3–23

```
IF DELFLAG
   CLEA
   ACCE "Deletions have been made. Make them "+;
   "PERMANENT? (Y/N) -> " TO DELFLAG
*
   IF DELFLAG
      RECA FOR .NOT. PERM
      PACK
   ENDI
*
ENDI
```

Here we use the combination of the DELETEd flag and the PERM field to PACK only those records that are to be permanently removed from the database with RECALL FOR condition and PACK. These two commands RECALL all database records that don't meet the condition (.NOT. PERM), leaving only the records we do wish to physically remove.

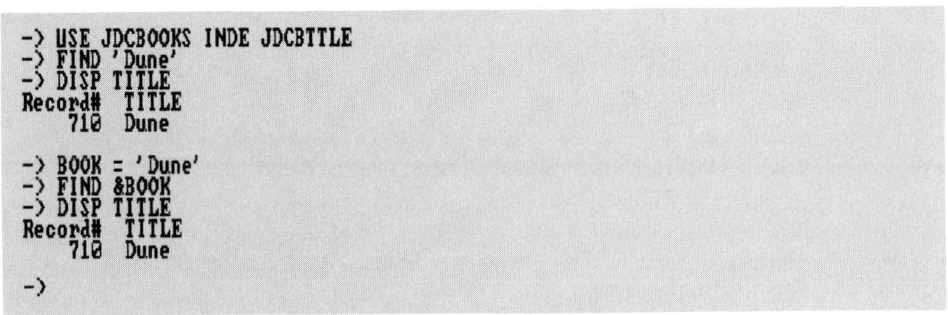

-> USE JDCBOOKS INDE JDCBTTLE
-> FIND 'Dune'
-> DISP TITLE
Record# TITLE
710 Dune
-> BOOK = 'Dune'
-> FIND &BOOK
-> DISP TITLE
Record# TITLE
710 Dune
->

Figure 3–11 You can FIND specific data by specifying what you want to find in a delimiter (FIND "Dune") or by using a variable (if BOOK = "Dune", you can FIND & BOOK).

THE FIND KERNEL

The most important part of editing and reviewing data is finding the record to edit or review. The user doesn't want to edit and review things randomly, nor does the user want to look through the database one record at a time until he or she finds the one record to work with. You must code to quickly locate either a single record or group of related records in a database. III PLUS has four commands that perform these functions; FIND, SEEK, LOCATE, and CONTINUE. The latter two commands are discussed in Chapter 5.

The first two commands, FIND and SEEK, are specific to INDEXed databases. FIND and SEEK will not work unless you have previously issued a command to USE a database's INDE index. FIND and SEEK share one important characteristic—they both look for the *first* occurrence of their object in the database. No matter how many times you FIND or SEEK, you will come to the first occurrence of the object you're FINDing or SEEKing, even if there are 3000 other occurrences of the same object in the database.

The major difference between FIND and SEEK is how each works. FIND requires either a delimited object or a variable name as the object and is best used with a single active database. SEEK isn't so fussy about the object it is SEEKing, and its properties lend it to working with a number of active databases. The FIND command is covered here, because it is the method of choice in the basic kernel. An example of a search using FIND is shown in Figure 3–11. The SEEK command is covered in Chapter 5.

The user is interested in quick access to specific records to review and edit data. What do we need to know about dBASE III PLUS's workings before we write the Find kernel?

We need to know that III PLUS INDEXes databases on the values in a specified field. INDEXing our BOOK database on the TITLE field gets us a database INDEXed alphabetically by title.

What if the database can't FIND what the user asked for? Then the kernel should be able to tell the user that the FIND was unsuccessful. Our assumptions for this code are:

1. The user knows what he or she is looking for.
2. dBASE III PLUS might not be able to FIND what the user is looking for.
3. The user needs to see, but not necessarily alter, what is found.
4. There is only one NDX file that will be used for each FIND.
5. We have already used SAY and GET on the screen.

Our kernel looks like this:

Listing 3–24

```
* Find KERNEL
@ 20,0 CLEA
ACCE "FIND > " TO KEYVALUE
FIND &KEYVALUE
*
IF .NOT. FOUND()
   @ 20,0 CLEA
   WAIT "I can't FIND " + KEYVALUE +;
        ". Perhaps you should SEARCH for it. "+;
    "Press any key to continue."
ELSE
   * DO GETS
   CLEA GETS
ENDI
* END OF Find KERNEL
```

This kernel starts by CLEARing whatever is below our SAY screen. Next it asks what the user wants to FIND. It then attempts to FIND what the user has specified. IF the user's request is .NOT. FOUND(), CLEAR the bottom of the screen and post an error message. This error message also points toward an alternative strategy for locating the desired record. Should dBASE III PLUS FIND the desired record, GET and CLEAR GETS that record's information and exit the kernel.

Often, one of our assumptions will go out the window the minute we begin developing an involved database management system. We assume there is only one open NDX file. Few large applications have databases INDEXed on a single field.

Keeping the subscription system as our model, let's assume we want to INDEX on the fields ACCT, LNAME, CITY, STATE, ZIP, and LEFT(ACCT,2)+LNAME+FNAME. That means there will be six NDX files for each database file (a similar situation would be INDEXing a receivables database on RECEIVED FROM, RECEIVED FOR, DATE DUE, DATE RECEIVED, PAYMENT METHOD, and AMOUNT OF PAYMENT fields). How can we expand our basic Find kernel to shift the NDX files? We use the DO CASE . . . OTHERWISE . . . ENDCASE, along with a few other commands, to create the following special block:

Listing 3–25

```
ACCE "FIND ACCT, LNAME, CITY, STATE, ZIP, or CODEKEY? -> " ;
     TO NDXFILE
NDXFILE = UPPER(NDXFILE)
*
DO CASE
   CASE NDXFILE = "ACCT"
      SET ORDE TO 1
   CASE NDXFILE = "LNAME"
      SET ORDE TO 2
   CASE NDXFILE = "CITY"
      SET ORDE TO 3
   CASE NDXFILE = "STATE"
      SET ORDE TO 4
   CASE NDXFILE = "ZIP"
      SET ORDE TO 5
   CASE NDXFILE = "CODEKEY"
      SET ORDE TO 6
   OTHE
      WAIT "That isn't a valid option. Press any key to continue."
ENDC
```

Listing 3–25 is specialized in that it is for the subscription system example we are using. But we want our kernel to be as generic as possible for use in different applications. The specialized command DO CASE . . . OTHERWISE . . . ENDCASE can be generalized by including Listing 3–26 at the very start of the work session:

Listing 3–26

```
NDXFIELD1 = first index field
NDXFIELD2 = second index field
NDXFIELD3 = third index field
NDXFIELD4 = fourth index field
NDXFIELD5 = fifth index field
NDXFIELD6 = sixth index field
NDXFIELD7 = seventh index field
NDXFILE = 1
```

The code stops at NDXFIELD7 because dBASE III PLUS only allows seven open NDX files per open database file. We can change that by using the SET INDEX TO command to change the open NDX files. The equivalencies in Listing 3–26 create seven variables with the names of seven fields. The DO CASE . . . OTHERWISE . . . ENDCASE command is then changed to:

Listing 3–27

```
@ 22,0 SAY "FIND 1-" + NDXFIELD1 + ", 2-"+;
 NDXFIELD2 + ", 3-" + NDXFIELD3 +;
```

Listing 3–27 (cont.)

```
    ", 4-" + NDXFIELD4 + ", 5-"+;
    NDXFIELD5 + ", 6-" + NDXFIELD6 +;
    ", or 7- " + NDXFIELD7 + " -> " ;
    GET NDXFILE PICT "9" RANG 1,7
READ
*
SET ORDE TO NDXFILE
```

This method GETs a number that corresponds to the desired field. That number is then used to SET the ORDER of the NDX files to a specific file. Notice that this method doesn't allow for error in the @ SAY GET command. It gives the user a PICTURE of the kind of answer we want and only lets the user respond with a number in a valid RANGE. It even SETs the ORDER TO the first NDXFILE should the user do nothing other than press the RETURN key.

Listing 3–27 is useful if there are going to be several different databases with several associated NDX files used in a given work session and you don't want to code Find kernels for each of the separate databases. If you're going to be working with one database that has several associated NDX files, the DO CASE . . . OTHERWISE . . . ENDCASE method is easier to manipulate and allows less room for error. But, coding for the most general, we could use:

Listing 3–28

```
NDXFIELD1 = first index field
NDXFIELD2 = second index field
NDXFIELD3 = third index field
NDXFIELD4 = fourth index field
NDXFIELD5 = fifth index field
NDXFIELD6 = sixth index field
NDXFIELD7 = seventh index field
NDXFILE = 1
```

at the beginning of our calling program. The Find kernel is then written as

Listing 3–29

```
* Find KERNEL EXPANDED FOR SEVERAL DBFS AND NDXES
@ 20,0 CLEA
@ 22,0 SAY "FIND 1-" + NDXFIELD1 + ", 2-" + NDXFIELD2 + ;
  ", 3-" + NDXFIELD3 + ", 4-" +    NDXFIELD4 + ", 5-" + ;
  NDXFIELD5 + ", 6-" + NDXFIELD6 + ", or       7- " + ;
  NDXFIELD7 + " -> " GET NDXFILE PICT "9" RANG 1,7
READ
*
SET ORDE TO NDXFILE
ACCE "FIND > " TO KEYVALUE
FIND &KEYVALUE
```

Listing 3–29 (cont.)

```
*
IF .NOT. FOUND()
   @ 20,0 CLEA
   WAIT "I can't FIND " + KEYVALUE + ;
        ". Perhaps you should SEARCH for it. " + ;
        "Press any key to continue."
ELSE
   * DO GETS
   CLEA GETS
ENDI
* END OF EXPANDED Find KERNEL
```

The Find kernel expanded for a single database with several NDX files, using the Subscription system as a model, is:

Listing 3–30

```
* Find KERNEL EXPANDED FOR A SINGLE DBF WITH NDXES
@ 20,0 CLEA
ACCE "FIND ACCT, LNAME, CITY, STATE, ZIP, or CODEKEY? -> " ;
     TO NDXFILE
NDXFILE = UPPER(NDXFILE)
*
DO CASE
   CASE NDXFILE = "ACCT"
      SET ORDE TO 1
   CASE NDXFILE = "LNAME"
      SET ORDE TO 2
   CASE NDXFILE = "CITY"
      SET ORDE TO 3
   CASE NDXFILE = "STATE"
      SET ORDE TO 4
   CASE NDXFILE = "ZIP"
      SET ORDE TO 5
   CASE NDXFILE = "CODEKEY"
      SET ORDE TO 6
   OTHE
      WAIT "That isn't a valid option. Press any key to continue."
ENDC
*
ACCE "FIND > " TO KEYVALUE
FIND &KEYVALUE
*
IF .NOT. FOUND()
   @ 20,0 CLEA
   WAIT "I can't FIND " + KEYVALUE +;
```

Listing 3–30 (cont.)

```
        ". Perhaps you should SEARCH for it. "+;
       "Press any key to continue."
ELSE
   * DO GETS
   CLEA GETS
ENDI
* END OF EXPANDED Find KERNEL
```

The Find kernel expanded for several databases and NDX files requires more code at the front end of our system, code that must be accessed with each change in database. Listing 3–30 shows how the basic Find kernel can be expanded for a single database situation.

All the code in this discussion has the limitation of FINDing only the *first* occurrence of the object of interest. What if the user wants the fifth occurrence? We use the contiguity of NDX files to address that problem and add a SKIP option to our calling program.

THE TRANSFER KERNEL

The last basic kernel to discuss is the Transfer kernel. This bit of code is used to transfer data from one database to another. Transferring data from one file to another is very useful when we want to investigate small portions of large databases or when we archive some portion of a database file. This occurs often in accounting systems, when monthly or yearly data is transferred from the working database to a historical database.

The important aspects of transferring data are:

1. knowing what has to be transferred.
2. knowing where the transferred data is coming from.
3. knowing where the transferred data is supposed to go.
4. knowing if we are creating a new target database, rewriting an old target database, or appending to an old target database.
5. the source database is already selected before the Transfer kernel is engaged.
6. we assume the user will either be allowed to tell the system what the transfer parameters are or that the entire situation is automated to the point where the user merely selects the Transfer option.

The heart of the Transfer kernel is the dBASE III PLUS COPY and APPEND commands.

Listing 3–31

```
* Transfer KERNEL
@ 20,0 CLEA
```

Listing 3–31 (cont.)

```
ACCE "What is the name of the target database? -> ";
 TO ARCHIVEFILE
ARCHIVEFILE = ARCHIVEFILE + ".DBF"
*
DO WHIL FILE(ARCHIVEFILE)
   OLDFILE = ARCHIVEFILE
   @ 20,0 CLEA
   ACCE "That file exists. Type another name,"+;
   " A(ppend) to the existing file, or D"+;
    "(elete) the existing file, or RETURN"+;
   "quit." TO ARCHIVEFILE
*
   DO CASE
      CASE ASC(ARCHIVEFILE) = 0
         RETU
      CASE UPPER(ARCHIVEFILE) = "D"
         ERAS &OLDFILE
         ARCHIVEFILE = OLDFILE
      CASE UPPER(ARCHIVEFILE) = "A"
         DATABASE = DBF()
         EXIT
      OTHE
         ARCHIVEFILE = ARCHIVEFILE + ".DBF"
   ENDC
*
ENDD
*
IF ":"$ARCHIVEFILE
   DEFAULT = LEFT(ARCHIVEFILE,1)
   SET DEFA TO &DEFAULT
ENDI
*
@ 20, 0 CLEA
ACCE "What are the transfer conditions? -> " TO CONDITIONS
*
DO WHIL TYPE(CONDITIONS) = "U"
   @ 20,0 CLEA
   ACCE "Those are not valid conditions. Type them"+;
   "again or RETURN to exit." TO CONDITIONS
*
   IF ASC(CONDITIONS) = 0
      RETU
   ENDI
*
ENDD
```

Listing 3-31 (cont.)

```
*
COUNT FOR &CONDITIONS TO TRANSCASE
*
DO WHIL TRANSCASE * RECS() + 89 + (NUMFIELDS * 32) > DISK()
   WAIT "There isn't enough room on the disk. "+;
   "(Q)uit or put a new disk in and T(ry "+;
   "again) -> " TO ANSWER
*
   IF UPPER(ANSWER) <> 'T'
      RETU
   ENDI
*
ENDD
*
IF UPPER(ARCHIVEFILE) = "A"
   USE &OLDFILE
   APPE FROM &DATABASE FOR &CONDITIONS
ELSE
   COPY TO &ARCHIVEFILE FOR &CONDITIONS
ENDI
* END OF Transfer KERNEL
```

The kernel begins by clearing the bottom of the screen and getting the name of a target file. If the user gives the target file a name similar to an existing file, he or she is given several options. The user can enter another name, APPEND to the existing file, DELETE the existing file and write a new file, or quit the Transfer kernel completely. All of these options are handled in a DO CASE . . . OTHERWISE . . . ENDCASE statement. If the user presses RETURN, which dBASE III PLUS interprets as having an ASCII value of 0, the kernel RETURNs to the calling program. Typing a D ERASEs the existing file. Typing an A tells III PLUS to prepare for an APPEND by getting the name of the in USE database, then EXIT the DO WHILE . . . ENDDO loop. The OTHERWISE condition of the DO CASE . . . OTHERWISE . . . ENDCASE statement handles renaming the target database.

Once that loop is passed, the kernel checks to see if the user is transferring to another disk drive. If so, it SETs the DEFAULT to that new drive.

We've accepted the target file and switched drives (if necessary). Now get the transfer CONDITIONs. If the CONDITIONs are not valid (if they're UNKNOWN to dBASE III PLUS), either get new CONDITIONs or quit the kernel.

The COUNT command and following DO WHILE . . . ENDDO loop check to make sure there is enough room on the target disk to hold all the data being transferred. The kernel COUNTs how many records in the source database meet the desired CONDITIONs. WHILE the number of desired records times the size of the record, plus 89, plus the number of fields times 32 is greater than the available DISK space, put up the error message. Where do these numbers come from?

TRANSCASE is the number of records to transfer.

RECS() is the size of a source record in bytes.

89 is the size of a dBASE III PLUS database file header block, in bytes.

NUMFIELDS is the number of fields per record. We must place this number in the Transfer kernel, as it depends on the database being transferred. If the Transfer kernel is going to be used for a number of databases, NUMFIELDS can be a SAVEd MEMORY variable.

32 is the size, in bytes, of a database field descriptor.

DISK() is the amount of free space on the default drive, in bytes (we SET the DEFAULT to the target drive earlier).

At this point the user can exit the Transfer kernel simply by pressing any key other than T. Notice that the kernel doesn't offer the option of transferring the entire source database to the target file. That is unnecessary, because the source database is already handled by the DOS COPY command. Programmers familiar with dBASE III PLUS may wonder why the kernel doesn't check for available disk space with the ERROR(56) function. That function only works once the transfer of data has started. No one wants to be 99 percent of the way through an APPEND or COPY and only then find out there isn't enough room on the target disk.

The actual transfer of information occurs in the IF . . . ELSE . . . ENDIF statement at the end of the kernel. IF the desired ARCHIVEFILE existed and was to be APPENDed, we USE the existing target file and APPEND from the source DATABASE FOR the desired CONDITIONS. If we're not APPENDing, we can COPY the desired information to the ARCHIVEFILE.

That is the basic Transfer kernel. As written, the Transfer kernel assumes an unINDEXed source database. Using an INDEXed database can improve the efficiency of this kernel immensely if the user wants transfer conditions based on the INDEXed field. The consideration is whether we want to let the user transfer from one NDX, several NDXes, or none. None is handled by the present code. If the source database is INDEXed with only one NDX file, there isn't much new code to be written. The user must know that instead of typing in a complete condition statement such as:

```
STATE = 'NH'
```

he or she only needs to type in NH (assuming the database is INDEXed on the STATE field). Our first job is to determine if the user typed in valid data for the INDEXed field. That is accomplished with:

Listing 3–32

```
DO WHIL TYPE("&CONDITIONS") # TYPE(INDEXFIELD)
  error messages and exit opportunity
ENDD
```

There aren't any relevant changes to the error messages that are internal to the DO WHILE . . . ENDDO loop. The next change comes directly before the COUNT statement.

Listing 3–33

```
FIND "&CONDITIONS"
*
IF .NOT. FOUND()
   WAIT "There are no matching conditions. Press "+;
   "any key to exit."
   RETU
ENDI
*
COUNT WHIL &CONDITIONS TO TRANSCASE
```

There's always the chance that what the user wants as the CONDITION doesn't exist in the source database, and the IF . . . ENDIF statement takes care of that possibility. The COUNT command is also modified; the FOR qualifier is replaced by a WHILE. The next change necessary to the Transfer kernel is the addition of another FIND "&CONDITIONS" before the actual transfer statements. This repositions the record pointer to the start of the desired records. Lastly, the FOR qualifiers in the transfer statements are replaced by WHILEs. The finished Transfer kernel for an INDEXed database is:

Listing 3–34

```
* Transfer KERNEL FOR AN INDEXED DATABASE
@ 20,0 CLEA
ACCE "What is the name of the target database? -> ";
TO ARCHIVEFILE
ARCHIVEFILE = ARCHIVEFILE + ".DBF"
*
DO WHIL FILE(ARCHIVEFILE)
   OLDFILE = ARCHIVEFILE
   @ 20,0 CLEA
   ACCE "That file exists. Type another name, "+;
        "A(ppend) to the existing file, or "+;
        "D(elete) the existing file, or RETURN "+;
        "to quit." TO ARCHIVEFILE
*
   DO CASE
      CASE ASC(ARCHIVEFILE) = 0
         RETU
      CASE UPPER(ARCHIVEFILE) = "D"
         ERAS &OLDFILE
         ARCHIVEFILE = OLDFILE
         EXIT
```

Listing 3–34 (cont.)

```
      CASE UPPER(ARCHIVEFILE) = "A"
         DATABASE = DBF()
         EXIT
      OTHE
         ARCHIVEFILE = ARCHIVEFILE + ".DBF"
   ENDC
*
ENDD
*
IF ":"ARCHIVEFILE
   DEFAULT = LEFT(ARCHIVEFILE,1)
   SET DEFA TO &DEFAULT
ENDI
*
@ 20, 0 CLEA
ACCE "What are the transfer conditions? -> " TO CONDITIONS
*
DO WHIL TYPE("&CONDITIONS") = TYPE(INDEXFIELD)
   @ 20,0 CLEA
   ACCE "Those are not valid conditions. Type "+;
   "them again or RETURN to exit." TO CONDITIONS
*
   IF ASC(CONDITIONS) = 0
      RETU
   ENDI
*
ENDD
*
FIND "&CONDITIONS"
*
IF .NOT. FOUND()
   WAIT "There are no matching conditions. Press "+;
   "any key to exit."
   RETU
ENDI
*
COUNT WHIL &CONDITIONS TO TRANSCASE
*
DO WHIL TRANSCASE * RECS() + 89 + (NUMFIELDS * 32) > DISK()
   WAIT "There isn't enough room on the disk. "+;
        "(Q)uit or put a new disk in and "+;
        "T(ry again) -> " TO ANSWER
*
   IF UPPER(ANSWER) <> 'T'
      RETU
```

Listing 3–34 (cont.)

```
   ENDI
*
ENDD
*
FIND "&CONDITIONS"
*
IF UPPER(ARCHIVEFILE) = "A"
   USE &OLDFILE
   APPE FROM &DATABASE WHIL &CONDITIONS
ELSE
   COPY TO &ARCHIVEFILE WHIL &CONDITIONS
ENDI
* END OF Transfer KERNEL FOR INDEXED DATABASE
```

The next set of modifications that you might consider are when the database is INDEXed to more than one NDX file. You can choose whether to limit the user's ability to choose those fields.

We assume the user has a basic knowledge of what each NDX file is INDEXed on. We make use of the SET ORDER TO command and the NDX() function.

Listing 3–35

```
@ 0,0 CLEA
? "Available NDX files are:"
N = 1
*
DO WHIL N < 8
   ? STR(N) + " -> " + NDX(N)
   N = N + 1
ENDD
*
@ 15,0 SAY "NDX file number -> " GET N PICT "9" RANGE 1,7
READ
SET ORDE TO N
* DO SAYS
* DO GETS
CLEA GETS
```

Listing 3–35 handles the available NDX files by the order assigned them when you designed the system. dBASE III PLUS will read the number the user selects and SET the ORDER of the NDX files TO that number. III PLUS lists null strings if there aren't seven NDX files. For the purists, a MEM variable can be created that passes the number of available NDX files to the Transfer kernel.

The rest of the kernel remains unchanged, except that a last line has been added just before the end of the kernel. We've SET the ORDER of the NDX files TO something other than the usual system setup, so we have to restore the natural order with SET ORDE TO 1.

The kernel is:

Listing 3–36

```
* Transfer KERNEL FOR A DATABASE WITH SEVERAL NDX FILES
@ 20,0 CLEA
ACCE "What is the name of the target database? -> ";
TO ARCHIVEFILE
ARCHIVEFILE = ARCHIVEFILE + ".DBF"
*
DO WHIL FILE(ARCHIVEFILE)
   OLDFILE = ARCHIVEFILE
   @ 20,0 CLEA
   ACCE "That file exists. Type another name, "+;
    "A(ppend) to the existing file, "+;
    "D(elete) the existing file, or RETURN to "+;
    "quit. ->" TO ARCHIVEFILE
*
   DO CASE
      CASE ASC(ARCHIVEFILE) = 0
         RETU
      CASE UPPER(ARCHIVEFILE) = "D"
         ERAS &OLDFILE
         ARCHIVEFILE = OLDFILE
      CASE UPPER(ARCHIVEFILE) = "A"
         DATABASE = DBF()
         EXIT
      OTHE
         ARCHIVEFILE = ARCHIVEFILE + ".DBF"
   ENDC
*
ENDD
*
IF ":"$ARCHIVEFILE
   DEFAULT = LEFT(ARCHIVEFILE,1)
   SET DEFA TO &DEFAULT
ENDI
*
@ 0,0 CLEA
? "Available NDX files are:"
N = 1
*
DO WHIL N < 8
   ? STR(N) + " -> " + NDX(N)
   N = N + 1
```

Listing 3–36 (cont.)

```
ENDD
*
@ 15,0 SAY "NDX file number -> " GET N PICT "9" RANGE 1,7
READ
SET ORDE TO N
* DO SAYS
* DO GETS
CLEA GETS
@ 20, 0 CLEA
ACCE "What are the transfer conditions? -> " TO CONDITIONS
*
DO WHIL TYPE("&CONDITIONS") = TYPE(INDEXFIELD)
   @ 20,0 CLEA
   ACCE "Those are not valid conditions. "+;
        "Type them again or RETURN to exit. -> " TO CONDITIONS
*
   IF ASC(CONDITIONS) = 0
      RETU
   ENDI
*
ENDD
*
FIND "&CONDITIONS"
*
IF .NOT. FOUND()
   WAIT "There are no matching conditions. Press any key to exit."
   RETU
ENDI
*
COUNT WHIL &CONDITIONS TO TRANSCASE
*
DO WHIL TRANSCASE * RECS() + 89 + (NUMFIELDS * 32) > DISK()
   WAIT "There isn't enough room on the disk. "+;
        "(Q)uit or put a new disk in and "+;
        "T(ry again) -> " TO ANSWER" *
   IF UPPER(ANSWER) <> 'T'
      RETU
   ENDI
*
ENDD
*
FIND "&CONDITIONS"
*
IF UPPER(ARCHIVEFILE) = "A"
   USE &OLDFILE
```

Listing 3–36 (cont.)

```
   APPE FROM &DATABASE WHIL &CONDITIONS
ELSE
   COPY TO &ARCHIVEFILE WHIL &CONDITIONS
ENDI
*
SET ORDE TO 1
* END OF Transfer KERNEL FOR DATABASE WITH SEVERAL NDX FILES
```

This kernel is now designed for transferring information when the source database has several possible NDX conditions to use in that transfer. It is important to remember that this kernel is so complex because it must error check both the user and the system. Next we'll see how to bring all these kernels together in a simple menu system.

A SIMPLE MENU SYSTEM

If you've followed the kernels up to now, you've seen that we've created small kernels of code to handle the commonest database applications. The last step of the process is to link all the small application specific kernels together. That is done with a simple menu system.

Menu systems have two parts. The first part displays the menu to the user and reads the option selected. The second part performs the desired action based on the user's choice. The physical size and shape of the screen menu system depends on your user's tastes and how much patience you have in programming. I make it a point to keep some of the database's information up on the screen at all times with the SAY and GET files, which means I use the lower portion of the screen for most menus. The menu options I offer in this simple system are Edit, Add, Delete, Find, and Transfer.

Remembering that the menu is contained at the bottom of the screen, code:

Listing 3–37

```
@ 20,0 TO 23,79
@ 21,1 SAY [  E -> Edit  A -> Add  D -> Dele  F -> ] + ;
         [Find  T -> Tran  Q -> Quit]
@ 23,34 SAY "select ->       "
@ 23,44 GET ANSWER PICT '!'
READ
```

which takes care of offering users choices and getting their choices to the program. The next part of the menu system is taking action based on the user's choices. That is done with a DO CASE . . . OTHERWISE . . . ENDCASE statement:

Listing 3–38

```
*
DO CASE
```

Listing 3–38 (cont.)

```
   CASE ANSWER = "Q"
*
      IF DELFLAG
         CLEA
         ACCE "Deletions have been made. Make them "+;
              "PERMANENT? (Y/N) -> " TO DELFLAG
*
         IF DELFLAG
            RECA FOR .NOT. PERM
            PACK
         ENDI
*
      ENDI
*
      RETU
   CASE ANSWER = "E"
      DO EDITOR       && Edit kernel
   CASE ANSWER = "A"
      DO ADDER                    && Add kernel
   CASE ANSWER = "D"
      DO DELETER                  && Delete kernel
   CASE ANSWER = "F"
      DO FINDER                   && Find kernel
   CASE ANSWER = "T"
      DO TRANSFER                 && Transfer kernel
   OTHE
      @ 20,0 CLEA
      WAIT "That isn't an option. Press any key to continue."
ENDC
*
```

The complete menu system only needs to know what variables it will use and which are carried into it. None are carried into it from the example used in this chapter, so the complete simple menu system is:

Listing 3–39

```
* SIMPLE MENU SYSTEM FOR SUBSCRIPTION SYSTEM
SET TALK OFF
SET PROC TO SUBSPRC
NUMFIELDS = 13
DBFILE = "SUBSCRIBER DATABASE"
PLACE = 40 - DBFILE/2
USE SUBS INDE SACCT,SLNAME,SCITY,SSTATE,SZIP,SCODEKEY
ANSWER = "Q"
DO SUBSAY
```

Listing 3–39 (cont.)

```
DO SUBGET
CLEA GETS
*
DO WHIL .T.
   @ 2,60 SAY IIF(DELETED(),"DELETED",SPACE(8)) +;
   IIF(PERM,"PERMANENT",SPACE(9))
   @ 20,0 CLEA
   @ 20,0 TO 23,79
   @ 21,1 SAY [  E -> Edit  A -> Add  D -> Dele  F]+;
     [ -> Find  T -> Tran  Q -> Quit]
   @ 23,34 SAY "select ->       "
   @ 23,44 GET ANSWER PICT '!'
   READ
*
   DO CASE
      CASE ANSWER = "Q"
*
         IF DELFLAG
            CLEA
            ACCE "Deletions have been made. Make "+;
                 "them PERMANENT? (Y/N) -> " TO DELFLAG
*
            IF DELFLAG
               RECA FOR .NOT. PERM
               PACK
            ENDI
*
         ENDI
*
         RETU
      CASE ANSWER = "E"
         DO EDITOR                            && Edit kernel
      CASE ANSWER = "A"
         DO ADDER                             && Add kernel
      CASE ANSWER = "D"
         DO DELETER                           && Delete kernel
      CASE ANSWER = "F"
         DO FINDER                            && Find kernel
      CASE ANSWER = "T"
         DO TRANSFER                          && Transfer kernel
      OTHE
         @ 20,0 CLEA
         WAIT "That isn't an option. Press any key to continue."
   ENDC
*
```

Listing 3–39 (cont.)

```
ENDD
* END OF SIMPLE MENU SYSTEM
```

What does the menu system do? We've gone to a lot of trouble to control the screen, so SET TALK OFF to make sure only the correct display appears on the screen. SET PROCEDURE TO procedure file, SUBPROC in this case, tells dBASE III PLUS where all the kernels for this application live (the SUBPROC procedure file is listed at the end of this section).

The next four lines are declarations to the MENU program assigning values to NUMFIELDS, DBFILE and PLACE, to USE the SUBS database and its NDX files, and create a menu program variable (which the menu system initializes with the Quit Program option).

The next two lines paint our initial screen. Next the program enters a DO WHILE . . . ENDDO loop to actually handle our menu selections. The loop begins with the DELETEd record message, then displays the menu options and GETS them from the user.

The last part of the program is a DO CASE . . . OTHERWISE . . . ENDCASE statement that performs the user's menu choice.

This menu offers all the options discussed in this chapter; it is efficient and tight. In a way, it is a kernel itself. We will use this very menu system to build our other, more complex menus later on in Chapters 5 and beyond.

The only part left to create is the procedure file, SUBPROC.PRG. That is done by stringing together our kernels, slightly modified for this application, and using standard dBASE III PLUS procedure file command syntax.

Listing 3–40

```
* SUBPROC.PRG PROCEDURE FILE FOR SUBSCRIPTION SYSTEM
*


PROC SUBSAY
CLEA
@  1,  0  TO 19, 79    DOUBLE
@  3,  1  TO  3, 78    DOUBLE
@ 13,  1  TO 13, 15
@ 13,  1  TO 13, 78
@  2, PLACE SAY DBFILE
@  2,65 SAY "# "
@  5,  2  SAY "ACCT"
@  5, 17  SAY "LNAME"
@  5, 41  SAY "FNAME"
@  7,  2  SAY "ADDRESS"
@  7, 38  SAY "ADDRESS1"
@  9,  2  SAY "BLDG"
@  9, 11  SAY "APT"
@  9, 19  SAY "LOT"
```

Listing 3-40 (cont.)

```
@  9, 28  SAY "CITY"
@  9, 50  SAY "STATE"
@  9, 60  SAY "ZIP"
@ 11,  2  SAY "HTEL"
@ 11, 21  SAY "WTEL"
@ 13, 32  SAY "SERVICES"
@ 15,  7  SAY "TIER1"
@ 15, 18  SAY "TIER2"
@ 15, 29  SAY "TIER3"
@ 15, 40  SAY "TIER4"
@ 15, 51  SAY "TIER5"
@ 15, 62  SAY "TIER6"
@ 16,  7  SAY "TIER7"
@ 16, 18  SAY "TIER8"
@ 16, 29  SAY "TIER9"
@ 16, 40  SAY "TIER10"
@ 16, 51  SAY "TIER11"
@ 16, 62  SAY "TIER12"
@ 18,  7  SAY "RATE"
@ 18, 26  SAY "CONVERTER"
@ 18, 51  SAY "HOOKED_UP"
* END OF SUBSAY

PROC SUBGET
@ 2,70 SAY STR(RECNO(),4,0)
@  5,  7  GET  SUBS->ACCT
@  5, 24  GET  SUBS->LNAME
@  5, 48  GET  SUBS->FNAME
@  7, 10  GET  SUBS->ADDRESS
@  7, 47  GET  SUBS->ADDRESS1  PICTURE "XXXXXXXXXXXXXXXXXXXXXXXXXXXXXX"
@  9,  7  GET  SUBS->BLDG
@  9, 15  GET  SUBS->APT
@  9, 23  GET  SUBS->LOT
@  9, 33  GET  SUBS->CITY
@  9, 56  GET  SUBS->STATE
@  9, 64  GET  SUBS->ZIP
@ 11,  7  GET  SUBS->HTEL  PICTURE "999-999-9999"
@ 11, 27  GET  SUBS->WTEL  PICTURE "999-999-9999"
@ 15, 13  GET  SUBS->TIER1
@ 15, 24  GET  SUBS->TIER2
@ 15, 35  GET  SUBS->TIER3
@ 15, 47  GET  SUBS->TIER4
@ 15, 58  GET  SUBS->TIER5
@ 15, 69  GET  SUBS->TIER6
@ 16, 13  GET  SUBS->TIER7
```

Listing 3–40 (cont.)

```
@ 16, 24  GET  SUBS->TIER8
@ 16, 35  GET  SUBS->TIER9
@ 16, 47  GET  SUBS->TIER10
@ 16, 58  GET  SUBS->TIER11
@ 16, 69  GET  SUBS->TIER12
@ 18, 15  GET  SUBS->RATE  PICTURE "999.99"
@ 18, 38  GET  SUBS->CONVERTER
@ 18, 62  GET  SUBS->HOOKED_UP
*
IF ERROR() <> 5
   READ
ELSE
   WAIT "I can't get that record. Press any key to continue."
ENDI
* END OF SUBGET


PROC EDIT
@ 20,0 CLEAR
@ 22,0 SAY "Press CTRL-W to save edit, CTRL-Q to"+;
  " quit without saving edit."
DO SUBGET
READ
* END OF Edit KERNEL


PROC ADD
COPY STRU TO TANK
SELE 2
USE TANK
FIELD1 = FIELD(1)
FIELD2 = FIELD(2)
FIELD3 = FIELD(3)
FIELD4 = FIELD(4)
FIELD5 = FIELD(5)
FIELD6 = FIELD(6)
FIELD7 = FIELD(7)
FIELD8 = FIELD(8)
FIELD9 = FIELD(9)
@ 20,0 CLEA
@ 22,0 SAY "Press CTRL-W to save and continue,"+;
 "CTRL-W at an empty screen to exit."
REPEATER = FIELD(1)
*
DO WHIL .T.
   APPE BLAN
   * DO GETS
```

Listing 3–40 (cont.)

```
   READ
*
   IF LEN(TRIM(&REPEATER) = 0
      DELE
      EXIT
   ENDI
*
   SET FUNC 2 TO TRIM(&FIELD1)+";"
   SET FUNC 3 TO TRIM(&FIELD2)+";"
   SET FUNC 4 TO TRIM(&FIELD3)+";"
   SET FUNC 5 TO TRIM(&FIELD4)+";"
   SET FUNC 6 TO TRIM(&FIELD5)+";"
   SET FUNC 7 TO TRIM(&FIELD6)+";"
   SET FUNC 8 TO TRIM(&FIELD7)+";"
   SET FUNC 9 TO TRIM(&FIELD8)+";"
   SET FUNC 10 TO TRIM(&FIELD9)+";"
ENDD
*
SET DELE ON
USE
SELE 1
APPE FROM TANK
SET DELE OFF
DO SUBGET
CLEA GETS
* END OF Add KERNEL

PROC DELETER
DELE
@ 20,0 CLEA
@ 22,0 SAY "Is this a PERMANENT deletion? ";
   GET PERM PICTURE "N"
READ
DELFLAG = .T.
* END OF Delete KERNEL

PROC FINDER
@ 20,0 CLEA
ACCE "FIND ACCT, LNAME, CITY, STATE, ZIP, or CODEKEY? -> " ;
     TO NDXFILE
NDXFILE = UPPER(NDXFILE)
*
DO CASE
   CASE NDXFILE = "ACCT"
      SET ORDE TO 1
```

Listing 3–40 (cont.)

```
   CASE NDXFILE = "LNAME"
      SET ORDE TO 2
   CASE NDXFILE = "CITY"
      SET ORDE TO 3
   CASE NDXFILE = "STATE"
      SET ORDE TO 4
   CASE NDXFILE = "ZIP"
      SET ORDE TO 5
   CASE NDXFILE = "CODEKEY"
      SET ORDE TO 6
   OTHE
      WAIT "That isn't a valid option. Press any key to continue."
ENDC
*
ACCE "FIND > " TO KEYVALUE
FIND &KEYVALUE
*
IF .NOT. FOUND()
   @ 20,0 CLEA
   WAIT "I can't FIND " + KEYVALUE +;
        ". Perhaps you should SEARCH for it. "+;
        "Press any key to continue."
ELSE
   DO SUBGET
   CLEA GETS
ENDI
* END OF Find KERNEL

PROC TRANSFER
@ 20,0 CLEA
ACCE "What is the name of the target database? -> ";
     TO ARCHIVEFILE
ARCHIVEFILE = ARCHIVEFILE + ".DBF"
*
DO WHIL FILE(ARCHIVEFILE)
   OLDFILE = ARCHIVEFILE
   @ 20,0 CLEA
   ACCE "That file exists. Type another name, "+;
        "A(ppend) to the existing file, "+;
        "D(elete) the existing file, or RETURN to "+;
        "quit. ->" TO ARCHIVEFILE
*
   DO CASE
      CASE ASC(ARCHIVEFILE) = 0
         RETU
```

Listing 3–40 (cont.)

```
      CASE UPPER(ARCHIVEFILE) = "D"
         ERAS &OLDFILE
         ARCHIVEFILE = OLDFILE
      CASE UPPER(ARCHIVEFILE) = "A"
         DATABASE = DBF()
         EXIT
      OTHE
         ARCHIVEFILE = ARCHIVEFILE + ".DBF"
   ENDC
*
ENDD
*
IF ":"$ARCHIVEFILE
   DEFAULT = LEFT(ARCHIVEFILE,1)
   SET DEFA TO &DEFAULT
ENDI
*
@ 0,0 CLEA
? "Available NDX files are:"
N = 1
*
DO WHIL N < 8
   ? STR(N) + " -> " + NDX(N)
   N = N + 1
ENDD
*
@ 15,0 SAY "NDX file number -> " GET N PICT "9" RANGE 1,7
READ
SET ORDE TO N
DO SUBSAY
DO SUBGET
CLEA GETS
@ 20, 0 CLEA
ACCE "What are the transfer conditions? -> " TO CONDITIONS
*
DO WHIL TYPE("&CONDITIONS") # TYPE(INDEXFIELD)
   @ 20,0 CLEA
   ACCE "Those are not valid conditions. "+;
        "Type them again or RETURN to exit. -> "+;
        TO CONDITIONS
*
   IF ASC(CONDITIONS) = 0
      RETU
   ENDI
*
```

Listing 3-40 (cont.)

```
ENDD
*
FIND "&CONDITIONS"
*
IF .NOT. FOUND()
   WAIT "There are no matching conditions. Press any key to exit."
   RETU
ENDI
*
COUNT WHIL &CONDITIONS TO TRANSCASE
*
DO WHIL TRANSCASE * RECS() + 89 + (NUMFIELDS * 32) > DISK()
   WAIT "There isn't enough room on the disk. "+;
        "(Q)uit or put a new disk in and T(ry again) -> " ;
        TO ANSWER
*
   IF UPPER(ANSWER) = "Q"
      RETU
   ENDI
*
ENDD
*
FIND "&CONDITIONS"
*
IF UPPER(ARCHIVEFILE) = "A"
   USE &OLDFILE
   APPE FROM &DATABASE WHIL &CONDITIONS
ELSE
   COPY TO &ARCHIVEFILE WHIL &CONDITIONS
ENDI
*
SET ORDE TO 1
* END OF Transfer KERNEL
* END OF PROCEDURE FILE
```

Note that the separate procedures are our kernels, slightly modified for this application. The dBASE III PLUS limit on separate procedures in a procedure file is 32. This file only contains eight separate procedures, three of which are unique to this application. In Chapter 5 and later chapters procedure files will be used as the primary reservoirs of kernels in applications.

SUMMARY

This chapter has provided you with an introduction to the basic kernels of code that execute 99 percent of database application tasks. The emphasis has been on coding in small, reusable modules that can be readily modified to handle a number of situations. These are the tools we put in our code library and use as necessary.

Throughout the rest of this book these kernels will be used and modified as needed to perform the different functions of inventory management, accounts receivable, subscriber list maintcnancc, and other applications.

CHAPTER

4

DATABASE DESIGNS

Those of you that have been programming for several months or years may wonder what this chapter is about. What are databases for specific designs?

Probably you have either been designing your databases for their specific jobs unconsciously, or you will read this chapter and learn why you *should* design your databases for specific jobs.

One thing I've emphasized in my lectures and articles is that microcomputers are going to start competing head to head with mini and mainframes in the office. But what do average users care about micro, mini, or mainframe? Their equation is simple. They want the speed and power of a mainframe for half the cost of a micro. It is your job to pack as much speed and power into the micro system as possible. Packing speed and power has a lot to do with how you design your database system, and that design has a lot to do with the databases you plan to use in your system.

This chapter begins by recognizing how different needs demand different solutions. Second, it explains why those different solutions are implemented. Third, it shows how to set things up so that a system can be efficient for both you and the user.

DIFFERENT DATABASES FOR DIFFERENT JOBS

A while back I helped a friend move a bush. We didn't have to move it very far, about ten feet. No big deal.

That's an oversimplification. The bush was about 7 feet tall and about 12 feet around. It was actually a bush trying hard to be a tree. We dug around the bush's roots, trying to keep as much dirt on them as possible to avoid root shock. Once we isolated the root cluster, I tried to use my shovel to pry the cluster (and hence the bush itself) up out of the hole.

I weigh about 185 pounds. I tried to pry the cluster up using an old short handled shovel. I owe my friend a new shovel, or at least a handle.

Don't beat around the bush, Joseph, what are you really trying to say? The moral of this story is that I did not use the right tool for the task of lifting the bush out of the soil. Instead I used the tool that was handy. It was a mistake.

Many good programmers use the wrong tool when they design database systems. They use the tool that is handy instead of getting the right tool for the job.

Imagine you are asked to design a database system for a magazine office. The database system must print mailing labels, take care of subscriber accounting, send notices to errant subscribers, and prepare renewal notices to subscribers approaching the end of their subscription. Your first priority, before you even begin to code or look for library modules to use as the basis of the system, is to determine how the database should look.

You should not, under any circumstances, use the same old database that you've used for your other, nonmagazine subscription system applications. You would be using the wrong tool for the job. How important is using specially designed databases for each application?

The application dictates the database design. Your client tells you to design a subscription system. You, in your greater wisdom and far ranging experience, know the client will need several different databases to do the job.

Specifically, your client asked that the database system:

1. print mailing labels.
2. perform subscriber accounting.
3. generate delinquent account notices.
4. prepare renewal notices.

Take each of those items singly. First, we are interested in printing mailing labels. A mailing label has very little information. It contains NAME, ADDRESS1, ADDRESS2, CITY, STATE, ZIP, and COUNTRY. It might also contain the subscription termination date (TERMDATE), a routing code (ROUTECODE), and an accounting code for the subscription system (ACCT). These last three items are not necessary to the actual mailing label, but might be useful when a subscriber calls the magazine to inquire about his or her account.

The database for generating mailing labels has very few fields. The important fields, ZIP and ACCT, are the first and second fields of the database. This decreases search time because dBASE III PLUS spends less time locating each field in each record.

What is the most important field shown in Figure 4–1? That's a trick question unless you know something about bulk mailings. The most important field for mailing labels is the ZIP. The post office insists that bulk mailings be separated by zip code.

What is the second most important field? That depends on your operation. If the magazine has an accounting code, then ACCT is the second most important field. If the client doesn't use accounting codes, then NAME is the second most important field. Why?

```
-> USE MAILING
-> LIST STRUC
Structure for database: D:MAILING.DBF
Number of data records:       0
Date of last update   : 11/17/86
Field  Field Name  Type       Width    Dec
    1  ZIP         Character     10
    2  ACCT        Character      7
    3  NAME        Character     30
    4  ADDRESS1    Character     30
    5  ADDRESS2    Character     30
    6  CITY        Character     30
    7  STATE       Character      2
    8  TERMDATE    Date           8
    9  ROUTECODE   Character     10
** Total **                     158
```

Figure 4–1 This is the structure of the mailing label database.

Because, as mentioned earlier, subscribers call up the magazine office to make inquiries about their account. This can range from changing the delivery address to an actual bookkeeping problem. The nature of the problem isn't your concern. What you must plan for is how the user will go from asking the caller "What is your account number?" to getting that person's information up on the screen for editing. At this point you should note that your database should always include an ACCT field. Very few operations can survive long or grow at all with out issuing account numbers, even if the numbers are nothing more than CARRJOSD03063 (CARRabisJOSephDavid03063) or _8CARRABISJOSEPH (LEFT(ACCT,2)+LNAME+FNAME). Designing a database to anticipate the future saves both you and your client headaches down the road.

Okay, we've isolated the two most important fields in this database. Why we've bothered to isolate the important fields is covered later in this chapter, because it has to do with knowing how dBASE III PLUS works. Next we look at our customer's second request, subscriber accounting.

What do we need in accounting? NAME or ACCT, BALANCE, last payment date (LASTPAYDT), last payment amount (LASTPAYAMT), termination date (TERMDATE), ACTIVE (as in active members/subscribers versus people whose membership or subscription has expired), start date (START), stop date (STOP), and restart date (RESTART). The accounting database, shown in Figure 4–2, contains only those fields necessary for accounting. The most important field, ACCT, is the first field in the database. It is followed by BALANCE and TERMDATE, because we know those fields will be queried often.

The next step is to do some set arithmetic on the fields used in the accounting database and the fields used in the mailing labels database. There should be only one field in common, NAME/ACCT. Because there is only one field in common,

```
-> USE ACCOUNTS
-> LIST STRUC
Structure for database: D:ACCOUNTS.DBF
Number of data records:        0
Date of last update   : 11/17/86
Field  Field Name  Type        Width    Dec
    1  ACCT        Character       7
    2  BALANCE     Numeric        10      2
    3  NAME        Character      30
    4  LASTPAYDT   Date            8
    5  LASTPAYAMT  Numeric        10      2
    6  TERMDATE    Date            8
    7  ACTIVE      Logical         1
    8  START       Date            8
    9  STOP        Date            8
** Total **                       91
```

Figure 4–2 Here is the structure of the accounting database.

you can probably get away with a separate database for the accounting needs of the magazine.

Let's consider the statement about database needs in its entirety. If the needs of the subscription system are small (there aren't that many subscribers and never will be), you can place all the fields listed so far in a single database. If the system is going to grow, you should separate the databases to help minimize access time (such design tips are discussed fully later in the chapter). Few operations want to remain stagnant, so we design for growth.

The other fields are fairly common in a subscription system. You want to know all subscribers' BALANCEs to send out delinquent payment notices, when and how much the last payments were, when the subscriptions terminate to send out renewal notices, when new subscribers start service, and when existing subscribers stop and restart service should they leave for vacations or the like. The ACTIVE field is a historical field your client will use to send "Have you missed your last three issues of *BLABBERMOUTH Monthly?*" letters to subscribers that haven't bothered to renew.

The accounting part of this system should have the ACCT field first. Next comes BALANCE. BALANCE is obviously important—you'll be sending out bills based on records that meet the condition "BALANCE <> 0." That condition is actually the most important part of the accounting. Your client doesn't want to send bills to everybody blindly. Your client is most interested in those subscribers that still owe a few shekels. Why not put that field first?

The answer is simple, and the best example is found in most personal checking accounts. How steady is the balance? If yours is like mine it jumps up and down. Occasionally the balance is negative, and once in a while there's enough money in the account to earn some interest. Individual balances in an accounting system are the same. They fluctuate according to the billing cycle. BALANCE should be high on the list of fields, as the user will be querying that field often, but it shouldn't be the first field in the database. Another important field is TERMDATE. People never know when their subscriptions end, and rarely will they send magazines money "just in case." The magazines have to tell them when they're about to end service.

Likewise, for continuity and ease of use you want the ACCT field prioritized in the database. You will be querying that field to answer subscriber questions, and more importantly, to match receivables to addresses for mailing.

The preceding paragraph set the groundwork for the next item our client wants. The company wants to send out delinquency notices. Easy enough. You have one database that shows whether the subscriber owes money and when the last payment was, and you have another database that lists the subscriber's address.

dBASE III PLUS provides a variety of ways you can transfer information from databases to paper. Here you want to find out who owes money, where they live, and send notices to their addresses telling them how much they owe.

One method of getting information from the databases to paper involves joining data from the two existing databases into a third. This third database is a synthesis of the fields in the mailing label and subscriber accounting databases. The premise here is that there are several hundred notices to go out. You don't necessarily want to tie up the computer and printer while dBASE III PLUS finds delinquent accounts, matches the records with unpaid balances to their corresponding addresses, then prints out notices. You want to take considerably less time by having dBASE III PLUS JOIN the necessary information from the two databases into a third, temporary database. That third database can then be used for an overnight print run.

Well, if you were going to do it overnight, why bother to create a third database? Because strange things happen overnight. "The database monster" only comes out at night. And its one goal in life is to mess up computers left standing alone, chugging away. I would prefer risking one easily reconstructed database than two quite important databases.

But, you say, that is what backups are for. True, and anyone who finds a cyberphobic user that backs up daily (prior to experiencing a massive disk failure) gets a free pizza.

Another method of sending out delinquent notices is to use the dBASE III PLUS SET RELATION TO and COPY DELIMITED commands to create a word processor compatible mail merge file. This method is well suited to companies that want to send personal notices to clients. The least pleasing option is to have the computer and printer tied up while the user sits there. It's aesthetically unsatisfactory, but sometimes necessary.

If you've been paying attention in preceding chapters, you know that this book emphasizes modular, structured coding. Our mythical client's last request is an excellent example of why modular, structured coding is so valuable.

This last request is the ability to send out renewal notices. Ideally, these notices should go out two to three months before termination would occur. No problem! dBASE III PLUS handles DATE arithmetic with no difficulty. What else is involved?

Remarkably little. You already developed this part of the application when you laid out the code for the delinquent notices module. The purpose of both requests is to get information from the databases to paper. Both requests look through the accounting database to find out who should get notices, then through the mailing label database to see where to send the notices. There is little that needs to be done to get this part up and running, once the delinquent notice module is active. In truth, you don't even need to write any more code. These two requests, sending out renewal and delinquency notices, can be done by the exact same piece of code. The only addition to the code written for the delinquency notice module is giving the user the ability to choose between renewal or delinquency notices, and that is what menus are for.

The point of this discussion is that you should design your databases before you design anything else. No matter how much code you write, your code will be executed as needed and is basically replaceable. Your databases, however, are irreplaceable. They should be designed for maximum efficiency and minimum access time from the beginning.

How do you design a database to maximize efficiency and minimize access time? That is covered next.

THE IMPORTANCE OF DATABASE DESIGN IN INDEXING AND SORTING

The last section concluded that database design is the most important part of developing a system. Here I will explain why that is so.

A database is useless unless someone, preferably the user, can get information out of it. The database is next to useless if the user has to sit and wait for the answer to queries. The best situation is where the user queries the database and gets the answer immediately. Sitting and waiting concerns disk access time and sloppy programming.

Let's look at disk access time first. dBASE III PLUS takes care of access time by SORTing and INDEXing its databases, and by reading chunks of a database into memory. You, as the system designer, must carefully design the database to let dBASE III PLUS efficiently SORT or INDEX it. How do you do this?

Consider a person with an extensive personal library (several thousand volumes). He wants to inventory his books and then produce lists. What would he be most interested in? Definitely TITLE. Probably AUTHOR/EDITOR and CATEGORY. These three fields would allow him to find exact titles, find books by author/editor, and find books by their subject matter.

That is to say, our user could either ask, "Do I have *The Odysseus Solution?*" or instruct dBASE III PLUS to "List all books by 'Mike Banks'," or "List all 'science fiction' books."

Each one of these queries is less specific than the one preceding it, but they do show an ordered method of getting information from a database. The first query (by actual title) is highly specific and reports on an existing situation. The second query (by author) lists several situations that match the selection criterion. The last query (by general category of fiction) is the most general search of the three and probably has the greatest number of matches.

Each one of the requests is also keyed to a specific field in the database. Note especially that the more general the request, the less specific the field searched. There is only one book entitled *The Odysseus Solution.* There are probably a few books by Mike Banks. There are probably lots of science fiction books.

So design the database from most specific to least specific. Put the most specific field at the top of the database. Getting information from the database requires queries that are specific. Locate that necessary information in a convenient place. Just as you keep your favorite tools in convenient places so you can find them quickly and easily, you should grant your database that same courtesy. Likewise, place fields that will be key but are somewhat less specific directly under the most specific fields.

Let me anthropomorphize dBASE III PLUS to give an example. You have designed a database so that a key field is perhaps the twentieth field in a file structure of 25 fields. You then tell dBASE III PLUS to either INDEX or SORT on that twentieth field.

There sits dBASE III PLUS in its office. Somebody has wheeled in 1,000 open topped barrels. You say, "About four-fifths of the way down in each barrel there is a piece of paper that tells you where we're going to store each barrel. Sort these barrels according to that piece of paper." You leave the room and dBASE III PLUS begins shoving its arm down into each barrel to find the piece of paper. It finds that piece of paper, copies the information from that paper onto a manifest, shoves the paper back in the barrel to the place where it found it, and goes to the next barrel. Every time it finds out what's in a barrel, it scans the manifest and rearranges the barrels it has already SORTed to make room for the new barrel.

Did I mention that these barrels contain the most foul detritus from the bottom of Lake Erie? You're off drinking coffee and dBASE III PLUS is calling you every name in RAM.

You could have helped dBASE III PLUS considerably if you put that piece of paper on the top of each barrel. dBASE III PLUS wouldn't have had to shove its arm in each barrel or write down on a manifest what was on the paper. It would still have to SORT the barrels, but it would have been happier doing it and the job would be completed in far less time.

Another part of proper design is realizing when a single NDX file can do the work of two or more NDX files. That is possible when two or more databases share the same number of records and have one field (the key field) in common. Remember the subscription system described earlier, in which we defined the need for two databases. One of the databases was used for mailing labels and the other for accounting.

Both of these databases shared the ACCT field. We would hope that there is a close similarity between everyone in the accounting database and everyone in the mailing database. (Remember in the last chapter that 5 percent of subscribers were never billed?)

Assume this close similarity takes the form of a one-to-one correspondence between the databases. For each record in the accounting database there is a unique corresponding record in the mailing label database. The two databases have an identical number of records, and the unique corresponding records have the ACCT field in common.

You need only INDEX one of the two databases to produce an NDX file that is valid for both. You INDEX on the common key field and have essentially INDEXed both databases.

But there are some caveats with this method. First, realize that you have to enter information to each database in the exact same order. If you enter information in the accounting database in the order A, B, C, D, E, then you have to enter information into the mailing label database as A, B, C, D, E. Second, INDEXing on a single, shared key field only works when you INDEX, not when you SORT. The reason has to do with the differences between SORTing and INDEXing a database.

dBASE III PLUS SORTs a database by physically rearranging its records. Given a database with records B, D, E, A, C, a SORT physically rearranges the records in the database to A, B, C, D, E. Obviously, SORTing one database has no effect on the record order of any other database.

INDEXing a database produces an auxiliary file that holds a logical listing of each record's location in the database. Given a database with records B, D, E, A, C, an INDEX produces an auxiliary file (an NDX file) with the following list:

A → 4
B → 1
C → 5
D → 2
E → 3

Given two databases with records B, D, E, A, C, the NDX listing can serve both databases. This logic applies to three, four, and even more databases. The only thing to remember is that each of the databases must share the same common key field and must have the same number of physical records.

After designing for efficient SORTing and INDEXing comes designing for efficient use of memory. The important concept here is that smaller packages are easier to move than large packages. When you were in school, did you carry all the books you'd need for the entire day's classes with you all day? I hope not. You probably knew your day's schedule and knew when you could make it back to your locker to drop off and pick up books.

Good. You are still you, but now your locker is the database and the books are the records in that database. Wasn't it a bear carrying those large chemistry and social studies texts? Didn't you prefer those paperbacks you read in English?

dBASE III PLUS is the same way. It prefers to work with small chunks of information, not large, awkward parcels. dBASE III PLUS will fly through databases with ten or so fields. It can even handle several open files of 10 to 20 fields with ease. Give it a single database with 40 or more fields per record and it will become lethargic and slovenly. This is due to the way dBASE III PLUS uses memory. It will read several complete records into memory if those records are small enough. That translates into several consecutively INDEXed or SORTed records. That in turn translates into fewer disk reads and writes per work session.

Finally comes sloppy programming. Preventing sloppy programming is the topic of the next section.

PREVENTING SLOPPY PROGRAMMING

The first discussion in this chapter dealt with designing the database before you design the code that operates it. The section just before this demonstrated the importance of database design in putting together a system. In particular, it concentrated on the importance of design in relation to dBASE III PLUS's INDEX and SORT commands. This discussion combines those two concepts in hopes of showing how to know what comes first and what comes second when you put together a database system.

Pretend that someone has come to you with a particular database need. You have listened to her story and asked the appropriate questions. You've observed her department's operations and talked with the people that will actually be using the finished product. After a few days of talking and observing, you've come away with a good understanding of the difference between what she said they needed and what they really need to get the job done.

Shortly after that fees are set, contracts signed, and hands shaken. You take off your suit, put on your work clothes, grab an armful of Twinkies and Coke, and go back to The Deep Cave Where All Good Programming Occurs.

Your first step is to sketch out what the finished product will look like. This doesn't yet involve flowcharts or logic diagrams. Right now you have to figure out how many parts the system will have. Let's go back to our magazine subscription system for a minute.

What did the customer ask for originally? The list had four specific needs:

1. print mailing labels.
2. perform subscriber accounting.
3. generate delinquent account notices.
4. prepare renewal notices.

How many parts is that, and can we break the parts down further? We know that we'll need at least two permanent and easily edited databases, one for mailing labels and the other for accounting. We'll also need a temporary, easily edited database for our overnight print runs. We've decided that we want the databases to carry only the information necessary for their specific purposes. The fact that we keep the databases small allows dBASE III PLUS to read in complete records or groups of records into memory. Having this information in memory decreases access time and improves memory management. So much for the databases. On to the code. We need a system to print mailing labels, do subscriber accounting, and send out both delinquent and renewal notices.

Did I ever tell you that disk space is at a premium these days? Disk space is almost on the same level as Will Rogers's view of land: It's so expensive because they stopped making it a while back.

You are not in business to get your client to buy more disk space. The client may have to eventually, but let's work the existing land as much as we can right now. That means getting as much information onto each sector of the disk as we can.

And that means doing the most with the least amount of code. Did you notice that there are two parts of code that print? Writing code for both pieces is a waste of time. Both parts can be options on a PRINTING menu. The separate options can generate simple forms or complex letters, it doesn't matter. The point is that you don't want to waste disk space, which also translates into wasted access time, which translates into poor memory management.

Good, we have a working picture of the separate parts of our system. The next part is to create a flowchart showing how the parts are linked. Obviously there is going to be some kind of master menu that links everything together (see Figure 4–3).

This is a flowchart of the parts of the program. It isn't a flowchart or pseudocode of the finished product. The purpose of this chart is to give you an idea of how many pieces make up the completed system and what databases are needed by each piece in the system.

The master menu has three major options on it. It must include Print, Accounting, and Quit. The Accounting option leads to a menu that includes Edit, Add, Delete, Pack, and Quit. These are the five options that are the backbone of any database application. Before getting to the accounting menu, however, realize that we want a one-to-one correspondence between the mail list database and the accounting database. We take care of that by opening both databases and linking them by the ACCT field. All editing, adding, deleting, and packing to either database are done here. Even if no information is placed in one of the databases, both must be opened to ensure a one-to-one correspondence.

The Printing menu has options for Labels, Delinquency Notices, Renewal Notices, and Quit. The first three of these options leads to another menu with options to Print, Review, and Quit. How they get there is different.

Our system prints labels directly from the mailing label database. That database is opened on the way to the last menu. If we select Print, our labels are printed. If we select Review, we are presented with another menu with Edit, Add, Delete, and Quit. Notice the missing Pack option? We don't want to permanently remove any records from this database, we only want to make them invisible to the print routine. That is accomplished by using DELETE on them and SETting DELETE ON. Once the print run is finished, the records are restored and no damage is done, our one-to-one correspondence still exists. What about adding records? New data can be placed in a temporary file that is later erased. The integrity of our mailing label database is therefore preserved.

The options to print delinquency and renewal notices first open the accounting and mailing label database to create a third, temporary database. This

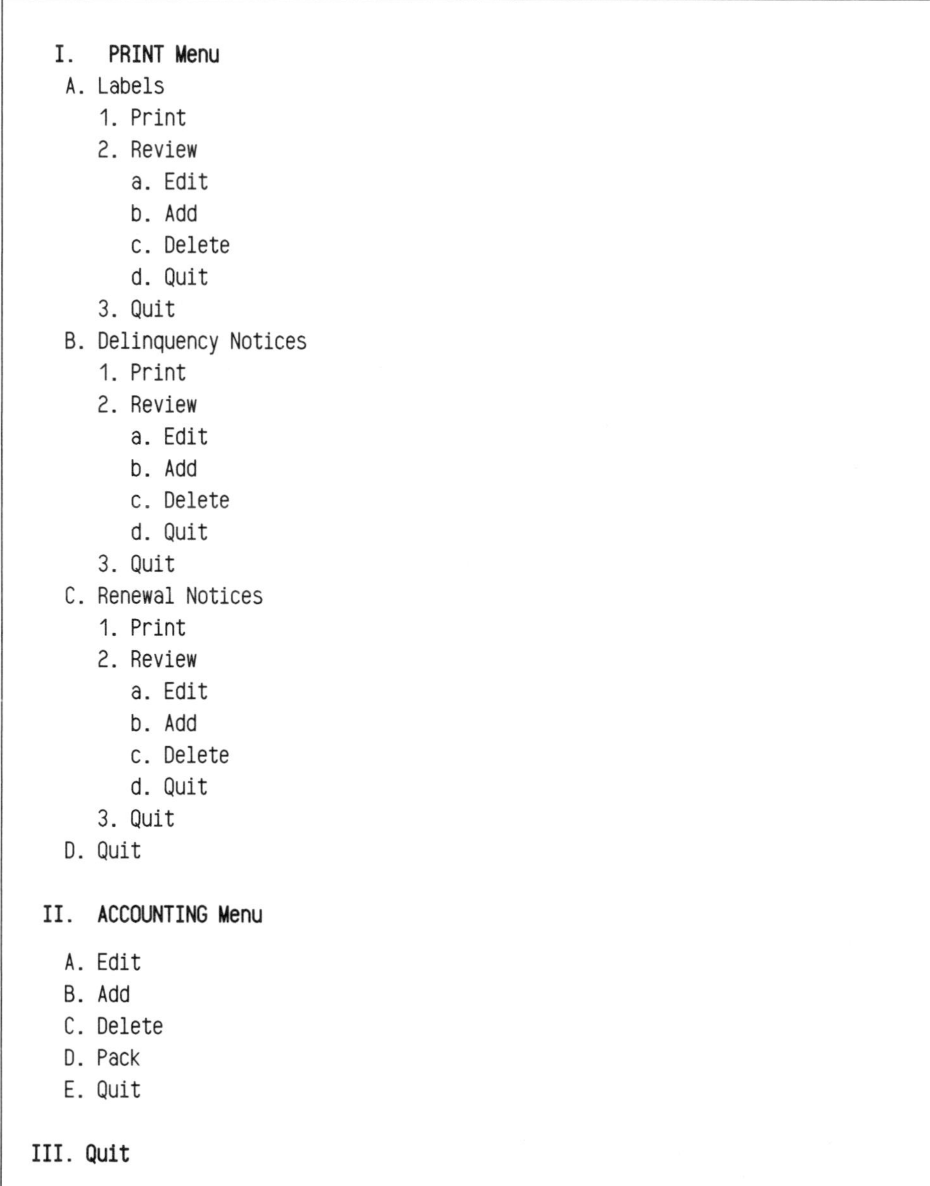

I. **PRINT Menu**
- A. Labels
  - 1. Print
  - 2. Review
    - a. Edit
    - b. Add
    - c. Delete
    - d. Quit
  - 3. Quit
- B. Delinquency Notices
  - 1. Print
  - 2. Review
    - a. Edit
    - b. Add
    - c. Delete
    - d. Quit
  - 3. Quit
- C. Renewal Notices
  - 1. Print
  - 2. Review
    - a. Edit
    - b. Add
    - c. Delete
    - d. Quit
  - 3. Quit
- D. Quit

II. **ACCOUNTING Menu**
- A. Edit
- B. Add
- C. Delete
- D. Pack
- E. Quit

III. **Quit**

Figure 4–3 This flowchart tracks the elements for our sample application.

database is used by the last menu to Print, Review, and Quit. Here, if we elect to Review our data, we review a temporary file. We can delete records as we did with the mailing label database and still not concern ourselves with packing, as this database is going to be erased at the end of the print run, anyway. Similar logic works with adding, only here we add directly to this third, temporary file.

The next step is what the rest of this book is about, the actual code that does all these wonderful things. But, although that is possibly the most time-consuming part of this operation, it will not be as time-consuming as it could be if you had not proceeded logically from the start, breaking your system into needs and seeing how each of those needs can be individually met, then combining similar functions into similar packages.

SUMMARY

This chapter was concerned with creating databases for specific designs. We started by recognizing that each application should get a separate system of databases. Auto part inventories are very different from a library system or the subscription system shown earlier in this chapter. No one database design can handle every need.

However, the principles of database design—putting the important and most unique fields at the top of the database—cross all systems and should be the guiding light for all design considerations. This is especially important in systems where records will be constantly queried in a variety of ways.

We also showed that design plays an important role in determining how many parts our system will have. Before we begin to code, we are interested in knowing how the different parts of our finished product will be tied together. This allows us the luxury of writing minimal code to do maximum work.

Chapter 5 elaborates on these principles and shows how judicious use of dBASE III PLUS commands can hasten development of database systems.

CHAPTER

5

ADVANCED KERNELS

Chapter 3 dealt with basic kernels of code, those chunks of code that can be used by various database systems regardless of what the system has to do. At the end of Chapter 3, a rudimentary menu system was developed. This chapter provides you with many more kernels.

Again, our goal is to create a basic editing system that is highly transportable and usable by a number of database systems. The code developed in this chapter and Chapter 3 will form the core of the applications developed in Part 2 in this book. Each application will have code specifically for the given application, but it will also use the code developed here and in Chapter 3 to do a major part of the work.

Also, note that not all kernels we develop are going to be used in every application. Some will be used so often they'll become de facto menu items. Others will be useful, but so application-specific that we'll place them on separate menus for each application.

Most people begin their DBMS programming work using a single database system. Such tasks as mailing lists are managed with single-database DBMS systems. The next step is to create kernels that handle more than one database at a time. This can be through editing (such as adding a record to a secondary database each time a record is added to a primary database), through field matching (such as making sure a secondary record exists for every primary record), or through updating one file based on the information in another file. This last method might involve the dBASE III PLUS UPDATE command, but might also be accomplished with other commands.

ADDING RECORDS TO TWO DATABASES AT A TIME

There is a hidden thought in this heading. It assumes you want to add records to one database that are somehow based on records in the other database.

We begin by considering what is involved in the operation.

- We build on our basic add kernel.
- It isn't necessary to append data to each open database.

There are several methods we can use. Our example will be from the subscriber/service system. The code is:

Listing 5–1

```
COPY STRUC TO TANK
SELE 6
USE TANK
REPEATER = FIELD(1)
DO SAVESCMS
*
IF [subscriber database file]$DBFILE
   SELE 2
   USE payments database file INDE account field NDX, other NDX
   COPY STRUC TO TANK2
   SELE 7
   USE TANK2
   TRUTH = .T.
   SELE 6
*
   DO WHIL .T.
      APPE BLAN
      DO &GETTER
      READ
*
      IF LEN(TRIM(&REPEATER)) = 0
         DELE
         EXIT
      ENDI
*
      @ 20,0 CLEA
      @ 22,0 SAY [ADD A NEW PAYMENT RECORD (Y/N)?  ] GET TRUTH
      READ
*
      IF TRUTH
         SELE 7
         CLEA
         APPE BLANK
         REPL account field WITH F->account field, name field WITH;
              F->namefield,other field WITH F->otherfield
         DO PAYSAY
         DO PAYGET2
         DO SAVESCMS
         READ
```

Listing 5–1 (cont.)

```
            SELE 6
            CLEA
            DO SUBSAY
         ENDI
*
DO SAVESCMS
   ENDD
*
   SELE 7
   USE
   SELE 2
   APPE FROM TANK2
   ERAS TANK2.DBF
ELSE * DBFILE # SUBSCRIPTIONS
*
   DO WHIL .T.
      APPE BLANK
      DO &GETTER
      READ
*
      IF LEN(TRIM(&REPEATER)) = 0
         DELE
         EXIT
      ENDI
*
   ENDD
*
ENDI
*
SELE 6
USE
SELE 1
SET DELE ON
APPE FROM TANK
SET DELE OFF
DO &GETTER
CLEA GETS
DO EDITMENU
ERAS TANK.DBF
```

Note first that we've built on the Add kernel developed in Chapter 3. We still copy the active database's structure to some temporary file. We still select a different work area and make the temporary file the currently selected database. The first new bit of code begins with DO SAVESCMS. You may remember that we placed messages and prompts on the screen. The DO SAVESCMS line calls one such message:

```
** SAVE ESCAPE MESSAGE
** SHOULD BE A PROCEDURE
*
@ 20,0 CLEA
@ 22,0 SAY [Press CTRL-W to save information, ESC to exit]
*
** EOF
```

The original Add kernel only needed to place this message on the screen once. The code as expanded to handle two databases needs to juggle messages and screens; thus, these two lines of code become a separately called routine. A strong recommendation is to place these two lines in a procedure file. An alternative is to always place your SAY and GET files on the same part of the screen. You wouldn't need to repeatedly call SAVESCMS, but you would need to include:

```
@ x0,y0 CLEA TO x1,y1
```

whenever you changed the screen. Note that X_0,Y_0 are the upper left coordinates of the cleared box, which terminates at the lower right coordinates X_1, Y_1.

The next block is where we begin determining how many databases we'll be adding data to. It is imperative that each new subscriber get a corresponding payment record. It is not imperative that each new payment record get a corresponding subscriber record. Why is that? We may be entering a payment record for an existing subscriber and don't want to duplicate subscriber information.

The new code starts by testing which database it's working with. The test is done by comparing a variable against something. DBFILE is a variable I use in many applications to hold the active database file's name. It is declared in a preceding program.

One could wonder why I don't use:

```
IF [subscriber database file]$DBF()
```

This line makes use of a dBASE III PLUS function and eliminates one variable from memory. I chose not to use that code because the test is performed after the temporary file is selected and placed in use.

Remember that this test is performed to determine if we'll be adding data to more than one file at a time or not. The results of the test determine how many work areas and temporary files must be opened and juggled.

Jumping to the ELSE statement, note that the remaining code is our simple Add kernel from Chapter 3. In other words, if we aren't working with the subscriber file, we aren't interested in adding data to more than one database at a time and can handle the whole operation in a single database mode. The first few lines of the IF . . . ELSE . . . ENDIF code block do nothing more than create our second temporary file in work area 7. Down the road we'll ask the user whether to add data to this database and get that answer in a logic variable. That variable, TRUTH, is initialized before data entry to either database begins. We also select the primary temporary file at this point.

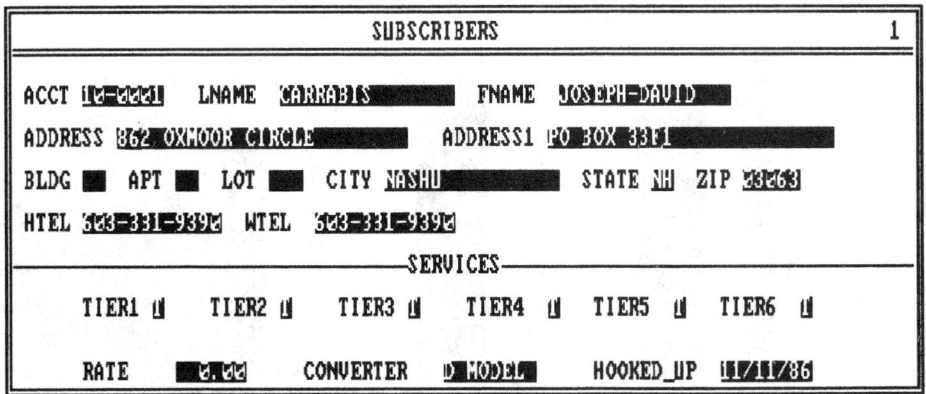

ADD A NEW PAYMENT RECORD (Y/N)? »

Figure 5–1 This figure is a data addition screen for a subscriber file. Figure 5–2 shows the corresponding payments file data addition screen. Note that three fields are copied from the subscriber file to the payments file.

Our interest is in the code that handles data entry to two databases simultaneously. The code proceeds as it did in the original Add kernel until we ask the user:

```
ADD A NEW PAYMENT RECORD (Y/N)?
```

The TRUTH variable we initialized before data entry now comes into play. The IF TRUTH code block is passed over if we don't wish to add a corresponding payment record. Adding a corresponding payment record activates some code that, when analyzed, is nothing more than the Add kernel in a different work area.

We start by selecting the temporary file's work area. We clear the screen and append a blank record to the secondary temporary file. This new record is supposed to correspond one to one with the new record just entered to the primary database, therefore replacing some of this file's fields with data from that file's fields. Here we replace the ACCT, LNAME, and FNAME fields. Figures 5–1 and 5–2 show the data addition screens for both of these files.

I make use of a nonstandard GET file, PAYGET2, in this code. My normal PAYGET file is:

Listing 5–2

```
PROC PAYGET
@ 2,73 SAY STR(RECNO(),5,0)
@  4,  8  GET  ACCT PICT '!!-!!!!'
@  4, 28  GET  LNAME
```

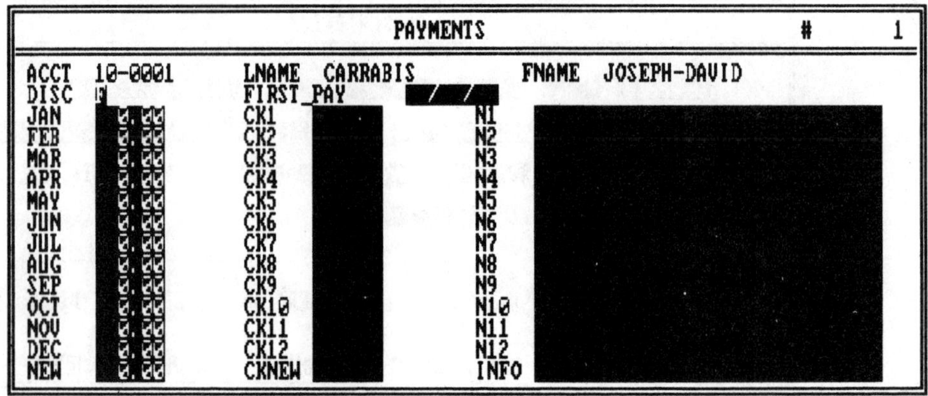

Type CTL-W to save information, ESCAPE to exit

Figure 5–2 This figure is a data addition screen for a payments file. Figure 5–1 shows the corresponding subscriber file data addition screen. Note that three fields are copied from the subscriber file to the payments file. The three fields chosen are also those used as an index key (LEFT(ACCT,2)+LNAME +FNAME).

Listing 5–2 (cont.)

```
@  4, 52  GET  FNAME
@  5,  8  GET  DISC
@  5, 35  GET  FIRST_PAY
@  6,  8  GET  JAN
@  6, 27  GET  CK1
@  6, 46  GET  N1
@  7,  8  GET  FEB
@  7, 27  GET  CK2
@  7, 46  GET  N2
@  8,  8  GET  MAR
@  8, 27  GET  CK3
@  8, 46  GET  N3
@  9,  8  GET  APR
@  9, 27  GET  CK4
@  9, 46  GET  N4
@ 10,  8  GET  MAY
@ 10, 27  GET  CK5
@ 10, 46  GET  N5
@ 11,  8  GET  JUN
@ 11, 27  GET  CK6
@ 11, 46  GET  N6
@ 12,  8  GET  JUL
@ 12, 27  GET  CK7
```

Listing 5-2 (cont.)

```
@ 12, 46  GET  N7
@ 13,  8  GET  AUG
@ 13, 27  GET  CK8
@ 13, 46  GET  N8
@ 14,  8  GET  SEP
@ 14, 27  GET  CK9
@ 14, 46  GET  N9
@ 15,  8  GET  OCT
@ 15, 27  GET  CK10
@ 15, 46  GET  N10
@ 16,  8  GET  NOV
@ 16, 27  GET  CK11
@ 16, 46  GET  N11
@ 17,  8  GET  DEC
@ 17, 27  GET  CK12
@ 17, 46  GET  N12
@ 18,  8  GET  NEW
@ 18, 27  GET  CKNEW
@ 18,46 GET INFO
*
```

This GET file is used for the majority of payment editing screens. The only changes made to generate the PAYGET2 file are:

Listing 5-3

```
@  4,  8  SAY  ACCT PICT '!!-!!!!'
@  4, 28  SAY  LNAME
@  4, 52  SAY  FNAME
```

These changes ensure that the three fields copied from the primary database are not edited.

A side question at this point. Is it necessary to have two separate GET files for the payments system? If you're beginning to think of minimizing your code, you'll say no, and you're right. We can include a flag to tell dBASE III PLUS whether we want to use the three SAY lines of code or the normal three lines found in the standard GET file. We don't even have to add more code to our expanded Add kernel to use that flag, which is an added benefit.

We start by recognizing that, in this system, there is only one time when the PAYGET2 file is used. PAYGET2 is used when data is being added to the payments database based on data just added to the subscriber database. We tell dBASE III PLUS that we want to ADD A NEW PAYMENT RECORD with a logic variable, TRUTH. The only time TRUTH is active is when we are adding data to both databases. The flag can be based on TRUTH and incorporated into the PAYGET file as:

Listing 5–4

```
PROC PAYGET
@ 2,73 SAY STR(RECNO(),5,0)
*
IF TRUTH
   @  4,  8  SAY  ACCT PICT '!!-!!!!'
   @  4, 28  SAY  LNAME
   @  4, 52  SAY  FNAME
ELSE
   @  4,  8  GET  ACCT PICT '!!-!!!!'
   @  4, 28  GET  LNAME
   @  4, 52  GET  FNAME
ENDI
*
@  5,  8  GET  DISC
@  5, 35  GET  FIRST_PAY
@  6,  8  GET  JAN
@  6, 27  GET  CK1
@  6, 46  GET  N1
@  7,  8  GET  FEB
@  7, 27  GET  CK2
@  7, 46  GET  N2
@  8,  8  GET  MAR
@  8, 27  GET  CK3
@  8, 46  GET  N3
@  9,  8  GET  APR
@  9, 27  GET  CK4
@  9, 46  GET  N4
@ 10,  8  GET  MAY
@ 10, 27  GET  CK5
@ 10, 46  GET  N5
@ 11,  8  GET  JUN
@ 11, 27  GET  CK6
@ 11, 46  GET  N6
@ 12,  8  GET  JUL
@ 12, 27  GET  CK7
@ 12, 46  GET  N7
@ 13,  8  GET  AUG
@ 13, 27  GET  CK8
@ 13, 46  GET  N8
@ 14,  8  GET  SEP
@ 14, 27  GET  CK9
@ 14, 46  GET  N9
@ 15,  8  GET  OCT
@ 15, 27  GET  CK10
@ 15, 46  GET  N10
```

Listing 5-4 (cont.)

```
@ 16,  8 GET NOV
@ 16, 27 GET CK11
@ 16, 46 GET N11
@ 17,  8 GET DEC
@ 17, 27 GET CK12
@ 17, 46 GET N12
@ 18,  8 GET NEW
@ 18, 27 GET CKNEW
@ 18,46 GET INFO
*
```

Be aware that each modification has its benefit and detriment. The benefit here is decreased code size. The detriment is a necessarily closer analysis of what happens to TRUTH throughout the system. Make sure TRUTH has a .F. value whenever PAYGET is called outside of this data addition block. The first and most obvious means of doing that is to place the line containing TRUTH = .F. at the end of this expanded Add kernel.

Let's return to the original problem of adding data to two databases in one pass. The original Add kernel made a point of testing a selected field to determine if data entry was over. The code given in this section does much the same thing. But where does it test a database field, and how often does it do it?

There is only one necessary test. One of the databases is designated as the primary database. You'll add data to the other databases based on data added to this database. Therefore, you only need to test the primary database to determine whether to exit the data entry code.

ADDING RECORDS TO MORE THAN TWO DATABASES AT A TIME

The next topic to investigate is adding data to more than two databases. You might guess that we're going to expand the code shown in the last section, and you're right.

There are three methods we're going to study for adding data to more than two databases at a time. The first assumes data is going to be added in a straight-line manner. An example of this occurs if you need to add data to several databases, and you know ahead of time something will be added to each of the several databases. You'll go from database A to B to C and so on until you've added some data to the last database in the series.

The second method assumes data doesn't need to be added to each database in the line, but some data from the primary database will be added to each file regardless of the user's movements through the add system. An example of this would be an expansion of the subscription system. We definitely need to copy three fields from the primary to the secondary database. Do we truly need to add more information when a record is first being entered? Not necessarily. We expand this to the point that several databases are similarly accessed.

The third (last) data addition method occurs when the user must consciously decide which of the several databases is going to be updated. This method assumes there isn't one-for-one tracking among the databases, and some other method—account numbers, for example—is going to be used to link records in different DBF files.

In all of these cases, we need to add two more conditions to our system. Those conditions can be appended to the first and second assumptions given previously.

- We must recognize some file limits. We can't use work area 10 if we have an open CAT file. This in turn means we can only add data to four databases at a time (four open databases and four temporary files). If there are no active CAT files, we can add data to five databases at a time.
- The primary database in a system will always be opened in work area 1. Its temporary file will be opened in work area 6. Second, third, and other databases will be opened in consecutive work areas as necessary.

Later, as we develop code for handling more databases than comfort will allow, some of these assumptions and conditions will have to be forfeited. We'll cross that bridge when we come to it.

Adding Data in a Straightline Manner

The first thing to study is a situation where we must add data to several databases, and each database needs to be accessed. We start with the code given in the previous section and expand.

Listing 5–5

```
&& This code assumes the some database has already been placed in
&& use in work area 1, and that database's GET and SAY files have
&& already been declared. The database in work area 1 isn't
&& necessarily the primary database. See the text for a fuller
&& explanation
COPY STRUC TO TANK
SELE 6
USE TANK
REPEATER = FIELD(1)
DO SAVESCMS
*
IF database is primary database
   SELE 2
   USE secondary database INDE related indexes
   COPY STRUC TO TANK2
```

Listing 5-5 (cont.)

```
   SELE 3
   USE third database INDE related indexes
   COPY STRUC TO TANK3
   SELE 4
   USE fourth database INDE related indexes
   COPY STRUC TO TANK4
   SELE 5
   USE fifth database INDE related indexes
   COPY STRUC TO TANK5
   SELE 7
   USE TANK2
   SELE 8
   USE TANK3
   SELE 9
   USE TANK4
   SELE 10
   USE TANK5
   SELE 6
*
   DO WHIL .T.
      APPE BLAN
      DO &GETTER                         && primary database's GET file
      READ
*
      IF LEN(TRIM(&REPEATER)) = 0
         DELE
         EXIT
      ENDI
*
      SELE 7
      CLEA
      APPE BLANK
      REPL necessary fields in secondary file
      DO secondary database's SAY file
      DO secondary database's GET file minus REPLACED fields
      DO SAVESCMS
      READ
      SELE 8
      CLEA
      APPE BLANK
      REPL necessary fields in third file
      DO third database's SAY file
      DO third database's GET file minus REPLACED fields
      DO SAVESCMS
      READ
```

Listing 5-5 (cont.)

```
      SELE 9
      CLEA
      APPE BLANK
      REPL necessary fields in fourth file
      DO fourth database's SAY file
      DO fourth database's GET file minus REPLACED fields
      DO SAVESCMS
      READ
      SELE 10
      CLEA
      APPE BLANK
      REPL necessary fields in fifth file
      DO fifth database's SAY file
      DO fifth database's GET file minus REPLACED fields
      DO SAVESCMS
      READ
      SELE 6
      CLEA
      DO &SAYER                    && primary database's SAY file
      DO SAVESCMS
   ENDD
*
   SELE 10
   USE
   SELE 9
   USE
   SELE 8
   USE
   SELE 7
   USE
   SELE 5
   APPE FROM TANK5
   SELE 4
   APPE FROM TANK4
   SELE 3
   APPE FROM TANK3
   SELE 2
   APPE FROM TANK2
   ERAS TANK5.DBF
   ERAS TANK4.DBF
   ERAS TANK3.DBF
   ERAS TANK2.DBF
ELSE * DBFILE # primary database
*
   DO WHIL .T.
```

Listing 5–5 (cont.)

```
      APPE BLANK
      DO &GETTER                                  && selected database's GET file
      READ
*
      IF LEN(TRIM(&REPEATER)) = 0
         DELE
         EXIT
      ENDI
*
   ENDD
*
ENDI
*
SELE 6
USE
SELE 1
SET DELE ON
APPE FROM TANK
SET DELE OFF
DO &GETTER                                        && selected database's GET file
CLEA GETS
DO EDITMENU
ERAS TANK.DBF
```

This code is a typical expansion of the code shown for adding data to two databases simultaneously. The code starts with the assumptions given earlier in the text.

First, what is a "primary" database? Earlier we noted that you may want to add data to several databases based on the addition of data to a single file, but not vice versa. For example, you have five databases, A, B, C, D, and E. If you add data to database A, you must add data to databases B, C, D, and E. However, adding data to database B doesn't mean you have to add data to A, C, D, or E. Similarly, adding data to C, D, or E doesn't mean you have to add data to any of the other databases. This is a typical straightline situation. Database A is your primary database. It is primary only in the sense that you need to add data to all the other files *if* you add data to this single file. You can add data to any of the other files and ignore A's existence, but not vice versa.

The listing determines if the primary database is active in work area 1 in the line:

```
IF database is primary database
```

You can use the two methods mentioned earlier for this test. Using:

```
IF [primary database]$DBF()
```

is a valid choice. But I elect not to use it due to the code preceding the test. That code concludes in work area 6, not work area 1, which is where the primary database is actually active. I would have to rewrite the lines before the test as:

Listing 5–6

```
DO SAVESCMS
SELE 1                  * new code line
*
IF [primary database]$DBF()
```

I would also need to include another line directly following the ELSE statement, should the database in work area 1 not be the primary database.

Listing 5–7

```
ELSE * [primary database]$DBF() -> FALSE
  SELE 6                              * new code line
*
  DO WHIL .T.
```

Again, the method of choice is to use a variable, such as DBFILE. This variable's value can change as different databases are opened in work area 1 by including the command DBFILE = DBF() when each database is opened in work area 1.

The code inside the IF block is expanded to hold the five accessed databases. Note that this is something necessarily unique to each application. You must name each database the code works with. You can use variables to declare your database names, but remember that every freedom increases your responsibility. dBASE III PLUS gives you the freedom to declare databases through macroized variables, but that increases your responsibility to reserve those variable names until the routine is through running.

The next new bit of code follows the &REPEATER test. Remember that this code models a straightline system. Data will be entered to all the databases if data is entered to the primary database. Because data will definitely be entered to the remaining databases if data is entered to the primary database, there is no need to include a line asking the user if that should be done.

Again, we must recognize the need to customize. Some situations will require the ability to *query* the user if data is to be added to the remaining databases. That code can be added with a few lines:

Listing 5–8

```
&& This code assumes the some database has already been placed in
&& use in work area 1, and that database's GET and SAY files have
&& already been declared. The database in work area 1 isn't
&& necessarily the primary database. See the text for a fuller
&& explanation
COPY STRUC TO TANK
SELE 6
```

Listing 5–8 (cont.)

```
USE TANK
REPEATER = FIELD(1)
DO SAVESCMS
*
IF database is primary database
   SELE 2
   USE secondary database INDE related indexes
   COPY STRUC TO TANK2
   SELE 3
   USE third database INDE related indexes
   COPY STRUC TO TANK3
   SELE 4
   USE fourth database INDE related indexes
   COPY STRUC TO TANK4
   SELE 5
   USE fifth database INDE related indexes
   COPY STRUC TO TANK5
   SELE 7
   USE TANK2
   SELE 8
   USE TANK3
   SELE 9
   USE TANK4
   SELE 10
   USE TANK5
   SELE 6
   TRUTH = .T.                                  && new line of code
*
   DO WHIL .T.
      APPE BLAN
      DO &GETTER                            && primary database's GET file
      READ
*
      IF LEN(TRIM(&REPEATER)) = 0
         DELE
         EXIT
      ENDI
*
** THE NEXT FOUR LINES ARE NEW
*
      @ 20,0 CLEA
      @ 22,0 SAY [ADD RELATED RECORDS (Y/N)?  ] GET TRUTH
      READ
*
      IF TRUTH          && new line of code, creates IF TRUTH block
```

Listing 5–8 (cont.)

```
            SELE 7
            CLEA
            APPE BLANK
            REPL necessary fields in secondary file
            DO secondary database's SAY file
            DO secondary database's GET file minus REPLACED fields
            DO SAVESCMS
            READ
            SELE 8
            CLEA
            APPE BLANK
            REPL necessary fields in third file
            DO third database's SAY file
            DO third database's GET file minus REPLACED fields
            DO SAVESCMS
            READ
            SELE 9
            CLEA
            APPE BLANK
            REPL necessary fields in fourth file
            DO fourth database's SAY file
            DO fourth database's GET file minus REPLACED fields
            DO SAVESCMS
            READ
            SELE 10
            CLEA
            APPE BLANK
            REPL necessary fields in fifth file
            DO fifth database's SAY file
            DO fifth database's GET file minus REPLACED fields
            DO SAVESCMS
            READ
            SELE 6
            CLEA
            DO &SAYER                      && primary database's SAY file
            DO SAVESCMS
         ENDI                      && new line, closes off IF TRUTH block
*
   ENDD
*
** THE REMAINDER OF THE CODE IS UNCHANGED.
*
```

These few lines increase the user's flexibility in adding data to the system. In practice, however, not much has been given to the user that wasn't already there. This code only queries the user if data is going to be added to the other databases,

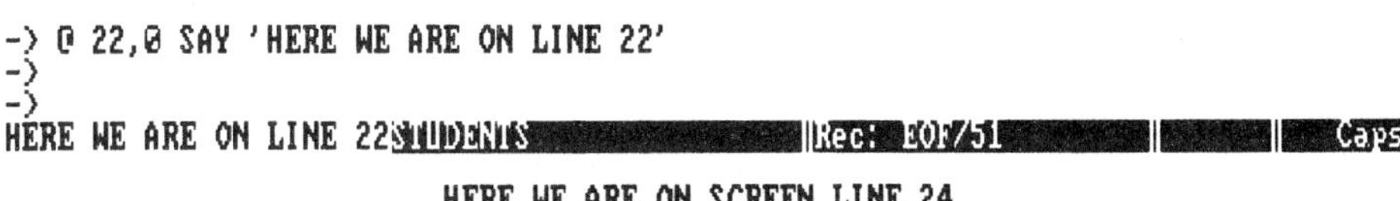

Figure 5–3 The SET STATUS ON and SET MESSAGE TO commands can be used to prompt the user, but you lose screen lines 22, 23, and 24 when you use these commands.

then enters a data addition code block based on the user's response. The same effect is achieved with no additional code simply by letting the user PRESS CTRL-W at each screen.

This point leads to another digression. Why not use the SET MESSAGE TO and SET STATUS ON commands to prompt and pass information to the user? This is a good question, and the answer has more to do with screen usage than the viability of these two commands. The dBASE III PLUS status line uses screen line 22. Anything displayed with the SET MESSAGE TO command is placed on screen line 24. The status line gives the user information on default drive, currently selected database, record number, and the toggle state of the INS, NUM LOCK, and CAPS LOCK keys. How much of that information is relative to data entry or editing? A guess would be everything but the last three items. Take a look at any of the SAY and GET file combinations, and you'll see that they provide you with as much information as necessary for the user to complete the task of data entry or editing. Feel free to use the SET STATUS ON and SET MESSAGE TO commands shown in Figure 5–3, but realize you'll lose three screen lines by doing so.

Systems That Share Fields in Several Databases

The second system builds off the data addition system described previously. Here we know ahead of time that data is going to be passed from a primary database to several other databases, but the user might not need to monitor the data being transferred. This example will build off the last example.

Listing 5–9

```
&& This code assumes the some database has already been placed in
&& use in work area 1, and that database's GET and SAY files have
&& already been declared. The database in work area 1 isn't
&& necessarily the primary database. See the text for a fuller
&& explanation
COPY STRUC TO TANK
SELE 6
USE TANK
REPEATER = FIELD(1)
DO SAVESCMS
*
```

Listing 5–9 (cont.)

```
IF database is primary database
   SELE 2
   USE secondary database INDE related indexes
   COPY STRUC TO TANK2
   SELE 3
   USE third database INDE related indexes
   COPY STRUC TO TANK3
   SELE 4
   USE fourth database INDE related indexes
   COPY STRUC TO TANK4
   SELE 5
   USE fifth database INDE related indexes
   COPY STRUC TO TANK5
   SELE 7
   USE TANK2
   SELE 8
   USE TANK3
   SELE 9
   USE TANK4
   SELE 10
   USE TANK5
   SELE 6
*
   DO WHIL .T.
      APPE BLAN
      DO &GETTER                        && primary database's GET file
      READ
*
      IF LEN(TRIM(&REPEATER)) = 0
         DELE
         EXIT
      ENDI
*
      SELE 7
      APPE BLANK
      REPL necessary fields in secondary file
      SELE 8
      APPE BLANK
      REPL necessary fields in third file
      SELE 9
      APPE BLANK
      REPL necessary fields in fourth file
      SELE 10
      APPE BLANK
      REPL necessary fields in fifth file
```

Listing 5–9 (cont.)

```
      SELE 6
   ENDD
*
   SELE 10
   USE
   SELE 9
   USE
   SELE 8
   USE
   SELE 7
   USE
   SELE 5
   APPE FROM TANK5
   SELE 4
   APPE FROM TANK4
   SELE 3
   APPE FROM TANK3
   SELE 2
   APPE FROM TANK2
   ERAS TANK5.DBF
   ERAS TANK4.DBF
   ERAS TANK3.DBF
   ERAS TANK2.DBF
ELSE * DBFILE # primary database
*
   DO WHIL .T.
      APPE BLANK
      DO &GETTER                                 && selected database's GET file
      READ
*
      IF LEN(TRIM(&REPEATER)) = 0
         DELE
         EXIT
      ENDI
*
   ENDD
*
ENDI
*
SELE 6
USE
SELE 1
SET DELE ON
APPE FROM TANK
SET DELE OFF
```

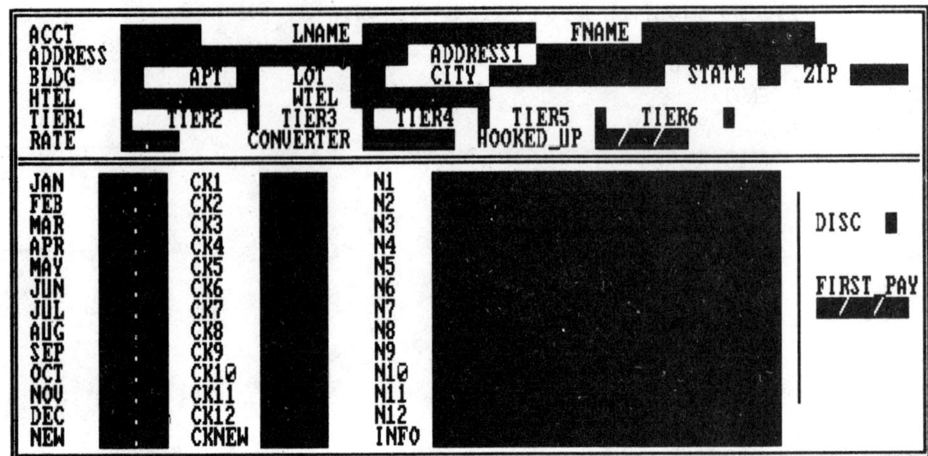

->

Figure 5–4 This screen is produced by the code shown in Listing 5–10. The screen and code help you to enter and edit data in two databases with one block of input or edit code.

Listing 5–9 (cont.)

```
DO &GETTER                                  && selected database's GET file
CLEA GETS
DO EDITMENU
ERAS TANK.DBF
```

Are you beginning to see how easy it is to take a proven piece of code and modify it—so far, slightly—to make it work in various situations? Good.

In this case, we're interested in passing data from a single database to several other databases. Unlike the code shown previously for straightline additions, this code assumes the user doesn't need to see what is going on or being added to each of the databases. How useful is this technique? Two uses have manifested themselves repeatedly, and those are shown here.

With dBASE III PLUS you can create format files that access several databases simultaneously. Such a format file, using the subscriber system as an example (see Figure 5–4), might be:

Listing 5–10

```
** MODI SCRE GENERATED FMT FILE
** SET DELI OFF, CLEA, HOUSEKEEPERS ADDED
*
CLEA
SET DEFA OFF
@ 2, 2  SAY "ACCT"
@ 2, 10  GET  SUBS->ACCT
```

Listing 5–10 (cont.)

```
@ 2, 25  SAY "LNAME"
@ 2, 31  GET  SUBS->LNAME
@ 2, 49  SAY "FNAME"
@ 2, 55  GET  SUBS->FNAME
@ 3,  2  SAY "ADDRESS"
@ 3, 10  GET  SUBS->ADDRESS
@ 3, 37  SAY "ADDRESS1"
@ 3, 46  GET  SUBS->ADDRESS1
@ 4,  2  SAY "BLDG"
@ 4, 10  GET  SUBS->BLDG
@ 4, 16  SAY "APT"
@ 4, 20  GET  SUBS->APT
@ 4, 25  SAY "LOT"
@ 4, 30  GET  SUBS->LOT
@ 4, 37  SAY "CITY"
@ 4, 42  GET  SUBS->CITY
@ 4, 59  SAY "STATE"
@ 4, 65  GET  SUBS->STATE
@ 4, 69  SAY "ZIP"
@ 4, 73  GET  SUBS->ZIP
@ 5,  2  SAY "HTEL"
@ 5, 10  GET  SUBS->HTEL
@ 5, 25  SAY "WTEL"
@ 5, 30  GET  SUBS->WTEL
@ 6,  2  SAY "TIER1"
@ 6, 10  GET  SUBS->TIER1
@ 6, 14  SAY "TIER2"
@ 6, 21  GET  SUBS->TIER2
@ 6, 24  SAY "TIER3"
@ 6, 31  GET  SUBS->TIER3
@ 6, 34  SAY "TIER4"
@ 6, 41  GET  SUBS->TIER4
@ 6, 44  SAY "TIER5"
@ 6, 51  GET  SUBS->TIER5
@ 6, 55  SAY "TIER6"
@ 6, 62  GET  SUBS->TIER6
@ 7,  2  SAY "RATE"
@ 7, 10  GET  SUBS->RATE
@ 7, 21  SAY "CONVERTER"
@ 7, 31  GET  SUBS->CONVERTER
@ 7, 41  SAY "HOOKED_UP"
@ 7, 51  GET  SUBS->HOOKED_UP
@ 9,  2  SAY "JAN"
@ 9,  8  GET  PAYMENTS->JAN
@ 9, 16  SAY "CK1"
```

Listing 5–10 (cont.)

```
@  9, 22  GET  PAYMENTS->CK1
@  9, 32  SAY "N1"
@  9, 37  GET  PAYMENTS->N1
@ 10,  2  SAY "FEB"
@ 10,  8  GET  PAYMENTS->FEB
@ 10, 16  SAY "CK2"
@ 10, 22  GET  PAYMENTS->CK2
@ 10, 32  SAY "N2"
@ 10, 37  GET  PAYMENTS->N2
@ 11,  2  SAY "MAR"
@ 11,  8  GET  PAYMENTS->MAR
@ 11, 16  SAY "CK3"
@ 11, 22  GET  PAYMENTS->CK3
@ 11, 32  SAY "N3"
@ 11, 37  GET  PAYMENTS->N3
@ 11, 70  SAY "DISC"
@ 11, 76  GET  PAYMENTS->DISC
@ 12,  2  SAY "APR"
@ 12,  8  GET  PAYMENTS->APR
@ 12, 16  SAY "CK4"
@ 12, 22  GET  PAYMENTS->CK4
@ 12, 32  SAY "N4"
@ 12, 37  GET  PAYMENTS->N4
@ 13,  2  SAY "MAY"
@ 13,  8  GET  PAYMENTS->MAY
@ 13, 16  SAY "CK5"
@ 13, 22  GET  PAYMENTS->CK5
@ 13, 32  SAY "N5"
@ 13, 37  GET  PAYMENTS->N5
@ 14,  2  SAY "JUN"
@ 14,  8  GET  PAYMENTS->JUN
@ 14, 16  SAY "CK6"
@ 14, 22  GET  PAYMENTS->CK6
@ 14, 32  SAY "N6"
@ 14, 37  GET  PAYMENTS->N6
@ 14, 70  SAY "FIRST_PAY"
@ 15,  2  SAY "JUL"
@ 15,  8  GET  PAYMENTS->JUL
@ 15, 16  SAY "CK7"
@ 15, 22  GET  PAYMENTS->CK7
@ 15, 32  SAY "N7"
@ 15, 37  GET  PAYMENTS->N7
@ 15, 70  GET  PAYMENTS->FIRST_PAY
@ 16,  2  SAY "AUG"
@ 16,  8  GET  PAYMENTS->AUG
```

Listing 5-10 (cont.)

```
@ 16, 16  SAY "CK8"
@ 16, 22  GET  PAYMENTS->CK8
@ 16, 32  SAY "N8"
@ 16, 37  GET  PAYMENTS->N8
@ 17,  2  SAY "SEP"
@ 17,  8  GET  PAYMENTS->SEP
@ 17, 16  SAY "CK9"
@ 17, 22  GET  PAYMENTS->CK9
@ 17, 32  SAY "N9"
@ 17, 37  GET  PAYMENTS->N9
@ 18,  2  SAY "OCT"
@ 18,  8  GET  PAYMENTS->OCT
@ 18, 16  SAY "CK10"
@ 18, 22  GET  PAYMENTS->CK10
@ 18, 32  SAY "N10"
@ 18, 37  GET  PAYMENTS->N10
@ 19,  2  SAY "NOV"
@ 19,  8  GET  PAYMENTS->NOV
@ 19, 16  SAY "CK11"
@ 19, 22  GET  PAYMENTS->CK11
@ 19, 32  SAY "N11"
@ 19, 37  GET  PAYMENTS->N11
@ 20,  2  SAY "DEC"
@ 20,  8  GET  PAYMENTS->DEC
@ 20, 16  SAY "CK12"
@ 20, 22  GET  PAYMENTS->CK12
@ 20, 32  SAY "N12"
@ 20, 37  GET  PAYMENTS->N12
@ 21,  2  SAY "NEW"
@ 21,  8  GET  PAYMENTS->NEW
@ 21, 16  SAY "CKNEW"
@ 21, 22  GET  PAYMENTS->NEWCK
@ 21, 32  SAY "INFO"
@ 21, 37  GET  PAYMENTS->INFO
@  1,  0  TO 22, 79    DOUBLE
@ 10, 68  TO 19, 68
@  8,  1  TO  8, 78    DOUBLE
*
** EOF
```

Systems That Add Data at the User's Discretion

This topic begins with a discussion of two new features incorporated in dBASE III PLUS. One is the text generation tool provided by the MODIFY SCREEN command, shown in Figure 5-5; the other is an unconventional use of the INKEY() function.

```
Set Up              Modify              Options            Exit  09:30:42 am
                                      ┌──────────────────────────┐
                                      │ Generate text file image │
                                      ├──────────────────────────┤
                                      │ Draw a window or line    │
                                      │  Single bar              │
                                      │  Double bar              │
                                      └──────────────────────────┘

MODIFY SCREEN  ||<D:>||5-11.SCR        ||Opt: 1/3        ||      ||    Caps
 Position selection bar - ↑↓. Select - ←┘. Leave menu - ↔. Blackboard - F10.
                    Generate a text file image of the blackboard.
```

Figure 5–5 Using the MODIFY SCREEN interface, you can generate a text image of the screen. This information is useful for documentation and editing purposes.

Few programmers make use of all the capabilities that dBASE III PLUS gives them. One feature, new with III PLUS and hence unknown and unnoticed by many programmers, is the text generation that you can do with one of the options on the MODIFY SCREEN interface.

Figure 5–6 was generated by III PLUS and corresponds to the screen and code shown in Figure 5–4 and Listing 5–10. The information in Figure 5–6 tells you many features about the screen and code that aren't obvious.

Consider Figure 5–4. We are called to modify the code after the system has been in place for several weeks/months/years. Do you remember exactly what's going on with each screen? Only if your memory is better than mine. Keeping the screen definition tells us this particular screen uses two databases and that there's no room for more information on that particular screen. We only use one screen page for the listed information, so we have two options for adding more fields.

First, we can create a format file and code as such. dBASE III PLUS allows format files up to 32 screens long and manages those screens with the cursor keys. The user can move between fields with the UP, RIGHT, DOWN, and LEFT ARROW keys. Movement from one screen to the next is done with the PG UP and PG DN keys.

That's all very well, but using format files and the SET FORMAT TO command negates much of our coding methodology. You can also use either the INKEY() function or the WAIT TO command to direct dBASE III PLUS to the proper screen. And that brings us right on track in this section.

The WAIT TO command and INKEY() function can use the function keys to allow up to 40 different branches. What am I talking about? Let's start by

Field definitions for Screen : 5-10.scr

Page	Row	Col	Data Base	Field	Type	Width	Dec
1	2	10	SUBS	ACCT	Character	7	
1	2	31	SUBS	LNAME	Character	15	
1	2	55	SUBS	FNAME	Character	15	
1	3	10	SUBS	ADDRESS	Character	25	
1	3	46	SUBS	ADDRESS1	Character	25	
1	4	10	SUBS	BLDG	Character	2	
1	4	20	SUBS	APT	Character	2	
1	4	30	SUBS	LOT	Character	3	
1	4	42	SUBS	CITY	Character	15	
1	4	65	SUBS	STATE	Character	2	
1	4	73	SUBS	ZIP	Character	5	
1	5	10	SUBS	HTEL	Character	12	
1	5	30	SUBS	WTEL	Character	12	
1	6	10	SUBS	TIER1	Logical	1	
1	6	21	SUBS	TIER2	Logical	1	
1	6	31	SUBS	TIER3	Logical	1	
1	6	41	SUBS	TIER4	Logical	1	
1	6	51	SUBS	TIER5	Logical	1	
1	6	62	SUBS	TIER6	Logical	1	
1	7	10	SUBS	RATE	Numeric	5	2
1	7	31	SUBS	CONVERTER	Character	8	
1	7	51	SUBS	HOOKED_UP	Date	8	
1	9	8	PAYMENTS	JAN	Numeric	6	2
1	9	22	PAYMENTS	CK1	Character	6	
1	9	37	PAYMENTS	N1	Character	30	
1	10	8	PAYMENTS	FEB	Numeric	6	2
1	10	22	PAYMENTS	CK2	Character	6	
1	10	37	PAYMENTS	N2	Character	30	
1	11	8	PAYMENTS	MAR	Numeric	6	2
1	11	22	PAYMENTS	CK3	Character	6	
1	11	37	PAYMENTS	N3	Character	30	
1	12	8	PAYMENTS	APR	Numeric	6	2
1	12	22	PAYMENTS	CK4	Character	6	
1	12	37	PAYMENTS	N4	Character	30	
1	13	8	PAYMENTS	MAY	Numeric	6	2
1	13	22	PAYMENTS	CK5	Character	6	
1	13	37	PAYMENTS	N5	Character	30	
1	14	8	PAYMENTS	JUN	Numeric	6	2
1	14	22	PAYMENTS	CK6	Character	6	
1	14	37	PAYMENTS	N6	Character	30	
1	15	8	PAYMENTS	JUL	Numeric	6	2
1	15	22	PAYMENTS	CK7	Character	6	
1	15	37	PAYMENTS	N7	Character	30	

Figure 5-6 This chart, created by III PLUS's Write Text option on the MODIFY SCREEN menu, provides documentation on field placement and size in FMT files.

```
1  16   8  PAYMENTS  AUG        Numeric      6  2
1  16  22  PAYMENTS  CK8        Character    6
1  16  37  PAYMENTS  N8         Character   30
1  17   8  PAYMENTS  SEP        Numeric      6  2
1  17  22  PAYMENTS  CK9        Character    6
1  17  37  PAYMENTS  N9         Character   30
1  18   8  PAYMENTS  OCT        Numeric      6  2
1  18  22  PAYMENTS  CK10       Character    6
1  18  37  PAYMENTS  N10        Character   30
1  19   8  PAYMENTS  NOV        Numeric      6  2
1  19  22  PAYMENTS  CK11       Character    6
1  19  37  PAYMENTS  N11        Character   30
1  20   8  PAYMENTS  DEC        Numeric      6  2
1  20  22  PAYMENTS  CK12       Character    6
1  20  37  PAYMENTS  N12        Character   30
1  11  76  PAYMENTS  DISC       Logical      1
1  15  70  PAYMENTS  FIRST_PAY  Date         8
1  21   8  PAYMENTS  NEW        Numeric      6  2
1  21  22  PAYMENTS  NEWCK      Character    6
1  21  37  PAYMENTS  INFO       Character   30

Content of page :  1

 ACCT     XXXXXXX        LNAME XXXXXXXXXXXXXXX   FNAME XXXXXXXXXXXXXXX
 ADDRESS XXXXXXXXXXXXXXXXXXXXXXXXX  ADDRESS1 XXXXXXXXXXXXXXXXXXXXXXXXX
 BLDG     XX    APT XX   LOT  XXX    CITY XXXXXXXXXXXXXXX  STATE XX  ZIP XXXXX
 HTEL     XXXXXXXXXXXX   WTEL XXXXXXXXXXXX
 TIER1    X   TIER2  X  TIER3  X  TIER4  X  TIER5  X   TIER6  X
 RATE     XXXXX      CONVERTER XXXXXXXX  HOOKED_UP XXXXXXXX

 JAN   XXXXXX  CK1   XXXXXX    N1   XXXXXXXXXXXXXXXXXXXXXXXXXXXXXX
 FEB   XXXXXX  CK2   XXXXXX    N2   XXXXXXXXXXXXXXXXXXXXXXXXXXXXXX
 MAR   XXXXXX  CK3   XXXXXX    N3   XXXXXXXXXXXXXXXXXXXXXXXXXXXXXX  DISC  X
 APR   XXXXXX  CK4   XXXXXX    N4   XXXXXXXXXXXXXXXXXXXXXXXXXXXXXX
 MAY   XXXXXX  CK5   XXXXXX    N5   XXXXXXXXXXXXXXXXXXXXXXXXXXXXXX
 JUN   XXXXXX  CK6   XXXXXX    N6   XXXXXXXXXXXXXXXXXXXXXXXXXXXXXX  FIRST_PAY
 JUL   XXXXXX  CK7   XXXXXX    N7   XXXXXXXXXXXXXXXXXXXXXXXXXXXXXX  XXXXXXXX
 AUG   XXXXXX  CK8   XXXXXX    N8   XXXXXXXXXXXXXXXXXXXXXXXXXXXXXX
 SEP   XXXXXX  CK9   XXXXXX    N9   XXXXXXXXXXXXXXXXXXXXXXXXXXXXXX
 OCT   XXXXXX  CK10  XXXXXX    N10  XXXXXXXXXXXXXXXXXXXXXXXXXXXXXX
 NOV   XXXXXX  CK11  XXXXXX    N11  XXXXXXXXXXXXXXXXXXXXXXXXXXXXXX
 DEC   XXXXXX  CK12  XXXXXX    N12  XXXXXXXXXXXXXXXXXXXXXXXXXXXXXX
 NEW   XXXXXX  CKNEW XXXXXX    INFO XXXXXXXXXXXXXXXXXXXXXXXXXXXXXX
```

Figure 5–6 (cont.)

WAIT TO FUNCTION KEY ASCII VALUES

FKEY	VALUE	ALT-VALUE	SHIFT-VALUE	CTRL-VALUE
F1	0	104	84	94
F2	255	105	85	95
F3	254	106	86	96
F4	253	107	87	97
F5	252	108	88	98
F6	251	109	89	99
F7	250	110	90	100
F8	249	111	91	101
F9	248	112	92	102
F10	247	113	93	103

INKEY() FUNCTION KEY ASCII VALUES

FKEY	VALUE	ALT-VALUE	SHIFT-VALUE	CTRL-VALUE
F1	28	104	84	94
F2	-1	105	85	95
F3	-2	106	86	96
F4	-3	107	87	97
F5	-4	108	88	98
F6	-5	109	89	99
F7	-6	110	90	100
F8	-7	111	91	101
F9	-8	112	92	102
F10	-9	113	93	103

Figure 5–7 The upper block is the ASCII values returned to the WAIT command by the function keys and the lower block is for the INKEY() function.

listing the ASCII values of the function keys for the INKEY() function and WAIT TO command shown in Figure 5–7.

A short program that demonstrates using INKEY() to capture function key ASCII values is shown in Listing 5–11.

Listing 5–11

```
** PRG TO DEMONSTRATE INKEY() FUNCTION
*
CLEA
I = 0
```

```
        28
        99
        28
        99
         0
        -2
       101
        -2
        28
       111
        -3
        96
       109
       101
       104
        97
       103
       101
       104
       101
        95
       103
*** INTERRUPTED ***
Called from - A:A-3.prg
Cancel, Ignore, or Suspend? (C, I, or S)
```

Figure 5–8 Use the INKEY() function to capture function keys for coding purposes.

Listing 5–11 (cont.)

```
*
DO WHIL .T.
   I = INKEY()
   ? I
ENDD
*
** EOF
```

This listing tells III PLUS to list at the screen either the value 0 or the value of the last key pressed. You can test the INKEY() values of any key using this program. Program execution is stopped by pressing the ESC key (see Figure 5–8).

How can this information be used to shuttle between input screens? Quite easily. Consider the following code:

Listing 5–12

```
** CODE EXAMPLE FOR USING INKEY() TO SHUTTLE BETWEEN INPUT
** SCREENS. THIS CODE ASSUMES YOU'LL WANT TO START WITH THE
** FIRST INPUT SCREEN AND INITIALIZES I TO 28 FOR THAT PURPOSE.
*
I = 28
ON ESCA EXIT
*
DO WHIL .T.
   CLEA
```

Listing 5–12 (cont.)

```
*
   DO CASE
*
** CASES FOR I = 28, -1 TO -9 CORRESPOND TO PRESSING AN FKEY
** BY ITSELF.
*
      CASE I = 28
         DO FIRSTSAY
         DO FIRSTGET
      CASE I = -1
         DO SECONDSAY
         DO SECONDGET
      CASE I = -2
         DO THIRDSAY
         DO THIRDGET
      CASE I = -3
         DO FOURTHSAY
         DO FOURTHGET
      CASE I = -4
         DO FIFTHSAY
         DO FIFTHGET
      CASE I = -5
         DO SIXTHSAY
         DO SIXTHGET
      CASE I = -6
         DO SEVENTHSAY
         DO SEVENTHGET
      CASE I = -7
         DO EIGHTHSAY
         DO EIGHTHGET
      CASE I = -8
         DO NINTHSAY
         DO NINTHGET
      CASE I = -9
         DO TENTHSAY
         DO TENTHGET
*
** CASES FOR I = 104 TO 113 CORRESPOND TO ALT-FKEY COMBINATIONS.
** CASES FOR I = 84 TO 93 CORRESPOND TO SHIFT-FKEY COMBINATIONS.
** CASES FOR I = 94 TO 103 CORRESPOND TO CTRL-FKEY COMBINATIONS.
*
   ENDC
*
   READ
   @ 22,0 SAY [PRESS F1->F10 FOR SCREENS 1->10, ];
```

Listing 5–12 (cont.)

```
             [ALT-F1->ALT-F10 FOR SCREENS 11]
   @ 23,0 SAY [->20, SHIFT-F1->SHIFT-F10 FOR SCREENS 21->30, ];
             [CTRL-F1->CTRL-F10 FOR]
   @ 24,0 SAY [SCREENS 31->40, OR ESCAPE TO EXIT INPUT MODE]
   OLD = I
*
   DO WHIL OLD = I
      I = INKEY()
   ENDD
*
ENDD
*
ON ESCA
*
** EOF
```

This code makes use of the INKEY() function to move between input screens. This can also be used for any editing function that requires multiple screen entry. Coding for more than 10 input screens follows the logic shown in the listing. You can achieve the same result using the WAIT TO command. A similar listing for that command is:

Listing 5–13

```
** CODE EXAMPLE FOR WAIT TO COMMAND TO SHUTTLE BETWEEN INPUT
** SCREENS. THIS CODE ASSUMES YOU'LL WANT TO START WITH THE
** FIRST INPUT SCREEN AND INITIALIZES I TO 0 FOR THAT PURPOSE.
*
I = 0
ON ESCA EXIT
*
DO WHIL .T.
   CLEA
*
   DO CASE
*
** CASES FOR I = 0, 255 TO 247 CORRESPOND TO PRESSING AN FKEY
** BY ITSELF.
*
      CASE I = 0
         DO FIRSTSAY
         DO FIRSTGET
      CASE I = 255
         DO SECONDSAY
         DO SECONDGET
      CASE I = 254
```

Listing 5–13 (cont.)

```
         DO THIRDSAY
         DO THIRDGET
      CASE I = 253
         DO FOURTHSAY
         DO FOURTHGET
      CASE I = 252
         DO FIFTHSAY
         DO FIFTHGET
      CASE I = 251
         DO SIXTHSAY
         DO SIXTHGET
      CASE I = 250
         DO SEVENTHSAY
         DO SEVENTHGET
      CASE I = 249
         DO EIGHTHSAY
         DO EIGHTHGET
      CASE I = 248
         DO NINTHSAY
         DO NINTHGET
      CASE I = 247
         DO TENTHSAY
         DO TENTHGET
*
** CASES FOR I = 104 TO 113 CORRESPOND TO ALT-FKEY COMBINATIONS.
** CASES FOR I = 84 TO 93 CORRESPOND TO SHIFT-FKEY COMBINATIONS.
** CASES FOR I = 94 TO 103 CORRESPOND TO CTRL-FKEY COMBINATIONS.
*
   ENDC
*
   READ
   @ 22,0 SAY [PRESS F1->F10 FOR SCREENS 1->10, ];
              [ALT-F1->ALT-F10 FOR SCREENS 11]
   @ 23,0 SAY [->20, SHIFT-F1->SHIFT-F10 FOR SCREENS 21->30, ];
              [CTRL-F1->CTRL-F10 FOR]
   WAIT [SCREENS 31->40, OR ESCAPE TO EXIT INPUT MODE] TO I
   I = ASC(I)
ENDD
*
ON ESCA
*
** EOF
```

The differences between using the INKEY() function and the WAIT TO command go deeper than just the I values necessary for both code blocks. The WAIT TO command captures values to the declared variable (I in this example).

```
   0
Press any key to continue...
 255
Press any key to continue...▪
 254
Press any key to continue...²
 253
Press any key to continue...ⁿ
 252
Press any key to continue...√
 251
Press any key to continue...·
 250
Press any key to continue...·
 249
Press any key to continue...°
 248
Press any key to continue...≈
 247
Press any key to continue...
*** INTERRUPTED ***
Called from - D:INKEYTST.prg
Cancel, Ignore, or Suspend? (C, I, or S) Cancel
Do cancelled
->
```

Figure 5–9 The WAIT TO block can place graphics characters on the screen when you don't want it to.

It doesn't capture the ASCII value of the key pressed, however. That means the programmer must make sure the line:

```
I = ASC(I)
```

is located somewhere prior to the CASE tests, or that each CASE tests for correct character input. The other difference involves coding to use the WAIT command for part of the prompt. Here:

```
WAIT [SCREENS 31->40, OR ESCAPE TO EXIT INPUT MODE] TO I
```

is used in place of:

```
@ 24,0 [SCREENS 31->40, OR ESCAPE TO EXIT INPUT MODE]
```

from the INKEY() code block. Also realize the WAIT TO block stops processing until a key is pressed. The INKEY() block uses a DO WHILE . . . ENDDO block to get the INKEY() value. Both blocks of code use the same logic and values for the ALT-, SHIFT-, and CTRL-function key combinations.

One other note on the WAIT TO command. Figure 5–9 shows that when you press a function key in response to a WAIT prompt, dBASE III PLUS echoes the function key's corresponding graphics character on the screen. That might prove aesthetically unsatisfactory. There are several solutions, but a strong suggestion would be to use the CURSOR2.BIN file available from Ashton-Tate. This is one of the several files available in the "dBASE PROGRAMMER'S UTILITIES" package. CURSOR2.BIN gives programmers the ability to turn the cursor on and off, and to make the cursor either normal or block shaped. The WAIT TO code block makes use of CURSOR2.BIN as follows:

Listing 5–14

```
** CODE EXAMPLE FOR WAIT TO COMMAND WITH CURSOR2.BIN FILE
** TO SHUTTLE BETWEEN INPUT SCREENS. THIS CODE ASSUMES YOU'LL
** WANT TO START WITH THE FIRST INPUT SCREEN AND INITIALIZES
** I TO 0 FOR THAT PURPOSE.
*
LOAD drive:\path(s)\CURSOR2
I = 0
ON ESCA EXIT
*
DO WHIL .T.
   CLEA
*
   DO CASE
*
** CASES FOR I = 0, 255 TO 247 CORRESPOND TO PRESSING AN FKEY
** BY ITSELF.
*
      CASE I = 0
         DO FIRSTSAY
         DO FIRSTGET
      CASE I = 255
         DO SECONDSAY
         DO SECONDGET
      CASE I = 254
         DO THIRDSAY
         DO THIRDGET
      CASE I = 253
         DO FOURTHSAY
         DO FOURTHGET
      CASE I = 252
         DO FIFTHSAY
         DO FIFTHGET
      CASE I = 251
         DO SIXTHSAY
         DO SIXTHGET
      CASE I = 250
         DO SEVENTHSAY
         DO SEVENTHGET
      CASE I = 249
         DO EIGHTHSAY
         DO EIGHTHGET
      CASE I = 248
         DO NINTHSAY
         DO NINTHGET
      CASE I = 247
```

Listing 5–14 (cont.)

```
        DO TENTHSAY
        DO TENTHGET
*
** CASES FOR I = 104 TO 113 CORRESPOND TO ALT-FKEY COMBINATIONS.
** CASES FOR I = 84 TO 93 CORRESPOND TO SHIFT-FKEY COMBINATIONS.
** CASES FOR I = 94 TO 103 CORRESPOND TO CTRL-FKEY COMBINATIONS.
*
   ENDC
*
   READ
   @ 22,0 SAY [PRESS F1->F10 FOR SCREENS 1->10, ];
              [ALT-F1->ALT-F10 FOR SCREENS 11]
   @ 23,0 SAY [->20, SHIFT-F1->SHIFT-F10 FOR SCREENS 21->30, ];
              [CTRL-F1->CTRL-F10 FOR]
*
** TURN THE CURSOR OFF.
*
   CALL CURSOR2 WITH '0'
   WAIT [SCREENS 31->40, OR ESCAPE TO EXIT INPUT MODE] TO I
*
** TURN THE CURSOR ON.
*
   CALL CURSOR2 WITH 'N'
   I = ASC(I)
ENDD
*
ON ESCA
*
** EOF
```

This code can also be modified to include the REPLACE blocks shown previously. The two situations that must be addressed involve different coding solutions. The first situation deals with one or more necessary fields being REPLACEd in each of the databases in the system. The second situation deals with fields being REPLACEd only in databases the user actually APPENDs to.

The first situation revolves around the placement of the READ command. Both the WAIT TO and INKEY() code solutions use a single READ command for all the GET files in the system. That necessitates placing a check after the READ command. This check determines if the user has accessed the first CASE (the first point of data entry and the data that must be carried to all the other databases). This check, as shown in Listing 5–15, provides a means of keeping a one-to-one correspondence among records even though the user doesn't necessarily add data to each record. With it, the user can add data only to records of definite interest, but it also updates each database as new information is entered to the primary file.

Listing 5–15

```
** CODE EXAMPLE FOR USING INKEY() TO SHUTTLE BETWEEN INPUT ;
   SCREENS. ASSUMPTIONS:                                    ;
 (1) YOU'LL WANT TO START WITH THE FIRST INPUT SCREEN ;
     SO INITIALIZE I TO 28 FOR THAT PURPOSE.          ;
 (2) YOU'RE GOING TO AUTOMATICALLY REPLACE FIELDS IN ALL ;
     NECESSARY DATABASES.
*
I = 28
ON ESCA EXIT
*
DO WHIL .T.
   CLEA
*
   DO CASE
*
** CASES FOR I = 28, -1 TO -9 CORRESPOND TO PRESSING AN FKEY
** BY ITSELF.
*
      CASE I = 28
         DO FIRSTSAY
         DO FIRSTGET
      CASE I = -1
         DO SECONDSAY
         DO SECONDGET
      CASE I = -2
         DO THIRDSAY
         DO THIRDGET
      CASE I = -3
         DO FOURTHSAY
         DO FOURTHGET
      CASE I = -4
         DO FIFTHSAY
         DO FIFTHGET
      CASE I = -5
         DO SIXTHSAY
         DO SIXTHGET
      CASE I = -6
         DO SEVENTHSAY
         DO SEVENTHGET
      CASE I = -7
         DO EIGHTHSAY
         DO EIGHTHGET
      CASE I = -8
         DO NINTHSAY
         DO NINTHGET
```

Listing 5–15 (cont.)

```
      CASE I = -9
         DO TENTHSAY
         DO TENTHGET
*
** CASES FOR I = 104 TO 113 CORRESPOND TO ALT-FKEY COMBINATIONS.
** CASES FOR I = 84 TO 93 CORRESPOND TO SHIFT-FKEY COMBINATIONS.
** CASES FOR I = 94 TO 103 CORRESPOND TO CTRL-FKEY COMBINATIONS.
*
   ENDC
*
   READ
*
   IF I = 28                         && then the first case was used
      SELE B
      APPE BLAN
      REPL fielda WITH A->fielda, fieldb WITH A->fieldb, ...
      SELE C
      APPE BLAN
      REPL fielda WITH A->fielda, fieldb WITH A->fieldb, ...
      SELE D
      APPE BLAN
      REPL fielda WITH A->fielda, fieldb WITH A->fieldb, ...
*
** CODE CONTINUES AS SUCH FOR AS MANY ACTIVE AREAS AS ARE NECESSARY.
*
   ENDI
*
   @ 22,0 SAY [PRESS F1->F10 FOR SCREENS 1->10, ];
              [ALT-F1->ALT-F10 FOR SCREENS 11]
   @ 23,0 SAY [->20, SHIFT-F1->SHIFT-F10 FOR SCREENS 21->30, ];
              [CTRL-F1->CTRL-F10 FOR]
   @ 24,0 SAY [SCREENS 31->40, OR ESCAPE TO EXIT INPUT MODE]
   OLD = I
*
   DO WHIL OLD = I
      I = INKEY()
   ENDD
*
ENDD
*
ON ESCA
*
** EOF
```

The check performed is determining the value of the variable I:

```
IF I = 28
```

then the first CASE statement was accessed, and all relative fields should be REPLACEd in other databases. Listing 5–15 shows the REPLACE block in the INKEY() code. It can be used in the WAIT TO code with one modification. The check must be:

```
IF I = 0
```

to work properly with the WAIT TO function key values.

The second situation is shown in Listing 5–16. That code only REPLACEs data in records if the user accesses a particular screen. That is, the user specifies the database to update simply by selecting a screen for data entry. There are 40 screens available, but only 10 databases. The programmer determines which screens correspond to which databases, then codes accordingly. The code makes use of much of the logic of Listing 5–15, but the IF . . . ENDIF block is replaced by a DO CASE . . . ENDCASE block to handle the 40 possible screens. Again, the INKEY() code was used in Listing 5–16. Changes for the WAIT TO code are the same as listed earlier; the check changed from I = 28 to I = 0.

Listing 5–16

```
** CODE EXAMPLE FOR USING INKEY() TO SHUTTLE BETWEEN INPUT ;
   SCREENS. ASSUMPTIONS:          ;
         (1) YOU'LL WANT TO START WITH THE FIRST INPUT SCREEN ;
             SO INITIALIZE I TO 28 FOR THAT PURPOSE.  ;
         (2) YOU'RE ONLY GOING TO REPLACE FIELDS IN DATABASES ;
             SPECIFIED BY THE USER.
*
I = 28
ON ESCA EXIT
*
DO WHIL .T.
   CLEA
*
   DO CASE
*
** CASES FOR I = 28, -1 TO -9 CORRESPOND TO PRESSING AN FKEY
** BY ITSELF.
*
      CASE I = 28
         DO FIRSTSAY
         DO FIRSTGET
      CASE I = -1
         DO SECONDSAY
         DO SECONDGET
      CASE I = -2
         DO THIRDSAY
```

Listing 5–16 (cont.)

```
            DO THIRDGET
         CASE I = -3
            DO FOURTHSAY
            DO FOURTHGET
         CASE I = -4
            DO FIFTHSAY
            DO FIFTHGET
         CASE I = -5
            DO SIXTHSAY
            DO SIXTHGET
         CASE I = -6
            DO SEVENTHSAY
            DO SEVENTHGET
         CASE I = -7
            DO EIGHTHSAY
            DO EIGHTHGET
         CASE I = -8
            DO NINTHSAY
            DO NINTHGET
         CASE I = -9
            DO TENTHSAY
            DO TENTHGET
*
** CASES FOR I = 104 TO 113 CORRESPOND TO ALT-FKEY COMBINATIONS.
** CASES FOR I = 84 TO 93 CORRESPOND TO SHIFT-FKEY COMBINATIONS.
** CASES FOR I = 94 TO 103 CORRESPOND TO CTRL-FKEY COMBINATIONS.
*
   ENDC
*
   READ
*
   DO CASE
*
** THIS CODE USES FOUR DATABASES AS AN EXAMPLE. THE FIRST      ;
   DATABASE USES SCREENS 1->10 CORRESPONDING TO I = 28,-1 -> -9 ;
   WHICH NEEDS NO UPDATING. SCREENS 11-20 ARE FOR DATABASE B,   ;
   21->30 ARE FOR DATABASE C, AND 31->40 ARE FOR DATABASE D.     ;
   B, C, AND D NEED UPDATING.
*
      CASE I > 103 .AND. I < 114
         SELE B
         APPE BLAN
         REPL fielda WITH A->fielda, fieldb WITH A->fieldb, ...
      CASE I > 83 .AND. I < 94
         SELE C
```

Listing 5–16 (cont.)

```
            APPE BLAN
            REPL fielda WITH A->fielda, fieldb WITH A->fieldb, ...
         CASE I > 93 .AND. I < 104
            SELE D
            APPE BLAN
            REPL fielda WITH A->fielda, fieldb WITH A->fieldb, ...
      ENDC
*
   @ 22,0 SAY [PRESS F1->F10 FOR SCREENS 1->10, ];
              [ALT-F1->ALT-F10 FOR SCREENS 11]
   @ 23,0 SAY [->20, SHIFT-F1->SHIFT-F10 FOR SCREENS 21->30, ];
              [CTRL-F1->CTRL-F10 FOR]
   @ 24,0 SAY [SCREENS 31->40, OR ESCAPE TO EXIT INPUT MODE]
   OLD = I
*
   DO WHIL OLD = I
      I = INKEY()
   ENDD
*
ENDD
*
ON ESCA
*
** EOF
```

CHECKING FOR DUPLICATIONS DURING DATA ENTRY

A problem that arises in a number of environments is validating data. There are many types of data validation. Commonly, code is inserted to ensure your program doesn't get numeric input when it's expecting character input, uppercase text when it's expecting lowercase text, and other such entry problems.

The type of validity checking we'll explore here concerns ensuring that new data doesn't duplicate old data. This type of data validation is very important in accounting systems. For example, you don't want two or more clients to be assigned the same account number.

Checking for Duplications Using Random Number Generators

We start by checking for duplications using key fields. A *key field* in a database is a field that is used for indexing or sorting purposes. It is special and used more often than any of the other fields in the database. There are two methods of ensuring there are no duplications of data in the key field when data is being entered.

The first and most obvious method is to make the program enter information into the key field. That is achieved by either having the computer generate new key field values as each new record is entered or having the program take necessary parts of other fields and enter that data into the key field.

Having the computer generate new values for the key field isn't as simple as it sounds. Do you want some kind of random number generation for the key field? Do you want some specific ordering pattern? Do you want the user to have access to the computer-generated value? This is a situation in which the subscriber system duplicates an accounting system on several levels, and we'll make use of that in demonstrating the code.

Our first block of code uses random number generation to create values in the key field:

Listing 5–17

```
** RANDOM NUMBER GENERATOR FOR AUTOMATIC KEY FIELD ENTRY.
*
SEED = VAL(LEFT(TIME(),AT(':',TIME()))) * ;
       VAL(SUBS(TIME(),AT(':',TIME()) + 1)) / ;
       VAL(RIGH(TIME(),AT(':',TIME()) - 1))
SEED = (SEED - INT(SEED)) * 100
ACCNUM = DTOC(DATE()) + '-' + LTRIM(STR(SEED))
*
** EOF
```

Listing 5–17 merely creates the random number. You'll notice that it derandomizes the actual ACCNUM number by including a DTOC() function. This is one method for guarding against duplications. The account number is randomized, but each day's entries will be coded by date. The line:

```
ACCNUM = DTOC(DATE()) + '-' + LTRIM(STR(SEED))
```

would normally go in your Add kernel. You then modify your Add code such that the SEED value is increased with each entry. An example is shown in Listing 5–18:

Listing 5–18

```
** MODIFIED Add KERNEL. BUILDS KEY FIELD FROM RANDOM NUMBER.
*
COPY STRUC TO TANK
SELE 6
USE TANK
@ 20,0 CLEA
@ 22,0 SAY "Press CTRL-W to save new information, ";
          "CTRL-Q to exit this mode."
REPEATER = FIELD(1)
*
```

Listing 5–18 (cont.)

```
DO WHIL .T.
   APPE BLAN
   REPL account field WITH DTOC(DATE()) + '-' + LTRIM(STR(SEED))
   DO &GETTER   && this GETTER file doesn't get the ACCOUNT field
   READ
*
   IF LEN(TRIM(&REPEATER)) = 0
      EXIT
   ENDI
*
   SEED = SEED + 1
ENDD
*
DELE
USE
SELE 1
SET DELE ON
APPE FROM TANK
SET DELE OFF
DO &GETTER
CLEA GETS
ERAS TANK.DBF
*
** EOF
```

This listing produces a screen similar to that shown in Figure 5–10. Note that this screen uses the subscriber system mentioned earlier in this book. Each succeeding record has a unique account number because dates are usually a one-shot deal, entropy being what it is. The SEED value is automatically increased each time a record is added. This prevents duplication in the ACCT field.

Checking for Duplications by Building Key Fields from Other Fields

An alternative method of programming nonduplicated field values is to build the key field (ACCT in this example) from other fields in the database. The ACCT field in the subscriber system is actually based on two separate values. It is a combination of the last two digits of the zip code (ZIP) and the last four digits of the home telephone number (HTEL). Provided those two fields are entered first, the ACCT field is generated with code in the following line of code:

```
REPL ACCT WITH RIGHT(ZIP,2) + '-' + RIGHT(HTEL,4)
```

The result of this code can be seen in Figure 5–11. There are necessary code changes to using this method of generating key field values, as shown here:

Listing 5-19

```
** MODIFIED Add KERNEL. BUILDS KEY FIELD FROM OTHER FIELDS.
*
COPY STRUC TO TANK
SELE 6
USE TANK
@ 20,0 CLEA
```

```
                              SUBSCRIBERS                              1

ACCT 12/02/86-12     LNAME  :               : FNAME  :               :
ADDRESS :                         : ADDRESS1 :                          :
BLDG :  : APT :  : LOT :  : CITY :               : STATE :  : ZIP :     :
HTEL :    -   -    : WTEL  :    -   -    :

     TIER1 : :  TIER2 : :  TIER3 : :  TIER4  : :  TIER5  : :  TIER6  : :
     TIER7 : :  TIER8 : :  TIER9 : :  TIER10 : :  TIER11 : :  TIER12 : :
     RATE    :     .    :  CONVERTER   :        :  HOOKED_UP  :  /  /  :
```

Type CTL-W to save new information, CTL-Q to exit this mode.

-\>

Figure 5-10 This is an example of the subscriber system using a random number generator to ensure nonduplicated key field values.

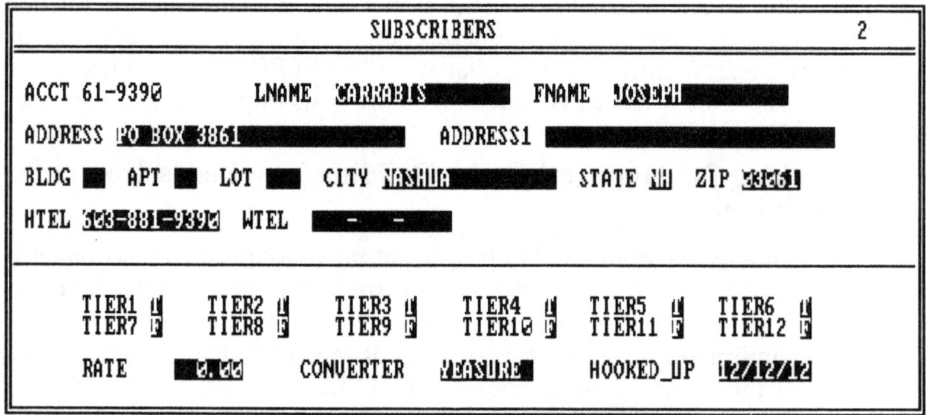

Type CTL-W to save new information, CTL-Q to exit this mode.

-\>

Figure 5-11 This screen is identical to that in Figure 5-10, except the ACCT field is built from parts of other fields.

Listing 5-19 (cont.)

```
@ 22,0 SAY "Press CTRL-W to save new information, ";
         "CTRL-Q to exit this mode."
REPEATER = FIELD(1)
*
DO WHIL .T.
   APPE BLAN
   DO &GETTER   && this GETTER file doesn't get the ACCOUNT field
   READ
*
   IF LEN(TRIM(&REPEATER)) = 0
      EXIT
   ENDI
*
   REPL account field WITH RIGH(field1,n) + '-' + RIGH(field2,m)
ENDD
*
DELE
USE
SELE 1
SET DELE ON
APPE FROM TANK
SET DELE OFF
DO &GETTER
CLEA GETS
ERAS TANK.DBF
*
** EOF
```

Note that Listing 5-19 is a bit more generic than Listing 5-18. The choice of fields to build the ACCT field from is yours to make, as are the parts of each field. ZIP was used because it provides for convenient geographic groupings. The last four digits of the home telephone number were used because telephone numbers are unique within a given exchange, which is also a geographic grouping.

Checking for Duplications Using a Historical NDX File

Most programmers would assume the method just described to be a fair way of ensuring nonduplication of the key field. In most cases their assumption is correct. However, nothing is sure in this life, and that brings us to the topic of scanning a historical index of the key field to actually test for duplications. This is where using a primary file and a temporary TANK file is especially handy. Consider Listing 5-20. This code is used when the primary database in work area 1 has an active NDX file. You can have more than one NDX file open. It is necessary that the active and first order NDX file be INDEXed on the field of interest. This example uses an account field:

Listing 5-20

```
** Add KERNEL MODIFIED TO CHECK EXISTING KEY FIELD VALUES
*
ON ESCA RETURN
COPY STRUC TO TANK
SELE 6
USE TANK
@ 20,0 CLEA
@ 22,0 SAY "Press CTRL-W to save information, CTRL-Q to exit"
SELE 6
*
DO WHIL .T.
   APPE BLAN
*
   DO WHIL .T.
      @ x,y GET account field
READ
*
      IF LEN(TRIM(account field)) = 0
         EXIT
      ELSE
         SELE 1
         SEEK F->account field
*
         IF FOUND()
            DO &GETTER
            CLEA GETS
            @ 20,0 CLEA
            WAIT [SORRY, WE'VE ALREADY GOT ONE OF THOSE. ] ;
                 [PRESS ANY KEY TO CONTINUE OR ESC TO EXIT.]
            @ 20,0 CLEA
            @ 22,0 SAY "Press CTRL-W to save information, ";
                       "CTRL-Q to exit."
            SELE F
            LOOP
         ELSE
            SELE F
            DO &GETTER
            READ
         ENDI
*
      ENDI
*
   ENDD
*
   IF LEN(TRIM(account field)) = 0
```

Listing 5–20 (cont.)

```
      EXIT
   ENDI
*
ENDD
*
DELE
USE
SELE 1
SET DELE ON
APPE FROM TANK
SET DELE OFF
DO &GETTER
CLEA GETS
ERAS TANK.DBF
*
** EOF
```

First, note that Listing 5–20 is missing the command:

```
REPEATER = FIELD(1)
```

This is intentional and due to the increased importance of the account field in this type of Add kernel. Again, your system doesn't have to poll an "account field," as this example does. The example here shows how to use the primary database's existing NDX files to ensure nonduplicated data entry.

CHECKING FOR PARALLEL ENTRIES

The earlier discussions in this chapter all deal with the topic of parallel data entry. Parallel data entry? What's that?

Parallel data entry occurs when you must duplicate data from any one database in other databases. Examples of parallel data entry shown in the situations described in the last three sections cover the need to copy:

1. a single field from a primary file to single fields in one or more secondary files.
2. several fields from a primary file to a single file or single fields in one or more secondary files.
3. several fields from a primary file to several fields in one or more secondary files.

All of this assumes you'll never make mistakes, and every entry that should be parallel will be. Ha!

People who have done lots of programming will nod knowingly at my next statement, and people who have done little programming will profit from it.

REAL WORLD FUNCTION 1: If it ain't happened yet, it's gonna.

COROLLARY TO REAL WORLD FUNCTION 1: If it hasn't happened to you yet, it should.

These truths were on the lost third tablet centuries ago, and some of us have rediscovered them through our own machinations. They apply to several aspects of life, not the least of which are critical disk failure and failed parallel data entry.

Here we're concerned with guarding against failed parallel data entry. We need some code that checks key fields in the primary database against key fields in some other database. In particular, we need to make sure there exists a one-to-one correspondence of records in two or more databases. This is done in several ways, discussed next.

Checking for Parallel Entries with Nonindexed Databases

One method we can use to check for parallelism is unique in that it doesn't make use of NDX files and still handles two or more databases. This method is excellent, provided the programmer can ensure that there will always be a one-to-one correspondence between the active data files. This might not always be the case, as is shown in later in this chapter.

This lack of correspondence is an important point and should be emphasized here. Any system that demands parallel, nonINDEXed data must also ensure that it deletes parallel records when the user does any deleting. Remember also that our chief concern in this code is to make sure there is an entry in the secondary files for each entry in the primary file.

Before showing the code, we should take a moment to explore the concept of parallel, nonINDEXed databases.

Say we have two databases. The databases contain separate information about the same subject. One file contains customer account data, and the other contains customer address information. Both databases have information on customers, but the information in each database is different. The only similarity between the two databases is one field, ACCOUNT (or ACCNUM or ACCT). Each customer has a record for account information and a parallel record for address information. Because this one-to-one correspondence exists between the two databases, and because this correspondence was designed to start the first time data was entered and be maintained ever after, we can create code like:

Listing 5–21

```
SELE 2
USE secondary database file
SELE 1
USE primary database file
SET RELA TO RECNO() INTO B
```

whenever we want to list information in both databases based on a common field or fields. This is demonstrated in Figure 5–12. Now, say something happened

```
-> SELE 2
-> USE PAYMENTS
-> SELE 1
-> USE SUBS
-> SET RELA TO RECNO() INTO B
-> LIST ACCT,B->ACCT
Record#  ACCT    B->ACCT
      1  3-0084  3-0084
      2  3-0091  3-0091
      3  3-0022  3-0022
      4  3-0025  3-0025
      5  3-0064  3-0064
      6  3-0068  3-0068
      7  3-0040  3-0040
      8  3-0042  3-0042
      9  3-0052  3-0052
     10  3-0094  3-0094
     11  3-0021  3-0021
     12  3-0001  3-0001
     13  3-0050  3-0050
     14  3-0059  3-0059
     15  3-0087  3-0087
     16  3-0078  3-0078
     17  3-0080  3-0080
     18  3-0018  3-0018
```

Figure 5–12 These two databases have a one-to-one correspondence on a single field and can therefore be linked using the SET RELA TO RECNO() command.

and we no longer had this one-to-one correspondence, such as occurs in Listing 5–22. Listing 5–22 is similar to Figure 5–12, but the one-to-one correspondence has gone out the window. Is there some code that can rebuild or reconstruct the missing records?

Listing 5–22

```
-> SELE 2
-> USE PAYMENTS
-> SELE 1
-> USE SUBS
-> SET RELA TO RECNO() INTO B
-> LIST ACCT,B->ACCT
Record#  ACCT    B->ACCT
      1  3-0084  3-0025
      2  3-0091  3-0064
      3  3-0022  3-0068
      4  3-0025  3-0040
      5  3-0064  3-0042
      6  3-0068  3-0052
      7  3-0040  3-0050
      8  3-0042  3-0059
      9  3-0052  3-0087
     10  3-0094
     11  3-0021
```

Listing 5–22 (cont.)

```
12   3-0001
13   3-0050
14   3-0059
15   3-0087
16   3-0078
17   3-0080
18   3-0018
19   3-0053
```

If all you need to do is make records to establish the one-to-one correspondence, yes, the code in Listing 5–23 will do that. If you need to replace data in the re-established records, that you must do. (It is worth noting that Figure 5–12 was made after Listing 5–22 was generated.)

Keeping to our theory of minimalist code, the kernel for this method is:

Listing 5–23

```
** KERNEL TO CHECK ON PARALLEL RECORDS USING NO NDX FILES
*
SELE 2
USE PAYMENTS
SELE 1
USE SUBS
SET RELA TO RECNO() INTO B
*
DO WHIL .NOT. EOF()
*
   IF ACCT # B->ACCT
      SELE 2
*
      IF EOF()
         APPE BLAN
      ELSE
         INSE BLAN BEFORE
      ENDI
*
      REPL ACCT WITH A->ACCT, LNAME WITH A->LNAME, FNAME WITH A->FNAME
   ENDI
*
   SELE 1
   SKIP
ENDD
*
** EOF
```

How does Listing 5–23 work? It makes use of our concept of parallel entries and takes that idea to the extreme. We start by recognizing the gaping hole in Listing

5–22. That hole means there are no more than nine records in the database in work arca B. By SETting a RELATION to RECNO() and not to the key field, we are telling ourselves that more often than not we're going to go over the edge of the file. In particular, we're going to go over the edge of the file in work area B.

We make sure things will get padded by testing whether we've gone over the edge of the file or not. If we have an end-of-file condition (IF EOF()) then APPEND a BLANK record. If we haven't gone over the edge of the file (ELSE), then we have a valid record number but the key fields don't match, so you should INSERT a BLANK record BEFORE the present record location. Then REPLACE the necessary fields.

Listing 5–23 is a specific example using the PAYMENTS and SUBS databases and the ACCT field as the key field for both. A generic block that you can modify is shown in Listing 5–24. Places to insert your own filenames and key fields for the variables are shown in lowercase.

Listing 5–24

```
** KERNEL TO CHECK ON PARALLEL RECORDS USING NO NDX FILES
*
SELE 2
USE secondary database file
SELE 1
USE primary database file
SET RELA TO RECNO() INTO B
TRUTH = .T.
CLEA
@ 10,0 SAY [RE-ESTABLISHING RECORD # ]
*
DO WHIL .NOT. EOF()
*
   IF key field in work area A # B->key field in work area B
      @ 10,33 SAY RECN()
      SELE 2
*
      IF EOF()
         APPE BLAN
      ELSE
         INSE BLAN BEFORE
      ENDI
*
      REPL field in B WITH A->corresponding field in A, ;
           other field in B WITH A->corresponding field in B, and so on
      @ 21,0 SAY [DO YOU WISH TO ENTER DATA INTO THIS RECORD? (Y/N)  ] GET TRUTH
      READ
*
      IF TRUTH
```

Listing 5–24 (cont.)

```
            CLEA
            DO &(secondary say file)
            DO &(secondary get file)
            READ
            CLEA
            @ 10,0 SAY [RE-ESTABLISHING RECORD # ]
         ENDI
*
   ENDI
*
   SELE 1
   SKIP
ENDD
*
** EOF
```

Listing 5–24 also includes code so the user can add data to the re-established record. This goes beyond the concept of kernels, but is useful and worth including. When the system detects a nonexistent record in the secondary database, the user now has the option of pulling that folder from the filing cabinet and adding data to the other fields as necessary.

This listing's blocks show this method being applied to two databases. The code can be expanded for use with any number of databases. The simplest method is to enclose Listing 5–24 in a loop that makes use of another dBASE III PLUS feature, the CATALOG file. The structure and data for a sample CATALOG file are shown in Figure 5–13. We make use of field 1 in the CATALOG file, PATH, as shown in Listing 5–25. Each pass through the loop uses another secondary file. There is no need to create new relations with each pass, because each file should have parallel records. Hence the command:

```
SET RELA TO RECNO() INTO B
```

will suffice each time. This code then becomes:

Listing 5–25

```
** KERNEL TO CHECK ON PARALLEL RECORDS USING NO NDX FILES.  ;
   THIS FILE USES SEVERAL SECONDARY FILES, EACH OF WHICH ARE ;
   LISTED IN A CAT FILE.
*
SELE 1
USE primary database file
SET CATA TO catalog file that contains names of secondary files
SELE 10
*
DO WHIL .NOT. EOF()
   USEFILE = J->PATH
```

```
Structure for database: D:5-29.cat
Number of data records:       4
Date of last update   : 12/04/86
Field  Field Name  Type       Width    Dec
    1  PATH        Character     70
    2  FILE_NAME   Character     12
    3  ALIAS       Character      8
    4  TYPE        Character      3
    5  TITLE       Character     80
    6  CODE        Numeric        3
    7  TAG         Character      4
** Total **                     181

-> DISP ALL
Record#  PATH
FILE_NAME    ALIAS    TYPE TITLE
                           CODE TAG
      1  D:subs.dbf
subs.dbf     SUBS     dbf  subscription records
                              1
      2  D:payments.dbf
payments.dbf PAYMENTS dbf  payment records that parallel subscription records
                              2
      3  D:newbooks.dbf
newbooks.dbf NEWBOOKS dbf  copy of 91 book records
```

Figure 5–13 The CAT files contain a field, PATH, that can be used in code to check for parallelism in several files.

Listing 5–25 (cont.)

```
   SELE 2
   USE &USEFILE          && opens secondary database file
   SELE 1
   SET RELA TO RECNO() INTO B
*
** THIS LINE STARTS THE ORIGINAL KERNEL AS SHOWN IN LISTING 5-23.

*
   DO WHIL .NOT. EOF()
*
      IF key field in work area A # B->key field in work area B
         SELE 2
*
         IF EOF()
            APPE BLAN
         ELSE
            INSE BLAN BEFORE
         ENDI
*
         REPL field in B WITH A->corresponding field in A, ;
              other field in B WITH A->corresponding field in B, and so on
      ENDI
*
      SELE 1
```

Listing 5–25 (cont.)

```
        SKIP
    ENDD
*
** THE ABOVE LINE ENDS THE KERNEL SHOWN IN LISTING 5-23.
*
    SELE 10
    SKIP
ENDD
*
** EOF
```

This listing emphasizes the use of the dBASE III PLUS CAT file. But note the only field being used is PATH. You can also create your own database file, one that contains only the PATH field. That is what many developers did before Ashton-Tate included the CAT file in III PLUS. The choice is yours to make, but the CAT file does allow for better housekeeping in other areas.

Another method for checking through several secondary files is based on there not being many secondary files to check through. In fact, the limit is nine secondary files. It starts by placing the secondary files in work areas 2 through 10, then enclosing Listing 5–23's code in a loop that goes through a new work area at each pass. That code is shown in Listing 5–26.

Listing 5–26

```
** KERNEL TO CHECK ON PARALLEL RECORDS IN UP TO NINE SECONDARY;
FILES USING NO NDX FILES
*
SELE 10
USE ninth secondary file
SELE 9
USE eighth secondary file
SELE 8
USE seventh secondary file
SELE 7
USE sixth secondary file
SELE 6
USE fifth secondary file
SELE 5
USE fourth secondary file
SELE 4
USE third secondary file
SELE 3
USE second secondary file
SELE 2
USE first secondary file
SELE 1
```

Listing 5-26 (cont.)

```
USE primary database file
ALIASVAL = 66                          && 66 is the ASCII value of 'b'
*
DO WHIL ALIASVAL < 75                  && 74 is the ASCII value of 'j'
   WORKAREA = CHR(ALIASVAL)
   SELE &WORKAREA
   SELE 1
   SET RELA TO RECNO() INTO B
*
** THIS LINE STARTS THE ORIGINAL KERNEL AS SHOWN IN LISTING 5-23.
*
   DO WHIL .NOT. EOF()
*
      IF key field in work area A # B->key field in work area B
         SELE 2
*
         IF EOF()
            APPE BLAN
         ELSE
            INSE BLAN BEFORE
         ENDI
*
         REPL field in B WITH A->corresponding field in A, ;
              other field in B WITH A->corresponding field in B, and so on
      ENDI
*
      SELE 1
      SKIP
   ENDD
*
** THE ABOVE LINE ENDS THE KERNEL SHOWN IN LISTING 5-23.
*
   ALIASVAL = ALIASVAL + 1
ENDD
*
** EOF
```

This code can be changed to handle fewer than nine secondary files by changing the SELECTed and USEd work areas and the upper limit of ALIASVAL in the line:

```
DO WHIL ALIASVAL = ASCII value of last selectable work area
```

Checking for Parallel Entries Using Key Fields

The next method is a little different in that it does make use of NDX files as well as key fields. However, this method is somewhat more complex, because we are juggling more files and our relation between the files is necessarily more complex. This is made even more complex even in theory when we realize we don't need parallel records, only parallel data. In other words, it doesn't matter *when* the parallel data is entered in the secondary files, all that matters is that parallel data was indeed entered. Information in record 15 of the primary file might be paralleled in record 96 of one secondary file, record 118 of the next secondary file, and so on.

We begin by listing the code that does the job.

Listing 5–27

```
** KERNEL TO CHECK FOR PARALLEL ENTRIES USING NDX FILES
*
SELE 2
USE secondary file INDE secondary file's NDX files
SELE 1
USE primary file INDE primary file's NDX files
SET RELA TO key field INTO B
*
DO WHILE .NOT. EOF()
*
   DO CASE
      CASE DELETED()
         SKIP
         LOOP
      OTHE
*
         IF key field in work area A = B->key field in work area B
            SKIP
            LOOP
         ELSE
            SELE 2
            APPE BLANK
            REPL key field in work area B WITH A->key field in work area A, ;
                 other field in work area B WITH A->parallel field in work area A;
                 and so on
         ENDI
*
         SELE 1
         SKIP
   ENDC
*
ENDD
*
** EOF
```

This code at first might appear to have more structure than necessary to do the job. For example, why do we use a DO CASE . . . OTHERWISE . . .

```
-> DISP STRUC
Structure for database: D:5-29.cat
Number of data records:       7
Date of last update   : 12/04/86
Field  Field Name  Type       Width    Dec
    1  PATH        Character     70
    2  FILE_NAME   Character     12
    3  ALIAS       Character      8
    4  TYPE        Character      3
    5  TITLE       Character     80
    6  CODE        Numeric        3
    7  TAG         Character      4
** Total **                     181

-> DISP ALL FILE_NAME,TYPE,CODE
Record#  FILE_NAME    TYPE CODE
      1  subs.dbf     dbf     1
      2  payments.dbf dbf     2
      3  newbooks.dbf dbf     3
      4  oldbooks.dbf dbf     4
      5  book.ndx     ndx     3
      6  sacct.ndx    ndx     1
      7  pacct.ndx    ndx     2

->
```

Figure 5–14 All CAT files have the same structure. We can use two fields, TYPE and CODE, to build code that selects NDX files based on activated DBF files.

ENDCASE block when there is only one CASE used? The DO CASE . . . OTHERWISE . . . ENDCASE construction is used because this is a kernel and kernels are modified for each application. There may be several different CASEs to be tested. Designing the code with the DO CASE . . . OTHERWISE . . . ENDCASE block allows us easy growth where necessary (an example of this is shown in Chapter 8).

Following the examples given for parallel entries in nonINDEXed databases, how would you alter Listing 5–27 to handle several databases with associated NDX files? The first method we'll demonstrate uses the dBASE III PLUS CATALOG file to provide our program with the names of necessary NDX files. The second method shows how to use the name of the database to build the names of the NDX files. The last method shown follows the outlines demonstrated with the last code for nonINDEXed databases; we use only nine secondary files and place them work areas 2 through 10.

We start by determining how dBASE III PLUS's CAT files link DBFs with their associated NDX files. Figure 5–14 shows both the structure and some fields from the previously designed CAT file.

Records were created in this particular CAT file when the following commands were issued:

```
USE SUBS
USE PAYMENTS
USE NEWBOOKS
USE OLDBOOKS
USE NEWBOOKS INDE BOOK
```

```
USE SUBS
INDE ON ACCT TO SACCT
USE PAYMENTS
INDE ON ACCT TO PACCT
```

Normally you'd enter DBF and its associated NDX files in a more precise manner, but this method shows how the CAT file can aid housekeeping, as mentioned earlier. The fields of interest in this discussion are shown in Figure 5–14 and are FILE_NAME, TYPE, and CODE. FILE_NAME is self-explanatory. TYPE is a three-character code defining what type of dBASE III PLUS file (DBF, NDX, VUE, FMT, FRM, QRY) is listed in the record. CODE tells dBASE III PLUS and us which records are linked.

Notice that record 5 has the BOOK.NDX file listed. Notice further that the CODE for record 5 is 3, which is also the record number for information on the file NEWBOOKS.DBF. Remember in the commands just given that we used:

```
USE NEWBOOKS INDE BOOK
```

The CAT file links auxiliary files to their primary use file by record number. The commands USE SUBS and INDE ON ACCT TO SACCT tell dBASE III PLUS to link the SACCT.NDX file to the SUBS.DBF file. Looking at Figure 5–14, we see that dBASE III PLUS has done just that. The CODE for SACCT.NDX is 1, the record number for information on SUBS.DBF. Likewise, PACCT.NDX's record, 7, has a CODE value of 2, the record number of PAYMENTS.DBF.

This is extremely useful application for our coding problem. We start by making sure the CAT file has an NDX file associated with it. This can be done after necessary data has been placed in the CAT file with the following interactive commands:

```
-> SET CATA TO name of catalog file
-> SELE 10
-> INDE ON CODE TO name of catalog NDX file
File not CATALOGed since SET CATALOG was OFF when the active database was USEd.
Press any key to continue...
-> && THE ABOVE IS A MESSAGE III PLUS DISPLAYS BECAUSE CATALOG FILES
-> && ARE 'SET,' NOT 'USED.'
```

You should know the following about INDEXing CATALOG files. First, III PLUS will not update the CAT file's NDX file when new files are opened or created in other work areas. This means you'd have to REINDEX the CAT file's NDX file each time you wanted to use it, providing changes were made to the CAT file. If no changes were made—no files were created or added to the CATALOG since the last INDEX—there is no need to REINDEX.

Let's return to the problem at hand. Remember that the CAT files we're working with here are special in that they only contain the names of secondary database files and associated NDX files. We can code to make use of that as shown in Listing 5–27.

Listing 5–28

```
** KERNEL TO CHECK FOR PARALLELISM USING INDEXED CATALOG FILE
*
SELE 1
USE primary file INDE primary file's NDX files
SELE 10
USE catalog file as described in text INDE catalog's NDX file
REIN
GOTO TOP
DO WHIL .NOT. EOF()
   USETHIS = .F.
*
   IF TYPE = 'DBF'
      COMMAND = 'USE ' + FILE_NAME
      MATCH = CODE
*
      DO WHIL CODE = MATCH
*
         IF TYPE = 'NDX'
            COMMAND = IIF(USETHIS, COMMAND + ', ' + FILE_NAME,;
                      COMMAND + ' INDE ' + FILE_NAME)
            USETHIS = .T.
         ENDI
*
         SKIP
      ENDD
*
      IF USETHIS
*
** KERNEL IN LISTING 5-27 STARTS HERE.
*
         SELE 2
         &COMMAND
         SELE 1
         SET RELA TO key field INTO B
*
         DO WHILE .NOT. EOF()
*
            DO CASE
               CASE DELETED()
                  SKIP
                  LOOP
               OTHE
*
                  IF key field in work area A = B->key field in work area B
                     SKIP
```

Listing 5–28 (cont.)

```
                    LOOP
                 ELSE
                    SELE 2
                    APPE BLANK
                    REPL key field in work area B WITH ;
                         A->key field in work area A, ;
                         other field in work area B WITH ;
                         A->parallel field in work area A;
                         and so on
                 ENDI
*
                 SELE 1
                 SKIP
           ENDC
*
        ENDD
*
** END OF KERNEL LISTED IN 5-27.
*
     ENDI
*
   ELSE
      SELE 10
      SKIP
   ENDI
*
ENDD
*
** EOF
```

Listing 5–28 may look somewhat complicated. Much of the complication comes from placing the kernel in Listing 5–27 inside the code. By itself, the code is shown in Listing 5–29. Listing 5–29 necessarily doesn't make use of a primary database file and is designed to be used with the catalog file shown earlier. Running Listing 5–29 produces the screen shown in Figure 5–15, demonstrating that matched DBFs and NDXes are opened, and only DBFs with associated NDX files are used. Below Listing 5–29's output is a LIST of the relevant data from the CAT file in Listing 5–26 (the file 5-26CAT).

Listing 5–29

```
** DEMONSTRATES USING INDEXED CATALOG FILE
*
SELE 10
USE 5-26CAT INDE 5-26CAT
REIN
GOTO TOP
```

```
-> DO 5-32
USE subs.dbf      INDE sacct.ndx    , SLNAME.ndx  , SFNAME.ndx
USE payments.dbf  INDE pacct.ndx
USE newbooks.dbf  INDE book.ndx     , NDAUDS.ndx
USE ACCOUNTS.dbf  INDE AACCT.ndx
->
-> LIST FILE_NAME,TYPE,CODE
Record#  FILE_NAME     TYPE CODE
      1  subs.dbf      dbf     1
      6  sacct.ndx     ndx     1
     10  SLNAME.ndx    ndx     1
     11  SFNAME.ndx    ndx     1
      2  payments.dbf  dbf     2
      7  pacct.ndx     ndx     2
      3  newbooks.dbf  dbf     3
      5  book.ndx      ndx     3
     12  NDAUDS.ndx    ndx     3
      4  oldbooks.dbf  dbf     4
      8  ACCOUNTS.dbf  dbf     5
      9  AACCT.ndx     ndx     5

->
```

Figure 5–15 This screen shows how Listing 5–29 can be used to surround the code in Listing 5–27 to use CATALOG files during tests for parallel data entry.

Listing 5–29 (cont.)

```
DO WHIL .NOT. EOF()
   USETHIS = .F.
*
   IF TYPE = 'DBF'
      COMMAND = 'USE ' + FILE_NAME
      MATCH = CODE
*
      DO WHIL CODE = MATCH
*
         IF TYPE = 'NDX'
            COMMAND = IIF(USETHIS, COMMAND + ', ' + FILE_NAME,;
                      COMMAND + ' INDE ' + FILE_NAME)
            USETHIS = .T.
         ENDI
*
         SKIP
      ENDD
*
      IF USETHIS
         ? COMMAND
         && code from 5-27 goes here
      ENDI
*
   ELSE
      SKIP
   ENDI
*
```

```
ENDD
*
** EOF
```

```
C:\LIBRARY>DIR

Volume in drive C has no label
Directory of  C:\LIBRARY

.           <DIR>       9-11-86  17:26
..          <DIR>       9-11-86  17:26
JDCBTTLE NDX   104448  30-11-86  17:04
JDCBATHR NDX   180736  30-11-86  17:04
JDCBEDTR NDX   188928  30-11-86  17:04
JDCBCTGY NDX   144384  30-11-86  17:04
JDCBSBJT NDX   184320  30-11-86  17:04
JDCBLIBR NDX   118784  30-11-86  17:04
JDCBOOKS DBF   623014  30-11-86  17:04
        7 File(s)  21995520 bytes free
```

Figure 5–16 Listing 5–30 works for directory files with similar names.

An alternative to this method can be used when you are moving from dBASE III PLUS to dBASE III systems. The alternative makes use of either a dBASE III PLUS CAT file or your own "CAT" file using a conventional DBF file. It has an advantage over the CAT file system shown in the listing because less loopable code is used, hence offering less chance for error. The heart of this code is shown in Listing 5–30.

Listing 5–30

```
SELE 10
USE catalog file
DBF = FILENAME
TAG = LEFT(FILENAME,4)
NDX1 = TAG + "first four-character NDX file code"
NDX2 = TAG + "second four-character NDX file code"
NDX3 = TAG + "third four-character NDX file code"
NDX4 = TAG + "fourth four-character NDX file code"
NDX5 = TAG + "fifth four-character NDX file code"
NDX6 = TAG + "sixth four-character NDX file code"
NDX7 = TAG + "seventh four-character NDX file code"
SELE 2
USE &DBFILE INDE &NDX1, &NDX2, &NDX3, &NDX4, &NDX5, &NDX6, &NDX7
```

This method relies on databases and index files sharing similar names or parts of names. An example from an inventory system makes use of a four-letter code as a pattern match for the rest of the files. This is shown in Figure 5–16.

Notice in Listing 5–30 that all seven files begin with JDCB. That is something designed from the start of the system and is totally intentional. All NDX files relating to the database JDCBOOKS share the first four characters in their names. This is useful in inventory systems, in which several subinventories often exist. An example of subinventories would be an automotive parts business that keeps Ford parts in warehouse 1, Chevy parts in warehouse 2, Chrysler parts in warehouse 3, Studebaker parts in a closet, and so on.

How do we build those NDX filenames? The code in Listing 5–30 opens up some kind of catalog file (again, either one you've created from a normal DBF file or one of III PLUS's CAT files) and creates a four-character TAG from the first four letters of the database filename. (Note: If you're using a III PLUS CAT file you'd use FILE_NAME, not FILENAME as shown in Listing 5–30). That TAG is then used to build up to seven NDX filenames. You can code for fewer than seven NDX files, but dBASE III PLUS maximum NDX file allowance is seven NDX files per database. Once the NDX files are named, we use work area 2 to open the database and associated NDX files. This code can be placed in our kernels to form:

Listing 5–31

```
** KERNEL TO CHECK FOR PARALLEL ENTRIES USING SEVERAL DATABASES, ;
   EACH WITH SEVERAL NDX FILES
*
SELE 1
USE primary file INDE primary file's NDX files
SELE 10
USE catalog file
*
DO WHIL .NOT. EOF()
   DBF = FILENAME
   TAG = LEFT(FILENAME,4)
   NDX1 = TAG + "first four-character NDX file code"
   NDX2 = TAG + "second four-character NDX file code"
   NDX3 = TAG + "third four-character NDX file code"
   NDX4 = TAG + "fourth four-character NDX file code"
   NDX5 = TAG + "fifth four-character NDX file code"
   NDX6 = TAG + "sixth four-character NDX file code"
   NDX7 = TAG + "seventh four-character NDX file code"
   SELE 2
   USE &DBFILE INDE &NDX1, &NDX2, &NDX3, &NDX4, &NDX5, &NDX6, &NDX7
   SELE 1
   SET RELA TO key field INTO B
*
   DO WHILE .NOT. EOF()
*
      DO CASE
         CASE DELETED()
            SKIP
            LOOP
```

Listing 5–31 (cont.)

```
        OTHE
*
           IF key field in work area A = B->key field in work area B
              SKIP
              LOOP
           ELSE
              SELE 2
              APPE BLANK
              REPL key field in work area B WITH A->key field in work area A, ;
                   other field in work area B WITH A->parallel field in work area A;
                   and so on
           ENDI
*
           SELE 1
           SKIP
      ENDC
*
   ENDD
*
   SELE 10
   SKIP
ENDD
*
** EOF
```

You'll note that Listing 5–31 presents less chance for errors in the loops than the previous code. Our last code block closely resembles the code shown in Listing 5–26 and is a synthesis of Listings 5–26 and 5–27. The logic is identical with that described earlier.

Listing 5–32

```
** KERNEL TO CHECK ON PARALLEL RECORDS IN UP TO NINE SECONDARY ;
   FILES USING NDX FILES
*
SELE 10
USE ninth secondary file INDE NDX file list
SELE 9
USE eighth secondary file INDE NDX file list
SELE 8
USE seventh secondary file INDE NDX file list
SELE 7
USE sixth secondary file INDE NDX file list
SELE 6
USE fifth secondary file INDE NDX file list
SELE 5
```

Listing 5–32 (cont.)

```
USE fourth secondary file INDE NDX file list
SELE 4
USE third secondary file INDE NDX file list
SELE 3
USE second secondary file INDE NDX file list
SELE 2
USE first secondary file INDE NDX file list
SELE 1
USE primary database file INDE NDX file list
ALIASVAL = 66                              && 66 is the ASCII value of 'b'
*
DO WHIL ALIASVAL < 75               && 74 is the ASCII value of 'j'
   WORKAREA = CHR(ALIASVAL)
   SELE &WORKAREA
   SELE 1
   SET RELA TO key field INTO B
*
   DO WHILE .NOT. EOF()
*
      DO CASE
         CASE DELETED()
            SKIP
            LOOP
         OTHE
*
      IF key field in work area A = B->key field in work area B
               SKIP
               LOOP
            ELSE
               SELE 2
               APPE BLANK
               REPL key field in work area B WITH A->key field in work area A, ;
                    other field in work area B WITH A->parallel field in work area A;
                    and so on
            ENDI
*
            SELE 1
            SKIP
      ENDC
*
   ENDD
*
   ALIASVAL = ALIASVAL + 1
ENDD
*
** EOF
```

DELETING PARALLEL DATA AND THE SET RELATION TO COMMAND

Many systems need the ability to delete records in one database based on deletions in another database. Two examples are accounting systems and subscription systems. Both require the ability to delete payment records when the actual account record has been removed.

For instance, consider a situation in which an account becomes inactive. It doesn't matter why the account becomes inactive, all that matters is that we know we no longer need that record in our active file. What do we do?

One of our options is to transfer the data to an inactive file. This allows us to keep the account information without cluttering up our active file. The other option is to permanently remove the inactive record. This should only be done if you're sure you'll never want to see that record again.

At this point allow me a soapbox. You are never *that* sure. You may have an accounting system and find a deadbeat among the AR. It's fine to remove that record from the active file, but don't get rid of it totally. Even if that person/company/group has given you penultimate heartache and headache, don't toss the data away. Remember that information isn't power, but use of information is. You don't know how the tides of fortune will affect that person/company/group. Someday such a client or customer may come to you with other needs. Wouldn't it be nice to say, "Gee, we have this unpaid balance. It was $1.35, but with interest it's now $6,395,816.37." That would give you much more satisfaction than merely saying, "Sorry, we can't take your order."

Likewise, I warn against tossing out AP records even when you haven't used a source for years. You might need that company's resources some day and hear its representative say, "Gosh, we have this unpaid balance. . . ." You can then go to your historical AP file and say, "Our records show that check is in the mail."

In any case, this section offers two methods for deleting parallel records in two or more databases. The first method permanently removes the records without backing them up. The second method allows for historical record keeping.

Both methods make use of the Delete kernel shown in Chapter 3. To recap the information there, the actual Delete kernel is the short piece of code:

Listing 5–33

```
CASE ANSWER = 'K'
   DELE
   DELS = .T.
   LOOP
```

This code is obviously intended to be part of a menu system. One line not shown in the listing, but nevertheless important to this discussion, is placed in the program prior to accessing the Delete kernel. It is:

```
DELS = .F.
```

This provides a flag to the system that something has been deleted from the current database, even when the current record isn't deleted. Note that the Delete kernel is accessed when the user presses K, as in "Kill."

Before going further, consider the convoluted logic that is used here. The following discussion isn't necessary to use the code successfully, but can help you understand how and where you would modify the code if necessary.

Systems that need to delete parallel data are the flip side of systems that must ensure that parallel information gets entered into a system. You don't normally want to delete a payment record just because an account record has been deleted. Why not? Payment records are used for much more than telling you who paid and when. They also tell you your income over time, your best and worst income periods, and more. You may want to get rid of a payment record from an immediate file, but you don't want to remove it permanently. Going the other direction is a different story.

You do want to remove an account record if you remove a payment record. Remember that we wanted to make sure there was a one-to-one correspondence from accounts to payments? Let's say that's a left to right operation:

```
ACCOUNTS -> PAYMENTS
```

That's during input. It also can be thought of as a logical formulation.

> IF we create an ACCOUNTS record, THEN we create a PAYMENTS record

That logical formulation can be continued with "If we create a PAYMENTS record, we don't necessarily create an ACCOUNTS record."

All is going well so far. Now we use the reverse mode. "If we delete an ACCOUNTS record, do we delete a PAYMENTS record?" No. How about "If we delete a PAYMENTS record, do we delete an ACCOUNT record?" Yes. Readers familiar with elementary logic will recognize this in the logic tables shown in Figure 5–17.

Note that the only FALSE case for:

~PAYMENTS -> ~ACCOUNTS

occurs when we delete a PAYMENTS record without deleting a corresponding ACCOUNTS record.

Deleting without Backing Up Data

Like this chapter's discussions of entering parallel data, we'll now address two avenues for making parallel deletions. First we'll investigate using nonINDEXed databases, then we'll study how to use INDEXed databases to aid the process of parallel deletions.

The first thing to explore is parallel records in nonINDEXed databases. This is similar to entering parallel records in nonINDEXed databases because we rely heavily on a one-to-one correspondence in record number as well as key fields in the parallel records.

	A	B	C
	ACCOUNTS	PAYMENTS	ACCOUNTS -> PAYMENTS
1	T	T	T
2	F	F	T
3	F	T	T
4	T	F	F

Using the Law of Transposition:

	C	D
	ACCOUNTS -> PAYMENTS	~PAYMENTS -> ~ACCOUNTS
1	T	T
2	T	T
3	T	T
4	F	F

And breaking down column D:

	D	E	F
	~PAYMENTS -> ~ACCOUNTS	~PAYMENTS	~ACCOUNTS
1	T	F	F
2	T	T	T
3	T	F	T
4	F	T	F

where column F is the logical opposite of column A and column E is the logical inverse of column B.

Figure 5–17 A logic table for deleting parallel records.

Listing 5–34

```
** CODE FOR DELETING PARALLEL, NONINDEXED RECORDS WITHOUT BACKUP
*
IF DELS
*
   DO CASE
      CASE database is secondary file
         SELE 2
         USE primary file
   SELE 1
         SET RELA TO RECNO() INTO B
         LOCA FOR DELETED()
*
```

Listing 5–34 (cont.)

```
         DO WHIL FOUN()
            SELE 2
            DELE
            SELE 1
            CONT
         ENDD
*
         SELE 2
         PACK
         SELE 1
   ENDC
*
   PACK
ENDI
*
** EOF
```

The code isn't difficult to follow. It starts with:

```
IF DELS
```

which lets you know that this code is used in conjunction with the Delete kernel shown in Listing 5–33. Readers will again notice a DO CASE . . . ENDCASE block with a single CASE statement. Yes, this does seem like a waste of code and processing time. Remember that you're seeing kernels, and these kernels are meant to either run as is or be expanded as necessary. It is easier to expand a DO CASE . . . ENDCASE block than any others III PLUS has to offer.

A nice feature is the III PLUS FOUND() function. Normally you'd have to code that block as:

```
DO WHIL .NOT. EOF()
```

That is acceptable, but also forces you to make sure you SET TALK OFF before you run the code. Not doing so forces dBASE III PLUS to send you a message when it reaches the end of the file, as shown in Figure 5–18.

Listing 5–34 has no checks to make sure the records are truly parallel. That is important. This code assumes the records are parallel to begin with. If that is not the case, you could be deleting nonparallel entries and not even know it until it's too late. The question to ask is, "Is it possible to ensure parallelism when you're deleting records?"

The answer is I don't know, nor is that question something I particularly want to answer. What has been done—and it's a poor substitute–is to check that both primary and secondary databases have the same number of records. Code for that is:

Listing 5–35

```
** CODE FOR DELETING PARALLEL, NONINDEXED RECORDS WITHOUT BACKUP
** CODE INCLUDES GLOBAL PARALLEL CHECK.
```

```
Record =       68
           68
Record =       80
           80
Record =       81
           81
Record =       82
           82
Record =       83
           83
Record =       84
           84
Record =       85
           85
Record =       86
           86
Record =       87
           87
Record =       88
           88
Record =       89
           89
End of LOCATE scope
we got out okay
->
```

Figure 5-18 You can use the dBASE III and III PLUS EOF() function as part of the test for DELETED() parallel records, but you must SET TALK OFF to avoid the End of LOCATE scope error message.

Listing 5-35 (cont.)

```
*
IF DELS
*
   DO CASE
      CASE database is secondary file
         SELE 2
         USE primary file
   TOTALBRECS = RECC()                        && new line
   SELE 1
*
** START OF RECORD COUNT ERROR CHECK.
*
         IF RECC() # TOTALBRECS
            && error message, exit from kernel, or run parallel check
         ENDI
*
** END OF RECORD COUNT ERROR CHECK.
*
         SET RELA TO RECNO() INTO B
         LOCA FOR DELETED()
*
         DO WHIL FOUN()
            SELE 2
```

Listing 5-35 (cont.)

```
            DELE
            SELE 1
            CONT
         ENDD
*
         SELE 2
         PACK
         SELE 1
   ENDC
*
   PACK
ENDI
*
** EOF
```

This check is the most global method to check for parallelism in nonINDEXed databases. You can have primary and secondary databases with an equal number of records and totally different information in each corresponding record. The best defense against using Listing 5-34's code and losing information is to force a check for parallel entries before you begin to delete anything. Adding this check to Listing 5-34 is no more complicated than dropping one of the kernels from the previous section (Listings 5-23 through 5-26) in at the appropriate place, either as a subroutine or part of the direct code. Using Listing 5-23's code directly in Listing 5-34's code, we get:

Listing 5-36

```
** CODE FOR DELETING PARALLEL, NONINDEXED RECORDS FROM ;
   DATABASES WITHOUT BACKUP. THIS CODE INCLUDES A CHECK FOR ;
   PARALLEL ENTRIES.
*
IF DELS
*
   DO CASE
      CASE database is secondary file
         SELE 2
         USE primary file
         TOTALBRECS = RECC()                    && new line
         SELE 1
*
** START OF RECORD COUNT ERROR CHECK
*
         IF RECC() # TOTALBRECS
*
** FOLLOWING CODE IS FROM LISTING 5-23.
*
```

Listing 5-36 (cont.)

```
        SET RELA TO RECNO() INTO B
*
        DO WHIL .NOT. EOF()
*
      IF key field # B->key field
            SELE 2
*
            IF EOF()
              APPE BLAN
            ELSE
              INSE BLAN BEFORE
            ENDI
*
            REPL key field in B WITH A->key field in A, and so on
          ENDI
*
          SELE 1
          SKIP
        ENDD
*
** END OF CODE FROM LISTING 5-23.
*
      ENDI
*
** END OF RECORD COUNT ERROR CHECK.
*
      LOCA FOR DELETED()
*
      DO WHIL FOUN()
        SELE 2
        DELE
        SELE 1
        CONT
      ENDD
*
      SELE 2
      PACK
      SELE 1
  ENDC
*
  PACK
ENDI
*
** EOF
```

How does one expand from the example of two databases to several? The methods for deleting parallel records are analogous to those used in entering parallel records—with one great exception. We need to know how far parallelism extends. Remember that deleting parallel records is a right to left operation. If we delete a secondary record we must delete the parallel primary record. What if parallelism exists among the secondary files?

Say you have five secondary databases. You relate your primary database to the first secondary database. You check for parallelism, then begin deleting matched records. But what if the records in all your other databases aren't parallel? That means you must first ensure that each secondary file is parallel to the primary file.

Hold on, it gets worse! Remember that deleting parallel records is a right to left operation. This means you not only have to make sure each of the secondary databases is parallel to the others and to the primary file, you must also make sure that records deleted from the first secondary database are also deleted from the second through fifth secondary databases.

Now you begin work on the second secondary file. Not only must you delete parallel records from the third through fifth secondary files, you must also go back to the first secondary file and delete records from that file. Imagine the looping necessary for tens of secondary files. It begins to sound like a job for Feynman diagrams, doesn't it?

The best solution for these matters is precognition. You should have mapped out your application thoroughly, if not rigorously, and should know much of what you'll need to code before you start. Experience has shown that parallelism is only necessary for parent-child relationships (one primary file related to one or more secondary files). Ashton-Tate has long followed that premise in its versions of dBASE. More recently, Clipper, the dBASE compiler from Nantucket Software, allows for several relations among files. More information on Clipper is given in Appendix A. For now we'll deal with the single parent-child parameters built into dBASE III PLUS.

All the methods for deleting parallel records from several files follow the logic of parallel entry. For brevity, only the method using nine secondary databases is shown here.

Listing 5-37

```
** CODE TO DELETE RECORDS FROM NINE SECONDARY NONINDEXED  ;
   DATABASES
*
SELE 10
USE ninth secondary file
SELE 9
USE eighth secondary file
SELE 8
USE seventh secondary file
SELE 7
USE sixth secondary file
SELE 6
USE fifth secondary file
```

Listing 5–37 (cont.)

```
SELE 5
USE fourth secondary file
SELE 4
USE third secondary file
SELE 3
USE second secondary file
SELE 2
USE first secondary file
SELE 1
USE primary database file
ALIASVAL = 66                               && 66 is the 'b'
DO WHIL ALIASVAL < 75                  && 74 is the ASCII value of 'j'
   WORKAREA = CHR(ALIASVAL)
   SELE &WORKAREA
   SELE 1
   SET RELA TO RECNO() INTO B
*
   IF DELS
*
      USE primary file
      TOTALBRECS = RECC()
      SELE 1
*
      IF RECC() # TOTALBRECS
*
         DO WHIL .NOT. EOF()
*
      IF key field # B->key field
               SELE 2
*
               IF EOF()
                  APPE BLAN
               ELSE
                  INSE BLAN BEFORE
               ENDI
*
               REPL key field in B WITH A->key field in A, and so on
      ENDI
*
      SELE 1
      SKIP
         ENDD
*
      ENDI
*
```

Listing 5–37 (cont.)

```
      SELE &WORKAREA      && new line for right to left relationships
      LOCA FOR DELETED()
*
      DO WHIL FOUN()
         SELE 1
         DELE
         SELE &WORKAREA   && necessary because secondary files are here
         CONT
      ENDD
*
      SELE 1
      PACK
      SELE &WORKAREA
      PACK
   ENDI
*
   ALIASVAL = ALIASVAL + 1
ENDD
*
** EOF
```

Much of this code has been explained elsewhere in this chapter. Do note the modifications in the latter part of the code. These changes are necessary because parallel deleting is a right to left operation, and we're using several secondary files. This code could delete from work area 1 to work area 2 if a CAT file was used to list the secondary files in work area 1.

Using Indexed Databases

Is there anything that much different or unique about deleting data from multiple INDEXed databases? Not really. The key, as always, is to use the SET RELATION TO command. The code is:

Listing 5–38

```
** CODE FOR PARALLEL INDEXED DELETIONS WITHOUT BACKUP
*
SELE 2
USE primary file INDE index file list
SELE 1
USE secondary file INDE secondary file list
SET RELA TO key field INTO B
LOCA FOR DELETED()
*
DO WHIL FOUN()
   SELE 2
   DELE
```

Listing 5-38 (cont.)

```
   SELE 1
   CONT
ENDD
*
SELE 2
PACK
SELE 1
PACK
*
** EOF
```

Remember that this code doesn't offer any backup, nor does it query the user if deletions are to be parallel. The assumption is that deletions are supposed to be parallel. A fully expanded version of this code is given later in this chapter. That code includes several prompts to make sure everything is acceptable before the program DELETEs any records from any database. This code is easily expanded to more than two databases using the outlines provided previously.

Backing Up Data while You Delete

Like the discussions on entering parallel data, this discussion addresses two avenues for making parallel deletions. First we'll investigate using nonINDEXed databases, then we'll study using INDEXed databases to aid the process of parallel deletions. The backup code is based on a single line of code:

```
COPY TO historical file FOR DELE()
```

This line is necessary for all systems that create a new historical database each time they are ready to make permanent historical deletions of the active database. The following line, on most databases, *does not work!*

```
APPE FROM active file FOR DELE()
```

I repeat, *this command doesn't back up records marked for deletion.* The point is shown in this list of records:

```
-> USE TANK
-> LIST TITLE
Record#  TITLE
      1 *Roget's University Thesaurus
      2 *Oxford American Dictionary
      3 *Words
      4 *American Heritage Dictionary
      5 *Webster's New World Dictionary
      6 *Book of Jargon, The
      7 *Bartlett's Familiar Quotations
```

```
        8 *Handbook of Good English, The
        9 *Roget's International Thesaurus
       10 *Dictionary of Philosophy and Religion
       11  Metamagical Themas
       12  Guardian
       13  History of Witchcraft and Demonology, The
       14  Soul of CP/M
       15  Other Worlds
       16  Godel, Escher, Bach
       17  Connections
       18  Essential Talmud, The
       19  Acts and Letters of the Apostles
       20  Dictionary of Christian Lore and Legend

-> USE TANK2
-> LIST TITLE

-> APPE FROM TANK FOR DELE()
No records added
-> APPE FROM TANK FOR TITLE = 'B'
      2 records added
-> LIST TITLE
Record#  TITLE
      1  Book of Jargon, The
      2  Bartlett's Familiar Quotations

-> USE TANK
-> COPY TO TANK2 FOR DELE()
TANK2.dbf already exists, overwrite it? (Y/N) Y
     10 records copied
-> USE TANK2
-> LIST TITLE
Record#  TITLE
      1  Roget's University Thesaurus
      2  Oxford American Dictionary
      3  Words
      4  American Heritage Dictionary
      5  Webster's New World Dictionary
      6  Book of Jargon, The
      7  Bartlett's Familiar Quotations
      8  Handbook of Good English, The
      9  Roget's International Thesaurus
     10  Dictionary of Philosophy and Religion
```

The APPEND command only works on DELETED records when specific fields in the database are referenced. Therefore, the APPEND command must be used with some variant of the PERM flag (introduced in Chapter 3). You could then use the APPEND command in code something like the following:

Listing 5–39

```
USE historical file
APPE FROM file to be packed FOR PERM
```

As mentioned in Chapter 3, use of the PERM flag involves adding an extra field to a database and a few extra lines of code, but not much else.

Using Nonindexed Databases

Much of this discussion reiterates points made earlier: The only new information involves the use of a Backup kernel.

The Backup kernel has many similarities to the Transfer kernel shown in Chapter 3. Both code blocks are used to take selected records from the active database to some other database. In the case of backing up data during the deletion and packing process, the criteria for backing up a record is quite simple; the record is deleted. Unlike the Transfer kernel of Chapter 3, you don't need to prompt the user for the transfer criteria, nor do you need to look for selected information in selected fields.

Our first example assumes you are creating a new historical database each time. This is often the case in accounting systems when you close out months, quarters, or years. You aren't making deletions in the sense of permanently getting rid of records; you are actually moving records from one database to another. Say you want to move all of 1986's records from the AP database to the AP86 database. This can be done with:

Listing 5–40

```
DELE FOR YEAR(RECDATE) # 1987
COPY TO AP86 FOR DELE()
PACK
```

Note that this listing is identical in function to the code:

Listing 5–41

```
COPY TO AP86 FOR YEAR(RECDATE) = 1986
DELE FOR YEAR(RECDATE) = 1986
PACK
```

Why choose one method over the other? The second method forces dBASE III PLUS to do the qualifying operation:

```
FOR YEAR(RECDATE) = 1986
```

twice. There is no need to make dBASE III PLUS go through a hoop more than it has to. The former listing makes good programming sense and makes use of one of III PLUS's strengths, the "hidden" DELETE flag.

It should be obvious that the principal part of backing up data during the deletion/packing process is the inclusion of the COPY command. That being the case, how do you back up data when deleting records from two parallel files? Consider the following code:

Listing 5–42

```
** CODE FOR DELETING PARALLEL, NONINDEXED RECORDS WITH BACKUP
** CODE DOESN'T INCLUDE CHECK FOR PARALLELISM.
*
IF DELS
*
   DO CASE
      CASE database is secondary file
         SELE 2
         USE primary file
         SELE 1
         SET RELA TO RECNO() INTO B
         LOCA FOR DELETED()
*
         DO WHIL FOUN()
            SELE 2
            DELE
            SELE 1
            CONT
         ENDD
*
         SELE 2
         COPY TO primary historical file FOR DELE()
         PACK
         SELE 1
   ENDC
*
   PACK
   COPY TO secondary historical file FOR DELE()
ENDI
*
** EOF
```

You can see that the only new code necessary is the two COPY commands. The first comes immediately before we PACK the primary file. The other comes immediately before we pack the secondary file. This code methodology follows for each of other nonINDEXed parallel deletion code blocks.

This discussion has been concerned with creating a new historical file each time a database is backed up. That might not always be the best method of handling a situation. You might be more interested in creating a historical file the first time you attempt to back up data, but then APPEND the historical file forever after. Can we code for that without adding the PERM field to our database? Yes, if we indeed will be deleting records for a specific condition. Any condition will do, but we can't use the DELETED() flag for our APPEND condition. We start with the following code:

Listing 5–43

```
USE database
*
IF .NOT. FILE("historical file")
   COPY STRU TO historical file
ENDI
*
USE historical file
APPE FROM database FOR condition && condition can't be deleted()
USE database
DELE FOR condition      && condition identical to above
PACK
```

This code performs two tasks. First, it makes sure the historical database is available to dBASE III PLUS. If the historical file can't be found, dBASE III PLUS creates a new one by copying the structure of the active file to a new historical file. Then the system appends the relevant records to the historical database and deletes those same records from the active file. This block of code can be dropped into any of our kernels without problems and can be rewritten to include user prompts for filenames and such.

Using Indexed Databases

One might guess that information in this section is a synthesis of information described earlier in Backing Up Data while You Delete and Using Nonindexed Databases—and that would be correct. There isn't much new information necessary to explaining the process of backing up records before you delete them. As when you want to use nonINDEXed databases, you need to add a line of code that tells dBASE III PLUS what to copy and where to. The advantage of using INDEXed databases is time savings. You can use the WHILE qualifier, which is a random ordered search, instead of the time-consuming FOR sequential search. Knowing this, we can rewrite Listing 5–42 as follows:

Listing 5–44

```
** CODE FOR DELETING PARALLEL, INDEXED RECORDS WITH BACKUP
** CODE DOESN'T INCLUDE CHECK FOR PARALLELISM.
** THIS CODE ASSUMES THE SECONDARY HISTORICAL FILE IS INDEXED.
*
IF DELS
*
   DO CASE
```

Listing 5-44 (cont.)

```
      CASE database is secondary file
         SEEK delete condition
         COPY TO secondary historical file WHILE delete condition
         SEEK delete condition
         DELE WHIL condition
         SELE 2
         USE primary file INDE ndx file list
         SELE 1
         USE secondary historical file INDE NDX file list
         SET RELA TO key field INTO B
*
         DO WHIL .NOT. EOF()
            SELE 2
            DELE
            SELE 1
            SKIP
         ENDD
*
         SELE 2
         COPY TO primary historical file FOR DELE()
         PACK
         SELE 1
   ENDC
*
   PACK
   COPY TO secondary historical file FOR DELE()
ENDI
*
** EOF
```

The significant difference between Listings 5–42 and 5–44 is in which files are related. Listing 5–42 relates files before deleting occurs. Listing 5–44 relates the secondary historical file to the primary file, then deletes records from the primary file. This is done principally for the speed advantage. We are juggling databases and records, but at least we're juggling smaller databases and fewer records. Note that this code can be easily modified to use the APPEND block shown in Listing 5–43. Situations involving several secondary files are easily handled by making simple modifications to the code.

DELETING NONPARALLEL DATA

The last section dealt with the fairly common problem of deleting parallel records from different databases. What methods can we use when we're deleting non-parallel records from different databases? The code to delete nonparallel records is shown in Listing 5–45. We begin by explaining the difference between parallel and nonparallel data.

Listing 5–45

```
** CODE FOR DELETING NONPARALLEL RECORDS
*
USE primary file INDE NDX file list
&& first NDX file above must use field common to both databases
SELE 2
USE secondary file
LOCA FOR primary filename = UPPE(LOCATION)
*
DO WHIL RECNO() <= RECCOUNT()
   SELE 3
*
** the following four lines create a temporary storage file ;
   for each of the secondary file's records
*
   USE PACKTANK     && structure file for temporary databases
   TEMPFILE = IIF(' '$LEFT(B->key field,8),LEFT(B->key field,;
                  AT(' ',B->key field)), LEFT(B->key field,8))
&& the above line creates a filename based on the secondary     ;
   file's key field
   COPY STRUC TO &TEMPFILE
   USE &TEMPFILE
&& the PARTLIST field is a character field containing the   ;
   reference numbers of items in inventory. The reference   ;
   numbers are also the item record numbers in the primary file.
   PARTLIST = TRIM(B->PARTLIST)
*
   DO WHIL LEN(PARTLIST) > 0
      SELE 1
*
      IF ","$PARTLIST
         GOTO VAL(LEFT(PARTLIST,AT(',',PARTLIST)))
         PARTLIST = SUBSTR(PARTLIST,AT(',',PARTLIST)+1)
      ELSE
         GOTO VAL(PARTLIST)
         PARTLIST = ""
      ENDI
*
      SELE 3
      APPE BLANK
      REPL NEXT 1 PARTTAG WITH A->PARTTAG
   ENDD * PARTLIST > 0
*
```

Listing 5–45 (cont.)

```
   SELE 2
   CONT
ENDD * RECNO <= RECCOUNT
*
SELE 1
PACK
SELE 2
LOCA FOR primary filename = UPPER(LOCATION)
*
DO WHIL RECNO() <= RECCOUNT()
   PARTLIST = ""
   TEMPFILE = IIF(' '$LEFT(B->key field,8),LEFT(B->key field,;
                  AT(' ', B->key field)-1) + ".DBF",;
                     LEFT(B->key field,8)+".DBF")
   SELE 3
   USE &TEMPFILE
*
   DO WHIL .NOT. EOF()
      SELE 1
      FINDER = search key && this search key can be constructed  ;
                            from any number of fields or    ;
                            memory variables in any open    ;
                            databases or memory
      SEEK FINDER
*
      IF .NOT. FOUND()
         SEEK partial search key
&& the partial search key mentioned above must be the first       ;
   characters in the search field
*
         IF .NOT. FOUND()
            SELE 3
            SKIP
            LOOP
         ENDI
*
      ENDI
*
      PARTLIST = IIF(LEN(PARTLIST)=0,LTRIM(STR(RECNO())),;
                 PARTLIST+','+LTRIM(STR(RECNO())))
      SELE 3
      SKIP
   ENDD * EOF
*
   USE
```

Listing 5-45 (cont.)

```
   SELE 2
   REPL NEXT 1 PARTLIST WITH M->PARTLIST
   ERASE &TEMPFILE
   CONT
ENDD * RECNO <= RECCOUNT
*
SELE 1
REIN
*
** END OF PACKER.PRG
```

Parallel records are records in different databases that share one or more fields. The fields may not share the same name in each of the databases, but they do share the same information. You might call the account number ACCT in one database and ACCTNUM in another and ACCOUNT in yet another. The *field names* are not the same, but the data in the fields—the exact *information* in each of these parallel databases—is. Each of the named fields in each of the parallel databases holds a one-to-one correspondence from record to record, from database to database, in the account number field. What we're doing is transferring information from one file to another according to some relation (you'll remember the constant use of SET RELATION TO and REPLACE commands in the previous sections).

Good. The concept of parallel data is clear. *Nonparallel data* occurs when a field in database B holds information from a nonparallel field in database A. An example would be a field, TARDY, which holds the account numbers of past due accounts. Both A→ACCT and B→TARDY, are character data, but the TARDY field is necessarily longer than the account number field. The example that will be shown here goes a step further. We create a character field and place numeric data in it. Nonparallel data systems don't transfer information so much as they store information. These systems are based on the following concepts:

1. Records are not linked by any relations.
2. The databases follow a right to left tracking order.
3. Records removed from the left file affect records in the right file, but records removed from the right file don't affect records in the left file.
4. The databases do have a common field, but that field doesn't serve a parallel purpose (there isn't a one-to-one correspondence between the databases).

Looking at those edicts you might see how this type of system works with inventory management. The code we'll use as our example is from an inventory management system with several warehouses. When inventory is permanently moved from one location to another, we find ourselves in a situation where we need to make deletions to a primary file, but update only the secondary file based on those deletions. We don't want to permanently remove records from the secondary file.

We start writing our code by recognizing nonparallel records only go one way (from item 2 of the list). We aren't interested in deleting a record in the primary file just because a record is being deleted in the secondary file. In fact, we'll only be deleting records from the primary file. We're interested in updating information in the secondary file based on the deletions made to the primary file.

This means we scan for information in the secondary file. The information we find shows any linkage to the primary file. In the example here, the secondary file contains a field, LOCATION, which is the name of the warehouse where the parts are located. What we're doing is using the warehouse name as the name of the primary database. This name is also in a character field in the secondary database.

However, we've not used a one-to-one correspondence between parts and warehouse items. There was good reason for not doing so. A warehouse might contain several thousand different items, and several thousand units of each item. Our secondary file is only concerned with where parts for a single good are (such as a fleet needing to know where individual items for maintenance and repair are located). We therefore need to create a temporary file that contains information synthesized from the primary and secondary files. In particular, because we're deleting inventory records from the primary file, we need to create temporary files for each record in our secondary file.

Now an aside. Anybody shrieking at the megadisk use that's occurring? Good. You should be. But think a bit further down the road. We're only creating temporary files for secondary records that are matched to the warehouse named in the primary file. This cuts down disk use a few degrees. A wise rule of thumb is: "Decrease files, increase buffers." This is a reference to the CONFIG.SYS file and is my way of telling you "The more buffers you have active, the less a program will hit the disk." Also, the more memory the better. Some dealers tell you there is no need to purchase over 640K of memory in a PC. There is if you can use a RAM or virtual disk. And a situation like this practically makes it mandatory. End of aside.

As mentioned earlier, the part number is also the record number. This part number doesn't have to be the catalog number or inventory number. It's just a simplified way of getting the code to work. Notice that the PARTLIST field is exactly that, a list of all the part numbers necessary for the particular item. It is also a character field, although it contains the record numbers for all the parts.

Remember that the temporary files need a different method of matching information in the primary and secondary databases? There are several aspects of inventory items that are unique. Such features as the record number (already used, so out of the question), inventory number, catalog number, and description are usually unique. This example uses the term PARTTAG as a generic expression. You'll use a field or field combination as dictated by your own application.

The juggling that occurs can be interesting and applied to a variety of code. We're breaking down a character field and using the information thus gleaned to provide record pointers. Later, when the primary database is packed, we'll use the record pointers to rebuild the character field. Another interesting feature is shown by the two SEEK commands.

The whole point to this code is to delete primary records while keeping continuity in the secondary file. What happens if we delete a record from the primary file the secondary file points to? Chances are we won't be able to perform a complex SEEK if that is done. Should that occur, SEEK by a less complex search key. For example, our supplier no longer stocks or ships a particular part, and it's no longer in our inventory. The part has been replaced by a new part, but with a similar identification. The simpler search key can be used to find new items, if necessary.

The last part of the code merely replaces the old PARTLIST field with the new PARTLIST data, closes the secondary file, and reindexes the primary file. How does this look with enough documentation to let the user know what's going on? That code is shown here:

Listing 5–46

```
* PACKER.PRG
*
CLEA
@ 4,0 TO 10,79 DOUBLE
@ 6,20 SAY [0. Quit without Changing Anything]
@ 7,20 SAY [1. Remove Deleted Entries]
@ 8,20 SAY [2. Remove All Entries]
@ 10,33 SAY " select      "
@ 10,42 GET selectnum PICT "9" RANG 0,2
READ
*
DO CASE
   CASE selectnum = 0
      RETURN
   CASE selectnum = 2
      FILENAME = SUBS(DBF(),AT(":",DBF()) + 1,  AT(".",DBF()) - 1) + ".OLD"
      COPY TO &FILENAME
      ZAP
   CASE selectnum = 1
      CLEA
*
      IF 'primary filename'$DBF()
         SET INDE TO necessary NDX file list
         SELE 2
         @ 2,0 SAY "CREATING TEMPORARY DATA FILES"
         @ 4,0 SAY "BUILDING FILE FOR ITEM -> "
         @ 5,0 SAY "SEARCHING FOR RECORD # "
         USE secondary file
         LOCA FOR UPPE(SUBS(primary file name)) = LOCATION
*
```

Listing 5-46 (cont.)

```
        DO WHIL RECNO() <= RECCOUNT()
           SELE 3
           USE PACKTANK
           TEMPFILE = IIF(' '$LEFT(B->key field,8),LEFT(B->key field,;
                          AT(' ',B->key field)), LEFT(B->key field,8))
           COPY STRUC TO &TEMPFILE
           USE &TEMPFILE
           @ 5,30 SAY SPACE(10)
           @ 4,30 SAY B->key field
           PARTLIST= TRIM(B->PARTLIST)
*
           DO WHIL LEN(PARTLIST) > 0
              @ 5,30 SAY "        "
              SELE 1
*
              IF ","$PARTLIST
                 GOTO VAL(LEFT(PARTLIST,AT(',',PARTLIST)))
                 PARTLIST = SUBSTR(PARTLIST,AT(',',PARTLIST)+1)
              ELSE
                 GOTO VAL(PARTLIST)
                 PARTLIST = ""
              ENDI
*
              @ 5,30 SAY RECNO()
              SELE 3
              APPE BLANK
              REPL NEXT 1 PARTTAG WITH A->PARTTAG
           ENDD * PARTLIST > 0
*
           SELE 2
           CONT
        ENDD * RECNO <= RECCOUNT
*
        CLEA
        @ 2,0 SAY "PACKING "+DBFILE+" TO REMOVE DELETED RECORDS"
        SELE 1
        PACK
        SELE 2
        CLEAR
        @ 2,0 SAY "RECREATING ITEM FILE LISTINGS"
        @ 4,0 SAY "RECREATING LIST FOR ITEM -> "
        @ 5,0 SAY "FINDING RECORD NUMBER FOR -> "
        LOCA FOR UPPE(SUBS(primary file name)) = LOCATION
*
        DO WHIL RECNO() <= RECCOUNT()
```

Listing 5–46 (cont.)

```
            PARTLIST = ""
            TEMPFILE = IIF(' '$LEFT(B->key field,8),LEFT(B->key field,;
                           AT(' ', B->key field)-1) +  ".DBF",;
                              LEFT(B->key field,8)+".DBF")
            @ 4,30 SAY B->key field
            SELE 3
            USE &TEMPFILE
            @ 5,30 SAY SPACE(40)
*
            DO WHIL .NOT. EOF()
               @ 5,30 SAY SPACE(40)
               SELE 1
               FINDER = B->key field+C->PARTTAG
               @ 5,30 SAY C->PARTTAG
               SEEK FINDER
*
               IF .NOT. FOUND()
                  SEEK C->PARTTAG
*
                  IF .NOT. FOUND()
                     SELE 3
                     SKIP
                     LOOP
                  ENDI
*
               ENDI
*
               PARTLIST = IIF(LEN(PARTLIST)=0,LTRIM(STR(RECNO())),;
                          PARTLIST+','+LTRIM(STR(RECNO())))
               SELE 3
               SKIP
            ENDD * EOF
*
            USE
            SELE 2
            REPL NEXT 1 PARTLIST WITH M->PARTLIST
            ERASE &TEMPFILE
            CONT
         ENDD * RECNO <= RECCOUNT
      ELSE
         SET TALK ON
         ? "PACKING DATABASE TO REMOVE DELETED RECORDS"
         PACK
         SET TALK OFF
```

Listing 5–46 (cont.)

```
     ENDI
*
ENDC
*
SELE 1
? "REINDEXING DATABASE"
REIN
*
** END OF PACKER.PRG
```

The one item not discussed in Listing 5–46 is whether EXACT should be ON or OFF. The ideal would be to SET EXACT ON. However, doing so implies you'll always be able to search records using the combined search key. If that were the case, we wouldn't need the second search key that uses only a partial match pattern. It isn't worth the time to constantly SET EXACT OFF and ON throughout the code, so I elect to ignore the command option entirely.

KERNELS FOR MOVING THROUGH DATABASES

Let's take a brief break from the intense sections so far in this chapter and look at some simple kernels for moving through a database. You've seen kernels to find specific data in a database; now we'll show some kernels for going there and back again. The three kernels shown here make use of the two primitive record movement commands, SKIP and GOTO. All three kernels are part of a larger menu system that will be shown at the end of this chapter.

Skipping Ahead

The first kernel is a simple, one-record movement kernel. It allows you to go from one record to the next, one at a time, and is based on the SKIP command. Note that this kernel follows the pattern set by the SET INDEX TO and SET ORDER TO commands. This gives this small piece of code some power. Consider a situation where you FIND the first occurrence of something in the database. If you can find it, you must be using an INDEXed database. If you're using an INDEXed database, each succeeding record will have the same key field or, at some point when the key field value changes, a possibly similar key field value. An example of this would be having 20 Manchester, MA addresses followed by 20 Mansfield, MA addresses. The key field does change, but the first characters in the key field, *Man,* don't.

With this kernel you can sequentially go from the first record that matches the search key to the next. This can be quite useful in large databases where a LOCATE command might be too time-expensive for real work purposes. The code is:

Listing 5–47

```
CASE ANSWER = 'S'
   SKIP
   DO &GETTER
   CLEA GETS
   LOOP
```

Skipping Back

What do you do after you've gone one record forward? You check what you've done by going one record back. The block of code given next has all the pros listed in the previous listing and is the reverse of that section's code. The last moved one record forward in the database. This section's code moves one record back.

Listing 5–48

```
CASE ANSWER = 'B'
   SKIP -1
   DO &GETTER
   CLEA GETS
   LOOP
```

Going to a Particular Record

Now that you can go forward one record and backward one record, as well as FIND any record according to a search key matching the contents of a key field, what's left? How about being able to go directly to a record as listed by record number? The code described next helps you to do that. Why would such code be useful?

You can LIST and DISPLAY information to the screen or printer. One assumes you'd only LIST or DISPLAY information you're interested in. Part of the information normally shown in LISTs and DISPLAYs is the record number where the information is found. This kernel allows you to use that information as part of a menu system command that quickly moves you to your target record:

Listing 5–49

```
CASE ANSWER = 'G'
   ACCE "Record Number -> " TO RECNUM
   GOTO VAL(RECNUM)
   DO &GETTER
   CLEA GETS
   @ 24,0 SAY SPACE(40)
   LOOP
```

The line:

```
@ 24,0 SAY SPACE(40)
```

is due to the placement of the editing menu (as shown at the end of this chapter), and the:

```
ACCE "Record Number -> " TO RECNUM
```

prompt. The SAY command erases the ACCE prompt without affecting the editing menu.

SEARCH USING THE LOCATE COMMAND

Most programmers and dBASE III and III PLUS system developers are aware of the power and flexibility of the SEEK and FIND commands. Using these commands, you can code very specific and exact searches of the database. However, greater power imposes greater restrictions on the use of that power.

Not everything you want to find in a database is going to be accessible to the FIND and SEEK commands. Those two commands need an NDX file to function properly, and unless you plan on INDEXing on every field you have in a given database structure, it is unlikely you can FIND and SEEK everything that will be of interest. A further restriction on the FIND and SEEK commands is their left to right matching pattern. This goes beyond the realm of SET EXACT ON or OFF. Both FIND and SEEK match the first left most characters to the right most characters. In other words, RI = RIG = RIGHT when EXACT is OFF. You couldn't FIND or SEEK something beginning at the fourth or fifth character of a field unless you really hobbled the INDEX command when you first INDEXed the database.

Is is possible to create code that will allow you to scan any field for anything in that field? That is what this discussion is about. Our interest here is to include code that works according to the following rules:

1. The code can be used with any database.
2. The code allows the user to scan any field in that database.
3. The code allows the user to scan for any occurrence of the requested information in the selected field in the database.
4. It would be nice, but not necessary, if the code checked the validity of the request before attempting the search.

With those rules in mind, consider the following code:

Listing 5–50

```
CASE ANSWER = 'L'
   @ 20,0 CLEA
   ACCE "Locate where? -> " TO LOCATEWHERE
   ACCE "Locate what? -> " TO LOCATEWHAT
   LOCA FOR "&LOCATEWHAT"$&LOCATEWHERE
   DO &GETTER
```

Listing 5–50 (cont.)

```
CLEA GETS
LOOP
```

Listing 5–50 is the first step in achieving our goal, as outlined earlier. This code can be used with any active and currently selected database; it allows the user to scan any field in the database; and it allows the user to scan for any occurrence of the requested information in selected fields in the database. How does it work?

First, the code is part of the ever-greater menu system we've been building. It clears the menu from the bottom of the screen with the first positioned CLEAR command. After that it prompts the user for information on what data to LOCATE and where that information can be found. The power of the code comes from the line:

```
LOCA FOR "&LOCATEWHAT"$&LOCATEWHERE
```

This command uses the LOCATE command and the $ (search for text string) function to create a logical test. Note that I'm not testing for the requested information to be at a specific position in the field. That kind of test would take the form:

```
LOCA FOR AT('&LOCATEWHAT',&LOCATEWHERE) # 0
```

This line is a valid method, but not the best. It simply takes up too much time when all we need to know is whether or not the requested data is in the specified field (as in "Yes, it's here" or "No, it's not here"). Does this actually work? Oh yes, quite well, as can be seen in Figure 5–19.

The bottom of Figure 5–19 shows the power of the $ function. I've progressively cut my search from *computer* to *puter* to *ter,* and $ returned .T. ("Yes, it's here") each time. Linking the use of LOCATE and $ creates a powerful and valuable tool. The next thing to do is expand our code to handle any problems that might arise. We'd also, of course, like to include escapes should the user change his or her mind. Taking the latter first, consider the following code:

Listing 5–51

```
   CASE ANSWER = 'L'
      @ 20,0 CLEA
      ACCE "Locate where? -> " TO LOCATEWHERE
      ACCE "Locate what? -> " TO LOCATEWHAT
*
      IF LEN(TRIM(LOCATEWHAT)) # 0 .AND. LEN(TRIM(LOCATEWHERE)) # 0
         LOCA FOR "&LOCATEWHAT"$&LOCATEWHERE
      ENDI
*
      DO &GETTER
      CLEA GETS
      LOOP
```

```
-> USE NEWBOOKS INDE NBAUDS
-> REIN
-> LIST AUDIENCE
Record#  AUDIENCE
      4  christian
      1  computer
      6  fantasy
      7  horror
     39  juvenile fantasy
     19  juvenile science fiction
      2  maine
      5  psychic
     17  science fiction
     47  star trek
     46  supernatural

-> SET INDE TO
-> 1
-> ? 'computer' $AUDIENCE
.T.
-> ? 'puter' $AUDIENCE
.T.
-> ? 'ter' $AUDIENCE
.T.
->
```

Figure 5–19 You can use the $ function with the LOCATE command to perform some exquisite searches that are unavailable to the FIND and SEEK commands.

This takes care of the user who wants to bail out before any LOCATE operation is performed. The IF . . . ENDIF test merely ensures that information was entered at each of the above prompts. If no information was entered to either, don't LOCATE. Coding to ensure that valid information has been entered is another matter entirely. We'll start by investigating the TYPE() function, shown here:

```
-> USE NEWBOOKS INDE NBAUDS
-> LIST AUDIENCE
Record#  AUDIENCE
      4  Christian
     65  Christian fiction
      1  computer
      6  fantasy
     81  fiction
      7  horror
     72  juvenile
     39  juvenile fantasy
     64  juvenile fiction
     19  juvenile science fiction
      2  maine
     86  mystery
      5  psychic
     69  religious
```

```
        17  science fiction
        71  short story collections
        47  star trek
        46  supernatural

-> SET INDE TO
-> LOCATEWHAT = 'Christian fiction'
-> LOCATEWHERE = 'AUDIENCE'
-> ? TYPE("LOCATEWHAT$LOCATEWHERE")
L
-> LOCATEWHAT = 37
-> ? TYPE("LOCATEWHAT$LOCATEWHERE")
U
-> LOCATEWHERE = 'PHILADELPHIA'
-> ? TYPE("LOCATEWHAT$LOCATEWHERE")
U
-> LOCATEWHAT = 'Christian fiction' -> ? TYPE("LOCATEWHAT$LOCATEWHERE")
L
```

A file, NEWBOOKS, is placed in USE with a UNIQUE NDX file, NBAUDS. The field of interest, AUDIENCE, is LISTed. What we want to do is find out if we can test the validity of a possible search before that search is performed. The NDX file is no longer necessary, so it's shut off with SET INDE TO. Two character variables, LOCATEWHAT and LOCATEWHERE, are created in the code. LOCATEWHERE is the name of the field of interest, AUDIENCE. LOCATEWHAT is what I want to find, *Christian fiction.* The line:

```
? TYPE("LOCATEWHAT$LOCATEWHERE")
```

is a test that tells me if my eventual request (as shown in Listings 5–50, 5–51, and eventually in 5–52) will be logical to dBASE III PLUS. Note: I'm not testing to see if the request will be positive and matches will be found. I'm only testing whether what I'm asking is a valid request. There is a difference. Anthropomorphizing a dialog between III PLUS and myself might result in:

> Joseph, knowing the answer might save the lives of millions, stared into III PLUS's eyes. "Am I allowed to ask this question?"
>
> III PLUS remembered her proud ancestors, the Developer's Release, dBASE III, dBASE II, back to lowly Vulcan, first born of the god Ratliff from the land of Ashton and Tate. She met Joseph's eyes.
>
> "Yes," she replied.

III PLUS could just have easily said "No, you can't ask that question." III PLUS says we can't ask a question by returning U (*U*NKNOWN) for the TYPE() function. That is more our concern at the moment. Continuing with the list of new books, I can enter a numeric or other noncharacter data type to LOCATEWHAT, and dBASE III PLUS will return U for the TYPE() test. But note what happens when both LOCATEWHAT and LOCATEWHERE are invalid, as in the last line of the booklist. TYPE() returns L, which means I could ask that question. Of course, if I did, dBASE III PLUS would get angry and never talk to me again. We must therefore first test for a valid LOCATEWHERE expression, then test for a valid LOCATE expression. Look at this interactive code:

```
-> USE NEWBOOKS
-> LIST STRUC
Structure for database: D:NEWBOOKS.dbf
Number of data records:       91
Date of last update   : 12/10/86
Field  Field Name  Type       Width    Dec
    1  NAME        Character     60
    2  AUDIENCE    Character     30
    3  ADDRESS1    Character     30
    4  ADDRESS2    Character     30
    5  CITY        Character     20
    6  STATE       Character      2
    7  COUNTRY     Character     20
    8  ZIPCODE     Character     10
    9  CONTACT     Character     30
   10  TITLE       Character     15
   11  DEAR        Character     20
   12  MSSMIN      Numeric       10
   13  MSSMAX      Numeric       10
   14  QUERY       Logical        1
   15  MANUSCRIPT  Logical        1
   16  DMP         Logical        1
   17  GOF         Logical        1
   18  SIMULSUBMT  Logical        1
   19  MISC        Character     65
   20  PHONENUMBR  Character     14
   21  SOURCE      Character     30
** Total **                     402

-> ? TYPE("NAME")
C
-> ? TYPE("QUERY")
L
-> ? TYPE("MSSMIN")
N
-> ? TYPE("REEBERSNORT")
U
```

As long as I ask for a valid field name, TYPE() returns the field type. Asking for a nonexistent field, REEBERSNORT, returns U. We have our test for LOCATEWHEREs. The test for the search condition follows from test for NEW-

BOOKS. All that is left is to add some lines to let the user know what's going on:

Listing 5–52

```
     CASE ANSWER = 'L'
        RELE LOCATEWHERE, LOCATEWHAT
        TRUTH = .F.
*
        DO WHIL TYPE('&LOCATEWHERE') = 'U' .AND. .NOT. TRUTH
           @ 20,0 CLEA
           @ 20,0 SAY [I NEED A VALID FIELD NAME]
           ACCE "Locate where? -> " TO LOCATEWHERE
*
           IF LEN(TRIM(&LOCATEWHERE)) = 0
              TRUTH = .T.
           ENDI
*
        ENDD
*
        DO WHIL TYPE("LOCATEWHAT$LOCATEWHERE") = 'U' .AND. .NOT. TRUTH
           @ 22,0 CLEA
           @ 22,0 SAY [I NEED A VALID EXPRESSION]
           ACCE "Locate what? -> " TO LOCATEWHAT
*
           IF LEN(TRIM(LOCATEWHAT)) = 0
              TRUTH = .T.
           ENDI
*
        ENDD
*
        IF .NOT. TRUTH
           LOCA FOR "&LOCATEWHAT"$&LOCATEWHERE
        ENDI
*
        DO &GETTER
        CLEA GETS
        LOOP
```

This code makes use of the TYPE() function to first test the validity of the LOCATEWHERE expression. As long as the user enters an invalid field name, the code remains in the first DO WHILE . . . ENDDO loop. The only out is to enter nothing, which causes III PLUS to exit the first loop. If the user left the first loop by declaring a valid field name, the program enters the second DO WHILE . . . ENDDO block. This block tests for a valid LOCATEWHAT expression. Again, the only ways out of the loop are either to enter a null or a valid response. You can add different user prompts. Note that the coding method uses only one set of the following three commands:

```
DO &GETTER
CLEA GETS
LOOP
```

The alternative is to code a separate three line block for each TYPE() text, or place the three lines in a PROCedure. Neither method is as elegant as the method shown.

UPDATE USING THE REPLACE COMMAND

The Edit kernel in Chapter 3 shows how to make one-shot changes to data in the current work area. That is useful, but can be limiting. No one enjoys having to edit record after record. Sometimes that is a necessary evil, but most often our editing follows a pattern. Perhaps we need to make a specific change to every record based on a condition, such as state, city, or part number. Is it possible to write some code that allows the user to enter data and have that data automatically update all relevant records in the database?

Of course it is. This is how we do it:

Listing 5–53

```
      CASE ANSWER = 'U'
         @ 20,0 CLEA
         ACCE [REPLACE WHAT FIELD?  ] TO REPLACER
*
         IF LEN(TRIM(REPLACER)) = 0
            @ 20,0 CLEA
            LOOP
         ENDI
*
         ACCE [REPLACE WITH  ] TO REPLACEWITH
*
         IF LEN(TRIM(REPLACEWITH)) = 0
            @ 20,0 CLEA
            LOOP
         ENDI
*
         ACCE "CONDITION  " TO CONDITION
*
         IF LEN(TRIM(CONDITION)) # 0
            LOCA FOR &CONDITION
*
            IF .NOT. FOUND()
               @ 20,0 CLEA
               LOOP
            ELSE
```

Listing 5-53 (cont.)

```
                SET FILT TO &CONDITION
            ENDI
*
            REPL &REPLACER WITH &REPLACEWITH

        ENDI
*
        @ 20,0 CLEA
```

This code is a fairly obvious use of a powerful command. We wanted something that would do a great deal of work with little effort on the user's part. Can the code be improved upon?

One thing that might improve the code is making the REPLACER memory variable a 10-character wide GET variable. The reason for this is that field names are limited to 10 characters in length. This step would ensure that we get a proper length field name. Another option is to use the TYPE() test shown previously. This test would ensure that we get an acceptable field name without bothering to check variable name length.

Notice three features of the code. It doesn't use the REPLACE command's FOR or WHILE qualifiers, nor does it specify a scope with a NEXT qualifier. And it appears I've coded to only allow one field's replacements at a pass. None of this is true, however.

The first feature, not using FOR or WHILE qualifiers, is answered with the use of the SET FILT TO &CONDITION command. This command is equivalent to a FOR qualifier on the REPLACE command. The second and third items have the same answer. The operative object of the REPLACE command is the macro &REPLACEWITH. When the code asks:

```
REPLACE WITH >
```

the user can answer:

```
replacement item(s) NEXT n
```

where *n* is some numeric expression. But there is a warning with this. You can include the NEXT qualifier, the dBASE III PLUS REST qualifier, your own FOR and WHILE qualifiers, and so forth, in the REPLACEWITH memory variable quite easily. Doing so can negate the effect of the SET FILT TO &CONDITION command. Also, including qualifiers in the REPLACEWITH memory variable means you design a sophisticated parser when and if you error check REPLACE-WITH.

The user can also include several replacements by answering with something like:

```
item1, field2 WITH item2, field3 WITH item3,...
```

and so on.

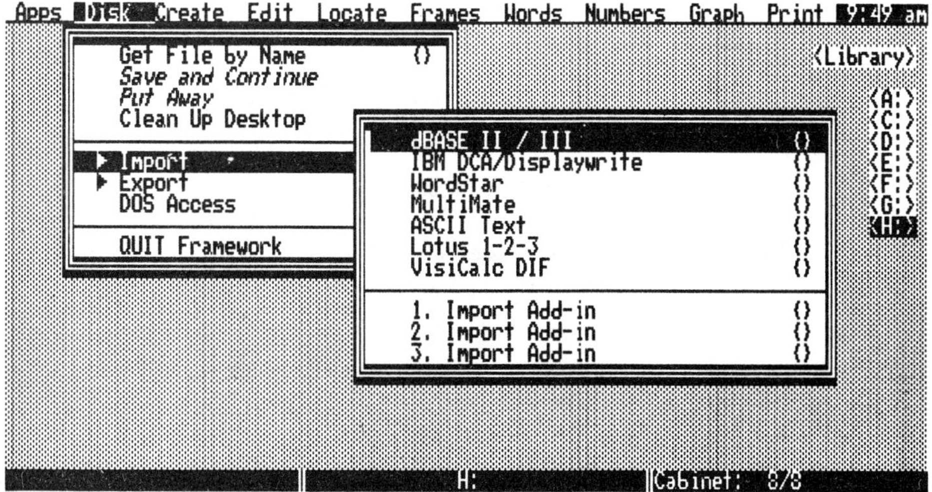

Figure 5–20 Framework II has a menu-driven interface to read and write dBASE files.

KERNELS AND CODE TO ACCESS FOREIGN FILES

There are occasions when it's important to access foreign data types. Perhaps you need to trade data between your spreadsheet and dBASE III PLUS, or III PLUS and a word processor, and so on. First let's spend a few moments exploring such exchanges.

There are some excellent products presently on the market that can read and write dBASE files. They handle dBASE II, dBASE III, Developers' Release, and dBASE III PLUS database files with no difficulties. These products include the GURU system from MDBS, the developers of the KnowledgeMan system, REFLEX, Q&A, and Ashton-Tate's own Framework II. These products run from the low-end price of REFLEX to GURU ($6,500!). What are the advantages and disadvantages of each?

For sheer compatibility and additional power not found in the dBASE III PLUS architecture, go with Framework II. See Figure 5–20 for an example of a Framework menu. You can run dBASE III PLUS from inside Framework II without exiting to DOS (Figure 5–21), read and write dBASE database files from an excellent menu system, create graphs from your database in a matter of seconds, and use your dBASE files as spreadsheets and incorporate your data directly into word processed documents in mailmerge and other forms. That is an incredible amount of power for one package. In addition, Framework II's additional commands and Pascal-like programming language do tasks with your data that aren't possible with other systems.

With Framework II you use your dBASE files for "reading, writing, and arithmetic," as you can do graphics, word processing, and spreadsheet work—three capabilities not contained in the dBASE III PLUS system.

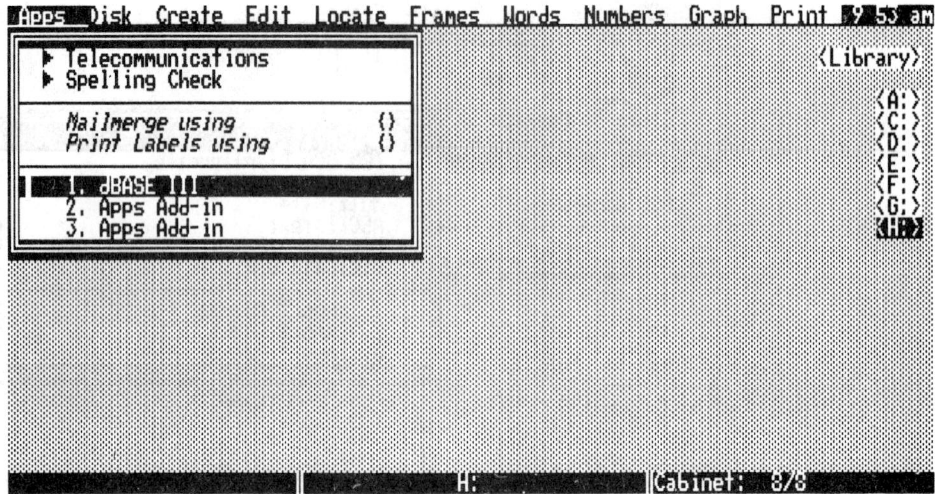

Run dBASE III within Framework II

Figure 5–21 Framework II can run the versions of dBASE directly from a menu, accessing them as subroutines.

Next down the scale is Symantec Software's Q&A. Q&A reads and writes dBASE files directly, but has no graphics or spreadsheet capabilities. Q&A is itself a *hierarchical* database system, as opposed to III PLUS's *relational* system. This means Q&A will only work with a single database file at a time. The advantage to Q&A is its powerful word processor and the "Intelligent Assistant," an AI interface that accepts commands in English. Q&A is a low-priced DBMS with some artificial intelligence capabilities. So, if you can't FIND, SEEK, or LOCATE what you're interested in with any of dBASE III PLUS's commands or the code shown in this book, you might be able to find it with Q&A's intelligence.

Borland International's REFLEX product lends dBASE III PLUS some powerful graphics features. Like Framework II, REFLEX reads and writes dBASE files and has a menu interface. Unlike Framework II, REFLEX only adds graphics and some spreadsheet-like capabilities to the dBASE III PLUS system. But the price is near unbeatable. For about $100 you can add beautiful graphics to your III PLUS application and make it menu-driven. For not much more money you can use a macro encoder (SuperKey, ProKey, KeyWorks, to name a few) and retain a III PLUS programmatic aspect of REFLEX while it runs.

With all this said, is it necessary to write code to let III PLUS read and write foreign files? Yes and no. Obviously, if you're developing your system from scratch, you don't care about such concerns and can tell your client/customer/supervisor to get Framework II (which works with dBASE III PLUS most easily of all products mentioned) and not worry about coding to access foreign structures.

However, you could be developing an application for an existing environment. Perhaps the clients are using Lotus 1-2-3 or Symphony, perhaps Multiplan, or a similar product. It is necessary to write code to access files in foreign formats in these cases. What does that code look like? The following listing is for an office that uses one product for spreadsheets and another for word processing. An example of this might be Multiplan for their number crunching and WordStar for their word crunching. The second listing assumes there are several foreign file formats that III PLUS must communicate with. One aspect of the last code that goes beyond the concept of kernels is the menu interface. I include it here because it is a nice touch and worth showing.

Listing 5–54

```
ANSWER = 'S'
@ 20,0 CLEA
@ 20,0 SAY [(W)ORD PROCESSOR FILE OR (S)PREADSHEET FILE? > ] GET ANSWER PICT '!'
READ
*
IF ANSWER = 'W'
   QUALIFY = [DELIM WITH delimiting character/BLANK]
ELSE
   QUALIFY = [foreign file type]        && could be SDF, DIF, SYLK, or WKS
ENDI
*
@ 20,0 CLEA
@ 20,0 SAY "DO YOU WANT TO (R)EAD OR (W)RITE DATA? > " GET ANSWER PICT '!'
READ
*
DO CASE
   CASE ANSWER = 'R'
      @ 20,0 CLEA
      @ 20,0 SAY "(C)REATE NEW FILE OR (A)DD TO EXISTING FILE? > " GET ANSWER PICT '!'
      READ
*
      IF ANSWER = 'C'
         ACCE [NEW FILENAME (8 CHAR MAX)? > ] TO NEWFILE
         SELE 2
         USE TEMPLATE   && existing file with necessary dbf structure for new data
         COPY STRUC TO &NEWFILE
      ELSE
         ACCE [EXISTING FILENAME (8 CHAR MAX)? > ] TO NEWFILE
      ENDI
*
      USE &NEWFILE
      ACCE [READ WHAT FILE (INCLUDE DRIVE AND PATH, IF NECESSARY)? > ] TO OTHERFILE
      APPE FROM &OTHERFILE &QUALIFY
      SELE 1
   CASE ANSWER = 'W'
      @ 20,0 CLEA
      @ 20,0 SAY [TARGET FILENAME (INCLUDE DRIVE AND PATH, IF NECESSARY)? > ] TO OTHERFILE
```

Listing 5–54 (cont.)

```
      COPY TO &OTHERFILE &QUALIFY
   OTHE
      @ 20,0 CLEA
      LOOP
ENDC
```

Remember that this listing is for a system that has a predefined spreadsheet package. The file TYPE is coded into Listing 5–54 in the first IF . . . ELSE . . . ENDIF block. Also note that we use a TEMPLATE database file when data is imported from another system. This template file is designed once and never changed, although databases derived from it can be changed. Using a template file ensures continuity and less confusion when the system is in place.

Some readers using the PFS product series may be curious how Listing 5–54 would change for that product. Most obviously, translations to and from the PFS products involve the IMPORT and EXPORT commands. The code becomes:

Listing 5–55

```
ANSWER = 'S'
@ 20,0 CLEA
@ 20,0 SAY [(W)ORD PROCESSOR FILE OR (S)PREADSHEET FILE? > ] GET ANSWER PICT '!'
READ
*
IF ANSWER = 'W'
   QUALIFY = [DELIM WITH delimiting character/BLANK]
ELSE
   QUALIFY = []
ENDI
*
@ 20,0 CLEA
@ 20,0 SAY "DO YOU WANT TO (R)EAD OR (W)RITE DATA? > " GET ANSWER PICT '!'
READ
*
DO CASE
   CASE ANSWER = 'R'
      @ 20,0 CLEA
      @ 20,0 SAY "(C)REATE NEW FILE OR (A)DD TO EXISTING FILE? > " GET ANSWER PICT '!'
      READ
*
         IF QUALIFY # []
*
            IF ANSWER = 'C'
               ACCE [NEW FILENAME (8 CHAR MAX)? > ] TO NEWFILE
               SELE 2
               USE TEMPLATE     && existing file with necessary dbf structure for new data
```

Listing 5–55 (cont.)

```
                COPY STRUC TO &NEWFILE
             ELSE
                ACCE [EXISTING FILENAME (8 CHAR MAX)? > ] TO NEWFILE
             ENDI
*
             USE &NEWFILE
          ENDI
*
      ACCE [READ WHAT FILE (INCLUDE DRIVE AND PATH, IF NECESSARY)? > ] TO OTHERFILE
*
      IF QUALIFY = []
         IMPO FROM &OTHERFILE PFS
      ELSE
         APPE FROM &OTHERFILE &QUALIFY
      ENDI
*
      SELE 1
        CASE ANSWER = 'W'
      @ 20,0 CLEA
      @ 20,0 SAY [TARGET FILENAME (INCLUDE DRIVE AND PATH, IF NECESSARY)? > ] TO OTHERFILE
*
      IF QUALIFY = []
         EXPO TO &OTHERFILE PFS
      ELSE
         COPY TO &OTHERFILE &QUALIFY
      ENDI
*
   OTHE
      @ 20,0 CLEA
      LOOP
ENDC
```

The next code block gives the user the opportunity to select the import and export target files. It is built off Listing 5–54, however. Yes, no matter what, I use existing code and modify as necessary!

Listing 5–56

```
ANSWER = 0
@  3, 20  TO 15, 60    DOUBLE
@  5, 26  SAY "0 -> Quit"
@  7, 26  SAY "1 -> Word Processing File"
@  8, 26  SAY "2 -> System File Format"
@  9, 26  SAY "3 -> VisiCalc File Format"
@ 10, 26  SAY "4 -> Multiplan File Format"
@ 11, 26  SAY "5 -> Lotus 1-2-3 File Format"
```

Listing 5–56 (cont.)

```
@ 12, 26  SAY "6 -> PFS Software File Format"
@ 15, 34  SAY "selection > <" GET ANSWER RANG 0,6
READ
*
DO CASE
   CASE ANSWER = 0
      CLEA
      LOOP
   CASE ANSWER = 1
      QUALIFY = [DELIM WITH delimiting character/BLANK]
   CASE ANSWER = 2
      QUALIFY = [SDF]
   CASE ANSWER = 3
      QUALIFY = [DIF]
   CASE ANSWER = 4
      QUALIFY = [SYLK]
   CASE ANSWER = 5
      QUALIFY = [WKS]
   CASE ANSWER = 6
      QUALIFY = []
ENDC
*
ANSWER = 'R'
CLEA
@ 1,0 SAY "DO YOU WANT TO (R)EAD OR (W)RITE DATA? > " GET ANSWER PICT '!'
READ
*
DO CASE
   CASE ANSWER = 'R'
      @ 20,0 CLEA
      @ 20,0 SAY "(C)REATE NEW FILE OR (A)DD TO EXISTING FILE? > " GET ANSWER PICT '!'
      READ
*
      IF QUALIFY # []
*
         IF ANSWER = 'C'
            ACCE [NEW FILENAME (8 CHAR MAX)? > ] TO NEWFILE
            SELE 2
            USE TEMPLATE       && existing file with necessary dbf structure for new data
            COPY STRUC TO &NEWFILE
         ELSE
            ACCE [EXISTING FILENAME (8 CHAR MAX)? > ] TO NEWFILE
         ENDI
*
         USE &NEWFILE
```

Listing 5–56 (cont.)

```
      ENDI
*
      ACCE [READ WHAT FILE (INCLUDE DRIVE AND PATH, IF NECESSARY)? > ] TO OTHERFILE
*
      IF QUALIFY = []
         IMPO FROM &OTHERFILE PFS
      ELSE
         APPE FROM &OTHERFILE &QUALIFY
      ENDI
*
      SELE 1
   CASE ANSWER = 'W'
      @ 20,0 CLEA
      @ 20,0 SAY [TARGET FILENAME (INCLUDE DRIVE AND PATH, IF NECESSARY)? > ]
        TO OTHERFILE
*
      IF QUALIFY = []
         EXPO TO &OTHERFILE PFS
      ELSE
         COPY TO &OTHERFILE &QUALIFY
      ENDI
*
   OTHE
      @ 20,0 CLEA
      LOOP
ENDC
```

HIDE USING THE SET FILT TO COMMAND

Often the need arises to "hide" information from the user or some level of users. The latter condition often occurs in networked applications, and the dBASE III PLUS PROTECT utility goes a long way in providing that ability. However, sometimes it is necessary to hide information merely in the sense of filtering a database. Perhaps you don't want to wade through several records and only want to READ, EDIT, CHANGE, LIST, DISPLAY, or REPLACE records that meet some condition. In other words, you want to hide inappropriate records from III PLUS and concentrate on records that meet some specific criteria.

This ability has been demonstrated in other listings in this book, but never explicitly shown as code in itself. There is nothing magical about the Hide kernel, and it is given here as a useful tool for database management.

Listing 5–57

```
@ 20,0 CLEA
ACCE [WHAT IS THE CONDITION? > ] TO CONDITION
```

Listing 5–57 (cont.)

```
*
IF LEN(TRIM(CONDITION)) = 0
   @ 20,0 CLEA
   LOOP
ELSE
   SET FILT TO &CONDITION
ENDI
*
```

This is indeed a simple piece of code, but don't underestimate its power. You can use this Hide kernel to select just a few records in a database containing several thousand records. Normally you might LOCATE such records, forcing dBASE III PLUS to scan every record from first to last until it matches the LOCATE condition. Using the Hide kernel, III PLUS accesses the desired records far more quickly than a LOCATE and several CONTINUE commands could. Once a FILTER is SET, any movement of the record pointer always goes to a record that meets the desired condition. You could, for example, use the Hide kernel to SET a FILTER on one or several fields, then use the LOCATE command on another field or fields. This would give you near surgical precision. This logic also follows for the FIND, REPLACE, DISPLAY, LIST, and similar commands.

One extra item can be added to a system using the Hide kernel. That item would be the line:

```
@ x,y SAY
;
IIF(LEN(TRIM(CONDITION))=0,SPAC(20);
[CONDITION EXISTS])
```

You could insert this line into whatever code paints the screen and is used to tell the user a condition exists on the active file. Naturally, the FILTER is turned off whenever a new database is made current. Final note: A neat trick with parallel files and the SET RELATION TO command is to SET the FILTER to something like:

parallel work area->field = data

With this, the user can HIDE data in the current work area based on data in other work areas.

PROTECTING DATABASES USING dBASE III PLUS UTILITIES AND THIRD PARTY SOFTWARE

Here we won't examine new kernels or code per se, but we'll explore some suggestions for a growing concern in office environments, namely data security. Several products have been introduced that offer some degree of security to the user, but it is important to remember that whatever one person does another can undo. My favorite anecdote about the protection business concerns a company that challenged anyone to break its file encryption algorithm. The managers offered cash prizes for the challenge and went bankrupt one month after their braggadocio!

There are several fairly inexpensive and useful ways to provide protection to dBASE III PLUS data. We'll look at three such methods. The first method is available to any dBASE III PLUS user with a hard disk and 640K of main memory. Even better, it comes in the standard dBASE III PLUS package and is better known as the PROTECT utility. This utility is normally reserved for network use, but that isn't all it can be used for. Any single-mode dBASE III PLUS user can employ PROTECT's abilities, provided the system has a hard disk and 640K of memory. The extra memory is necessary, as you'll be running the network version of III PLUS even though you won't be on a network. A detailed explanation of this is beyond the scope of this book, but is covered well in the III PLUS documentation.

The second method is also workable to any PC user, doesn't require much extra memory, but does require memory above 320K. It involves the use of files such as Norton's FA.COM file and the dBASE Programmer's Utility CHMOD.EXE file. These files provide some database security, as you can use them to change the attributes of a file. One of the attributes you can change is whether the file is hidden or archived. *Archived files* are available to anyone and shown in directory listings. Hidden files are equally available, but don't show up in directory listings.

The last protection scheme covered in this section is a utility available from Ashton-Tate and included in the dBASE PROGRAMMER'S UTILITIES package. A file in that package, PROTECT.BIN, and its DOS file counterpart, DPROTECT.EXE prevent unauthorized access to files by making them incompatible with dBASE III PLUS. You can use these files to protect and unprotect III PLUS files as necessary.

The dBASE III PLUS PROTECT Utility

The PROTECT.EXE utility, housed on Administrator Disk 1 in the standard dBASE III PLUS package, is a useful tool that you can use to set a variety of parameters for file access. It is normally used by the network manager to set access levels to III PLUS files on the file server. You can make use of the PROTECT.EXE utility even in single-user mode, but you must be using the III PLUS network version. Don't let this confuse you. Remember that you can use the network version of III PLUS as a single user, provided you have 640K of memory and a hard disk system.

The PROTECT.EXE opens up with a screen similar to the III PLUS sign on screen. Once that passes, you're using the network manager mode and are asked to enter a password. Once you enter it, you're given the opportunity to confirm that password, as Figure 5–22 shows.

The next step for PROTECT.EXE is to enter the various passwords that will be associated with the user (yourself or whomever you're designing the system

```
dBASE ADMINISTRATOR Password Security System

Please reenter password to confirm
```

Figure 5–22 The PROTECT.EXE utility asks you to confirm your password before giving you access to the security management screen.

for—a process shown in Figure 5–23), and last, to designate the files that are to be protected with this utility (shown in Figure 5–24).

Full documentation on this utility is included in the III PLUS package. There are disadvantages to using PROTECT.EXE, however. The utility writes a file, DBSYSTEM.DB, with the access codes for each file. This file is read whenever III PLUS's networked version is started. Once this file is read, the network version knows who should gain access to files and who shouldn't, even in single-user mode. However, the files can still be accessed by anyone using single-user dBASE III PLUS. A single-mode network user starts III PLUS with the command:

```
ACCESS M=
```

followed by the necessary parameters. But here we're talking about using the networked version's protection algorithms, which means anyone sitting down at the single machine can load in single-user III PLUS, type in the command:

```
dBASE
```

```
Users                          Files                          Exit  02:44:34 am

Login name
Password
Group name

Account name
Access level              1

Store user profile

Delete user from group

PROTECT     <C:>     Opt: 1/7
Position selection bar - ↑↓.  Select - ←┘.  Leave menu - ←→.
Enter the login name for this user.
```

Figure 5–23 With PROTECT.EXE, you assign passwords and levels of access to users of your application.

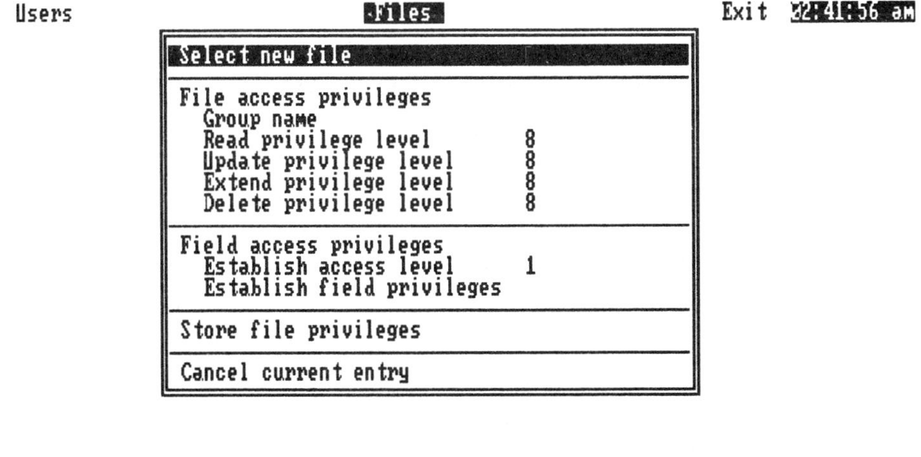

Figure 5–24 You also use PROTECT.EXE to assign levels of protection to individual database files.

at the DOS prompt, and read the files. Single-user III PLUS never looks for the DBSYSTEM.DB file. There is also another problem. You can completely defeat DBSYSTEM.DB's protection simply by erasing the file. If this is your method of choice, please also read on for the discussion of hiding the DBSYSTEM.DB file.

Locking Files with Third Party Software

As both products mentioned in the introduction to this section are third party packages, I won't spend much time on them. They are mentioned due to their ability to protect databases and other dBASE III PLUS files by hiding them from snoopy users. Both programs, and others similar to them, work by changing file attributes.

What are file attributes? Each file on either a floppy or hard disk has a group of flags. Right beside the filename you might imagine a pixie. All the long life of this pixie, it wanted to join the navy. Why? It always wanted to wave those flags that are used for some ship-to-ship communication. Now the pixie has its chance. It stands beside the file's name and waves flags matching those shown in Figure 5–25.

As listed, these flags tell DOS if a file is *read only* (no one can write to this file), *hidden* (this file isn't listed with any directory listing command, such as DIR or CAT), *archive* (anybody can do anything with this file, such as read it, write to it, or delete it) or *system* (DOS can use it but not too many others). It might be worth it to write a short routine that sets your database attributes to *hidden system* when your work session is over and resets the attributes to *archive* when you start a work session. This is not difficult to do and can be transparent to the

```
D:\>c:\db3\utility\chmod

CHMOD Version 1.0 [1-20-86]    Copyright (C) 1986 by LSP, Inc.
Usage: CHMOD [/attri]  [dr:][\path]filename
  attri = attribute codes grouped without spaces.
     Attribute bit       Set   Clear
       read only         r+    r-
       hidden            h+    h-
       archive           a+    a-
       system            s+    s-

Example:  Display Attributes only:
             chmod myfile.xyz
          Clear read only bit and set archive bit:
             chmod /r-a+ c:myfile.abc

D:\>
```

Figure 5–25 The help screen for the CHMOD.EXE.file, used to change file attributes.

user by directing the output of the CHMOD or FA files to the NUL device. These commands can be issued through a BAT file or in a dBASE III PLUS PRG file with the RUN/! command.

The dBASE PROGRAMMER'S UTILITIES PROTECT.BIN and DPROTECT.EXE Files

Two utilities in the dBASE PROGRAMMER'S UTILITIES package are available from Ashton-Tate. The two files, PROTECT.BIN and DPROTECT.EXE, are nothing more than a LOADable BINary version and a DOS-level version of the same file. Both protect databases by making them unreadable by III PLUS. This process is shown in Figure 5–26.

```
-) DIR
Database Files    # Records    Last Update      Size
ACCOUNTS.DBF       Not a dBASE III PLUS file.             413
NEWBOOKS.DBF             91    12/10/86        37288
MSSFILE.DBF              13    10/13/86         3033
PAYMENTS.DBF              0    11/25/86         1442
TANK.DBF                 10    12/07/87         7178
SUBS.DBF                  2    12/02/86         1142
OLDBOOKS.DBF             91    12/03/86        37288

  87784 bytes in     7 files.
3072000 bytes remaining on drive.

-) CALL PROTECT WITH 'F,ACCOUNTS.DBF'
-) DIR
Database Files    # Records    Last Update      Size
ACCOUNTS.DBF              1    11/24/86          413
NEWBOOKS.DBF             91    12/10/86        37288
MSSFILE.DBF              13    10/13/86         3033
PAYMENTS.DBF              0    11/25/86         1442
TANK.DBF                 10    12/07/87         7178
SUBS.DBF                  2    12/02/86         1142
OLDBOOKS.DBF             91    12/03/86        37288
```

Figure 5–26 The PROTECT files make the DBF files alternately readable and unreadable by dBASE III PLUS.

This figure shows the BIN file being CALLed from inside dBASE III PLUS. Note that the first DIR listing shows ACCOUNTS.DBF as "Not a dBASE III PLUS file." After CALLing PROTECT, the ACCOUNTS.DBF file is listed as a valid dBASE III PLUS database.

DISPLAYING DATA TO THE SCREEN AND PRINTER

We now return to the concept of kernels in order to DISPLAY data. Why would we want to DISPLAY data? Perhaps you want to view data, but don't want to change it. Perhaps you want to see a cross listing of information on screen or just make a printout for referencing against other lists. Sometimes a quick visual error check is all a database needs, and repeated LOCATEs and CONTINUEs would take too long. The possibilities are endless. A simplified DISPLAY kernel is:

Listing 5–58

```
     CASE ANSWER = 'D'
        @ 20,0 CLEA
        ACCE "Display What -> " TO DISPLAYWHAT
*
        IF LEN(TRIM(DISPLAYWHAT)) = 0
           @ 20,0 CLEA
           LOOP
        ENDI
*
        TRUTH = .T.
        @ 21,0 CLEA
        ACCE "DISP FOR -> " TO DISPLAYFOR
        READ
*
        IF LEN(TRIM(DISPLAYFOR)) # 0
           SET FILT TO &DISPLAYFOR
           DISPLAYFOR = 'FOR' + DISPLAYFOR
        ENDI
*
        @ 21,0 CLEA
        @ 21,0 SAY [DO YOU WANT THIS PRINTED (Y/N)?  ] GET TRUTH
        READ
*
        IF TRUTH
           TOPRINT = 'TO PRINT'
           EJECT
        ELSE
           TOPRINT = []
           CLEA
```

Listing 5–58 (cont.)

```
        ENDI
*
        DISP &DISPLAYWHAT &DISPLAYFOR &TOPRINT
*
        IF TRUTH
           EJECT
        ENDI
*
        CLEA
        DO &FRAMER
        DO &GETTER
        CLEA GETS
*
        @ 21,0 CLEA
        SET FILT TO
        LOOP
```

Again, note my use of macros to create complex commands from user-supplied information. In particular, I've SET a FILTER with the DISPLAYFOR variable, then added 'FOR' to the variable's value. Then I can use it in the command:

```
DISP &DISPLAYWHAT &DISPLAYFOR &TOPRINT
```

without adding the necessary FOR qualifier to the command itself. Why was this done? As the code stands, it will run whether or not DISPLAYFOR has any real value. If you don't include FOR in DISPLAYFOR, the command becomes:

```
DISP &DISPLAYWHAT FOR &DISPLAYFOR &TOPRINT
```

That can cause problems, because III PLUS will look for something to be qualified, even if nothing is supposed to be.

A COMPLETE EDITOR FILE

This entire chapter and Chapter 3 have shown you a wide variety of kernels. The one thing lacking is a comprehensive demonstration of them in working code. Now we'll address that need. The file shown here contains a sample of the kernels designed to make a complete EDITOR file. The EDITOR file can be used as a subroutine or placed in a PROCedure file. A Clipper compatible version of this file is also listed in Appendix A.

Listing 5–59

```
* EDIT.PRG
* CALLS EDITMENU FROM PROCEDURE FILE
```

Listing 5–59 (cont.)

```
*
DO &FRAMER
DO &GETTER
CLEA GETS
DO EDITMENU
ANSWER = 'X'
DELS = .F.
*
DO WHIL .T.
   @ 0,0 SAY SPACE(80)
   @ 24,0 SAY SPACE(80)
   @  2,60 SAY IIF(DELETED(),"DELETED",SPACE(7))
   @ 23,34 SAY " select   "
   @ 23,43 GET ANSWER PICT '!'
   READ
*
   DO CASE
      CASE .NOT. ANSWER $ 'XQKRSBEOCGDFLAU'
         @ 20,0 CLEA
         WAIT [NOT ONE OF THE OPTIONS. PRESS ANY KEY TO CONTINUE.]
         @ 20,0 CLEA
         DO EDITMENU
         LOOP
      CASE ANSWER = 'X'
         CANC           && programmer's bail out
      CASE ANSWER = 'Q'
*
         IF DELS
            @ 20,0 CLEA
            @ 21,0 SAY [SOME RECORDS HAVE BEEN DELETED FROM THIS FILE.]
            @ 23,0 SAY [DO YOU WISH TO REMOVE THEM PERMANENTLY (Y/N)?  ] GET DELS
            READ
*
            DO CASE
               CASE DELS .AND. [secondary database]$DBFILE
                  @ 21,0 CLEA
                  @ 21,0 SAY [DO YOU WISH TO DELETE CORRESPONDING DATA IN THE primary
                    FILE (Y/N)?  ] GET DELS
                  READ
*
                  IF DELS
                     SELE 1
                     SET RELA TO key field INTO B
                     LOCA FOR DELETED()
*
```

Listing 5-59 (cont.)

```
                    DO WHIL .NOT. EOF()
                       SELE 2
                       DELE
                       SELE 1
                       CONT
                    ENDD
*
                    SELE 2
                    PACK
                 ENDI
*
                 SELE 1
                 PACK
              CASE DELS
                 PACK
        ENDC
*
     ENDI
*
     RETU
  CASE ANSWER = 'K'
     DELE
     DELS = .T.
     LOOP
  CASE ANSWER = 'R'
     RECA
     LOOP
  CASE ANSWER = 'S'
     SKIP
     DO &GETTER
     CLEA GETS
     LOOP
  CASE ANSWER = 'B'
     SKIP -1
     DO &GETTER
     CLEA GETS
     LOOP
  CASE ANSWER = 'E'
     @ 20,0 CLEA
     @ 22,0 SAY "Press CTRL-W to save edit, ESC to exit"
     DO &GETTER
     READ
     DO EDITMENU
     LOOP
  CASE ANSWER = 'O'
```

Listing 5-59 (cont.)

```
      COPY NEXT 1 TO TANK
      APPE FROM TANK
      DO &GETTER
      CLEA GETS
      LOOP
   CASE ANSWER = 'C'
      SET ORDER TO 0
      CONT
      DO &GETTER
      CLEA GETS
      SET ORDER TO 1
      LOOP
   CASE ANSWER = 'G'
      ACCE "Record Number -> " TO RECNUM
      GOTO VAL(RECNUM)
      DO &GETTER
      CLEA GETS
      @ 24,0 SAY SPACE(40)
      LOOP
   CASE ANSWER = 'D'
      @ 20,0 CLEA
      ACCE "Display What -> " TO DISPLAYWHAT
*
      IF LEN(TRIM(DISPLAYWHAT)) = 0
         @ 20,0 CLEA
         DO EDITMENU
         LOOP
      ENDI
*
      TRUTH = .T.
      @ 21,0 CLEA
      ACCE "Display for -> " TO DISPLAYFOR
      READ
*
      IF LEN(TRIM(DISPLAYFOR)) # 0
         SET FILT TO &DISPLAYFOR
         DISPLAYFOR = 'FOR' + DISPLAYFOR
      ENDI
*
      @ 21,0 CLEA
      @ 21,0 SAY [DO YOU WANT THIS PRINTED (Y/N)?  ] GET TRUTH
      READ
*
      IF TRUTH
         TOPRINT = 'TO PRINT'
```

Listing 5–59 (cont.)

```
            EJECT
         ELSE
            TOPRINT = []
            CLEA
         ENDI
*
         DISP &DISPLAYWHAT &DISPLAYFOR &TOPRINT
*
         IF TRUTH
            EJECT
         ENDI
*
         CLEA
         DO &FRAMER
         DO &GETTER
         CLEA GETS
*
         @ 21,0 CLEA
         SET FILT TO
         DO EDITMENU
         LOOP
      CASE ANSWER = 'F'
         @ 20,0 CLEAR
         ACCE "Find &KEYFIELD  " TO TOFIND
         SEEK TOFIND
*
         IF .NOT. FOUND()
           @ 24,50 SAY "Record Number ->  END  "
           @ 0,0 SAY "I can't FIND that entry. Perhaps you should LOCATE it."
           CALL DELAY WITH CHR(1)
         ENDI
*
         DO &GETTER
         CLEA GETS
         DO EDITMENU
         LOOP
      CASE ANSWER = 'L'
         SET ORDER TO 0
         @ 20,0 CLEA
         ACCE "Locate what? -> " TO LOCATEWHAT
         ACCE "Locate where? -> " TO LOCATEWHERE
         LOCA FOR "&LOCATEWHAT"$&LOCATEWHERE
         SET ORDER TO 1
         DO &GETTER
         CLEA GETS
```

Listing 5–59 (cont.)

```
         DO EDITMENU
         LOOP
      CASE ANSWER = 'A'

COPY STRUC TO TANK
         SELE 6
         USE TANK
         @ 20,0 CLEA
         @ 22,0 SAY "Press CTRL-W to save information, ESC to exit"
*
         IF [primary database]$DBFILE
            SELE 2
            USE secondary database INDE index file list
            COPY STRUC TO TANK2
            SELE 7
            USE TANK2
            TRUTH = .T.
            GETTER = [edited primary GETTER file]
*
            DO WHIL .T.
               SELE 6
               APPE BLAN
*
               DO WHIL .T.
                  DO primary GETTER file
                  CLEA GETS
                  @ 5,7 GET key field
                  READ
*
                  IF LEN(TRIM(key field)) = 0
                     EXIT
                  ENDI
*
                  SELE 1
                  SEEK  F->key field
*
                  IF FOUND()
                     DO primary GETTER file
                     CLEA GETS
                     @ 20,0 CLEA
                     @ 20,0 SAY [SORRY, WE'VE ALREADY GOT ONE OF THOSE.]
                     CALL DELAY WITH CHR(1)
                     @ 20,0 CLEA
                     @ 22,0 SAY "Press CTRL-W to save information, ESC to exit"
```

Listing 5–59 (cont.)

```
            ELSE
               SELE F
               EXIT
            ENDI
*
            SELE F
         ENDD
*
         IF LEN(TRIM(key field)) = 0
            DELE
            EXIT
         ENDI
*
         DO &GETTER
         READ
         @ 20,0 CLEA
         @ 22,0 SAY [ADD A NEW RECORD TO secondary database (Y/N)?  ] GET TRUTH
         READ
*
         IF TRUTH
            SELE 7
            CLEA
            APPE BLANK
            REPL key field WITH F->key field, other field WITH
            F->other field, etc.
            DO secondary SAY file
            DO secondary GETTER file
            @ 20,0 CLEA
            @ 22,0 SAY [Press CTRL-W to save information, ESC to exit]
            READ
            SELE 6
            CLEA
            DO primary SAY file
         ENDI
*
         @ 20,0 CLEA
         @ 22,0 SAY [Press CTRL-W to save information, ESC to exit]
      ENDD
*
      SELE 7
      USE
      SELE 6
      USE
      SELE 2
      APPE FROM TANK2
```

Listing 5-59 (cont.)

```
            ERAS TANK2.DBF
            GETTER = [primary GETTER file]
         ELSE * DBFILE # primary database
            REPEATER = FIELD(1)
*
            DO WHIL .T.
               APPE BLANK
               DO &GETTER
               READ
*
               IF LEN(TRIM(&REPEATER)) = 0
                  DELE
                  EXIT
               ENDI
*
            ENDD
*
         ENDI
*
         USE
         SELE 6
         USE
         SELE 1
         SET DELE ON
         APPE FROM TANK
         SET DELE OFF
         DO &GETTER
         CLEA GETS
         DO EDITMENU
         ERAS TANK.DBF
      CASE ANSWER = 'U'
         @ 20,0 CLEA
         ACCE [Replace What Field?  ] TO REPLACER
*
         IF LEN(TRIM(REPLACER)) = 0
            @ 20,0 CLEA
            DO EDITMENU
            LOOP
         ENDI
*
         ACCE [Replace With  ] TO REPLACEWITH
*
         IF LEN(TRIM(REPLACEWITH)) = 0
            @ 20,0 CLEA
            DO EDITMENU
```

Listing 5–59 (cont.)

```
            LOOP
         ENDI
*
         ACCE "CONDITION  " TO CONDITION
*
         IF LEN(TRIM(CONDITION)) # 0
            LOCA FOR &CONDITION
*
            IF .NOT. FOUND()
               @ 20,0 CLEA
               WAIT "NOTHING MATCHES THAT CONDITION. PRESS ANY KEY TO CONTINUE..."
               @ 20,0 CLEA
               DO EDITMENU
               LOOP
            ELSE
               SET FILT TO &CONDITION
            ENDI
*
            REPL &REPLACER WITH &REPLACEWITH

         ENDI
*
         @ 20,0 CLEA
         DO EDITMENU
   ENDC
*
ENDD
*
** END OF EDIT.PRG
```

All of these kernels have been explained in other parts of the book. The only thing not shown here is the EDITMENU file that is often called in the code. I place this file in a PROCedure file, because it is called often during a work session. The EDITMENU code is:

Listing 5–60

```
PROC EDITMENU
@ 20,0 TO 23,79 DOUBLE
@ 21,1 SAY [  E -> EDIT  B -> BACK  S -> SKIP  G -> GOTO  K -> KILL  R -> RSTR  Q -
> QUIT]
@ 22,1 SAY [  F -> FIND  L -> LOCA  C -> CONT  D -> DISP  O -> COPY  A -> ADD   U -
> UPDA]
*
```

SUMMARY

This chapter concludes Part 1 of the book, which has concerned kernels of code that perform specific tasks in several different environments. The kernels developed here and the ones shown in Chapter 3 will find repeated use in the listings given in the rest of the book. Chapter 6 begins to demonstrate how kernels can be linked to form completed applications.

P A R T

2

The Systems

The remaining chapters in this book contain actual applications that were written for different environments using dBASE III PLUS. Here are some facts you should know before you begin copying code:

No database structures are given in the code.

Key fields are described.

Index files are described.

REPORT and LABEL FORM files are not described.

The code works as listed and is designed to be generic.

Modifications are encouraged.

The reasons for these decisions might not be obvious. I don't provide database structures because I've explained how databases should be designed in Part 1, Chapter 4 of this book and want you to design your own databases. You know far better than I what exact fields and information you'll need. I can provide you with code that will help you manage those databases, but that's about it.

I describe key fields because they are necessary to the code. I tell you what you should INDEX or SORT on, not the name of the field. Again, that is your decision. All I can tell you is the type of information that should go into that field. A similar logic follows for NDX files.

REPORT and LABEL FORM files are not described, except where they link into the code. You have a better idea than I of what you want LABELed and REPORTed, so you can design the files. As long as your FORM files work properly, you can drop them into the code where indicated and things will work beautifully.

The code in the following chapters works as written. But it is also generic. Like the white and black cans of vegetables you get at the grocery, the code in the following chapters looks and works like real dBASE III PLUS code. There is good reason for that—it *is* real dBASE III PLUS code. But designing something that will fit every application means it fits none of them perfectly. The code listed will probably provide you with 85 to 90 percent of your application. You'll get

100 percent of your application if you're not too choosy. But modifications are encouraged. I say you'll get 85 to 90 percent because there are aspects like screen names, filenames, field names, GETTER and SAYER files, and so on, that you'll need to fill in. You can even study what I've done and improve upon it to make code highly specific to your application.

CHAPTER

6

INVENTORY SYSTEM

The inventory system in this chapter is designed to handle several types of inventory needs. It can also be used to handle inventory from several locations in a master file while it keeps information on the separate locations in several location-specific files.

WHAT IS AN INVENTORY SYSTEM?

Inventory systems have one and only one function in the world: They tell you where you put it.

You may want an inventory system that tells you that information in a variety of ways. You may want an inventory system that tells you where you put it at several times during the trafficking process. None of that is really as important as the overriding function of an inventory system. An inventory system should first and foremost answer "Where is it?"

The system in this chapter shows a method for keeping track of things on the shelf, in process, and during sales. These are the three parts of inventory control that are common to all inventory systems. As mentioned in the introduction to Part 2, no report forms are described. You can easily design these FRM files to report the specific information of interest.

DESIGNING AN INVENTORY SYSTEM

The most important part of the inventory system is the initial design. Good inventory management is essential to any business that exists on item sales. Imagine going to Sears for something and being told, "Gee, I think we have one of those . . . somewhere." Chances are it would be the last time Sears saw your business.

As with any database management system, you must first decide what data is important. A suggestion is to recognize inventory as a three-part system. First you need to be up to date on the physical inventory. This means you need a database that does nothing but provide information on how many items are left on the shelf and in what warehouse those items can be found.

Second, you want to know where items are during the shipping and ordering process. There are few situations more infuriating to a client than hearing, "Yeah, well, I'm pretty sure we shipped that yesterday, but it may be on today's truck." When a customer calls up wanting to know where a purchase is, you should be able to tell him or her with fair accuracy. That is one of Federal Express's major advertising points. That company's COSMOS system can tell you exactly where your package is and when you can expect to get it.

Third, you want to poll your inventory to determine what you should re-stock, what's moving, what's dead, what should go on sale, and so on.

How do these factors come into play? Remember the earlier advice to design your system around the data you want to work with? Your first concern is the inventory itself. You want to create a database that holds at least the following information:

```
Item number
Item name
Item location (warehouse, if necessary)
Stock number (if different from item number)
Inventory
Reorder value
Distributor id
Distributor name
Distributor address
Distributor city
Distributor state
Distributor zip
Contact name (distributor's sales person)
Contact's phone number
```

Note that this isn't necessarily all the information you need in the database, but it provides what many people consider the minimum information for such a system.

The next consideration is the order tracking database. Obviously, that will contain data on what was ordered, who ordered it, and where the item(s) are in the delivery process. A minimum amount of information for that might be:

```
Item number
Stock number (if different from item number)
Item name
When ordered
```

```
When shipped
Item's original location (warehouse, if necessary)
Item's last verified location
Who verified last location
When last location verified
Customer id
Customer name
Customer address
Customer city
Customer state
Customer zip
Contact name
Contact's phone number
Number purchased
Number shipped
Number back ordered
Customer's number in back order priority
```

Again, this is what many would consider mandatory information. You should edit it to suit your needs.

The last part, reporting on your inventory, isn't really something you need a database for. Careful planning of the two database structures identified so far can yield incredible amounts of information. You can see when items move, when items are stagnant, seasonal fluxes, how quickly items go through the process, and so on. The system described here does make use of a historical database. This file merely serves to keep the two databases in main usage at a workable size.

This example should provide you with a launching point for your own database designs. Remember that databases with too many fields (more than 20) can be cumbersome. Most people would rather deal with 2,000 tiny lizards than one two-ton lizard. dBASE III PLUS is the same way, so design accordingly.

USING THE KERNELS TO BUILD THE SYSTEM

Now we come to the fun part—for me—of the book. I get to tell you what kernels from earlier parts of the book you might use to design your basic editing system. Next, we create some new features specifically for the application. Last, we'll put it all together.

What basic editing features are of interest for an inventory system? Most obviously, we'll need a menu option to Quit from the editor back to the main menu system. We want to Kill (DELETE) and Recall records that are killed by mistake. Our general-purpose record pointer movement functions, Skip, Back, and Go To, are also necessary. More selective record pointer positioning commands are also necessary for selective and quick searches. Thus, we include Locate, Continue, and Find. We'll always need to Edit the records. We'll be duplicating records based on item name, number, distributor data, and other such field types, so Copy is a nice option to include. Not everything we want to know about our databases will be coded into report forms, so we include a Display option. The DBMS would be worthless unless data could be added to it, so include an Add option.

Anything else? Oh yes. Remember that this is an inventory management system we're talking about. We need a Track option to help us monitor inventory throughout the ordering process.

Before showing you the modifications to the kernels, I'll give you some warnings. We won't PACK the database every time we Quit the editor. The reason has to do with the nature of inventory systems. There are times we want to DELETE records because we're out of stock, don't want to reorder, are locked at a certain price, and so on. None of those reasons are good enough to permanently remove the record from the database. We'll use a separate PACKing routine to handle that situation. Tied directly into this is the lack of a DELS flag in the Kill kernel. Again, we don't want to be asked if we want to permanently remove records from the database; thus, there is no need for DELS. We wrote our kernels in Part 1 of the book. The modifications to them are shown next.

MODIFYING THE SYSTEM

In case you haven't noticed, things are moving fairly quickly now. And well they should. Remember, most of the work has been done in the previous chapters. Now we make use of the tools we've been developing all along.

Earlier we listed the kernels necessary for an inventory DBMS editor. The editor is the core of any application, and this is no exception. What modifications are necessary to the kernels? Consider Listing 6–1.

Listing 6–1

```
* EDIT.PRG
* CALLS EDITMENU FROM PROCEDURE FILE
*
DO EDITMENU
ANSWER = 'X'
*
DO WHIL .T.
   @ 0,0 SAY SPACE(80)
   @  2,60 SAY IIF(DELETED(),"DELETED",SPACE(7))
   @ 23,34 SAY "select ->      "
   @ 23,44 GET ANSWER
   READ
   ANSWER = UPPER(ANSWER)
*
   DO CASE
      CASE ANSWER = 'X'
         CANC            && programmer's bailout
```

Listing 6-1 (cont.)

```
CASE ANSWER = 'Q'
   RETU
CASE ANSWER = 'K'
   DELE
   LOOP
CASE ANSWER = 'R'
   RECA
   LOOP
CASE ANSWER = 'S'
   SKIP
   DO &GETTER
   CLEA GETS
   LOOP
CASE ANSWER = 'B'
   SKIP -1
   DO &GETTER
   CLEA GETS
   LOOP
CASE ANSWER = 'E'
   @ 20,0 CLEA
   @ 22,0 SAY "Press CTRL-W to save edits,"+;
              " CTRL-Q to quit without saving edits"
   DO &GETTER
   READ
   DO EDITMENU
   LOOP
CASE ANSWER = 'O'
   COPY NEXT 1 TO TANK
   APPE FROM TANK
   LOOP
CASE ANSWER = 'C'
   SET ORDER TO
   CONT
   SET ORDER TO 1
   DO &GETTER
   CLEA GETS
   LOOP
CASE ANSWER = 'G'
   ACCE "Record Number -> " TO RECNUM
   GOTO VAL(RECNUM)
   DO &GETTER
   CLEA GETS
   @ 24,0 SAY SPACE(40)
   LOOP
CASE ANSWER = 'D'
```

Listing 6–1 (cont.)

```
        @ 20,0 CLEA
        ACCE "Display What -> " TO DISPLAYWHAT
*
        IF LEN(TRIM(DISPLAYWHAT)) = 0
           @ 20,0 CLEA
           DO EDITMENU
           LOOP
        ENDI
*
        TRUTH = .T.
        @ 21,0 CLEA
        ACCE "Display for -> " TO DISPLAYFOR
        READ
*
        IF LEN(TRIM(DISPLAYFOR)) # 0
           SET FILT TO &DISPLAYFOR
           DISPLAYFOR = 'FOR' + DISPLAYFOR
        ENDI
*
        @ 21,0 CLEA
        @ 21,0 SAY [DO YOU WANT THIS PRINTED (Y/N)?  ] GET TRUTH
        READ
*
        IF TRUTH
           TOPRINT = 'TO PRINT'
           EJECT
        ELSE
           TOPRINT = []
           CLEA
        ENDI
*
        DISP &DISPLAYWHAT &DISPLAYFOR &TOPRINT
*
        IF TRUTH
           EJECT
        ENDI
*
        CLEA
        DO &FRAMER
        DO &GETTER
        CLEA GETS
*
        @ 20,0 CLEA
        SET FILT TO
        DO EDITMENU
```

Listing 6–1 (cont.)

```
         LOOP
      CASE ANSWER = 'F'
         @ 20,0 CLEAR
*
         DO CASE
            CASE [inventory database name]$UPPE(DBF())
               ACCE "Find 1-key field a, 2-key field b, 3-key field c,"+;
               "4-key field d, 5-key field e, 6-key field f"+;
               "or 7-key field g? -> " TO TOFIND
               SET ORDE TO VAL(TOFIND)
               @ 20,0 CLEA
               ACCE "Find > " TO TOFIND
            CASE [order database name]$UPPE(DBF())
               ACCE "Find 1-key field a, 2-key field b, 3-key field c,"+;
               "4-key field d, 5-key field e, 6-key field f"+;
               "or 7-key field g? -> " TO TOFIND
               SET ORDE TO VAL(TOFIND)
               @ 20,0 CLEA
               ACCE "Find > " TO TOFIND
           OTHE
              INDEXKEY = FIELD(1)
              ACCE "Find &INDEXKEY > " TO TOFIND
         ENDCASE
*
         SEEK TOFIND
*
         IF .NOT. FOUND()
           @ 24,50 SAY "Record Number ->  END  "
           @ 0,0 SAY "I can't FIND that entry. Perhaps you should LOCATE it."
           DO POOL
         ENDI
*
         DO &GETTER
         CLEA GETS
         DO EDITMENU
         LOOP
      CASE ANSWER = 'L'
         SET ORDER TO 0
         @ 20,0 CLEA
         ACCE "Locate what? -> " TO LOCATEWHAT
         ACCE "Locate where? -> " TO LOCATEWHERE
         LOCA FOR "&LOCATEWHAT"$&LOCATEWHERE
         SET ORDER TO 1
         DO &GETTER
         CLEA GETS
```

Listing 6–1 (cont.)

```
         DO EDITMENU
         LOOP
      CASE ANSWER = 'A'
         COPY STRUC TO TANK
         SELE 2
         USE TANK
         @ 20,0 CLEA
         @ 22,0 SAY "Press CTRL-W to save information, CTRL-Q to exit"
         REPEATER = FIELD(1)
*
         DO WHIL .T.
            APPE BLAN
            DO &GETTER
            READ
*
            IF [inventory database name]$UPPE(DBF())
*
               IF LEN(TRIM(&REPEATER)) = 0 .AND. LEN(TRIM(secondary key field)) = 0
                  DELE
                  EXIT
               ENDI
*
               TRUTH = .F.
               SELE 1
               SEEK B->key field
*
               DO WHIL FOUN()
                  TRUTH = .T.
                  KEYFIELD = found key field value
                  @ 20,0 CLEA
                  WAIT [SORRY, WE'VE GOT ONE OF THOSE. PRESS ANY KEY TO CONTINUE...]
                  @ x,y GET KEYFIELD
                  READ
                  SEEK KEYFIELD
               ENDD
*
               SELE 2
               REPL key field  WITH IIF(TRUTH, KEYFIELD, key field)
            ELSE
*
               IF LEN(TRIM(&REPEATER)) = 0
                  DELE
                  EXIT
               ENDI
*
```

Listing 6-1 (cont.)

```
            ENDI * DBFILE = inventory database
*
         ENDD
*
         USE
         SELE 1
         SET DELE ON
         APPE FROM TANK
         SET DELE OFF
         DO &GETTER
         CLEA GETS
         DO EDITMENU
         ERAS TANK.DBF
      CASE ANSWER = 'T'
*
         IF order database name $UPPE(DBF(0))
            @ 0,0 SAY "That isn't one of the options. Try again"
            DO POOL
            LOOP
         ELSE
            DO TRACK
         ENDI
*
      OTHE
         @ 0,0 SAY "That isn't one of the options. Try again"
         DO POOL
   ENDC
*
ENDD
*
** END OF EDIT.PRG
```

The modifications aren't major and the code itself is easily explained. The X option is the programmer's bailout. The Q option simply returns the user to the previous menu. The database is not PACKed at this Quit option. That is handled by a different menu system. Because there is no PACKing, there is no DELS flag under the Kill option. The S and B options are the standard record pointer movement options. E is a standard Edit option. Likewise for O, which cOpies a record in the database. The Continue option shuts off any active NDX files with the SET ORDE TO command before it CONTINUEs through the database. G is also our standard Go To option. The Display module is as shown and explained earlier.

This brings us to the Find kernel. This kernel is recoded to handle several NDX files. The code here shows seven possible NDX files, dBASE III PLUS's maximum allowed per active DBF file. The module then SETs the NDX file ORDER to the user's NDX file preference. The two databases of major concern are the inventory and order databases, but a DO CASE . . . OTHE . . . ENDCASE block is used in case the system grows.

The Locate kernel returns to our previously described logic. The next item of interest is recoding the Add kernel. We want to make sure items added to the inventory only create new records if no previous record exists for the item. This is an example of input error checking, described in Chapter 5. We use the method of checking a key field against a historical database. This code uses the inventory database in work area 1 to provide a historical profile of all items in the inventory. Also note that valid input to the inventory database is determined by checking two data fields, not one, which was the method shown earlier. Checking over two data fields gives the user the option of entering information based on name and an as-yet-undetermined item number.

The last item of interest is the Track option. This is a singularly important part of an inventory system and, as shown, shifts III PLUS's attention to a separate file. That file is shown later in this chapter.

ORDER TRACKING

The part of the inventory system we'll study here is the Tracking program. This option is listed as part of the EDITOR module shown earlier.

Listing 6–2

```
* TRACK.PRG
* CALLED FROM EDIT.PRG
*
TRUTH = .T.
*
DO WHIL .T.
   SELE 1
*
   DO CASE
      CASE location field or other identifier = 'tag based on data of interest'
         SELE 2
         USE inventory database INDE NDX file keyed on interest
*        this could also be a SET FILTER TO command, depending on your needs
      CASE location field or other identifier = 'tag based on data of interest'
         SELE 2
         USE inventory database INDE NDX file keyed on interest
*        this could also be a SET FILTER TO command, depending on your needs
*     CASE more cases could follow, depending on need
   ENDC
*
   @ 20,0 TO 23,79 DOUBLE
   @ 21,1 SAY [  S -> Start Track  A -> Add To Track  E -> End Track     ]
   @ 22,1 SAY [  L -> List Track  H -> Show History  Q -> Quit          ]
```

Listing 6–2 (cont.)

```
   @ 23,34 SAY "select ->       "
   @ 23,44 GET ANSWER PICT '!'
   READ
*
   DO CASE
      CASE ANSWER = 'Q'
         @ 20,0 CLEA
         DO EDITMENU
         SELE 2
         USE
         SELE 1
         RETU
      CASE ANSWER = 'S'
         IDNUM = variable type and form based on corresponding database field
         SELE 2
         @ 21,0 CLEA
*
         DO WHIL .T.
            @ 21,0 SAY 'ITEM ORDERED -> ' GET IDNUM PICT 'picture based on data field'
            READ
            SEEK IDNUM
*
            IF FOUND()
               EXIT
            ENDI
*
            WAIT [WE DON'T HAVE ANY OF THOSE. 'RETURN']+;
                 [TO QUIT, ANY OTHER KEY TO CONTINUE...] TO AGAIN
*
            IF LEN(TRIM(AGAIN)) = 0
               EXIT
            ENDI
*
         ENDD
*
         IF .NOT. FOUN()
            @ 20,0 CLEA
            LOOP
         ENDI
*
         SELE 1
         APPE BLAN
         REPL necessary fields in order database with information from inventory database
*             several of the fields in the order database will be automatically
*             filled when you find the ordered item and begin the tracking process
```

Listing 6-2 (cont.)

```
        DO order getter file
        READ
     CASE ANSWER = 'A'
        @ 21,0 CLEA
        ACCE 'TRACKING FOR CUSTOMER -> ' TO CUSTID
&& this is a customer identification tag
        SET FILT TO customer identification field = CUSTID
        GOTO BOTT
        COPY TO TANK
        APPE FROM TANK
        ERAS TANK.DBF
        REPL date field with DATE(), time field with TIME()
        DO order say file
        DO edited order get file
        READ
     CASE ANSWER = 'E'
        @ 21,0 CLEA
        ACCE 'TRACKING FOR CUSTOMER -> ' TO CUSTID
&& this is a customer identification tag
        SET FILT TO customer identification field = CUSTID
        SET DEVI TO PRINT
        GOTO TOP
*
        DO WHILE .NOT. EOF()
           DO order format file && this is a combination SAY and GET file for printing purpose
           SKIP
        ENDD
*
        @ 21,0 CLEA
        @ 21,0 SAY [ARE WE CLOSING THIS ORDER TRACK TODAY? (Y/N) -> ] GET TRUTH
        READ
*
        IF TRUTH
           SKIP -1
           COPY NEXT 1 TO TANK
           APPE FROM TANK
           ERAS TANK.DBF
           SET DEVI TO SCRE
           DO order say file
           REPL necessary fields with information to close out this order track
           DO order get file
           READ
           SET DEVI TO PRIN
           DO order format file from above
           SET DEVI TO SCRE
```

Listing 6–2 (cont.)

```
        ENDI
*
        @ 21,0 CLEA
        @ 21,0 SAY 'COPY THIS ORDER TRACK TO historical DATABASE? (Y/N) -> ';
              GET TRUTH
        READ
*
        IF TRUTH
           SELE 1
           FILENAME = DBF()
           USE
           SELE 3
           DO GETFILE
           APPE FROM &FILENAME FOR CUSTID = filter condition
           USE
           SELE 1
           SET VIEW TO &FILENAME
        ENDI
*
     CASE ANSWER = 'L'
        @ 21,0 CLEA
        ACCE 'TRACKING FOR CUSTOMER -> ' TO CUSTID
&& this is a customer identification tag
        SET FILT TO customer identification field = CUSTID
        @ 22,0 SAY 'DO YOU WANT THIS PRINTED (Y/N)? -> ' GET TRUTH
        TOPRINT = IIF(TRUTH,'TO PRINT',[])
        DISP ALL field list &TOPRINT
*
        COMMAND = IIF(TRUTH,'EJEC',[])
        &COMMAND
        WAIT
        SET FILT TO
        CLEA
        DO order say file
        DO order get file
        CLEA GETS
     CASE ANSWER = 'H'
        SELE 3
        DO GETFILE
        CLEA
        ACCE 'SHOW RECORDS FOR indicative field name -> ' TO CUSTID
*
&&      The CUSTID memory variable above is used to create a condition filter
&&      The "indicative field name" is whatever field you'll scan over
&&      when looking for historical records
```

Listing 6–2 (cont.)

```
*
        SET FILT TO indicative field = CUSTID
        @ 21,0 CLEA
        ACCE "Do you want a P(rintout) or S(creen listing)? (P/S) -> " TO YORN
*
        IF UPPER(YORN) = "P"
           SET CONS OFF
           SET PRIN ON
           ?CHR[this line can contain control codes for different printing modes]
           REPO FORM report form file 1 TO PRINT
           ?CHR[this line can contain control codes to return to normal print mode]
           SET PRIN OFF
           SET CONS ON
        ELSE
           CLEA
           REPO FORM report form file 2 PLAIN
           WAIT
           CLEA
           DO order say file
           DO order get file
           CLEA GETS
        ENDI
*
**THE TWO REPORT FORMS CAN BE IDENTICAL. I SHOW TWO DIFFERENT REPORT FORM FILES
**BECAUSE YOU MAY WANT TO DESIGN ONE WIDE CARRIAGE FORM FOR THE PRINTER AND ANOTHER,
**80-CHARACTER WIDE REPORT FOR SCREEN LISTINGS.
*
   ENDCASE
*
ENDD
*
* END OF TRACK.PRG
```

The code does one task; it tells the user where an inventory item is in the order process. Basically, the order process involves following an item from the point of purchase to the point of delivery. In manufacturing/inventory systems this might also entail tracking the item during production. For those with such a need, this code can be used for production tracking.

We start by creating a local variable, TRUTH. This variable is declared in several routines, but is local to each. The entire TRACK module is contained in a DO WHILE . . . ENDDO block. Each time we pass through the block we return to work area 1 and determine which inventory database NDX files should be prioritized. The same need can be met with a SET FILTER TO condition command. The reason is simple: the order database may be quite large. We don't want to tax dBASE III PLUS by having it juggle two large files that are all too randomly ordered. We alleviate that concern by having it load into the PC's buffers only the necessary parts of the files.

The order database is, of course, a listing of several orders. However, each order may comprise several records. Each separate record contains information on where the order is in the process. The tracking process begins when the order is accepted. Option S creates a new record in the order database; the record contains information on what was purchased and by whom. The next option is Add. Every time new information on the item is entered the Add option is used. As the item moves through the order process, records are added. Depending on the nature of your inventory, you may have a starting and ending order track record or several hundred (again, consider Federal Express's COSMOS system). Note that the Add option is similar to the Copy kernel shown earlier—with two exceptions. I've included space to date and time stamp each record, something also mentioned in the next paragraph. Why date and time stamp each record? It provides better tracking, of course.

After starting and adding to the TRACK module, we might want to end the track. We determine who we're tracking for and then print out all relevant records. Each record in the tracking process is printed out separately, and it is usually worth including a DATE() and TIME() stamp on the printouts. The next part of the code deals with whether the track is being closed. Doing so causes the TRACK module to first create a last record for this track. Next, it asks if the track is to be copied to a historical database. The historical database holds all past completed tracks.

The List option merely provides a quick means of seeing where things are in the inventory order system. I code around a DISPLAY command. It is also possible to code around a BROWSE command. I suggest not doing so, because the user can accidentally edit a BROWSEd record or records. The editing capability may be something you need, however, and BROWSE would be the command of choice. Also, BROWSE can't be coded into a worthy printing option.

The last option, H, generates reports of past orders. I show two separate REPORT FORMS being used, but you can use a single report. Two different reports allow you to design one form to make use of a wide carriage printer, the other for screen use.

INVENTORY STATUS

Another valuable part of inventory systems is the ability to get reports based on inventory status. It's not worth much if you don't know what you have where, or can't find the information in ways that are useful. This module can actually be considered a reporting kernel, as the basic form will be repeated in other work sessions.

Listing 6–3

```
* INVENTORY STATUS REPORTER
*
```

Listing 6–3 (cont.)

```
SELE 1
USE inventory database INDE NDX file list
HEADER = SPACE(40)
TOPRINT = [PLAI]
*
DO WHILE .T.
   CLEAR
   @ 2, 0 TO 19,79 DOUBLE
   @ 3, 8 SAY [I N V E N T O R Y   S T A T U S   R E P O R T   G E N E R A T O R]
   @ 4,1 TO 4,78 DOUBLE
   @ 7,28 SAY IIF(TO PRINT = [TO PRIN],[1. List to Printer/screen],;
                            [1.  List to Screen/printer])
   @  8,28 SAY [2. Listing Method One]
   @  9,28 SAY [3. Listing Method Two]
   @ 10,28 SAY [4. Listing Method Three]
   @ 11,28 SAY [5. Listing Method Four]
   @ 12,28 SAY [6. Listing Method Five]
   @ 13,28 SAY [7. Listing Method Six]
   @ 14,28 SAY [8. Listing Method Seven]
   @ 15,28 SAY [9. Set Report Criteria]
   @ 17, 28 SAY '0. EXIT'
   @ 21, 0 SAY "PRESENT REPORT CRITERIA IS: " + HEADER
   ANSWER = 0
   @ 19,33 SAY " select ->      "
   @ 19,44 GET ANSWER PICT "9" RANG 0,9
   READ
*
** YOU CAN INCLUDE MORE OPTIONS BY HAVING A CHARACTER INPUT, ONE OF WHICH LOADS IN
** ANOTHER SCREEN OF OPTIONS
*
** THE FOLLOWING DO CASE...ENDCASE BLOCK HANDLES THREE MENU OPTIONS,
** LIST TO AND SET REPORT CRITERIA FOR THE INVENTORY REPORTS
*
   DO CASE
      CASE ANSWER = 0
         SET FILT TO
         SET ORDE TO 1
         RETU
      CASE ANSWER = 1
*
         IF TO PRINT = [TO PRIN]
            TOPRINT = [PLAI]
         ELSE
            TOPRINT = [TO PRIN]
         ENDI
```

Listing 6–3 (cont.)

```
*
      CASE ANSWER = 9
         CLEA
         DO inventory say file
         DO inventory get file
         CLEA GETS
         LIMITFIELD = SPACE(10)
         LIMITVALUE = SPACE(60)
         LIMITEQUAL = .T.
         @ 20,0
         @ 21,0 SAY "What is the LIMITING field? -> " GET LIMITFIELD
         @ 22,0 SAY "What is the LIMITING value? -> " GET LIMITVALUE
         @ 23,0 SAY "Should LIMITING field = LIMITING value? (Y/N) -> ";
                GET LIMITEQUAL PICT "Y"
         READ
         LIMITFIELD = TRIM(LIMITFIELD)
         LIMITVALUE = TRIM(LIMITVALUE)
*
         IF LEN(LIMITFIELD) = 0
            SET FILT TO
            HEADER = SPACE(40)
            LOOP
         ENDI
*
         IF LEN(LIMITVALUE) = 0
*
            IF LIMITEQUAL
               SET FILT TO LEN(TRIM(&LIMITFIELD)) = 0
               HEADER = LIMITFIELD+" = "+LIMITVALUE
            ELSE
               SET FILT TO LEN(TRIM(&LIMITFIELD)) <> 0
               HEADER = LIMITFIELD+" <> "+LIMITVALUE
            ENDIF
*
         ELSE
*
            IF LIMITEQUAL
               SET FILT TO &LIMITFIELD = "&LIMITVALUE"
               HEADER = LIMITFIELD+" = "+LIMITVALUE
            ELSE
               SET FILT TO &LIMITFIELD <> "&LIMITVALUE"
               HEADER = LIMITFIELD+" <> "+LIMITVALUE
            ENDIF
*
         ENDI
```

Listing 6–3 (cont.)

```
*
        LOOP
   ENDC
*
   IF PRINTERON
      SET CONS OFF
   ENDI
*
&& The following DO CASE...ENDCASE block handles report generation
*
   DO CASE
      CASE ANSWER = 2
         SET ORDER TO 1
         REPO FORM file 1 HEAD "&HEADER" &TOPRINT
      CASE ANSWER = 3
         SET ORDER TO 2
         REPO FORM file 2 HEAD "&HEADER" &TOPRINT
      CASE ANSWER = 4
         SET ORDE TO 3
         REPO FORM file 3 HEAD "&HEADER" &TOPRINT
      CASE ANSWER = 5
         SET ORDER TO 4
         REPO FORM file 4 HEAD "&HEADER" &TOPRINT
      CASE ANSWER = 6
         SET ORDE TO 5
         REPO FORM file 5 HEAD "&HEADER" &TOPRINT
      CASE ANSWER = 7
         SET ORDE TO 6
         REPO FORM file 6 HEAD "&HEADER" &TOPRINT
      CASE ANSWER = 8
         SET ORDE TO 7
         REPO FORM file 7 HEAD "&HEADER" &TOPRINT
   ENDCASE
*
   SET CONS ON
*
ENDD
*
** EOF
```

Like much of my other code, this listing makes a great deal of use of dBASE III PLUS's macro abilities. It begins with two VARIABLES: HEADER and TOPRINT (TO PRINT). The working code is contained in a DO WHILE . . . LOOP . . . ENDDO block and makes use of the REPORT command's TO PRINT and PLAIN options.

The first menu line is an IIF() function that reports on the status of the TO PRINT flag. This flag doesn't tell III PLUS if the printer is physically on or attached to the system. It merely indicates the user's desired output destination—if something goes to the printer, the SAY LIST TO PRINTER/screen, else SAY LIST TO SCREEN/printer.

This code offers seven different report formats from the present menu. I emphasize that these are report formats. There are seven offered because each different report can be developed around each of the seven available NDX files that III PLUS allows for each database. But basing reports on NDX files is not the only means for specialized reporting that this menu system provides. Consider option 9, Set Report Criteria. This option lets the user custom design a filter for the system. Note that more CASEs can be added to the system, which is discussed later in this chapter.

The code is broken into two DO CASE . . . ENDCASE blocks. The reason is the IF . . . ENDIF block that separates the two DO CASE . . . ENDCASE blocks. We are handling two different functions with each DO CASE . . . ENDCASE block. The first block handles only the three housekeeping options, Quit, LIST TO device, and Set Report Criteria. These are screen-oriented options that don't require any actual reporting; hence, it isn't important whether we SET CONSOLE ON or OFF, provided the CONSOLE is always ON when these options are being used. Do note that the first DO CASE . . . ENDCASE block is designed around our concept of most-often-called functions before rarely called functions. This means Quit is called more often than setting a LIST device is called, which in turn is more often than setting a REPORT criterion.

Option 0 is a simple Quit option. We make sure any FILTERs are disengaged and the NDX file ORDER is SET back to 1 before RETURNing to the calling program. Option 1 is a toggle triggered by the PRINTERON flag. If the printer is on, then the toggle makes it .F. and builds one of our macro expressions, TOPRINT, with the value PLAI(n). If the printer is not on, then the toggle makes it .T. and gives the TOPRINT the value TO PRIN(t).

Option 9 is a spiffy little block that creates a filter condition and a HEADER for our REPORTS. We begin by CLEARing the screen and putting up the inventory SAY and GET files. No editing is allowed on this screen, however, so we CLEAR GETS. These screens are put up only to show the user what field names and data types are available to build the report criterion. The code at present only allows for equal and unequal options. Other code is shown later, in Listing 6–5. This code works by accepting values from the user, using the values in macro expressions, then creating a HEADER and FILTER based on the macros. This is handled in an IF . . . ENDIF block based on the passed value of LIMITVALUE. If there is no LIMITing VALUE we're only interested in whether or not the LIMITFIELD has data, else we're interested in whether the LIMITFIELD's data matches the LIMITVALUE's. Also note the bailout condition, which is based on no LIMITFIELD being entered.

This brings us to the PRINTERON toggle that either SETs the CONSOLE OFF for REPORTING TO the PRINTER or leaves the CONSOLE ON and REPORTs PLAIN to the screen. Note the responding SET CONSOLE ON command at the end of the following DO CASE . . . ENDCASE block. Each of the following CASEs has two commands. The first command SETs the ORDER of the NDX files to facilitate the REPORT format. Each REPORT is generated with a macro HEADER and TOPRINT variables.

Changes to this code use files not included in the dBASE III PLUS package, but which were mentioned in Chapter 5 and are useful to the system developer. Two that will be mentioned are Borland International's REFLEX program and Ashton-Tate's dBASE PROGRAMMER'S UTILITIES' SAVESCR.BIN file.

Taking the latter first, say we want to use several menu screens to handle several report formats. We can build those screens into a quick access system using the SAVESCR.BIN file. The beginning of our code is modified to:

Listing 6–4

```
* INVEREPO.PRG INVENTORY STATUS REPORTER
*
SELE 1
USE inventory database INDE NDX file list
HEADER = SPACE(40)
TOPRINT = [PLAI]
LOAD SAVESCR
SET CONS OFF
** SAY first menu screen
CALL SAVESCR WITH 'S1'
CLEA
** SAY second menu screen
CALL SAVESCR WITH 'S2'
CLEA
** SAY third menu screen
CALL SAVESCR WITH 'S3'
CLEA
** SAY fourth menu screen
CALL SAVESCR WITH 'S4'
CLEA
** SAY fifth menu screen
CALL SAVESCR WITH 'S5'
SET CONS ON
SAVESCREEN = 1
*
DO WHILE .T.
   CLEA
   CALL SAVESCR WITH 'R'+LTRIM(STR(SAVESCREEN))
   @ 7,28 SAY IIF(TO PRINT = [TO PRIN],[1. List to Printer/screen],;
                             [1.  List to Screen/printer])
   @ 21, 0 SAY "PRESENT REPORT CRITERION IS: " + HEADER
   ANSWER = '0'
   @ 19,33 SAY " select ->      "
   @ 19,44 GET ANSWER PICT "!"
```

Listing 6–4 (cont.)

```
   READ
*
** THE FOLLOWING DO CASE...ENDCASE BLOCK NOW HANDLES FOUR MENU OPTIONS, QUIT, SCREEN SAVE,
** LIST TO, AND SET REPORT CRITERIA FOR THE INVENTORY REPORTS
*
   DO CASE
      CASE ANSWER = '0'
         SET FILT TO
         SET ORDE TO 1
         RETU
      CASE ANSWER = 'N'
         SAVESCREEN = IIF(SAVESCREEN = 5, 1, SAVESCREEN + 1)
         LOOP
      CASE ANSWER = '1'
*
         IF TO PRINT = [TO PRINT]
            TOPRINT = [PLAI]
         ELSE
            TOPRINT = [TO PRIN]
         ENDI
*
      CASE ANSWER = '9'
         CLEA
         DO inventory say file
         DO inventory get file
         CLEA GETS
         LIMITFIELD = SPACE(10)
         LIMITVALUE = SPACE(60)
         LIMITEQUAL = .T.
         @ 21,0 SAY "What is the LIMITING field? -> " GET LIMITFIELD
         @ 22,0 SAY "What is the LIMITING value? -> " GET LIMITVALUE
         @ 23,0 SAY "Should LIMITING field = LIMITING value? (Y/N) -> ";
                GET LIMITEQUAL PICT "Y"
         READ
         LIMITFIELD = TRIM(LIMITFIELD)
         LIMITVALUE = TRIM(LIMITVALUE)
*
         IF LEN(LIMITFIELD) = 0
            SET FILT TO
            HEADER = SPACE(40)
            LOOP
         ENDI
*
         IF LEN(LIMITVALUE) = 0
*
```

Listing 6–4 (cont.)

```
            IF LIMITEQUAL
               SET FILT TO LEN(&LIMITFIELD) = 0
               HEADER = LIMITFIELD+" = "+LIMITVALUE
            ELSE
               SET FILT TO LEN(&LIMITFIELD) <> 0
               HEADER = LIMITFIELD+" <> "+LIMITVALUE
            ENDIF
*
         ELSE
*
            IF LIMITEQUAL
               SET FILT TO &LIMITFIELD = "&LIMITVALUE"
               HEADER = LIMITFIELD+" = "+LIMITVALUE
            ELSE
               SET FILT TO &LIMITFIELD <> "&LIMITVALUE"
               HEADER = LIMITFIELD+" <> "+LIMITVALUE
            ENDIF
*
         ENDI
*
         LOOP
   ENDC
*
   IF TO PRINT = [TO PRIN]
      SET CONS OFF
   ENDI
*
** THE FOLLOWING DO CASE...ENDCASE BLOCK HANDLES REPORT GENERATION
** AND CAN BE MODIFIED TO HANDLE SEVERAL MORE REPORTS
*
   DO CASE
      CASE ANSWER = '2'
         SET ORDE TO 1
         REPO FORM file 1 HEAD "&HEADER" &TOPRINT
      CASE ANSWER = '3'
         SET ORDE TO 2
         REPO FORM file 2 HEAD "&HEADER" &TOPRINT
      CASE ANSWER = '4'
         SET ORDE TO 3
         REPO FORM file 3 HEAD "&HEADER" &TOPRINT
      CASE ANSWER = '5'
         SET ORDE TO 4
         REPO FORM file 4 HEAD "&HEADER" &TOPRINT
      CASE ANSWER = '6'
         SET ORDE TO 5
```

Listing 6–4 (cont.)

```
         REPO FORM file 5 HEAD "&HEADER" &TOPRINT
      CASE ANSWER = '7'
         SET ORDE TO 6
         REPO FORM file 6 HEAD "&HEADER" &TOPRINT
      CASE ANSWER = '8'
         SET ORDE TO 7
         REPO FORM file 7 HEAD "&HEADER" &TOPRINT
   ENDCASE
*
   SET CONS ON
*
ENDD
*
** END OF INVEREPO.PRG
```

Each of the screens contains the lines normally running from screen position 2,0 to 19,79. In addition to the lines shown in Listing 6–3, they include the line:

```
@ 16,28 SAY [N. Next Screen]
```

The first DO CASE . . . ENDCASE block then gets another CASE. This new CASE argument handles the screens. Note that Listing 6–4 uses five screens, because five is SAVESCR's limit. Note that this code block still uses the criteria selection method shown in Listing 6–3. Also note that each CASE condition is set off in single quotes. Remember that we're working with character—not numeric—input in this revised code.

Another suggestion I've mentioned is to incorporate Borland International's REFLEX product in your system. REFLEX reads and writes dBASE III PLUS files easily and provides a dynamic graphics interface for your data. Per necessity, however, your system must have considerably more memory than 256K to run REFLEX alone. Again, this is a strong suggestion to expand to 640K and beyond. As an example of REFLEX's power and use, look at Figure 6–1.

Revising the criteria generator isn't a difficult procedure. The new code is:

Listing 6–5

```
         CLEA
         DO inventory say file
         DO inventory get file
         CLEA GETS
         LIMITFIELD = SPACE(10)
         LIMITVALUE = SPACE(60)
         @ 21,0 SAY "What is the LIMITING field? -> " GET LIMITFIELD
         @ 22,0 SAY "What is the LIMITING value? -> " GET LIMITVALUE
         READ
         LIMITFIELD = TRIM(LIMITFIELD)
*
```

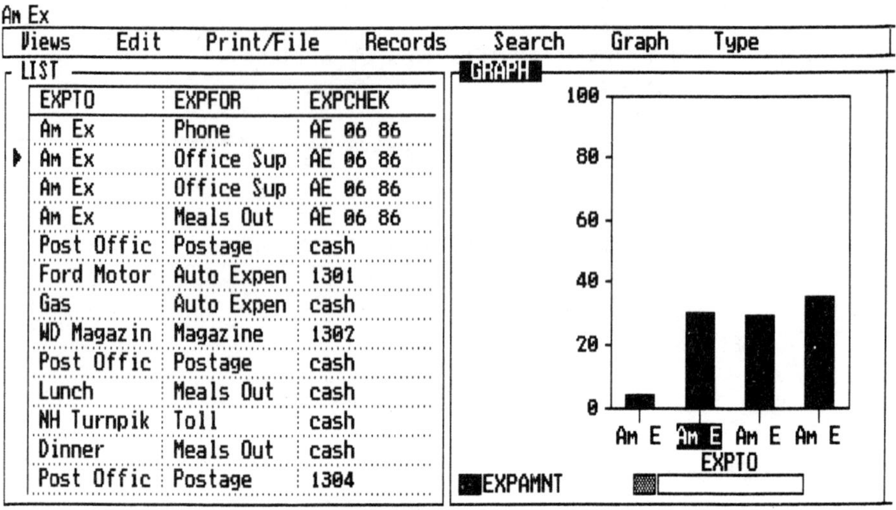

Figure 6–1 This screen was created with Borland's REFLEX, a low-cost, high-power graphics tool that can be useful in inventory situations because graphics make it easier to visually spot trends. Note the spreadsheet-like display on the left of the screen and the bar chart on the right.

Listing 6–5 (cont.)

```
         IF LEN(LIMITFIELD) = 0
            SET FILT TO
            HEADER = SPACE(40)
            LOOP
         ENDI
*
         LIMITVALUE = TRIM(LIMITVALUE)
         LIMITRELATE = 'E'
         @ 20,0 CLEA
         @ 20,  0  TO 24, 79
         @ 20, 15  SAY " LIMITING FIELD TO LIMITING VALUE RELATIONSHIP "
         @ 22, 10  SAY "= -> E   <> -> N   < -> L   > -> G   <= -> T   >= -> R"
         @ 24, 30  SAY " select -> <- "
         @ 24,40 GET LIMITRELATE PICT '!'
         READ
*
         IF LEN(LIMITVALUE) = 0
*
            DO CASE
               CASE LIMITRELATE = 'E'
                  SET FILT TO LEN(&LIMITFIELD) = 0
                  HEADER = LIMITFIELD+" = "+LIMITVALUE
               CASE LIMITRELATE = 'N'
```

Listing 6–5 (cont.)

```
                SET FILT TO LEN(&LIMITFIELD) <> 0
                HEADER = LIMITFIELD+" <> "+LIMITVALUE
             OTHE
                @ 20,0 CLEA
                WAIT [SORRY, YOU CAN'T DO THAT. PRESS ANY KEY TO CONTINUE...]
                LOOP
          ENDC
*
       ELSE
*
          DO CASE
             CASE TYPE('&LIMITFIELD') = 'N'
*
                DO CASE
                   CASE LIMITRELATE = 'E'
                      SET FILT TO &LIMITFIELD = VAL(LIMITVALUE)
                      HEADER = LIMITFIELD+" = "+LIMITVALUE
                   CASE LIMITRELATE = 'N'
                      SET FILT TO &LIMITFIELD <> VAL(LIMITVALUE)
                      HEADER = LIMITFIELD+" <> "+LIMITVALUE
                   CASE LIMITRELATE = 'L'
                      SET FILT TO &LIMITFIELD < VAL(LIMITVALUE)
                      HEADER = LIMITFIELD+" < "+LIMITVALUE
                   CASE LIMITRELATE = 'G'
                      SET FILT TO &LIMITFIELD > VAL(LIMITVALUE)
                      HEADER = LIMITFIELD+" > "+LIMITVALUE
                   CASE LIMITRELATE = 'T'
                      SET FILT TO &LIMITFIELD <= VAL(LIMITVALUE)
                      HEADER = LIMITFIELD+" <= "+LIMITVALUE
                   CASE LIMITRELATE = 'R'
                      SET FILT TO &LIMITFIELD >= VAL(LIMITVALUE)
                      HEADER = LIMITFIELD+" >= "+LIMITVALUE
                   OTHE
                      @ 20,0 CLEA
                      WAIT [YOU CAN'T DO THAT. PRESS ANY KEY TO CONTINUE...]
                      LOOP
                ENDC
*
          CASE TYPE('&LIMITFIELD') = 'C'
*
             DO CASE
                   CASE LIMITRELATE = 'E'
                      SET FILT TO &LIMITFIELD = "&LIMITVALUE"
                      HEADER = LIMITFIELD+" = "+LIMITVALUE
                   CASE LIMITRELATE = 'N'
```

Listing 6–5 (cont.)

```
                    SET FILT TO &LIMITFIELD <> "&LIMITVALUE"
                    HEADER = LIMITFIELD+" <> "+LIMITVALUE
                 CASE LIMITRELATE = 'L'
                    SET FILT TO &LIMITFIELD < "&LIMITVALUE"
                    HEADER = LIMITFIELD+" < "+LIMITVALUE
                 CASE LIMITRELATE = 'G'
                    SET FILT TO &LIMITFIELD > "&LIMITVALUE"
                    HEADER = LIMITFIELD+" > "+LIMITVALUE
                 CASE LIMITRELATE = 'T'
                    SET FILT TO &LIMITFIELD <= "&LIMITVALUE"
                    HEADER = LIMITFIELD+" <= "+LIMITVALUE
                 CASE LIMITRELATE = 'R'
                    SET FILT TO &LIMITFIELD >= "&LIMITVALUE"
                    HEADER = LIMITFIELD+" >= "+LIMITVALUE
                 OTHE
                    @ 20,0 CLEA
                    WAIT [YOU CAN'T DO THAT. PRESS ANY KEY TO CONTINUE...]
                    LOOP
              ENDC
*
        OTHE
           @ 20,0 CLEA
           WAIT [YOU CAN'T DO THAT. PRESS ANY KEY TO CONTINUE...]
     ENDC

*
  ENDI
*
  LOOP
```

Much of this code proceeds as before. The new code is contained in the expanded IF . . . ELSE . . . ENDIF block with its DO CASE . . . OTHE . . . ENDCASE blocks. If there is no LIMITVALUE variable, then the only two options are Equal and Not Equal. However, if there is a LIMITVALUE we must concern ourselves with the LIMITFIELD's TYPE. The code can only work on two field types, numeric and character. Any other field type isn't valid. With the IF . . . ELSE . . . ENDIF block and its associated DO CASE . . . OTHE . . . ENDCASE blocks we can to set criteria for both numeric and character data fields.

SALES INFORMATION

The sales information system is actually the same code as the inventory status report system. The only difference is that the sales code works on the ORDER database and the historical database. The necessary code changes are shown in

Listing 6–6. Note that this code uses the expansions shown in Listings 6–4 and 6–5.

Listing 6–6

```
* SALEREPO.PRG SALES INFORMATION REPORTER
*
DBFILE = SPAC(8)
HEADER = SPAC(40)
TOPRINT = [PLAI]
LOAD SAVESCR
SET CONS OFF
** SAY first menu screen
CALL SAVESCR WITH 'S1'
CLEA
** SAY second menu screen
CALL SAVESCR WITH 'S2'
CLEA
** SAY third menu screen
CALL SAVESCR WITH 'S3'
CLEA
** SAY fourth menu screen
CALL SAVESCR WITH 'S4'
CLEA
** SAY fifth menu screen
CALL SAVESCR WITH 'S5'
SET CONS ON
SAVESCREEN = 1
*
DO WHILE .T.
   CLEA
   CALL SAVESCR WITH 'R'+LTRIM(STR(SAVESCREEN))
   @ 7,28 SAY IIF(TO PRINT = [TO PRIN],[1. LIST TO PRINTER/screen],;
                              [1. LIST TO SCREEN/printer])
   @ 21, 0 SAY "PRESENT REPORT CRITERIA IS: " + HEADER
   @ 22,0 SAY [USING DATABASE -> ] + DBFILE
   ANSWER = '0'
   @ 19,33 SAY " select ->       "
   @ 19,44 GET ANSWER PICT "!"
   READ
*
** THE FOLLOWING DO CASE...ENDCASE BLOCK NOW HANDLES FOUR MENU OPTIONS, QUIT, SAVE SCREEN,
** LIST TO, AND SET REPORT CRITERIA FOR THE ORDER REPORTS
*
   DO CASE
      CASE ANSWER = '0'
         SET FILT TO
```

Listing 6–6 (cont.)

```
            SET ORDE TO 1
            RETU
         CASE ANSWER = 'D'
            DO GETFILE
            CLEA
            LOOP
         CASE ANSWER = 'N'
            SAVESCREEN = IIF(SAVESCREEN = 5, 1, SAVESCREEN + 1)
            LOOP
         CASE ANSWER = '1'
*
            IF TO PRINT = [TO PRIN]
               TOPRINT = [PLAI]
            ELSE
               TOPRINT = [TO PRIN]
            ENDI
*
         CASE ANSWER = '9'
            CLEA
            DO order say file
            DO order get file
            CLEA GETS
            LIMITFIELD = SPACE(10)
            LIMITVALUE = SPACE(60)
            @ 21,0 SAY "What is the LIMITING field? -> " GET LIMITFIELD
            @ 22,0 SAY "What is the LIMITING value? -> " GET LIMITVALUE
            READ
            LIMITFIELD = TRIM(LIMITFIELD)
*
            IF LEN(LIMITFIELD) = 0
               SET FILT TO
               HEADER = SPACE(40)
               LOOP
            ENDI
*
            LIMITVALUE = TRIM(LIMITVALUE)
            LIMITRELATE = 'E'
            @ 20,0 CLEA
            @ 20,  0  TO 24, 79
            @ 20, 15  SAY " LIMITING FIELD TO LIMITING VALUE RELATIONSHIP "
            @ 22, 10  SAY "= -> E   <> -> N   < -> L   > -> G   <= -> T   >= -> R"
            @ 24, 30  SAY " select -> <- "
            @ 24,40 GET LIMITRELATE PICT '!'
            READ
*
```

Listing 6–6 (cont.)

```
        IF LEN(LIMITVALUE) = 0
*
          DO CASE
            CASE LIMITRELATE = 'E'
              SET FILT TO LEN(&LIMITFIELD) = 0
              HEADER = LIMITFIELD+" = "+LIMITVALUE
            CASE LIMITRELATE = 'N'
              SET FILT TO LEN(&LIMITFIELD) <> 0
              HEADER = LIMITFIELD+" <> "+LIMITVALUE
            OTHE
              @ 20,0 CLEA
              WAIT [SORRY, YOU CAN'T DO THAT. PRESS ANY KEY TO CONTINUE...]
              LOOP
          ENDC
*
        ELSE
*
          DO CASE
            CASE TYPE('&LIMITFIELD') = 'N'
*
              DO CASE
                CASE LIMITRELATE = 'E'
                  SET FILT TO &LIMITFIELD = VAL(LIMITVALUE)
                  HEADER = LIMITFIELD+" = "+LIMITVALUE
                CASE LIMITRELATE = 'N'
                  SET FILT TO &LIMITFIELD <> VAL(LIMITVALUE)
                  HEADER = LIMITFIELD+" <> "+LIMITVALUE
                CASE LIMITRELATE = 'L'
                  SET FILT TO &LIMITFIELD < VAL(LIMITVALUE)
                  HEADER = LIMITFIELD+" < "+LIMITVALUE
                CASE LIMITRELATE = 'G'
                  SET FILT TO &LIMITFIELD > VAL(LIMITVALUE)
                  HEADER = LIMITFIELD+" > "+LIMITVALUE
                CASE LIMITRELATE = 'T'
                  SET FILT TO &LIMITFIELD <= VAL(LIMITVALUE)
                  HEADER = LIMITFIELD+" <= "+LIMITVALUE
                CASE LIMITRELATE = 'R'
                  SET FILT TO &LIMITFIELD >= VAL(LIMITVALUE)
                  HEADER = LIMITFIELD+" >= "+LIMITVALUE
                OTHE
                  @ 20,0 CLEA
                  WAIT [YOU CAN'T DO THAT. PRESS ANY KEY TO CONTINUE...]
                  LOOP
              ENDC
*
```

Listing 6-6 (cont.)

```
            CASE TYPE('&LIMITFIELD') = 'C'
*
               DO CASE
                  CASE LIMITRELATE = 'E'
                     SET FILT TO &LIMITFIELD = "&LIMITVALUE"
                     HEADER = LIMITFIELD+" = "+LIMITVALUE
                  CASE LIMITRELATE = 'N'
                     SET FILT TO &LIMITFIELD <> "&LIMITVALUE"
                     HEADER = LIMITFIELD+" <> "+LIMITVALUE
                  CASE LIMITRELATE = 'L'
                     SET FILT TO &LIMITFIELD < "&LIMITVALUE"
                     HEADER = LIMITFIELD+" < "+LIMITVALUE
                  CASE LIMITRELATE = 'G'
                     SET FILT TO &LIMITFIELD > "&LIMITVALUE"
                     HEADER = LIMITFIELD+" > "+LIMITVALUE
                  CASE LIMITRELATE = 'T'
                     SET FILT TO &LIMITFIELD <= "&LIMITVALUE"
                     HEADER = LIMITFIELD+" <= "+LIMITVALUE
                  CASE LIMITRELATE = 'R'
                     SET FILT TO &LIMITFIELD >= "&LIMITVALUE"
                     HEADER = LIMITFIELD+" >= "+LIMITVALUE
                  OTHE
                     @ 20,0 CLEA
                     WAIT [YOU CAN'T DO THAT. PRESS ANY KEY TO CONTINUE...]
                     LOOP
               ENDC
*
            OTHE
               @ 20,0 CLEA
               WAIT [YOU CAN'T DO THAT. PRESS ANY KEY TO CONTINUE...]
         ENDC
*
      ENDI
*
      LOOP
   ENDC
*
   IF PRINTERON
      SET CONS OFF
   ENDI
*
** THE FOLLOWING DO CASE...ENDCASE BLOCK HANDLES REPORT GENERATION
** AND CAN BE MODIFIED TO HANDLE SEVERAL MORE REPORTS.
*
   DO CASE
```

Listing 6–6 (cont.)

```
        CASE ANSWER = '2'
           SET ORDER TO 1
           REPO FORM file 1 HEAD "&HEADER" &TOPRINT
        CASE ANSWER = '3'
           SET ORDER TO 2
           REPO FORM file 2 HEAD "&HEADER" &TOPRINT
        CASE ANSWER = '4'
           SET ORDE TO 3
           REPO FORM file 3 HEAD "&HEADER" &TOPRINT
        CASE ANSWER = '5'
           SET ORDER TO 4
           REPO FORM file 4 HEAD "&HEADER" &TOPRINT
        CASE ANSWER = '6'
           SET ORDE TO 5
           REPO FORM file 5 HEAD "&HEADER" &TOPRINT
        CASE ANSWER = '7'
           SET ORDE TO 6
           REPO FORM file 6 HEAD "&HEADER" &TOPRINT
        CASE ANSWER = '8'
           SET ORDE TO 7
           REPO FORM file 7 HEAD "&HEADER" &TOPRINT
    ENDCASE
*
    SET CONS ON
*
ENDD
*
** END OF SALEREPO.PRG
```

Each screen includes one more line:

```
@ 18,28 SAY [D. Select Database]
```

This option is used to select one of the order databases. The system described in this chapter uses an active and a historical database, but a larger system might use a different database for each warehouse or inventory type. Selecting databases is actually done through the GETFILE routine located in INVENTORY.PRC file.

AN INVENTORY SYSTEM

The following code composes a generic but complete inventory control system. That means it handles the basics of inventory management and can be used as a "kernel" in developing your own inventory control system.

The system starts with a main menu generator:

Listing 6–7

```
* INVENTORY.PRG MAIN MODULE
*
CLOS ALL
CLEA ALL
*
* FEATURES TURNED ON
SET DELI ON
SET ESCA ON
SET INTE ON
*
* FEATURES TURNED OFF
SET BELL OFF
SET CONF OFF
SET STAT OFF
SET SAFE OFF
SET TALK OFF
*
REST FROM INVENTORY
SET PATH TO &CPATH
SET DEFA TO &CDRIVE
SET PROC TO INVENTORY.PRC
SET DELI TO '><'
*
ON ERROR DO ERRORMSS
*
NEWDRIVE = CDRIVE
NEWPATH = CPATH
DBFILE = SPACE(10)
PLACE = 0
*
DO WHILE .T.
   CLEAR
   @ 2, 0 TO 14,79 DOUBLE
   @ 3,31 SAY "INVENTORY SYSTEM"
   @ 4,1 TO 4,78 DOUBLE
   @  7,20 SAY [1. Editing Menu]
   @  8,20 SAY [2. Inventory Reports Menu]
   @  9,20 SAY [3. Sales Reports Menu]
   @ 10,20 SAY [4. INVENTORY Utilities]
   @ 12,20 SAY '0. Exit'
   STORE 0 TO ANSWER
   @ 14,33 SAY " select     "
   @ 14,41 GET ANSWER PICTURE "9" RANGE 0,5
   READ
*
```

Listing 6–7 (cont.)

```
    DO CASE
       CASE ANSWER = 0
          SAVE TO INVENTORY
          QUIT
       CASE ANSWER = 1
          DO GETFILE
          DO &SAYER
          DO &GETTER
          CLEA GETS
          DO EDIT
       CASE ANSWER = 2
          DO GETFILE
          DO INVEREPO
       CASE ANSWER = 3
          DO GETFILE
          DO SALEREPO
       CASE ANSWER = 4
          DO UTILMAIN
    ENDCASE
*
ENDD
*
** END OF INVENTORY.PRG
```

This main menu must set the system for all the work that will follow; hence, it starts with III PLUS commands that SET features ON and OFF, CLOSE the system's work areas, and CLEAR everything from everywhere. This is called the "tabula rasa effect."

Now that we've lobotomized the system, we can fill it with information we want it to have. This is done with:

```
REST FROM INVENTORY
```

This MEM file has all the necessary memory variables, path and drive specifications, and so on, to start the work session. Also note that the listing uses SET PROC TO INVENTORY.PRC.

By now you should be realizing that the listings keep uniform filenames. All necessary files for the system have different extensions, but start with INVENTOR(Y). The databases have different names, as will the index files, but all historical databases will have an HST extension, all order databases will have an ODR extension, and all inventory databases will have an INV extension.

The rest of the file is a straightforward menu system and doesn't need explanation. The INVEREPO and SALEREPO files were discussed previously.

What is the INVENTORY.PRC file? I use the PRC extension to separate regular PRG files from procedure files. This file contains all the procedures necessary to the inventory system:

Listing 6–8

```
** INVENTORY.PRC PROCEDURE FILE
**
PROC GETFILE
CLEA
SET CATA TO INVENTOR    && only eight characters are used in the CAT filename
SET VIEW TO ?
PLACE = 40-LEN(TRIM(DBF()))/2
*
&& all historical databases have an HST extension
&& all order databases have an ODR extension
&& all inventory databases have an INV extension
*
DO CASE
   CASE [HST]$UPPE(DBF())
      SAYER = [HISTOSAY]
      GETTER = [HISTOGET]
   CASE [ODR]$UPPE(DBF())
      SAYER = [ORDERSAY]
      GETTER = [ORDERGET]
   CASE [INV]$UPPE(DBF())
      SAYER = [INVENSAY]
      GETTER = [INVENGET]
ENDC
*
PROC EDITMENU
@ 20,0 TO 23,79 DOUB
@ 21,1 SAY;
[  E -> Edit  B -> Back  S -> Skip  G -> Goto  K -> Kill  R -> Rstr
Q -> Quit]
@ 22,1 SAY;
[  F -> Find  L -> Loca  C -> Cont  D -> Disp  O -> Copy
A -> Add               ]
*
IF [ODR]$UPPE(DBF())
  @ 22,69 SAY "T -> TRCK"
ENDI
*
PROC INVENSAY
CLEA
@  2, PLACE SAY DBF()
*
** SAY STATEMENTS FROM YOUR INVENTORY SAY FILE
*
@  3,   1  TO  3, 78    DOUBLE
@  1,   0  TO 18, 79    DOUBLE
```

Listing 6–8 (cont.)

```
*
PROC INVENGET
*
** GET STATEMENTS FROM YOUR INVENTORY GET FILE
*
@ 24, 50  SAY "Record Number -> " + STR(RECNO(),4,0)
*
PROC ORDERSAY
@  2, PLACE SAY DBF()
*
** SAY STATEMENTS FROM YOUR ORDER GET FILE
*
@  3,  1  TO  3, 78    DOUBLE
@  1,  0  TO 18, 79    DOUBLE
*
PROC ORDERGET
*
** GET STATEMENTS FROM YOUR ORDER GET FILE
*
@ 24, 50  SAY "Record Number -> " + STR(RECNO(),4,0)
*
PROC HISTOSAY
@  2, PLACE SAY DBF()
*
** SAY STATEMENTS FROM YOUR HISTORICAL SAY FILE
*
@  3,  1  TO  3, 78    DOUBLE
@  1,  0  TO 18, 79    DOUBLE
*
PROC HISTOGET
*
** GET STATEMENTS FROM YOUR HISTORICAL GET FILE
*
@ 24, 50  SAY "Record Number -> " + STR(RECNO(),4,0)
*
PROC GETFIELD
KEYFIELD = 0
CLEA
*
** THERE ARE SEVEN KEY FIELD OPTIONS DUE TO SEVEN POSSIBLE NDX FILES.
*
@  4, 24  SAY "SELECT A KEY FIELD FROM THE MENU"
@  6, 31  SAY "1 > XXXXXXXXXX"
@  7, 31  SAY "2 > XXXXXXXXXX"
@  8, 31  SAY "3 > XXXXXXXXXX"
```

Listing 6–8 (cont.)

```
@  9, 31  SAY "4 > XXXXXXXXXX"
@ 10, 31  SAY "5 > XXXXXXXXXX"
@ 11, 31  SAY "6 > XXXXXXXXXX"
@ 12, 31  SAY "7 > XXXXXXXXXX"
@ 15, 31  SAY "0 > QUIT "
@ 17, 32  SAY " KEY FIELD    "
@  3, 10  TO 17, 69    DOUBLE
*
DO CASE
   CASE [HST]$UPPE(DBF())
*
** THESE KEY FIELDS CORRESPOND TO A HISTORICAL DATABASE.
*
      @ 6,36 SAY key field 1
      @ 7,36 SAY key field 2
      @ 8,36 SAY key field 3
      @ 9,36 SAY key field 4
      @ 10,36 SAY key field 5
      @ 11,36 SAY key field 6
      @ 12,36 SAY key field 7
   CASE [ODR]$UPPE(DBF())
*
** THESE KEY FIELDS CORRESPOND TO AN ORDER DATABASE.
*
      @ 6,36 SAY key field 1
      @ 7,36 SAY key field 2
      @ 8,36 SAY key field 3
      @ 9,36 SAY key field 4
      @ 10,36 SAY key field 5
      @ 11,36 SAY key field 6
      @ 12,36 SAY key field 7
   CASE [INV]$UPPE(DBF())
*
** THESE KEY FIELDS CORRESPOND TO AN INVENTORY DATABASE.
*
      @ 6,36 SAY key field 1
      @ 7,36 SAY key field 2
      @ 8,36 SAY key field 3
      @ 9,36 SAY key field 4
      @ 10,36 SAY key field 5
      @ 11,36 SAY key field 6
      @ 12,36 SAY key field 7
ENDC
*
@ 17,44 GET KEYFIELD PICT '9' RANG 0,7
```

Listing 6–8 (cont.)

```
READ
*
IF KEYFIELD = 0
   RETU
ELSE
   SET ORDE TO KEYFIELD
ENDI
*
PROC ERRORMSS
*
DO CASE
   CASE ERROR() = 1
      @ 0,0 SAY "That file doesn't exist on drive "+NEWDRIVE
      DO POOL
      RETU TO MASTER
   CASE ERROR() = 4
      @ 24,50 say "Record Number ->  END  "
      @ 0,0 SAY "You're at the end of the file now. "
   CASE ERROR() = 5
      @ 24,50 say "Record Number ->  END  "
      @ 0,0 SAY "You can't CONTINUE any further. You're at the end. ."
   CASE ERROR() = 38
      @ 24,50 say "Record Number -> 0   "
      @ 0,0 SAY "You can't go any further. You're at the beginning now. "
   CASE ERROR() = 42
      @ 0,0 SAY "You must LOCATE before you can CONTINUE. "
   CASE ERROR() = 114
      CLEAR
      @ 10,10 TO 20,70 DOUBLE
      @ 15,15 SAY "The INDEX file is damaged, excuse me while I REINDEX."
      REIN
   CASE ERROR() = 125
      @ 0,0 SAY "Please turn the PRINTER ON."
   OTHE
      @ 0,0 SAY "I've encountered an unknown error. Please try again."
ENDC
*
DO POOL
*
PROC POOL
LAPS = 0
*
DO WHILE LAPS < WAITTIME
   LAPS = LAPS + 1
ENDD
```

Figure 6–2 Here is a typical VIEW file selection screen.

Listing 6–8 (cont.)

```
*
RETU
*
** END OF INVENTORY.PRC PROCEDURE FILE
```

There are several procedures in this file. The first one, GETFILE, is used to load the appropriate DBF and associated NDX files into the work area. This is done with the CAT and VUE files available in III PLUS. Note that the CAT file is specifically called by an eight-character filename, not INVENTORY but INVENTOR. This is important with CAT files. A VUE file is selected with the SET VIEW TO ? command. Depending on the number of VUE files designed into your system, the screen looks something like that shown in Figure 6–2.

The advantage to this method is in accessing one file, the VUE file, and letting that file open the necessary DBF and NDX files. The only task left is to determine which SAY and GET files will be needed. That is handled in the DO CASE . . . ENDCASE block.

The EDITMENU procedure has been discussed in earlier sections of this text. Each of the SAY and GET files can be developed according to your needs. The kernels of the files are shown in the PRC file.

The next interesting bit of code is GETFIELD. This is used heavily in the utility portion of this code and elsewhere. It is designed to help the user select an option based on the key fields available in NDX files, as shown in Figure 6–3. These blanks are 10 characters long, the length of the longest possible database field name. However, multiple key field entries can be included with longer blanks. A DO CASE . . . ENDCASE block handles the possibilities of historical, order, and inventory database key fields. The NDX file ORDER is SET based on the selected KEYFIELD. I often replace the "key field n" with the FIELD(n) function. I also make use of this later on, but note that it depends on the design of the database. Obviously you can't do it if your key fields aren't the first seven fields in the database (but they should be, you know).

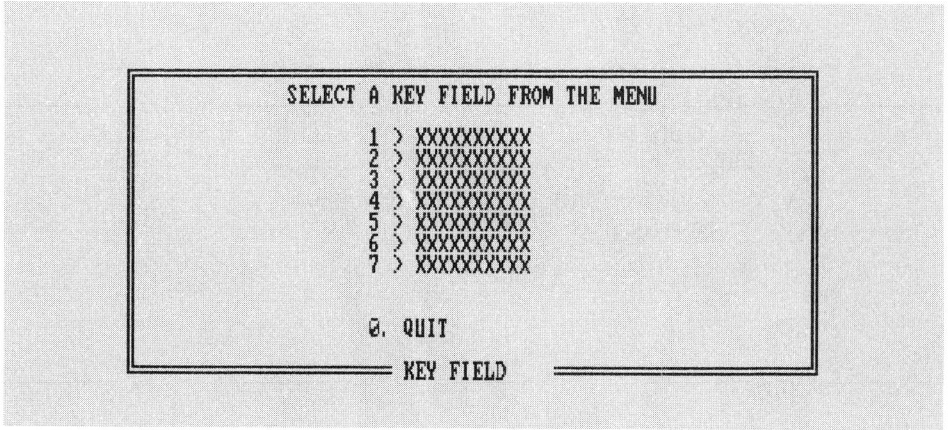

Figure 6–3 The key field selection menu can be used to SET the ORDER of the NDX files.

The last bit of interesting code is the ERRORMSS procedure. This is an abrupt version of a much longer file that contains all of dBASE III PLUS's possible error messages. These error messages were selected from watching the most common mistakes made by users.

The next routine shown in INVENTORY.PRG is the UTILMAIN.PRG file. This is the MAIN utility file and not terribly impressive. However, the utility PRG files are highly transportable and do a great deal of work; hence, they are worth investigating.

Listing 6–9

```
** UTILMAIN.PRG INVENTORY UTILITY MAIN MENU
*
DO WHILE .T.
   CLEAR
   @ 2, 0 TO 19,79 DOUBLE
   @ 3, 11 SAY [I N V E N T O R Y   U T I L I T I E S   M A I N   M E N U]
   @ 4,1 TO 4,78 DOUBLE
   @ 7,26 SAY [1. System Functions]
   @ 8,26 SAY [2. Inventory Functions]
   @ 17, 26 SAY '0. Exit'
   STORE 0 TO ANSWER
   @ 19,33 SAY " select     "
   @ 19,42 GET ANSWER PICTURE "9" RANGE 0,9
   READ
*
   DO CASE
      CASE ANSWER = 0
         RETURN
      CASE ANSWER = 1
```

Listing 6–9 (cont.)

```
         DO UTILSYS
      CASE ANSWER = 2
         DO UTILINV
      OTHE
         @ 0,0 SAY "That isn't an option. Try again."
         DO POOL
   ENDC
*
ENDD
*
RETURN
*
** END OF: UTILMAIN.PRG
```

The next file we'll investigate is the second and more interesting of those listed in UTILMAIN.PRG, namely UTILINV.PRG:

Listing 6–10

```
** UTILINV.PRG INVENTORY UTILITIES
*
STORE NEWDRIVE TO SOURCE,TARGET
*
DO WHILE .T.
   CLEAR
   @ 2, 0 TO 19,79 DOUBLE
   @ 3,15 SAY [I N V E N T O R Y   U T I L I T I E S   M E N U]
   @ 4,1 TO 4,78 DOUBLE
   @  7,26 SAY [1. Set Source and Target Drives]
   @  8,26 SAY [2. Purge a File]
   @  9,26 SAY [3. Import a File (ASCII)]
   @ 10,26 SAY [4. Export a File(ASCII)]
   @ 11,26 SAY [5. Reindex a File]
   @ 12,26 SAY [6. Create a New File]
   @ 13,26 SAY [7. Delete an Old File]
   @ 14,26 SAY [8. Extract a File]
   @ 15,26 SAY [9. Merge a File]
   @ 17, 26 SAY '0. Exit'
   STORE 0 TO ANSWER
   @ 19,33 SAY " select     "
   @ 19,42 GET ANSWER PICTURE "9" RANGE 0,9
   @ 21,0 SAY "Current SOURCE drive is -> " + SOURCE
   @ 23,0 SAY "Current TARGET drive is -> " + TARGET
   READ
*
   DO CASE
```

Listing 6–10 (cont.)

```
      CASE ANSWER = 0
         RETURN
      CASE ANSWER = 1
         @ 20,0 CLEA
         @ 21,0 SAY "New SOURCE drive is -> " GET SOURCE
         @ 23,0 SAY "New TARGET drive is -> " GET TARGET
         READ
         TARGET = TARGET + ":"
         SOURCE = SOURCE + ":"
         SET DEFA TO &SOURCE
      CASE ANSWER = 2
         DO GETFILE
         CLEA
         @ 1,0 TO 10,79 DOUBLE
         @ 3,20 SAY [0. QUIT WITHOUT CHANGING ANYTHING]
         @ 5,20 SAY [1. REMOVE DELETED ENTRIES]
         @ 7,20 SAY [2. REMOVE ALL ENTRIES]
         @ 10,33 SAY " select      "
         @ 10,42 GET ANSWER PICTURE "9" RANGE 0,2
         READ
*
         DO CASE
            CASE ANSWER = 2
               ZAP
            CASE ANSWER = 1
               CLEA
               SET TALK ON
               PACK
               SET TALK OFF
         ENDC
*
      CASE ANSWER = 3
         DO GETFILE
         CLEA
         ? "Available SOURCE files are:"
         TXT = SOURCE + "*.TXT"
         DIR &TXT
         ACCE "Which file do you want to IMPORT? -> " TO IMPORTFILE
         IMPORTFILE = SOURCE + TRIM(IMPORTFILE)
         COPY STRUC TO TANK
         SELE 2
         USE TANK
         SET TALK ON
         APPE FROM &IMPORTFILE DELIM WITH ,
         SET TALK OFF
```

Listing 6–10 (cont.)

```
         CLEA
*
         TEXT
            I'm going to list the first 10 and last 10 entries to your printer.
            This will give you a chance to confirm that things went where you wanted
            them to go. If things went where they should, I will place the IMPORTED
            data in the current database.
         ENDT
*
         WAIT
         1
         LIST NEXT 10 TO PRINT
         GOTO BOTT
         SKIP -10
         LIST NEXT 10 TO PRINT
         TRUTH = .T.
         @ 10,0 SAY "Okay to IMPORT this data?" GET TRUTH
         READ
*
         IF TRUTH
            USE
            SELE 1
            SET TALK ON
            APPEN FROM TANK
            SET TALK OFF
         ELSE
            USE
            SELE 1
         ENDI
*
         ERAS TANK.DBF
      CASE ANSWER = 4
         CLEA
         DO GETFILE
         CLEA
         ACCE "What name do you want for the EXPORTED file (8 CHAR MAX)? -> ";
              TO EXPORTFILE
         DO GETFIELD
         THIS = FIELD(KEYFIELD)
         ACCE "EXTRACT &THIS > " TO TOFIND
         EXPORTFILE = TARGET + TRIM(EXPORTFILE)
         SEEK TOFIND
         SET TALK ON
*
         IF TYPE('&THIS') = 'N'
```

Listing 6–10 (cont.)

```
            COPY TO &EXPORTFILE DELIM WHILE &THIS = TOFIND
         ELSE
            COPY TO &EXPORTFILE DELIM WHILE &THIS = '&TOFIND'
         ENDI
*
         SET TALK OFF
      CASE ANSWER = 5
         DO GETFILE
         SET TALK ON
         REIN
         SET TALK OFF
      CASE ANSWER = 6
         CLEA
*
         TEXT
            I need an appropriate file on which to base the new file's structure.
            Please select a file type (HST, ODR, or INV) from the list on the next
            screen.

         ENDT
*
         WAIT
         DO GETFILE
         CLEA
         DO GETFIELD
         SELE 2
         FILENAME = SPAC(8)
         @ 10,0 SAY "What is the new database name (8 characters)? - " GET FILENAME
         READ
         TAG = LEFT(FILENAME,4)
         NEWFILE = TARGET + TRIM(FILENAME) + RIGH(DBF(),4)
         COPY STRUC TO &NEWFILE
         NDX1 = TARGET + TAG + "file 1 tag"
         NDX2 = TARGET + TAG + "file 2 tag"
         NDX3 = TARGET + TAG + "file 3 tag"
         NDX4 = TARGET + TAG + "file 4 tag"
         NDX5 = TARGET + TAG + "file 5 tag"
         NDX6 = TARGET + TAG + "file 6 tag"
         NDX7 = TARGET + TAG + "file 7 tag"
         USE &NEWFILE
*
** The FOLLOWING CAN BE MULTIPLE KEY FIELD LISTS.
*
         INDE ON key field 1 TO &NDX1
         INDE ON key field 2 TO &NDX2
```

Listing 6–10 (cont.)

```
      INDE ON key field 3 TO &NDX3
      INDE ON key field 4 TO &NDX4
      INDE ON key field 5 TO &NDX5
      INDE ON key field 6 TO &NDX6
      INDE ON key field 7 TO &NDX7
      SET CATA TO INVENTOR
      CREA VIEW FROM ENVI &FILENAME
      SET CATA TO
      USE
   CASE ANSWER = 7
      CLEA
      DO GETFILE
      ERASER = DBF()
      NDX1 = NDX(1)
      NDX2 = NDX(2)
      NDX3 = NDX(3)
      NDX4 = NDX(4)
      NDX5 = NDX(5)
      NDX6 = NDX(6)
      NDX7 = NDX(7)
      CLOSE DATA
      SET CATA TO INVENTOR
      FILENAME = LEFT(MERGER,AT('.',MERGER) + 1) + '.VUE'
      ERAS &FILENAME
      ERAS &ERASER
      ERAS &NDX1
      ERAS &NDX2
      ERAS &NDX3
      ERAS &NDX4
      ERAS &NDX5
      ERAS &NDX6
      SET CATA TO
   CASE ANSWER = 8
      CLEA
      DO GETFILE
      FILENAME = SPAC(8)
      @ 21,0 SAY "What is the new database name? (8 chars) - " GET FILENAME
      READ
      NEWFILE = TARGET + TRIM(FILENAME) + RIGH(DBF(),4)
      TAG = LEFT(FILENAME,4)
      NDX1 = TARGET + TAG + "file 1 tag"
      NDX2 = TARGET + TAG + "file 2 tag"
      NDX3 = TARGET + TAG + "file 3 tag"
      NDX4 = TARGET + TAG + "file 4 tag"
      NDX5 = TARGET + TAG + "file 5 tag"
```

Listing 6–10 (cont.)

```
        NDX6 = TARGET + TAG + "file 6 tag"
        NDX7 = TARGET + TAG + "file 7 tag"
        DO GETFIELD
        THIS = FIELD(KEYFIELD)
        ACCE "EXTRACT &THIS > " TO TOFIND
        SEEK TOFIND
        SET EXAC ON
        CLEAR
        SET TALK ON
*
        IF TYPE('&THIS') = 'N'
           COPY TO &NEWFILE WHILE &THIS = TOFIND
        ELSE
           COPY TO &NEWFILE WHILE &THIS = '&TOFIND'
        ENDI
*
        SET EXAC OFF
        SELE 2
        USE &NEWFILE
*
** THE FOLLOWING CAN BE MULTIPLE KEY FIELD LISTS.
*
        INDE ON key field 1 TO &NDX1
        INDE ON key field 2 TO &NDX2
        INDE ON key field 3 TO &NDX3
        INDE ON key field 4 TO &NDX4
        INDE ON key field 5 TO &NDX5
        INDE ON key field 6 TO &NDX6
        INDE ON key field 7 TO &NDX7
        SET CATA TO INVENTOR
        CREA VIEW FROM ENVI &FILENAME
        SET CATA TO
        USE
        SET TALK OFF
        SELE 1
        CLEA
        YORN = .F.
        @ 5,0 SAY "Delete and remove the records from the old database? " GET YORN
        READ
*
        IF YORN
           SET EXAC ON
           SEEK TOFIND
*
           IF TYPE('&THIS') = 'N'
```

Listing 6–10 (cont.)

```
          DELE WHILE &THIS = TOFIND
        ELSE
          DELE WHILE &THIS = '&TOFIND'
        ENDI
*
        PACK
        SET EXAC OFF
      ENDI
*
   CASE ANSWER = 9
      CLEA
      WAIT [Please select a target file from the next screen. Press any key when ready...]
      SELE 1
      DO GETFILE
      CLEA
      WAIT [Please select a source file from the next screen. Press any key when ready...]
      SELE 2
      DO GETFILE
      MERGER = DBF()
      NDX1 = NDX(1)
      NDX2 = NDX(2)
      NDX3 = NDX(3)
      NDX4 = NDX(4)
      NDX5 = NDX(5)
      NDX6 = NDX(6)
      NDX7 = NDX(7)
      USE
      SELE 1
      APPE FROM &MERGER
      TRUTH = .F.
      CLEA
      @ 10,0 SAY [DO YOU WANT TO ERASE ] + MERGER + [? ] GET TRUTH
      READ
*
      IF TRUTH
         SET CATA TO INVENTOR
         FILENAME = LEFT(MERGER,AT('.',MERGER) + 1) + '.VUE'
         ERAS &FILENAME
         ERAS &MERGER
         ERAS &NDX1
         ERAS &NDX2
         ERAS &NDX3
         ERAS &NDX4
         ERAS &NDX5
         ERAS &NDX6
```

Listing 6–10 (cont.)

```
            ERAS &NDX7
            SET CATA TO
         ENDI
*
      OTHE
         @ 0,0 SAY [Not a valid choice, sorry. Try again.]
         DO POOL
   ENDC
*
ENDD
*
RETU
*
** END OF UTILINV.PRG
```

As you can see, the options are quite varied, but all deal with file rather than system options. Option 1 is a straightforward PATHing code block. Option 2 shows why we didn't include the DELS flag and PACK commands in the EDIT module. The code for option 2 in itself is a kernel. Note that both PACK and ZAP commands are included. You may wish to include a warning or two about them in the code.

Option 3 provides a way to import ASCII data. Note that this code could easily be modified with the kernel to import foreign files other than ASCII. It is currently designed only to work with comma (,) delimited files. A useful feature is the TEXT ... ENDTEXT screen and code. This helps users see if they've properly accessed the data.

Option 4 is the flip side of option 3, which imports data from an ASCII file. Here we export to an ASCII file. As before, this code can be modified with the kernel to COPY TO various foreign file types. Note the TYPE() test at the end of the option. This ensures proper COPY command use.

Option 5 merely REINDEXes databases. It is included because accidents happen more often to NDX files than to any other kind.

Option 6 creates new databases and associated index files from nothing—quite an impressive feat. It gets a database structure from the GETFILE procedure, strips the new file's name to the necessary parts to build new DBF and NDX filenames, loads them into a VUE file, and *voilá!*

Option 7 is a dangerous one. The user can select it to ERASE files from the disk. The method isn't involved and is designed around the use of macros, along with the DBF() and NDX() functions.

Option 8 creates new files but does so by taking parts of other files. It is based on option 6's code, but also has extra code to delete the extracted records in the original DBF file.

The last option, 9, is the other side of extracting one database from another. Option 9 merges databases. This option is a synthesis of Option 7 and other code. Note that any deletions necessitate updating the VUE file list and CAT file.

The last file to consider is the UTILSYS.PRG system utilities file. This file only performs two operations. First, it lets the user determine the wait time on error messages. This wait time is a necessary element of the POOL procedure listed at the end of INVENTORY.PRC. I should point out that I prefer to use the dBASE PROGRAMMER'S UTILITIES DELAY.BIN file for such tasks. This LOADable file is called with one line of code, allows for alterable wait times as procedure POOL does, but is a cleaner method than the one shown here.

The second function of UTILSYS.PRG is to set default path and drive specifications. These settings are done through memory variables kept in the INVENTORY.MEM file and otherwise declared in the INVENTORY.PRG main menu file.

Listing 6–11

```
** UTILSYS.PRG UTILITIES SYSTEM
*
DO WHILE .T.
   CLEAR
   @ 2, 0 TO 19,79 DOUBLE
   @ 3, 5 SAY [I N V E N T O R Y   S Y S T E M   U T I L I T I E S   M E N U]
   @ 4,1 TO 4,78 DOUBLE
   @  7,26 SAY [1. Set Message Wait Time (SET AT)]+ STR(WAITLENGTH,4) + [(SECONDS)]
   @  8,26 SAY [2. Set Default Drive and Path]
   @ 17, 26 SAY '0. Exit'
   STORE 0 TO ANSWER
   @ 19,33 SAY " select     "
   @ 19,42 GET ANSWER PICTURE "9" RANGE 0,9
   READ
*
   DO CASE
      CASE ANSWER = 0
         RETURN
      CASE ANSWER = 1
         @ 20,0 CLEA
         @ 21,0 SAY "The current ERROR MESSAGE wait time is about "+;
                  "STR(WAITLENGTH,4)+" seconds."
         @ 23,0 SAY "How long would you like to wait (seconds)? -> " GET WAITLENGTH
         READ
         WAITTIME = INT(WAITLENGTH * 5.2) && The value 5.2 is system dependent
      CASE ANSWER = 2
         @ 20,0 CLEA
         @ 21,0 SAY "The current PATH is -> "+CPATH+;
". The current DEFAULT DRIVE is "+CDRIVE
         @ 22,0 SAY "Which PATH should be the DEFAULT PATH? -> " GET CPATH
         @ 23,0 SAY "Which DRIVE should be the DEFAULT? -> " GET CDRIVE
         READ
         SET DEFA TO &CDRIVE
```

Listing 6–11 (cont.)

```
         SET PATH TO &CPATH
      OTHE
         @ 0,0 SAY [That isn't an option!]
         DO POOL
   ENDC
*
ENDD
*
RETU
*
** END OF UTILSYS.PRG
```

SUMMARY

There you have the code necessary to start you on your way to a functional inventory management system. The code can be used as it stands, but experimentation is the best way to learn.

Remember that you must design your databases first then let the code fit them. Giving you the code might seem a backwards method, but you will have no problems if you follow the rules listed in Part 1 of this book.

CHAPTER

7

CLIENT/PERSONNEL RECORD KEEPING

A client/personnel service system is based on doing something that dBASE III PLUS—in fact, all of the versions of dBASE—cannot do well. We're going to use III PLUS to study large text fields. The typical client service system is designed to handle large amounts of textual data. This data can be personnel records, medical records, dental records, psychiatric care records, legal records, student records—any information that is usually entered into a word processor (this is a hint as to how this problem is addressed in the dBASE III PLUS world).

THE SPECIAL REQUIREMENTS FOR DESIGNING LARGE DATABASES

You might guess that any system dealing with large amounts of text is going to contain large databases. I don't mean databases containing several records, I mean records containing several fields. One way around this with dBASE III PLUS is the memo field. Even so, the nature of text-based databases still demands large database design. This is where the concepts of masterbase and database are brought to bear.

The other problem of large text systems is having to search for specific data throughout the entire system. The normal III PLUS system doesn't allow for rapid textual searches of memo fields, and that will present an initial problem for us. Several solutions will be offered.

Breaking Large Databases into Manageable Sizes

One of the problems with personnel/client service systems is privacy and the access of privileged information. This is an area that breeds confusion. Am I talking about law cnforcement agencies coming in and subpoenaing records? No, here we mean sectioning the database into areas where access is restricted on a need-to-know basis.

Let's hypothesize a client system for a small psychiatric office. As open-minded as we are in our society, few people want the world to know they've had psychiatric care. How do we ensure that only the right eyes see the information and the right hands enter it? And once we've segregated the databases as such, how do we make the security system hold together as it should?

The first method to consider is using more than one database, but maintaining the same key field between them. A situation such as described for the psychiatrist would use a database for all the bookkeeping functions keyed to some client number. The other database would contain the doctor's notes, the patient's profile and medical history, and also be keyed on the same client number. This method requires several databases and open work areas.

Another method is to use a single large database structure and protect fields in the file with passwords. This can be done with an FMT file or similarly coded GET and SAY files. A secretary, for example, can enter all the data necessary for his or her needs and then be prompted to enter a password to get to other parts of the database, perhaps on another data entry screen. This is also a situation where dBASE III PLUS's PROTECT utility can be of service, even on a single-user system.

The PROTECT utility (which comes in every dBASE III PLUS package, not just the network version) is used by the network manager to tell III PLUS which users can access various levels of specific DBF files. Don't let *network manager* in the last sentence throw you. You don't have to be running a network to make use of some of the network features. You only need a computer with 640K minimum memory and a hard disk to use dBADMINISTRATOR, the network version of III PLUS, even in single-user mode. This type of application begs the use of a hard disk, so I'll assume you have one. The 640K of memory might be a problem. Having both lets you take advantage of the PROTECT utility. You—the developer/designer/programmer—can use the PROTECT utility when you're setting up the system to determine who gets access to what. If you're a consultant, you could guarantee job security by not telling the office personnel how to make adjustments to the DBSYSTEM.DB file (the file created by PROTECT.EXE to govern file access)! But professional ethics dictate that we tell who will have governance of the DBSYSTEM.DB file and show him or her how such maintenance should be.

What if you don't have enough memory to use III PLUS in the networked single-user mode? Then you must resort to using III PLUS in single-user mode, without the features of PROTECT.EXE and dBADMINISTRATOR, and design your own password system. This isn't as difficult as it sounds. Figure 7–1 shows a sample screen for such a system.

The files that generate this screen are shown in Listings 7–1 and 7–2. The database structures are shown in Figure 7–2a and Figure 7–2b.

Listing 7–1

```
** SAMPLE SAY FILE FOR PASSWORD PROTECTED DATA ENTRY
*
@  2,  2  SAY "USER_NAME"
@  2, 14  SAY  PASSINFO->USER_NAME
@  2, 42  SAY "PASSWORD"
```

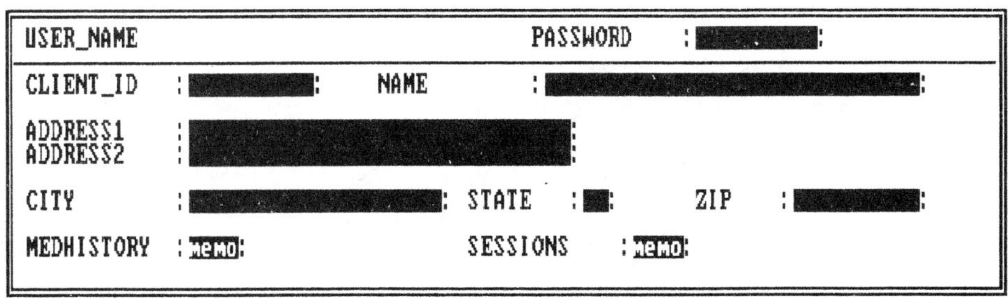

->

Figure 7–1 This sample screen illustrates how passwords protect sensitive database fields in a large database system.

Listing 7–1 (cont.)

```
@  4,  2  SAY "CLIENT_ID"
@  4, 30  SAY "NAME"
@  6,  2  SAY "ADDRESS1"
@  7,  2  SAY "ADDRESS2"
@  9,  2  SAY "CITY"
@  9, 37  SAY "STATE"
@  9, 55  SAY "ZIP"
@ 11,  2  SAY "MEDHISTORY"
@ 11, 37  SAY "SESSIONS"
@  1,  0  TO 13, 79    DOUBLE
@  3,  1  TO  3, 78
*
** EOF
```

Listing 7–2

```
** SAMPLE GET FILE FOR PASSWORD PROTECTED DATA ENTRY
*
SET CONS OFF
@  2, 54  GET  PASSINFO->PASSWORD
SET CONS ON
@  4, 14  GET  CLNTDATA->CLIENT_ID
@  4, 42  GET  CLNTDATA->NAME
@  6, 14  GET  CLNTDATA->ADDRESS1
@  7, 14  GET  CLNTDATA->ADDRESS2
@  9, 14  GET  CLNTDATA->CITY
```

```
Structure for database: D:CLNTDATA.dbf
Number of data records:        0
Date of last update   : 12/29/86
Field  Field Name  Type       Width    Dec
    1  CLIENT_ID   Character     10
    2  NAME        Character     30
    3  ADDRESS1    Character     30
    4  ADDRESS2    Character     30
    5  CITY        Character     20
    6  STATE       Character      2
    7  ZIP         Character     10
    8  MEDHISTORY  Memo          10
    9  SESSIONS    Memo          10
** Total **                     153
```

(a)

```
Structure for database: D:PASSINFO.dbf
Number of data records:        0
Date of last update   : 12/29/86
Field  Field Name  Type       Width    Dec
    1  USER_NAME   Character     20
    2  PASSWORD    Character     10
    3  ACCSLEVEL   Numeric        3
** Total **                      34
```

(b)

Figure 7–2 (a) *A sample medical history database structure.*
(b) *The structure of the necessary DBF files used to create password protection.*

Listing 7–2 (cont.)

```
@ 9, 45  GET  CLNTDATA->STATE
@ 9, 62  GET  CLNTDATA->ZIP
READ
*
IF PASSINFO->ACCSLEVEL > 1
   @ 11, 14  GET  CLNTDATA->MEDHISTORY
   READ
*
   IF PASSINFO->ACCSLEVEL = 3
      @ 11, 49  GET  CLNTDATA->SESSIONS
      READ
   ELSE
      @ 11,49 SAY [ACCESS DENIED]
   ENDI
*
```

Listing 7-2 (cont.)

```
ELSE
   @ 11,14 SAY [ACCESS DENIED]
ENDI
*
** EOF
```

All of these approaches address a single need—breaking a large database structure into smaller, manageable files. Part 1 of this book contains specific information on that process and the lines along which databases should be broken. The personnel/client record keeping system poses the extra problems of security.

A strong suggestion for programmers wishing to address this need is to recognize how data will be added to the database(s). Account data—something not included in the 7-1 and 7-2 listings—will take the form of new records for each patient's visit and a separate master record of up-to-date account information. Mailing information will be a single record and remain as such. Medical history and session information are large text fields, and this tells us something about them. Instead of appending a new record every time data is added, data is directly added to the existing record's information. Thus, each record grows, but the number of records does not. This problem is partially solved by dBASE III PLUS's use of DBT (memo field) files.

Remember that each DBF file can have several memo fields, but all the memo fields will be contained in a single DBT file. Searching through such a file for specific data isn't easily done, and you may wish to create several different DBFs, each linked by a common field, with each separate DBF containing a single memo field. An algorithm is given later in this chapter for finding information in DBT files.

Searching Large Text Fields

So how does one scan the data in a memo field? Unfortunately, we can't FIND, SEEK, or LOCATE information in it using standard III PLUS. What are we to do?

There are actually several options available. The first option is to create a memo field and a concomitant "key word" field. The key word field contains what the user thinks are significant arrows/markers/identifiers into the memo field. Such a structure might be that in Figure 7-3.

Note that the structure for CLNTDATA has been modified to include two key word fields, one for MEDHISTORY and the other for SESSIONS. These fields are each 254 characters wide, which can make them cumbersome, but in dBASE III PLUS you can scroll through them with the PICT '@Sn' function. An example of using the MODI SCRE command to add the '@Sn' PICTURE FUNCTION is shown in Figure 7-4.

The GET and SAY fields would then be modified to:

Listing 7-3

```
** GET FILE MODIFIED WITH KEY WORD FIELDS
*
```

```
Structure for database: D:CLNTDATA.dbf
Number of data records:       3
Date of last update   : 12/29/86
Field  Field Name  Type       Width    Dec
    1  CLIENT_ID   Character     10
    2  NAME        Character     30
    3  ADDRESS1    Character     30
    4  ADDRESS2    Character     30
    5  CITY        Character     20
    6  STATE       Character      2
    7  ZIP         Character     10
    8  MEDIKEY     Character    254
    9  MEDHISTORY  Memo          10
   10  SESSIONKEY  Character    254
   11  SESSIONS    Memo          10
** Total **                     661
```

Figure 7-3 This structure, similar to that of Figure 7-2a, adds the MEDIKEY and SESSIONKEY fields to enable users to search memo fields.

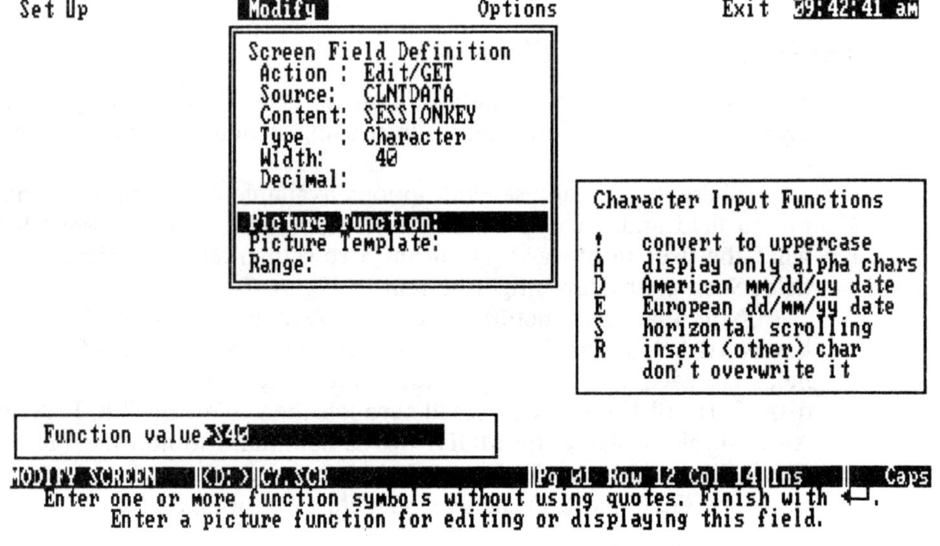

Figure 7-4 With the MODIFY SCREEN command, you can set a field to a displayed width less than the field width, then use the cursor keys to scroll through the field.

Listing 7–3 (cont.)

```
@  2, 54  GET  PASSINFO->PASSWORD
@  4, 14  GET  CLNTDATA->CLIENT_ID
@  4, 42  GET  CLNTDATA->NAME
@  6, 14  GET  CLNTDATA->ADDRESS1
@  7, 14  GET  CLNTDATA->ADDRESS2
@  9, 14  GET  CLNTDATA->CITY
@  9, 45  GET  CLNTDATA->STATE
@  9, 62  GET  CLNTDATA->ZIP
@ 11, 14  GET  CLNTDATA->MEDIKEY  FUNCTION "S40"
@ 11, 68  GET  CLNTDATA->MEDHISTORY
@ 12, 14  GET  CLNTDATA->SESSIONKEY  FUNCTION "S40"
@ 12, 68  GET  CLNTDATA->SESSIONS
*
** EOF
```

Listing 7–4

```
** SAY FILE MODIFIED WITH KEY WORD FIELDS
*
@  2,  2  SAY "USER_NAME"
@  2, 14  SAY  PASSINFO->USER_NAME
@  2, 42  SAY "PASSWORD"
@  4,  2  SAY "CLIENT_ID"
@  4, 30  SAY "NAME"
@  6,  2  SAY "ADDRESS1"
@  7,  2  SAY "ADDRESS2"
@  9,  2  SAY "CITY"
@  9, 37  SAY "STATE"
@  9, 55  SAY "ZIP"
@ 11,  2  SAY "MEDIKEY"
@ 11, 55  SAY "MEDIHISTORY"
@ 12,  2  SAY "SESSIONKEY"
@ 12, 55  SAY "SESSIONS"
@  1,  0  TO 14, 79    DOUBLE
@  3,  1  TO  3, 78
*
** EOF
```

which produce a screen like that shown in Figure 7–5.

Still, it is impossible to FIND or SEEK anything in a 254-character field. III PLUS has an INDEXing limit of 100 characters. INDEXing on a 254-character field requires a command like:

```
INDE ON LEFT(key word field, 100) TO NDX file
```

This is a serviceable solution, but still unsatisfactory. The major flaw is that both FINDing and SEEKing require a left-justified search pattern. You can't FIND or SEEK something in the middle of the key word field.

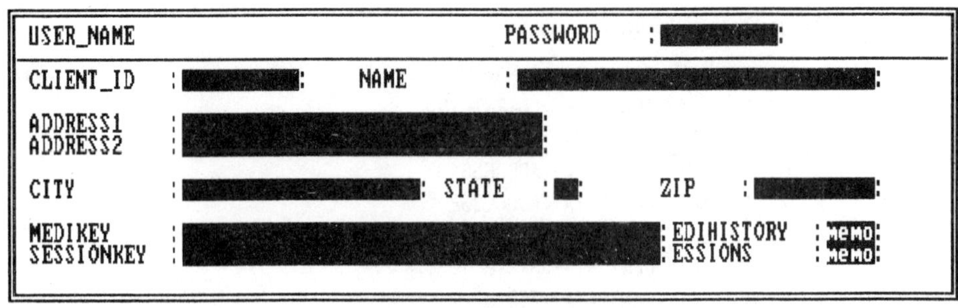


```
->
```

Figure 7–5 This screen is modified from that of Figure 7–1 and includes the scrolled key word fields.

That problem is alleviated with the Locate kernel. The basis of the Locate kernel is the command:

```
LOCA FOR 'text to match'$field to match text in
```

In other words, to find *dyslexia* as a key word in the MEDIKEY field requires the command:

```
LOCA FOR 'dyslexia'$MEDIKEY
```

If the word *dyslexia* (and remember that case is important! *Dyslexia* doesn't match *DYSLEXIA* nor *dyslexia*) is in the MEDIKEY field of any record, it will turn up.

You can quickly pseudocode a keyed field search of a memo field in near III PLUS syntax as follows:

Listing 7–5

```
GET search string
LOCATE FOR 'search string'$keyed field
*
IF FOUND
   EDIT memo field, keyed field?
*
   IF YES
      EDIT
   ENDIF
*
   CONTINUE?
```

Listing 7-5 (cont.)

```
*
   IF YES
      CONTINUE
   ELSE
      EXIT
   ENDI
*
ENDI
```

This method makes good use of dBASE III PLUS commands and hints at a method around some memo field limitations. You can use the kernels and suggestions included in this book to create the search algorithm, but someone has done much of the work for you. LSEARCH version 3.2, available from Tom Lewinson, President, Thinker's Apprentice, 392 Central Park West #12X, New York, NY 10025 (212/222-5050), is a package of dBASE III PLUS executable code, complete with documentation, that rapidly identifies which records/fields/lists satisfy a user-supplied key word or phrase. The program runs as fast as III PLUS will allow and is completely menu-driven. Having programs supplied in III PLUS executable ASCII PRG files, you directly incorporate Lewinson's logic and code into your own applications. Nice and slick. Some programmers may question the need for such a product until they try coding a similar algorithm themselves. Coding this solution yourself is a good learning experience, but your time programming can be put to better and more profitable use by availing yourself of the right tools.

Next, after the methods involving the LOCATE command and Lewinson's LSEARCH package, is instructing III PLUS to use an external word processor, line editor, or text editor. This requires more than 256K memory and is itself a good reason to upgrade.

dBASE III PLUS's CONFIG.DB file contains two separate commands to access external editors. The first is TEDIT. This is the command that tells dBASE III PLUS an external word processor is going to handle all the MODI COMM and MODI FILE commands. The other CONFIG.DB command, and the one more interesting to us at the moment, is WP. This is the command that tells dBASE III PLUS what external word processor will be used to edit memo fields. This is a near necessity in the applications covered in this chapter.

The III PLUS package includes a primitive but serviceable text editor. It doesn't have the ability to perform text searches and pattern matches, as can most editors. The solution is to use the CONFIG.DB WP command to incorporate a word processor into the III PLUS memo field system. With a word processor available, the user can also print the memo field, save parts of the field to other files, and so on.

This sounds good, but still not good enough. The problem we now have is the way dBASE III PLUS incorporates word processors and memo fields. The memo field file is actually a series of minifiles, each some multiple of 512 bytes in size. Whenever you create a III PLUS DBF file with one or more DBT fields, III PLUS automatically creates an associate DBT file. This DBT file contains all the memo field information. The input screen form for a memo field, as shown in Figures 7–1 and 7–5, is really just the word *memo*. However, behind the word *memo* is the starting block of the memo field's data in the DBT file.

For example, say you create a file with a single memo field and place data in each field in the first 10 records of the database. Not only is there data in each of the CHARACTER, NUMERIC, DATE, and LOGICAL fields, but there is somewhere between 1 and 511 bytes of textual data in each record's memo field as well. dBASE III PLUS keeps track of which block contains which record's data with lists like this:

```
DBF RECORD        DBT BLOCK

    1                 1
    2                 2
    3                 3
    4                 4
    5                 5
    6                 6
    7                 7
    8                 8
    9                 9
    10                10
```

There is a one-to-one correspondence between the record number and 512-byte block number, because III PLUS reserves memo field data in 512-byte blocks. Even if you only enter two letters in the field, III PLUS reserves 512 bytes for it. It's shamefully wasteful, but you learn to live with some features.

What happens when you add more than 512 bytes of information to a memo field? III PLUS keeps track automatically, but your pointers may look something like this:

```
DBF RECORD        DBT BLOCK

    1                 1             && 2 blocks of data entered
    2                 3
    3                 4
    4                 5
    5                 6             && 2 blocks of data entered
    6                 8
    7                 9
    8                 10
    9                 11            && 2 blocks of data entered
    10                13
```

How does III PLUS know all this? The DBT file header (described in the dBASE III PLUS documentation) tells III PLUS the location of the next available

512-byte block. This information is stored in the first four bytes of the file header and is in least-significant-digit-first form. How's that again? Consider counting from 1 to 20, but place the least significant digit of each number first. In other words, give each number a two-digit representation. This means there's room for each number to be represented by a tens digit and a ones digit. Of the two digits representing each number, the ones digit is the least significant. Why? Because any multiple of ten is larger than that same multiple times one (1 × 10 > 1 × 1, 2 × 10 > 2 × 1, and so on). Remember that the following displays are only samples; if we count from 1 to 20 and list the least significant digit first we have the following:

TWO DIGIT REPRESENTATION	LEAST SIGNIFICANT DIGIT FIRST
0 1	1 0
0 2	2 0
0 3	3 0
0 4	4 0
0 5	5 0
0 6	6 0
0 7	7 0
0 8	8 0
0 9	9 0
1 0	0 1
1 1	1 1
1 2	2 1
1 3	3 1
1 4	4 1
1 5	5 1
1 6	6 1
1 7	7 1
1 8	8 1
1 9	9 1
2 0	0 2

The least significant digits column can be translated into hexadecimal format, as shown:

LEAST SIGNIFICANT DIGIT FIRST	HEXADECIMAL REPRESENTATION
1 0	1 0 0 0
2 0	2 0 0 0
3 0	3 0 0 0
4 0	4 0 0 0
5 0	5 0 0 0
6 0	6 0 0 0

```
7 0          7 0 0 0
8 0          8 0 0 0
9 0          9 0 0 0
0 1          A 0 0 0
1 1          B 0 0 0
2 1          C 0 0 0
3 1          D 0 0 0
4 1          E 0 0 0
5 1          F 0 0 0
6 1          0 1 0 0
7 1          1 1 0 0
8 1          2 1 0 0
9 1          3 1 0 0
0 2          4 1 0 0
```

That display can be extended up to hexadecimal value FFFF (decimal value 65535), which you can display if you wish. (Remember that a real HEX display has the form "00 00 00 00.")

The point of this whole discussion is to show you an algorithm for breaking up a DBT file for searching purposes. That algorithm is:

1. Build DBT filename from DBF filename.
2. Determine positions of 512-byte memo blocks in DBT file.
   a. Read block positions from appropriate memo field in DBF file.
   b. Accumulate separate block positions until you reach the end of the file.
3. Accumulate memo field data into word processable file.

You can use this algorithm to code in C, BASIC, or whatever language you're most comfortable with. The point is to create a file that can be easily searched for key words and phrases without having to create a secondary key word field in the DBF file. Following the steps just listed, you can translate the data in memo fields into a single document. You can include flags that merge some of the DBF data with the DBT data in the word processable file. This would make later identification of clients or personnel much easier.

Again, you should be asking if anyone has already done this or something similar to this. And, yes, someone has. The company that has done this to some degree is Seaside Software, P.O. Box 31, Perry, FL 32347 (800)3-ASKSAM. That phonenumber should give you an idea of the firm's product, AskSam. AskSam is a text-oriented database system that allows you to perform quick, highly specific searches on any text data. The searches are fast and accurate, the program is easy to learn and use, and, best of all, there is a program on the company's bulletin board that pulls dBASE III PLUS files into the AskSam format. According to Mike McKinney, vice-president of Seaside Software, the file reads the dBASE DBF structure, creates a field screen for the AskSam system, queries the user where things should go on the screen and in the file, then begins the job of

```
MEMOVIEW 1.1              Copyright (c) 1985 by Proud Products

              DBF filename in use ... CLNTDATA

              1.  Find a string.
              2.  Change DBF filename.
              3.  Memo field to search : MEDHISTORY
              4.  Exit.

              SELECTION >>> 1
          STRING TO FIND >>> Dyslexia
```

Figure 7–6 Using the MEMOVIEW.COM file, you can view fields that match the search string.

importing. AskSam can be a powerful tool for programmers with this type of application and is worth consideration when large amounts of text data need to be scanned for cross-referenced information.

This, of course, brings to mind the area of scanning several memo fields for similar data. So far we've covered making concomitant key word fields, using a word processor to study individual memo fields, and using another program to perform high-speed cross references of data.

The last topic to cover is creating a feature that tells you where your desired information is even if it can't let you see the specific information. This is similar to using a card catalog in a library. The card catalog tells you the desired book is in the library, but it doesn't show you the book itself.

A similar approach within a database system would be to scan through a DBT file for specific information and then either generate a report showing that information and where you got it or somehow mark the DBF file so you'll know where to look in the DBT file. This is handled by a series of files available through the DATA BASED FORUM, from Data Based Solutions, Inc., 1975 Fifth Ave., Suite 105, San Diego, CA 92101, (619) 236-1182. The files are grouped under the topic of MEMOSRCH as MEMOVIEW.COM, MEMOREPT.COM, and MEMOFILE.COM.

Each of these files are written in Turbo Pascal and can be executed from inside dBASE III PLUS with the RUN/! command. With the first file you can view on the screen any memo fields that match the search string. An example of this screen is shown in Figure 7–6.

This is good, but you can't edit that information or otherwise use it. The second file sends memo fields and their record numbers (*not* their block numbers) to an ASCII file that can be edited with a word processor or printed. The last file, MEMOFILE.COM, is more like the card catalog.

MEMOFILE.COM works because you first modify your DBF file to include a logical field, MEMOMARK, as the first field in the database. MEMOFILE then scans memo fields and places a true in records with memo fields that match the search string. What a nice feature!

Several methods for scanning large text fields for specific data have been presented here. The important thing to remember, of course, is to design your database to make the best use of the tools available.

DESIGNING A CLIENT SERVICE SYSTEM

Now we can get back to the problem of designing the system. As always, we consider what we have readily available in our tool kit and build any new tools we need.

We'll be using our usual editing kernels: Quit, Add, Edit, Kill, Recall, Go to, Skip, and so on. We're also going to add an Update kernel. This kernel will help us do rapid edits of specified database fields based on specific patterns. (The Update kernel was first shown in Chapter 5.)

A few more lines of code must be included to handle the needs discussed in Searching Large Text Fields earlier in this chapter. We are particularly interested in seeing memo field data that somehow matches a search pattern. One method that can be coded from exiting kernels makes use of the key word field concept. Basically we modify the Locate kernel so that it works on a specific field or fields. When the search string is FOUND(), you are given access to the memo field. This code has the form:

Listing 7–6

```
      CASE ANSWER = 'M'
         RELE LOCATEWHERE, LOCATEWHAT
         TRUTH = .F.
*
         DO WHIL TYPE('&LOCATEWHERE') # 'M' .AND. .NOT. TRUTH
            @ 20,0 CLEA
            @ 20,0 SAY [I NEED A VALID FIELD NAME]
            ACCE "Use which memo field -> " TO LOCATEWHERE
*
            IF LEN(TRIM(&LOCATEWHERE)) = 0
               TRUTH = .T.
            ENDI
*
         ENDD
*
** THE FOLLOWING BLOCK IS USED IF THERE IS MORE THAN ONE MEMO FIELD IN THE DATABASE
*
         DO CASE
            CASE LOCATEWHERE = memo field 1
               LOCATEWHERE = memo field 1's key word field's name
            CASE LOCATEWHERE = memo field 2
               LOCATEWHERE = memo field 2's key word field's name
*
** YOU CAN INCLUDE AS MANY CASE STATEMENTS AS ARE NECESSARY
*
         ENDC
*
         DO WHIL TYPE("LOCATEWHAT$LOCATEWHERE") = 'U' .AND. .NOT. TRUTH
```

Listing 7–6 (cont.)

```
          @ 22,0 CLEA
          @ 22,0 SAY [I NEED A VALID EXPRESSION]
          ACCE "Locate what? -> " TO LOCATEWHAT
*
          IF LEN(TRIM(LOCATEWHAT)) = 0
             TRUTH = .T.
          ENDI
*
       ENDD
*
       IF .NOT. TRUTH
          LOCA FOR "&LOCATEWHAT"$&LOCATEWHERE
*
          DO WHIL FOUN()
             DO &GETTER
             @ 20,0 CLEA
             @ 20,0 SAY [RECORD MATCHES SEARCH STRING.]+;
                        [DO YOU WISH TO EDIT? (Y/N) -> ] GET TRUTH
             READ
*
             IF TRUTH
                DO memo format file
                @ 20,0 SAY [CONTINUE TO NEXT MATCHING RECORD? (Y/N) -> ] GET TRUTH
                READ
*
                IF .NOT. TRUTH
                   EXIT
                ENDI
*
                CONT
             ENDI
*
          ENDD
*
       ENDI
*
       DO &GETTER
       CLEA GETS
       LOOP
```

Careful readers will notice that this code has a great deal in common with Listing 5–52, the Search Using Locate kernel. The only modifications are those necessary to ensure that only memo fields are used and to allow editing of the matched memo fields. The one part of the code that may be new to some is this command:

```
DO memo format file
```

A memo format file is not tremendously different from any other format file, provided you realize you can't do the normal @ SAY GET combination. What you can do is something like this:

Listing 7–7

```
** MEMO FORMAT FILE
*
@ x,y SAY [PRESS CTRL-PG DN TO EDIT MEMO, CTRL-PG UP TO END EDIT]
@ z,t GET memo field
*
** EOF
```

An alternative to this code is to use the SET STATUS ON and SET MESSAGE TO commands:

Listing 7–8

```
** ALTERNATIVE MEMO FORMAT FILE
*
SET STAT ON
SET MESS TO [PRESS CTRL-PG DN TO EDIT MEMO, CTRL-PG UP TO END EDIT]
&& Start of @ SAY GET commands
*
** EOF
```

What other parts of the system should be considered? Do we wish to keep records (account or similar information) separate from histories (memo field based information)? If so, do we wish to keep records (account or similar information) separate from histories (memo field based information)? If such is the case—and it usually is easier to design to separate databases for these purposes—we'll be using parallel, INDEXed databases. We must make sure we include a Quit kernel and a Kill kernel that use the DELS flag to make sure all associated DBFs have similar records deleted. But we don't want to make permanent deletions from the editor. The data is too sensitive and begs a good backup with a DELETE procedure of its own. Our Add kernel must also reflect the use of parallel, INDEXed databases, and be able to check for previously used identification numbers (remember that data confidentiality is important here, perhaps more so than in other systems).

Three concerns for this system—billing, invoicing, and accounts receivable—deal with its use in client record keeping and aren't part of the personnel record system. The billing part must keep records of all visits, what is done, who does what, how long it takes, what rates apply, and so on. This data is then used by the invoicing system to generate bills and prepare them for mailing. Once invoiced, the data should go to the AR file and possibly a historical file.

As stated earlier, confidentiality is important. We therefore break the database system into four or more separate databases. The first is the client database. This database includes the following information:

ID number
Name
(In the case of patients, you may include a "care of" field)
Address
City
State
Zip
Phone

The next database is the first memo field file; it holds either confidential or semiprivate matter. This database should include:

ID number (identical to the client database)
Name
(Again, a care of field might be appropriate here)
Phone
Memo field or fields should follow

and should be UNIQUEly INDEXed.

Here is where we directly address the question of confidentiality. We can keep different levels of information from different users by creating different databases for the various confidentiality levels. Office help can only access the client database, the next higher level of employee can access the client database, and the first level of memo field files. From there the system continues with more access levels, depending on the levels of confidentiality needed. This chapter will deal with two levels of memo field files. All the memo field files contain the same basic structure, with identification number the most important field for database purposes. Note that you can easily modify the code in this chapter for several levels of files by using the multiple file kernels listed in Chapter 5. Actual confidentiality and access levels are addressed by a password file. This file should include nothing more than each user's name, password, and access level.

Our billing database is what we depend on to keep track of what's going on moneywise. This information should be included:

ID number (as in previous files)
Date of visit
Length of visit
Purpose of visit
Rate

Fee

The last database to concern ourselves with is the one that keeps track of whether we got paid—certainly a prime consideration! This is our accounts receivable (AR) database. The structure should include:

ID number (as in previous files)

Date of service

Fee (from billing database)

Date of invoice

The invoicing system makes use of both the billing and AR databases.

The AR database has a similar structure to the billing database. A handy feature to include is an automatic update of past due accounts based on data entered. In other words, if we receive partial payment, the AR GET file should automatically update the PAST DUE field.

This system uses CHARACTER fields for all identification fields. Many such systems INDEX each database on two separate fields. The first is the client/patient/member/worker identification field. The other is the carrier field. This last field is most often used when we service a client but bill our time to another entity, such as an insurance agency. As always, these database skeletons are for you to build on.

We keep all this in mind as we go to the next part of this chapter, using the kernels to build the system.

USING THE KERNELS TO BUILD THE EDITING SYSTEM

Our first task is to put together the central editor for this system. Remember that most of the work in any system is done by the editing module. Each application has some specific code that will be written directly for it, but most day-to-day activities are carried out by this core of routines. Based on the earlier discussion, we string our modules into the following editor.

Listing 7–9

```
* EDIT.PRG
* CALLS EDITMENU FROM PROCEDURE FILE
*
DO EDITMENU
DELS = .F.
ANSWER = 'X'
*
DO WHIL .T.
   @ 0,0 SAY SPACE(80)
```

Listing 7–9 (cont.)

```
   @  2,60 SAY IIF(DELETED(),"DELETED",SPACE(7))
   @ 23,34 SAY "select ->       "
   @ 23,44 GET ANSWER
   READ
   ANSWER = UPPER(ANSWER)
*
   DO CASE
      CASE ANSWER = 'X'
         CANC
      CASE ANSWER = 'Q'
*
         IF DELS .AND. $DBF()
            @ 20,0 CLEA
            @ 21,0 SAY [DO YOU WISH TO DELETE ]+;
                       [PARALLEL RECORDS IN MEMO FILES? (Y/N) -> ] GET DELS
            READ
*
            IF DELS
               SELE 2
               USE first client memo file INDE NDX file list
               SELE 3
               USE second client memo file INDE NDX file list
*
** YOU WOULD DECLARE OTHER CLIENT MEMO FILES AND WORK AREAS HERE
*
               N = 66
*
               DO WHIL N < 68                && N serves as a work area counter
                  WORKAREA = CHR(N)
                  SELE &WORKAREA
                  SELE 1
                  SET RELA TO key field INTO B
                  SET FILT TO DELE()
                  GOTO TOP
*
                  DO WHIL .NOT. EOF()
                     SELE &WORKAREA
                     DELE
                     SELE 1
                     SKIP
                  ENDD
*
                  SELE &WORKAREA
                  USE
                  N = N + 1
```

Listing 7-9 (cont.)

```
               ENDD
*
            ENDI
*
         ENDI
*
         SELE 1
         RETU
      CASE ANSWER = 'K'
         DELE
         DELS = .T.
         LOOP
      CASE ANSWER = 'R'
         RECA
         LOOP
      CASE ANSWER = 'S'
         SKIP
         DO &GETTER
         CLEA GETS
         LOOP
      CASE ANSWER = 'B'
         SKIP -1
         DO &GETTER
         CLEA GETS
         LOOP
      CASE ANSWER = 'E'
         @ 20,0 CLEA
         @ 22,0 SAY "Press CTRL-W to save edits,"+;
                    " CTRL-Q to quit without saving edits"
         DO &GETTER
         READ
         DO EDITMENU
         LOOP
      CASE ANSWER = 'O'
         COPY NEXT 1 TO TANK
         APPE FROM TANK
         LOOP
      CASE ANSWER = 'C'
         SET ORDER TO
         CONT
         SET ORDER TO 1
         DO &GETTER
         CLEA GETS
         LOOP
      CASE ANSWER = 'G'
```

Listing 7–9 (cont.)

```
         ACCE "Record Number -> " TO RECNUM
         GOTO VAL(RECNUM)
         DO &GETTER
         CLEA GETS
         @ 24,0 SAY SPACE(40)
         LOOP
      CASE ANSWER = 'D'
         @ 20,0 CLEA
         ACCE "Display What -> " TO DISPLAYWHAT
*
         IF LEN(TRIM(DISPLAYWHAT)) = 0
            @ 20,0 CLEA
            DO EDITMENU
            LOOP
         ENDI
*
         TRUTH = .T.
         @ 21,0 CLEA
         ACCE "DISP FOR -> " TO DISPLAYFOR
         READ
*
         IF LEN(TRIM(DISPLAYFOR)) # 0
            SET FILT TO &DISPLAYFOR
            DISPLAYFOR = 'FOR' + DISPLAYFOR
         ENDI
*
         @ 21,0 CLEA
         @ 21,0 SAY [DO YOU WANT THIS PRINTED (Y/N)?  ] GET TRUTH
         READ
*
         IF TRUTH
            TOPRINT = 'TO PRINT'
            EJECT
         ELSE
            TOPRINT = []
            CLEA
         ENDI
*
         DISP &DISPLAYWHAT &DISPLAYFOR &TOPRINT
*
         IF TRUTH
            EJECT
         ENDI
*
         CLEA
```

Listing 7-9 (cont.)

```
          DO &FRAMER
          DO &GETTER
          CLEA GETS
          SET FILT TO
          DO EDITMENU
          LOOP
       CASE ANSWER = 'F'
          @ 20,0 CLEAR
          INDEXKEY = FIELD(1)
          ACCE "Find &INDEXKEY > " TO TOFIND && field 1 is the ID NUMBER field
          SEEK TOFIND
*
          IF .NOT. FOUND()
            @ 24,50 SAY "Record Number ->  END  "
            @ 0,0 SAY "I can't FIND that entry. Perhaps you should LOCATE it."
            DO POOL
          ENDI
*
          DO &GETTER
          CLEA GETS
          DO EDITMENU
          LOOP
       CASE ANSWER = 'L'
          RELE LOCATEWHERE, LOCATEWHAT
          TRUTH = .F.
*
          DO WHIL TYPE('&LOCATEWHERE') = 'U' .AND. .NOT. TRUTH
             @ 20,0 CLEA
             @ 20,0 SAY [I NEED A VALID FIELD NAME]
             ACCE "Locate where? -> " TO LOCATEWHERE
*
             DO CASE
                CASE LEN(TRIM(&LOCATEWHERE)) = 0
                   TRUTH = .T.
                CASE TYPE('&LOCATEWHERE') = 'M'
                   @ 20,0 CLEA
                   WAIT [YOU HAVE TO USE 'M']+
                        [FOR MEMO FIELDS. PRESS ANY KEY TO CONTINUE...]
                   TRUTH = .T.
             ENDC
*
          ENDD
*
          DO WHIL TYPE("LOCATEWHAT$LOCATEWHERE") = 'U' .AND. .NOT. TRUTH
             @ 22,0 CLEA
```

Listing 7-9 (cont.)

```
          @ 22,0 SAY [I NEED A VALID EXPRESSION]
          ACCE "Locate what? -> " TO LOCATEWHAT
*
          IF LEN(TRIM(LOCATEWHAT)) = 0
             TRUTH = .T.
          ENDI
*
       ENDD
*
       IF .NOT. TRUTH
          LOCA FOR "&LOCATEWHAT"$&LOCATEWHERE
       ENDI
*
       DO &GETTER
       CLEA GETS
       LOOP
    CASE ANSWER = 'A'
       COPY STRUC TO TANK
       SELE 6
       USE TANK
       REPEATER = FIELD(1)
*
       IF [client database]$DBF()
          SELE 2
          USE memo field file 1 INDE related indexes
          COPY STRUC TO TANK2
          SELE 3
          USE memo field file 2 INDE related indexes
          COPY STRUC TO TANK3
          SELE 7
          USE TANK2
          SELE 8
          USE TANK3
          SELE 6
       ENDI
*
       @ 20,0 CLEA
       @ 22,0 SAY "Press CTRL-W to save information, CTRL-Q to exit"
*
       DO WHIL .T.
          APPE BLAN
          DO &GETTER
          READ
*
          IF LEN(TRIM(&REPEATER)) = 0
```

Listing 7-9 (cont.)

```
                DELE
                EXIT
             ELSE
                TRUTH = .F.
                SELE 1
                SEEK F->key field
*
                DO WHIL FOUN()
                   TRUTH = .T.
                   KEYFIELD = found key field value
                   @ 20,0 CLEA
                   WAIT [SORRY, WE'VE GOT ONE OF THOSE. PRESS ANY KEY TO CONTINUE...]
                   @ x,y GET KEYFIELD
                   READ
                   SEEK KEYFIELD
                ENDD
*
                SELE 6
                REPL id number WITH IIF(TRUTH, KEYFIELD, id number)
                SELE 7
                APPE BLANK
                REPL id number WITH F->id number, name WITH F->name,;
                                    phone WITH F->phone
                SELE 8
                APPE BLANK
                REPL id number WITH F->id number, name WITH F->name,;
                                    phone WITH F->phone
                SELE 6
             ENDI
*
          ENDD
*
          IF [client database]$DBF()
             SELE 8
             USE
             SELE 7
             USE
             SELE 3
             APPE FROM TANK3
             SELE 2
             APPE FROM TANK2
             ERAS TANK3.DBF
             ERAS TANK2.DBF
          ENDI
*
```

Listing 7–9 (cont.)

```
         SELE 1
         SET DELE ON
         APPE FROM TANK
         SET DELE OFF
         DO &GETTER
         CLEA GETS
         DO EDITMENU
         ERAS TANK.DBF
      CASE ANSWER = 'U'
         @ 20,0 CLEA
         ACCE [REPLACE WHAT FIELD?  ] TO REPLACER
*
         DO CASE
            CASE LEN(TRIM(&REPLACER)) = 0
               @ 20,0 CLEA
               LOOP
            CASE TYPE('&REPLACER') = 'M'
               @ 20,0 CLEA
               WAIT [YOU CAN'T UPDATE MEMO FIELDS. PRESS ANY KEY TO CONTINUE...]
               LOOP
         ENDC
*
         ACCE [REPLACE WITH  ] TO REPLACEWITH
*
         IF LEN(TRIM(REPLACEWITH)) = 0
            @ 20,0 CLEA
            LOOP
         ENDI
*
         ACCE "CONDITION  " TO CONDITION
*
         IF LEN(TRIM(CONDITION)) # 0
            LOCA FOR &CONDITION
*
            IF .NOT. FOUND()
               @ 20,0 CLEA
               WAIT [THAT CONDITION DOESN'T EXIST. PRESS ANY KEY TO CONTINUE...]
               LOOP
            ELSE
               SET FILT TO &CONDITION
            ENDI
*
            REPL &REPLACER WITH &REPLACEWITH

         ENDI
```

Listing 7-9 (cont.)

```
*
        @ 20,0 CLEA
      CASE ANSWER = 'M'
*
         IF .NOT. [memo field file 1 memo field file 2]$DBF()
            @ 0,0 SAY "This option only works on memo field files. Try again"
            DO POOL
            LOOP
         ELSE
            RELE LOCATEWHERE, LOCATEWHAT
            TRUTH = .F.
*
            DO WHIL TYPE('&LOCATEWHERE') # 'M' .AND. .NOT. TRUTH
            @ 20,0 CLEA
            @ 20,0 SAY [I NEED A MEMO FIELD NAME]
            ACCE "Use which memo field -> " TO LOCATEWHERE
*
            IF LEN(TRIM(&LOCATEWHERE)) = 0
               TRUTH = .T.
            ENDI
*
         ENDD
*
** THE FOLLOWING BLOCK IS USED IF THERE IS MORE THAN ONE MEMO FIELD IN THE DATABASE
** AND MAKES USE OF THE FIELD() FUNCTION, WHICH ALLOWS FOR MORE THAN ONE MEMO FIELD
** FILE TO BE USED. NOTE THAT THE MEMO FIELDS AND THEIR ASSOCIATED KEY WORD FIELDS
** MUST SHARE THE SAME POSITION IN ALL MEMO FIELD DATABASES.
*
         DO CASE
            CASE LOCATEWHERE = FIELD(first memo field)
               LOCATEWHERE = FIELD(first memo field's key word field number)
            CASE LOCATEWHERE = FIELD(second memo field)
               LOCATEWHERE = FIELD(second memo field's key word field number)
*
** YOU CAN INCLUDE AS MANY CASE STATEMENTS AS ARE NECESSARY.
*
         ENDC
**
         DO WHIL TYPE("LOCATEWHAT$LOCATEWHERE") = 'U' .AND. .NOT. TRUTH
            @ 22,0 CLEA
            @ 22,0 SAY [I NEED A VALID EXPRESSION]
            ACCE "Key word? -> " TO LOCATEWHAT
*
            IF LEN(TRIM(LOCATEWHAT)) = 0
               TRUTH = .T.
```

Listing 7–9 (cont.)

```
          ENDI
*
        ENDD
*
        IF .NOT. TRUTH
          LOCA FOR "&LOCATEWHAT"$&LOCATEWHERE
*
          DO WHIL FOUN()
            DO &GETTER
            @ 20,0 CLEA
            @ 20,0 SAY [RECORD MATCHES SEARCH STRING.]+;
                    [DO YOU WISH TO EDIT? (Y/N) -> ] GET TRUTH
            READ
*
            IF TRUTH
              DO MEMO format file
              @ 20,0 SAY [CONTINUE TO NEXT MATCHING RECORD? (Y/N) -> ] GET TRUTH
              READ
*
              IF .NOT. TRUTH
                EXIT
              ENDI
*
              CONT
            ENDI
*
          ENDD
*
        ENDI
*
        DO &GETTER
        CLEA GETS
      OTHE
        @ 0,0 SAY "That isn't one of the options. Try again"
        DO POOL
    ENDC
*
ENDD
*
** END OF EDIT.PRG
```

Much of the editor has been explained in the descriptions of the various kernels. There are a few points of interest here, however.

The Quit option has been expanded to do more than just return from the editor to a calling program. In particular, it now handles parallel deletions from the primary database to the secondary database. But the nature of this data is too sensitive to be PACKed directly and is saved for another menu system.

Nevertheless, we're going to use the QUIT module to perform the parallel deletions on the two memo field databases mentioned earlier in this chapter. Remember that your system can have as many or as few memo field files as needed. The DO WHILE . . . ENDDO loop that performs these deletions is built around the command:

```
SELE &WORKAREA
```

This is a trick mentioned earlier and put to good use here. Rather than code a delete loop for each memo field file, this macroized SELECT command lets us create a work area counter, N, and use the same loop for all memo fields. Doing so provides for easy expanding or shrinking as more files are added or removed from the system. This follows the procedures outlined and described in Chapter 5.

The Kill, Recall, Skip, and Back kernels are unchanged. The Edit kernel is also unchanged, but do remember that the memo field files have different GET and SAY files associated with them. This is especially true if you're using an external word processor as part of the memo field system.

The Copy, Continue, and Go To kernels are unchanged. The Display kernel is unchanged, but remember that DISPLAYing a memo field will do strange things to your monitor or printer (using a DISPLAY TO PRINT qualifier). You may want to include the:

```
SET MEMO TO n
```

command as part of your start-up file. This command can be easily included in a UTILITIES menu. An alternative is to use the CONFIG.DB MEMOWIDTH command. You can use the CONFIG.DB command and also use SET MEMO TO from a menu to over ride the CONFIG.DB default. The SET MEMO TO command is included in the utilities code for this section. III PLUS has a default memo width of 50 characters.

Note this final caveat before we leave the Display option. No attempt is made to make sure the user is attempting to DISPLAY FOR a proper condition.

The Find option is written to work with information in the first field in each database. This is a point originally mentioned in Chapter 4. The most important field in any database should be the first field in the database, at least for INDEXing and SORTing purposes.

The Locate option is similar to Chapter 5's Locate kernel but has a DO CASE . . . ENDCASE block added. This block incorporates:

```
TRUTH = .T.
```

as an exiting line plus a test to ensure that the user isn't trying to LOCATE on a memo field, which is an invalid function in dBASE III PLUS.

The Add kernel is modeled after the parallel, INDEXed data entry kernels shown in Chapter 5. In this case, however, we assume initial data entry is to the client database or the billing database, not to the memo field files. Because of that assumption, no editing of the memo field files occurs. This is coded as:

```
IF [client database]$DBF()
```

Such a line negates the need for access level checks and only copies (REPLACEs) the necessary fields in the memo field files. Again, because of the need for confidentiality, a check is included to make sure each new record in the primary file has a new ID number. This is done in the IF . . . ELSE . . . ENDIF block. As long as we can find our new ID number in the primary database we can DO WHIL FOUN() and continue until a nonrepetitive ID number is entered. You may want to include code to EXIT this loop should the user become frustrated.

We've included an Update kernel in this editor. The Update kernel was first discussed in Chapter 5 and is modified here with a DO CASE . . . ENDCASE block similar to that added to the Locate kernel. We test that the user isn't trying to Update a memo field. Programmers/developers/designers, take note of this. dBASE III PLUS will tell you you've REPLACEd (we use the REPLACE command in the Update kernel) information in the memo field, but won't perform the operation. Consider Figure 7–7.

The CLNTDATA.DBF file is in USE and contains two memo fields. The contents of the memo fields are shown with the ? query. The command REPL MEDHISTORY WITH SESSIONS is entered and III PLUS tells us the command has been properly executed. But, when we again query the MEDHISTORY memo field we see nothing has changed. III PLUS would tell us if something had gone wrong, as shown in the rest of the listing. There we use a text string memory variable as our WITH replacement and are told:

```
Data type mismatch.
```

So, the moral is to make sure updates don't occur to memo fields.

The last module in the editor is the MEMO SEARCH module. This module was described earlier in the chapter. The only thing left is to show the EDITMENU for this application.

Listing 7–10

```
PROC EDITMENU
@ 20,0 TO 23,79 DOUB
@ 21,1 SAY [  E -> Edit  B -> Back  S -> Skip  G -> Goto  K -> Kill  R -> Rstr]+;
          [Q -> Quit]
@ 22,1 SAY [  F -> Find  L -> Loca  C -> Cont  D -> Disp  O -> Copy  A -> Add]+;
          [U -> Upda]
*
```

The first thing we're met with is having more options than our present menu system can handle. This means we have to create code to revolve our menu

```
-> USE CLNTDATA
-> DISP STRUC
Structure for database: D:CLNTDATA.dbf
Number of data records:       3
Date of last update   : 12/30/86
Field  Field Name  Type       Width    Dec
    1  CLIENT_ID   Character     10
    2  NAME        Character     30
    3  ADDRESS1    Character     30
    4  ADDRESS2    Character     30
    5  CITY        Character     20
    6  STATE       Character      2
    7  ZIP         Character     10
    8  MEDIKEY     Character     40
    9  MEDHISTORY  Memo          10
   10  SESSIONKEY  Character     40
   11  SESSIONS    Memo          10
** Total **                     233

-> ? MEDHISTORY
MEDICAL HISTORY RECORD 1

-> ? SESSIONS
SESSIONS RECORD 1

-> REPL MEDHISTORY WITH SESSIONS
   1 record replaced
-> ? MEDHISTORY
MEDICAL HISTORY RECORD 1

-> SESSIONS = [THIS IS A TEXT STRING ]
THIS IS A TEXT STRING

-> REPL MEDHISTORY WITH M->SESSIONS
Data type mismatch.?

REPL MEDHISTORY WITH M->SESSIONS
```

Figure 7–7 MEMO fields must be edited, they can't be REPLACed.

options, but also allow any option to be executed—even if it's not listed on the present screen. That poses no problem. We include:

```
CASE ANSWER = 'N'
```

in our editor and break our EDITMENU PROCedure into two parts, as follows:

Listing 7–11

```
CASE ANSWER = 'N'
   EDITFLAG = IIF(EDITFLAG, .F., .T.)
   DO EDITMENU
   LOOP
```

This of course means you'll include the line:

```
EDITFLAG = .T.
```

at the top of the editor. This CASE should be the first CASE in the editor, even before the QUIT module. Over time CASE ANSWER = 'N' will be used less and less, but it will be the primary use CASE for the first few weeks of system USE.

The EDITMENU PROCedure is modified to:

Listing 7–12

```
PROC EDITMENU
@ 20,0 TO 23,79 DOUB
@ 21,1 SAY IIF(EDITFLAG, [  E -> Edit  B -> Back  S -> Skip  G -> Goto  K -> Kill]+;
[R -> Rstr  Q -> Quit], [  F -> Find  L -> Loca  C -> Cont  D -> Disp  O ->]+;
[Copy  A -> Add   U -> Upda])
@ 22,1 SAY  [                 M -> Memo Search                   N -> Next ]
*
```

MODIFYING THE SYSTEM

Now that the editor is complete, we can begin to address the other needs of the system. We've already mentioned the subsystems, but what do they involve?

The main menu will of course provide access to the other menus. It should also include something that gets the access level of the current user before doing anything else. As mentioned earlier, this is handled nicely with the dBASE III PLUS PROTECT.EXE utility. That utility requires using the dBADMINISTRATOR part of the dBASE III PLUS system, 640K of memory, and a hard disk. Those are some disadvantages (others were mentioned earlier). This chapter will approach the method from a straight coding process. Note that *any*one with enough time and patience can defeat *any* protection method. Allow me a strong statement to developers, however.

One of the packages offered by Ashton-Tate and mentioned previously is the dBASE PROGRAMMER'S UTILITIES. One of the programs in that package is PROTECT.BIN. This is a LOADable BIN file and can be CALLed anytime during the III PLUS work session. PROTECT.BIN works by making database files alternately readable and unreadable by dBASE III PLUS, thus protecting them from snooping eyes. Even the coding methods I'll demonstrate in this chapter can be easily overridden by anyone who simply enters III PLUS at the

DOS prompt and USEs the databases of interest. The PROTECT.BIN file would make such a step more difficult, because the PROTECTed file can't be read by III PLUS—period. Now, you can argue that anyone looking at your code will see the LOAD and CALL to PROTECT.BIN and realize what's going on. True. That's why I always recommend using DBC and DBL, the Coder and Linker utilities included in the dBASE III PLUS package and discussed in the Runtime+ section of Ashton-Tate's *Programming with dBASE III PLUS* manual. These programs pseudocompile and link your III PLUS ASCII code into a compressed form that is nearly impossible to read, thus preventing all but the most diligent from reading your ASCII PRG files and seeing the LOAD and CALL statements.

Back to the main menu. Once the access level is set, the program should let the user enter a client record system, a billing system, an invoice system, and an AR system; it also should provide a utilities option. I keep accounts receivable separate from billing and invoice because of the coding methodology I use.

The billing system keeps records of cost per visit. That's the main job of the billing system. Invoicing is the act of totaling the patient/client/carrier-specific records in the billing system and sending that information to the patient/client/carrier and into an AR file. This is the point when records from billing become historical. Totaled billing information goes into the AR file when invoices are sent out. In truth, the invoicing system doesn't have its own database. It makes use of the system's other databases. The invoicing system checks for past due accounts in the AR file and includes that information in new invoices when the system scans the billing records.

The AR system only performs three functions. It edits data, reports past due accounts, and provides for PACKing the database.

The utility is a different story. It must handle altering passwords, editing archived files, and the other, more mundane housekeeping routines necessary to the system.

Each subsystem except UTILITY must make backup files whenever PACKing occurs. This means checking for existing filenames and APPENDing to existing files or creating new files as necessary.

Now, with modifications outlined, we begin coding.

CLIENT RECORDS

The first concern is working with the actual client records. Remember that the system allows for different levels of sensitivity of client records. The first level, which can be defined as ACCESS = 1, contains address and similar information. The second level, ACCESS = 2, contains more sensitive information. ACCESS = 3 level information, for the system developed here, is the top level and contains the most confidential information. So, there are three levels. What does the code look like?

Listing 7–13

```
** CLIENT MAIN MENU SYSTEM
*
```

Listing 7–13 (cont.)

```
DO WHILE .T.
   CLEAR
   @ 2, 0 TO 14,79 DOUBLE
   @ 3,21 SAY [C L I E N T   R E C O R D   S Y S T E M]
   @ 4,1 TO 4,78 DOUBLE
   @  7,24 SAY [1. Edit Client Accounts]
   @  8,24 SAY [2. Remove Deleted Records from ] + DBF()
*
** YOU CAN HAVE AS MANY LEVELS OF THE NEXT LINE AS YOUR SYSTEM REQUIRES.
*
   @  9,24 SAY IIF(ACCESS > 1, [3. Edit Client History], [])
   @ 10,24 SAY IIF(ACCESS = 3, [4. Edit Client (next level file)], [])
   @ 12,24 SAY '0. EXIT'
   ANSWER = 0
   @ 14,33 SAY " select      "
   @ 14,42 GET ANSWER PICTURE "9" RANGE 0, ACCESS + 1
   READ
*
   DO CASE
      CASE ANSWER = 0
         CLOS DATA
         RETURN
      CASE ANSWER = 1
*
         IF PAST
*
** I USE THE NAME 'CLIENTS.OLD' FOR THE FIRST LEVEL BACKUP FILE. YOU CAN USE WHATEVER
** NAME YOU WISH, BUT CHANGE THE CODE ACCORDINGLY. DO NOTE THAT THIS SYSTEM'S
** HISTORICAL BACKUP NDX FILES USE THE EXTENSION NDO.
*
            IF .NOT. FILE('CLIENTS.OLD')
               @ 20,0
               WAIT [NO HISTORICAL FILES EXIST FOR THIS DATA.]+;
                    [PRESS ANY KEY TO CONTINUE...]
               LOOP
            ELSE
               USE CLIENTS.OLD INDE client identification NDX file.NDO,;
                                     carrier identification NDX file.NDO
            ENDI
*
         ELSE
            USE clients database INDE client identification NDX file,;
                                     carrier identification NDX file
         ENDI
*
```

Listing 7-13 (cont.)

```
            PLACE = 40-LEN(DBF())/2
            SAYER = [CLIENSAY]
            GETTER = [CLIENGET]
            DO EDIT
         CASE ANSWER = 2
*
            IF PAST
               @ 20,0
               WAIT [You can't delete records from a backup file.]+;
                    [Press any key to continue...]
            ELSE
               DO PACKER
            ENDI
*
         CASE ANSWER = 3 .AND. ACCESS > 1
*
            IF PAST
*
** I USE THE NAME 'CLMEMO1.OLD' FOR THE SECOND-
LEVEL BACKUP FILE. YOU CAN USE WHATEVER
** NAME YOU WISH, BUT CHANGE THE CODE ACCORDINGLY. DO NOTE THAT THIS SYSTEM'S
** HISTORICAL BACKUP NDX FILES USE THE EXTENSION NDO.
*
               IF .NOT. FILE('CLMEMO1.OLD')
                  @ 20,0
                  WAIT [NO HISTORICAL FILES EXIST FOR THIS DATA.]+;
                       [PRESS ANY KEY TO CONTINUE...]
                  LOOP
               ELSE
                  USE CLMEMO1.OLD INDE CLMEMO1.NDO
&& This level file only needs a single NDX file
               ENDI
*
            ELSE
*
** THE FIRST-LEVEL MEMO FIELD DATABASE IS THE SECOND-LEVEL ACCESS FILE.
** IT HAS ONLY ONE NDX FILE.
*
               USE FIRST-LEVEL MEMO FIELD DATABASE INDE FIRST-LEVEL MEMO FIELD NDX FILE
            ENDI
*
            PLACE = 40-LEN(DBF())/2
            SAYER = [MEMO1SAY]
            GETTER = [MEMO1GET]
            DO EDIT
```

Listing 7–13 (cont.)

```
      CASE ANSWER = 4 .AND. ACCESS = 3
*
         IF PAST
*
** I USE THE NAME 'CLMEMO2.OLD' FOR THE THIRD-LEVEL BACKUP FIELD.
** YOU CAN USE WHATEVER NAME YOU WISH,
** BUT CHANGE THE CODE ACCORDINGLY.
** DO NOTE THAT THIS SYSTEM'S HISTORICAL
** BACKUP NDX FILES USE THE EXTENSION NDO.
*
            IF .NOT. FILE('CLMEMO2.OLD')
               @ 20,0
               WAIT [NO HISTORICAL FILES EXIST FOR THIS DATA.]+;
                    [PRESS ANY KEY TO CONTINUE...]
               LOOP
            ELSE
               USE CLMEMO2.OLD INDE CLMEMO2.NDO && This level file only
                                                && needs a single NDX file

            ENDI
*
         ELSE
*
** THE SECOND-LEVEL MEMO FIELD DATABASE IS THE THIRD-LEVEL ACCESS FILE.
** IT HAS ONLY ONE NDX FILE.
*
            USE SECOND-LEVEL MEMO FIELD DATABASE;
            INDE SECOND-LEVEL MEMO FIELD NDX FILE
         ENDI
*
         PLACE = 40-LEN(DBF())/2
         SAYER = [MEMO2SAY]
         GETTER = [MEMO2GET]
         DO EDIT
      OTHE
         @ 20,0
         WAIT [SORRY, YOU CAN'T DO THAT. PRESS ANY KEY TO CONTINUE...]
         LOOP
   ENDCASE
*
   DO &SAYER
   DO &GETTER
   CLEA GETS
   DO EDIT
ENDDO T
```

Listing 7-13 (cont.)

```
*
** END OF CLMAIN.PRG
```

This code is not difficult to understand, but there are some highlights worth special attention.

First, the last two detail lines of the menu are generated with IIF() and not simply declared as they normally would be. The third and fourth options are actually based on the access level of the user. This access level is entered on the main menu. In addition to that, the RANG qualifier on the GET ANSWER command is also based on the user's access level. This is one means of restricting user activity. The other method, also included in this code, is in the CASE statements and discussed later.

Option 0 does something not done in Chapter 6's system; it CLOSEs all the DATAbases before returning to the calling program.

Option 1 works on a logical flag, PAST. This flag is declared in the main menu and changed in the UTILCLNT utility system. Once this flag is set to .T., the entire system works on the historical files. When the flag is .F., all current files are used. The flag's sole purpose in the system is to flag III PLUS that backup files are going to be used instead of normal work files. The backup files are not the archived files, they are historical databases. The term *historical* is literally that—past databases that don't have current information in them. This logical flag can be found in most of the modules in this chapter.

Option 2 provides the PACKing and ZAPping commands normally included in the DELS flag and editor Quit options. However, we don't want to DELETE records from our backup files, so we again use our PAST flag. Here the PAST flag tells us we can't permanently DELETE records from a historical file.

Earlier I mentioned using the RANG qualifier to restrict access to files. The other method is shown in CASEs 3 and 4. The second argument to each CASE is based on the user's access level.

The last note concerns the last four lines of the DO WHILE . . . ENDDO loop. These are the four lines that actually do work on the files and are similar to the commands used in earlier chapters.

CLIENT BILLING

The billing module is based on the concept of a billing database comprised of records of client visits or meetings. The code is:

Listing 7-14

```
** BILLING SYSTEM MAIN MODULE
*
SAYER = [BILLSAY]
GETTER = [BILLGET]
*
```

Listing 7–14 (cont.)

```
IF PAST
*
** I USE THE NAME 'BILLING.OLD' FOR THE BACKUP FILE. YOU CAN USE WHATEVER
** NAME YOU WISH, BUT CHANGE THE CODE ACCORDINGLY. DO NOTE THAT THIS SYSTEM'S
** HISTORICAL BACKUP NDX FILES USE THE EXTENSION NDO.
*
   IF .NOT. FILE('BILLING.OLD')
      @ 20,0
      WAIT [NO HISTORICAL FILES EXIST FOR THIS DATA. PRESS ANY KEY TO CONTINUE...]
      RETU
   ELSE
      USE BILLING.OLD INDE client identification NDX file.NDO,;
                           carrier identification field NDX file.NDO.
   ENDI
*
ELSE
   USE billings database INDE client identification NDX file,;
                              carrier identification NDX file
ENDI
*
PLACE = 40-LEN(DBF())/2
*
DO WHILE .T.
   CLEAR
   @ 2, 0 TO 15,79 DOUBLE
   @ 3,27 SAY [B I L L I N G   S Y S T E M]
   @ 4,1 TO 4,78 DOUBLE
   @  7,29 SAY [1. Edit Billing Records]
   @  8,29 SAY [2. Record Client(patient, etc.) Visit]
   @  9,29 SAY [3. Print Client(patient, etc.) Record]
   @ 10,29 SAY [4. Print Carrier Record]
   @ 11,29 SAY [5. Remove Deleted Records]
   @ 13, 29 SAY '0. Exit'
   ANSWER = 0
   @ 15,33 SAY " select     "
   @ 15,42 GET ANSWER PICTURE "9" RANGE 0,5
   READ
*
   DO CASE
      CASE ANSWER = 0
         CLOS DATA
         RETURN
      CASE ANSWER = 1
         DO &SAYER
         DO &GETTER
```

Listing 7–14 (cont.)

```
         CLEA GETS
         DO EDIT
      CASE ANSWER = 2
         ID = SPAC(length of client id field in database)
*
** THE FOLLOWING @ SAY GET CAN INCLUDE A PICT FUNCTION IF NECESSARY.
*
         @ 20,0 SAY [What is the patient/worker/member/client's ID? -> ] GET ID
         READ
         SET FILT TO ID = TRIM(client id field)
         GO BOTT
*
         IF client id field # ID
            @ 22,0
            WAIT [I can't find that ID. Press any key to continue...]
         ELSE
            COPY NEXT 1 TO TANK
            SELE 2
            USE TANK
            SET MENU ON
            SET STAT ON
            SET MESS TO [PRESS CTRL-W TO SAVE RECORD,]+;
                        [CTRL-Q TO QUIT WITHOUT SAVING RECORD]
*
** IT IS NECESSARY TO USE A FMT FILE TO MAKE USE OF THE READKEY()
** FUNCTION IN THE FOLLOWING CODE.
*
            SET FORM TO BILLING
&& This FMT file is merely the SAY and GET files combined
            EDIT
*
            IF READ() # 12
               SELE 1
               APPE FROM TANK
            ENDI
*
            SET FORM TO
            SET MESS TO
            SET STAT OFF
            SET MENU OFF
            USE
            SELE 1
            SET FILT TO
            ERAS TANK.DBF
         ENDI
```

Listing 7–14 (cont.)

```
*
         LOOP
      CASE ANSWER = 3
         ID = SPAC(length of client id field)
*
** THE FOLLOWING @ SAY GET CAN INCLUDE A PICT FUNCTION IF NECESSARY.
*
         @ 20,0 SAY [What is the patient/worker/member/client's ID? -> ] GET ID
         READ
         SET FILT TO ID = TRIM(client id field)
         GO TOP
*
         IF client id field # ID
            @ 22,0
            WAIT [I can't find that ID. Press any key to continue...]
         ELSE
            REPO FORM FRM filename
         ENDI
*
         SET FILT TO
         LOOP
      CASE ANSWER = 4
*
** THIS CASE USES A CARRIER FIELD, SOMETHING NOT NECESSARY IN EVERY DATABASE DESIGN.
*
         ID = SPAC(length of carrier id field)
*
** THE FOLLOWING @ SAY GET CAN INCLUDE A PICT FUNCTION IF NECESSARY.
*
         @ 20,0 SAY [What is the carrier ID? -> ] GET ID
         READ
         SET FILT TO ID = TRIM(carrier identification field)
         GO TOP
*
         IF carrier identification field # ID
            @ 22,0
            WAIT [I can't find that ID. Press any key to continue...]
         ELSE
            REPO FORM FRM filename
         ENDI
*
         SET FILT TO
         LOOP
      CASE ANSWER = 5
*
```

Listing 7–14 (cont.)

```
        IF PAST
           @ 20,0
           WAIT [You can't delete records from a backup file.]+;
                [Press any key to continue...]
        ELSE
           DO PACKER
        ENDI
*
   ENDCASE
*
ENDDO T
*
** END OF BILLING.PRG
```

The code starts by determining the PAST flag, as was done in the previous section. The code is mundane until we work with CASE ANSWER = 2.

The problem is to only work with records of interest. In particular, records of interest are those dealing with a single client. We "find" the records of interest by SETting a FILTER on the client identification field. If there are no previous records for that client, one must be added. That is done on the editing menu. Here we're only interested in recording a new visit. We GO to the BOTTOM of the database, where we determine if any previous records exist. If they do, we COPY the last record (the one on the BOTTOM of the file) to a temporary TANK file and EDIT it. We EDIT because it frees the user to only alter necessary fields instead of entering an entirely new record.

How do we know if the user has quit editing and doesn't want to add the record to the billing database? We use the READKEY() function. If the user exits any full screen editing mode (such as one initiated with the SET FORMAT TO FMT file command) with a CTRL-Q, READKEY() returns a value of 12 (no editing performed) or 268 (editing performed).

CASEs 3 and 4 perform print listings of data in the file and use the "find" method of CASE 2. CASE 5 is identical to the DELETE CASE for client records.

INVOICING

The invoicing system requires a bit more code, but is not a difficult system to code.

Listing 7–15

```
** INVOICE SYSTEM MAIN MODULE
*
SELE 1
*
** THE BILLING DATABASE HAS TWO NDX FILES. THE FIRST INDEXED ON THE CLIENT
```

Listing 7–15 (cont.)

```
** IDENTIFICATION FIELD, THE SECOND IS INDEXED ON THE CARRIER IDENTIFICATION FIELD,
** AND THE CLIENT IDENTIFICATION FIELD.
** THIS IS NECESSARY FOR LARGER GROUPING REQUIREMENTS.
*
IF PAST
*
** I USE THE NAME 'BILLING.OLD' FOR THE BACKUP FILE. YOU CAN USE WHATEVER
** NAME YOU WISH, BUT CHANGE THE CODE ACCORDINGLY. DO NOTE THAT THIS SYSTEM'S
** HISTORICAL BACKUP NDX FILES USE THE EXTENSION NDO.
*
   IF .NOT. FILE('BILLING.OLD')
      @ 20,0
      WAIT [NO HISTORICAL FILES EXIST FOR THE BILLING DATA.]+;
           [PRESS ANY KEY TO CONTINUE...]
      RETU
   ELSE
      USE BILLING.OLD INDE client identification NDX file.NDO,;
                           carrier identification field NDX file.NDO
   ENDI
*
ELSE
   USE billing database INDE client identification NDX file,;
                             carrier identification NDX file
ENDI
*
SELE 2
*
IF PAST
*
** I USE THE NAMED 'CLIENT.OLD' FOR THE BACKUP FILE. YOU CAN USE WHATEVER
** NAME YOU WISH, BUT CHANGE THE CODE ACCORDINGLY. DO NOT THAT THIS SYSTEM'S
** HISTORICAL BACKUP NDX FILES USE THE EXTENSION NDO.
*
   IF .NOT. FILE('CLIENT.OLD')
      @ 20,0
      WAIT [NO HISTORICAL FILES EXIST FOR THE CLIENT DATA.]+;
           [PRESS ANY KEY TO CONTINUE...]
      RETU
   ELSE
      USE CLIENT.OLD INDE client identification NDX file.NDO,;
                          carrier identification field NDX file.NDO
   ENDI
*
ELSE
   USE client database INDE client identification NDX file,;
```

Listing 7–15 (cont.)

```
                           carrier identification NDX file
ENDI
*
SELE 3
*
** The AR DATABASE HAS TWO NDX FILES BASED ON CRITERIA
** IDENTICAL TO THE BILLING DATABASE.
*
IF PAST
*
** I USE THE NAME 'AR.OLD' FOR THE BACKUP FIELD. YOU CAN USE WHATEVER
** NAME YOU WISH, BUT CHANGE THE CODE ACCORDINGLY. DO NOTE THAT THIS SYSTEM'S
** HISTORICAL BACKUP NDX FILES USE THE EXTENSION NDO.
*
   IF .NOT. FILE('AR.OLD')
      @ 20,0
      WAIT [NO HISTORICAL FILES EXIST FOR THE AR DATA. PRESS ANY KEY TO CONTINUE...]
      RETU
   ELSE
      USE AR.OLD INDE client identification NDX file.NDO,;
                carrier identification field NDX file.NDO
   ENDI
*
ELSE
   USE ar database INDE client identification NDX file,;
                    carrier identification NDX file
ENDI
*
** WORK AREA 4 IS RESERVED FOR TEMPORARY DATABASES IN THIS MODULE.
*
DO WHILE .T.
   CLEAR
   @ 2, 0 TO 15,79 DOUBLE
   @ 3,27 SAY [I N V O I C E   S Y S T E M]
   @ 4,1 TO 4,78 DOUBLE
   @  7,23 SAY [1. Edit Invoices]
   @  8,23 SAY [2. Invoice Patient]
   @  9,23 SAY [3. Invoice Carrier]
   @ 10,23 SAY [4. Update Accounts Receivable File]
   @ 11,23 SAY [5. Remove Deleted Records]
   @ 13, 23 SAY '0. Exit'
   ANSWER = 0
   @ 15,33 SAY " select     "
   @ 15,42 GET ANSWER PICTURE "9" RANGE 0,6
   READ
```

Listing 7–15 (cont.)

```
*
   DO CASE
      CASE ANSWER = 0
         CLOS DATA
         RETURN
      CASE ANSWER = 1
*
** THIS CAN SERVE AS AN EDIT OF THE BILLING FILE USING DIFFERENT SAY AND GET FILES
*
         SELE 1
         PLACE = 40-LEN(DBF())/2
         SAYER = [INVOISAY]
         GETTER = [INVOIGET]
         DO &SAYER
         DO &GETTER
         CLEA GETS
         DO EDIT
      CASE ANSWER = 2
         SELE 1
*
** YOU MAY WANT TO PRINT ONE INVOICE FOR A PARTICULAR CLIENT, BUT IF YOU PRINT
** ALL THE INVOICES YOU SHOULD UPDATE AR (OPTION 4 IN THIS MENU).
*
         ID = SPAC(length of client identification field)
*
** THE FOLLOWING @ SAY GET CAN INCLUDE A PICT FUNCTION IF NECESSARY.
*
         @ 20,0 SAY [What is the patient/worker/member/client's ID]+;
                    [('*' for all)? -> ] GET ID
         READ
*
         IF TRIM(ID) = '*'
            SET FILT TO LEN(TRIM(carrier identification field) = 0
*
            DO WHIL .NOT. EOF()
               ID = A->client identification field
               COPY TO TANK WHIL client identification field = ID
               SET RELA TO client identification field INTO B
               SET DEVI TO PRIN
*
** YOU WOULD PLACE CODE HERE TO PRINT OUT THE CLIENT
** ADDRESS INFORMATION FROM WORK AREA 2
*
               SET DEVI TO SCRE
               SET RELA TO client identification field INTO C
```

Listing 7–15 (cont.)

```
            SELE 4
            USE TANK
            INSE BLAN BEFO
            REPL necessary fields in TANK WITH data from accounts receivable file
            SET CONS OFF
            REPO FORM BILLING NOEJ TO PRINT
            SET CONS ON
            SELE 1
         ENDD
*
      ELSE
         SET FILT TO ID = TRIM(client identification field)
         COPY TO TANK
         SELE 2
         SEEK ID
         SET DEVI TO PRIN
*
** YOU WOULD PLACE CODE HERE TO PRINT OUT THE NAME, ADDRESS, CITY, STATE, ETC.,
** FIELDS FROM THE CLIENT DATABASE. THIS CODE DEPENDS ON THE FORMS YOU USE IN YOUR
** APPLICATIONS.
*
         SET DEVI TO SCRE
         SELE 3
         SEEK ID
         SELE 4
         USE TANK
         GO TOP
         INSE BLAN BEFO
*
&& The next line copies any previous balance due information into TANK
*
         REPL necessary fields in temporary TANK WITH information in AR file
         ENDI
*
** THE FRMS SHOULD BE GROUPED BY CLIENT/PATIENT/MEMBER/
** AND SO ON AND SET TO EJECT AFTER THE LAST PAGE.
*
         SET CONS OFF
         REPO FORM BILLING NOEJ TO PRIN
         SET CONS ON
         USE
      ENDI
*
      SELE 1
      SET FILT TO
```

Listing 7–15 (cont.)

```
          ERAS TANK.DBF
        CASE ANSWER = 3
          SELE 3
          SET ORDE TO 2
          SELE 2
          SET ORDE TO 2
          SELE 1
          SET ORDE TO 2
*
&& You may want to print one invoice for a particular carrier, but if you print
&& all the invoices you should update AR (option 4 on this menu)
*
          ID = SPAC(length of carrier identification field)
*
** THE FOLLOWING @ SAY GET CAN INCLUDE A PICT FUNCTION IF NECESSARY.
*
          @ 20,0 SAY [What is the carrier's ID ('*' for all)? -> ] GET ID
          READ
*
          IF TRIM(ID) = '*'
*
            DO WHIL .NOT. EOF()
              ID = A->carrier identification field
              COPY TO TANK WHIL carrier identification field = ID
              SET RELA TO carrier identification field INTO B
              SET DEVI TO PRIN
*
&& You would place code here to print out the client address
&& information from work area 2
*
              SET DEVI TO SCRE
              SET RELA TO carrier identification field INTO C
              SELE 4
              USE TANK
              INSE BLAN BEFO
              REPL necessary fields in TANK WITH data from accounts receivable file
              SET CONS OFF
              REPO FORM CBILLING NOEJ TO PRINT
              SET CONS ON
              SELE 1
            ENDD
*
            ERAS TANK2.DBF
          ELSE
*
```

Listing 7–15 (cont.)

```
** THE FOLLOWING @ SAY GET CAN INCLUDE A PICT FUNCTION IF NECESSARY.
*
            @ 20,0 SAY [What is the carrier's ID? -> ] GET ID
            READ
            SET FILT TO ID = TRIM(carrier id field)
            COPY TO TANK
            SELE 2
            SEEK ID
            SET DEVI TO PRIN
*
&& You would place code here to print out the name, address, city, state, and so on,
&& fields from the client database. This code depends on the forms you use in your
&& application
*
            SET DEVI TO SCRE
            SELE 3
            SEEK ID
            TRUTH = FOUN()
            SELE 4
            USE TANK
            GO TOP
*
            IF TRUTH
               INSE BLAN BEFO
**
&& The next line copies any previous balance due information into TANK
*
               REPL necessary fields in temporary TANK database;
                    WITH FOUND() information in AR file
            ENDI
*
** THIS FRM FILE IS DIFFERENT FROM THE FRM FILE USED IN CASE 2.
** THIS ONE IS GROUPED ON CLIENT/PATIENT/MEMBER ID OR NAME
** AND SHOULD EJECT FOR EACH CLIENT/PATIENT/MEMBER.
*
            SET CONS OFF
            REPO FORM CBILLING NOEJ TO PRIN
            SET CONS ON
            USE
         ENDI
*
         ERAS TANK.DBF
         SELE 3
         SET ORDE TO 1
         SELE 2
```

Listing 7–15 (cont.)

```
         SET ORDE TO 1
         SELE 1
         SET ORDE TO 1
         SET FILT TO
      CASE ANSWER = 4
*
&& This code assumes all invoices are sent out periodically.
&& This means your billing cycle
&& is weekly, biweekly, monthly, quarterly, and so on
*
         SELE 1
         TOTA ON client identification field TO TANK FOR;
              LEN(TRIM(carrier identification field)) = 0
         SELE 4
         USE TANK
         INDE ON client identification field TO TANK
         SELE 3
*
** REMEMBER TO ADD FIELDS WHILE YOU UPDATE.
*
         UPDA ON client identification field FROM D REPL;
              necessary fields WITH data from TANK
         SELE 4
         SET RELA TO client identification field INTO C
         GO TOP
*
** THE FOLLOWING DO WHILE...ENDDO LOOP MAKES SURE
** EVERYTHING IS COPIED FROM TANK TO THE AR DATABASE.
*
         DO WHIL .NOT. EOF()
*
            IF client identification field # C->client identification field
               SELE 3
               APPE BLAN
               REPL necessary fields in ar database WITH data from TANK
               SELE 4
            ENDI
*
            SKIP
         ENDD
*
         USE
*
** THE NEXT LINE IS MEANT TO BE USED WITH SAFETY OFF.
** THIS NEXT SECTION IS IDENTICAL TO THE ABOVE CODE,
```

Listing 7–15 (cont.)

```
** BUT WORKS ON THE CARRIER FIELD INSTEAD OF THE CLIENT FIELD.
*
        SELE 1
        TOTA ON carrier identification field TO TANK FOR;
             LEN(TRIM(carrier identification field)) # 0
        SELE 4
        USE TANK
        INDE ON carrier identification field TO TANK
        SELE 3
        SET ORDE TO 2
        UPDA ON carrier identification field FROM D REPL;
             necessary fields WITH data from TANK
        SELE 4
        SET RELA TO carrier identification field INTO C
        GO TOP
*
** THE FOLLOWING DO WHILE...ENDDO LOOP MAKES SURE
** EVERYTHING IS COPIED FROM TANK TO THE AR DATABASE.
*
        DO WHIL .NOT. EOF()
*
           IF carrier identification field # C->carrier identification field
              SELE 3
              APPE BLAN
              REPL necessary fields in ar database WITH data from TANK
              SELE 4
           ENDI
*
           SKIP
        ENDD
*
        USE
        SELE 3
        SET ORDE TO 1
        ERAS TANK.DBF
        ERAS TANK.NDX
        SELE 1
        USE historical billing file INDE historical billing file NDX
        APPE FROM billing database
        USE billing database INDE client identification NDX file,;
                                  carrier identification NDX file
*
&& The following code places some extra responsibility on the user. You must decide
&& if it is advisable in your application's environment
*
```

Listing 7–15 (cont.)

```
         TRUTH = .F.
         SET COLOR TO W+
         CLEA
         @ 10,0 SAY [AR FILE UPDATED AND BILLING FILE COPIED TO BACKUP FILE.]
         SET COLO TO W*+
         @ 12,0 SAY [ALL ]
         SET COLO TO W+
         @ 12,4 SAY [RECORDS WILL BE ]
         SET COLO TO W+*
         @ 12,20 SAY [DELETED]
         SET COLO TO W+
         @ 12,27 SAY [ UNLESS YOU SPECIFY OTHERWISE.]
         @ 14,0 SAY [OKAY TO DELETE ALL RECORDS? (Y/N) -> ] GET TRUTH
         READ
*
         IF TRUTH
            DELE ALL
            @ 20,0 SAY [YOU MUST USE OPTION 5 FROM THE]+;
                       [NEXT MENU TO MAKE THESE DELETIONS PERMANENT]
            WAIT
         ENDI
*
         SET COLO TO
      CASE ANSWER = 5
         SELE 1
*
         IF PAST
            @ 20,0
            WAIT [You can't delete records from a backup file.]+;
                 [Press any key to continue...]
         ELSE
            DO PACKER
         ENDI
*
   ENDCASE
*
ENDDO T
*
** END OF INVOICE.PRG
```

The invoicing system makes use of the three principal databases of the system: client records, billings, and accounts receivable. Each of these is tested with a PAST flag before the actual invoice system menu is presented.

Option 1 is actually another means of working on the billings database. It is included for consistency more than anything else. Do note that different SAY and GET files are used for this option than are used in the billing system. This provides the programmer with the ability to mask data from the user, should that be necessary.

Options 2 and 3 both serve to print invoices. Option 2 goes to the client; Option 3 goes to the carrier. The carrier option is included for systems that do billings to organizations, such as insurance agencies, that pay client bills in groups. Both 2 and 3 can invoice a single client/carrier or all clients/carriers.

Option 2, which handles invoicing clients without carriers, ensures that it does so by SETting a FILTER on the carrier identification field. In particular, it makes sure only records with no carrier information are available. The next step is to determine if the user wants to invoice all clients or just one in particular.

All clients are handled by printing REPORTs based on client identification fields. Data from the billing database is COPYed to a temporary TANK file. A RELATIONship is established on the client identification field into work area B, the client database. Information from work area B is used to create a header at the top of the page in the printer. You need to supply the code for this based on your printer forms. A RELATIONship is then established on the client identification field into work area C, the accounts receivable file. Data from that file, if any exists, is copied to TANK and placed at the top of the database. If there is no data to copy, no problem: PAST DUE = $0.00. REPORTs are then generated. Some time is saved in generating by SETting the CONSOLE OFF during printing.

What if we're only interested in one client? We SET a FILTER to the particular client identification field of interest. Instead of SETting RELATIONs into other work areas, we SEEK the data of interest. From there the code proceeds much like before.

Option 3 is the carrier version of option 2.

Option 4 covers updating the accounts receivable file. The first part of the code creates a TOTALs file. This TOTALs file is used with the UPDATE command. Note that the UPDATE command only works on records with matching client identification fields. What do we do if previously nonexisting records are now in the TOTALs file? We SET a RELATION on the client identification field in work area C, the accounts receivable database. Starting at the TOP of the TOTALs database, we go from record to record, checking client IDs in the TOTALs database against those in the accounts receivable database. Whenever they don't match, we APPEND data from the TOTALs file to accounts receivable.

That takes care of clients without carriers. Now we do the same for carriers. The next step is to move data from the billings database to the historical billings database. The next big problem is letting the user know he or she should use option 5 on the menu to PACK the database. That is done by displaying some blinking words on the screen.

Option 5 is the DELETER option, as described earlier in the chapter.

AR—ACCOUNTS RECEIVABLE

The AR module isn't particularly noteworthy. It does three things and three things only.

Listing 7–16

```
** ACCOUNTS RECEIVABLE SYSTEM
*
SAYER = [ACRECSAY]
GETTER = [ACRECGET]
*
IF PAST
*
&& I use the name 'AR.OLD' for the backup field. You can use whatever
&& name you wish, but change the code accordingly. Do note that this system's
&& historical backup NDX files use the extension NDO.
*
   IF .NOT. FILE('AR.OLD')
      @ 20,0
      WAIT [NO HISTORICAL FILES EXIST FOR THIS DATA. PRESS ANY KEY TO CONTINUE...]
      LOOP
   ELSE
      USE ar.OLD INDE client identical NDX file.NDO,;
                      carrier identification field NDX file.NDO
   ENDI
*
ELSE
   USE ar database INDE client identification NDX file,;
                        carrier identification NDX file
ENDI
*
PLACE = 40-]LEN(DBF())/2
*
DO WHILE .T.
   CLEAR
   @ 2, 0 TO 13,79 DOUBLE
   @ 3,15 SAY [A C C O U N T S   R E C E I V A B L E   S Y S T E M]
   @ 4,1 TO 4,78 DOUBLE
   @  7,28 SAY [1. Edit Records]
   @  8,28 SAY [2. Print Past Due Report]
   @  9,28 SAY [3. Remove Deleted Records]
   @ 11, 28 SAY '0. Exit'
   ANSWER = 0
   @ 13,33 SAY " select     "
   @ 13,42 GET ANSWER PICTURE "9" RANGE 0,3
   READ
*
   DO CASE
      CASE ANSWER = 0
         CLOS DATA
         RETURN
```

Listing 7-16 (cont.)

```
      CASE ANSWER = 1
         DO &SAYER
         DO &GETTER
         CLEA GETS
         DO EDIT
      CASE ANSWER = 2
*
&& This option can be coded two different ways. The simpler method is to assume all
&& records are past due; therefore, you print out all records. The other method is to
&& read the system date--assuming it is accurate--and print out all records past
&& your environment's billing cycle (15 days, 30 days, and so on).
&& The following line addresses the latter case. The former case is handled simply by
&& the REPO FORM line.
&& The variable, BILLCYCLE, is initialized by the programmer/developer/designer
&& and modified through the UTILCLNT utility menu
*
         SET FILT TO invoiced date field < DATE()-]BILLCYCLE
         REPO FORM PASTDUE NOEJ TO PRINT
      CASE ANSWER = 3
*
         IF PAST
            @ 20,0
            WAIT [You can't delete records from a backup file.]+;
                 [Press any key to continue...]
         ELSE
            DO PACKER
         ENDI
*
   ENDCASE
*
ENDDO T
*
** END OF ACCREC.PRG
```

The code starts with the same PAST test used in the billings and invoice systems. Option 1 is a straightforward editor. Option 2 prints past due reports and can be either a single-line command or two lines. Note that the AR file, unlike the billings database, has single records per carrier or client. Option 3 is the DELETER discussed previously.

UTILITIES

Of all the subsystems in the CLIENT/PERSONNEL tracking system, the utilities are the most elaborate. We start with a main menu similar to that shown in Chapter 6.

Listing 7–17

```
** UTILMAIN.PRG CLIENT UTILITY MAIN MENU
*
DO WHILE .T.
   CLEAR
   @ 2, 0 TO 19,79 DOUBLE
   @ 3, 14 SAY [C L I E N T   U T I L I T I E S   M A I N   M E N U]
   @ 4,1 TO 4,78 DOUBLE
   @ 7,26 SAY [1. System Functions]
   @ 8,26 SAY [2. Client Functions]
   @ 17, 26 SAY '0. EXIT'
   ANSWER = 0
   @ 19,33 SAY " select     "
   @ 19,42 GET ANSWER PICTURE "9" RANGE 0,9
   READ
*
   DO CASE
      CASE ANSWER = 0
         RETURN
      CASE ANSWER = 1
         DO UTILSYS
      CASE ANSWER = 2
         DO UTILCLNT
      OTHE
         @ 0,0 SAY "That isn't an option. Try again."
         DO POOL
   ENDC
*
ENDD
*
** END OF UTILMAIN.PRG
```

This main menu can branch to two submenus. The first to explore is system utilities. This code is:

Listing 7–18

```
** UTILSYS.PRG UTILITIES SYSTEM
*
DO WHILE .T.
   CLEAR
   @ 2, 0 TO 19,79 DOUBLE
   @ 3, 8 SAY [C L I E N T   S Y S T E M   U T I L I T I E S   M E N U]

   @ 4,1 TO 4,78 DOUBLE
   @  7,26 SAY [1. Set Message Wait Time (SET AT ] + STR(WAITLENGTH,4) + [ SECONDS)]

   @  8,26 SAY [2. Set Default Drive and Path]
```

Listing 7–18 (cont.)

```
   @  9,26 SAY [3. Set Date Type (SET AT ] + DATETYPE
   @ 17, 26 SAY '0. Exit'
   ANSWER = 0
   @ 19,33 SAY " select     "
   @ 19,42 GET ANSWER PICTURE "9" RANGE 0,3
   READ
*
   DO CASE
      CASE ANSWER = 0
         RETURN
      CASE ANSWER = 1
         @ 20,0 CLEA
         @ 21,0 SAY "The current ERROR MESSAGE wait time is about "+;
                    STR(WAITLENGTH,4)+" seconds."

   @ 23,0 SAY "How long would you like to wait (seconds)? -> " GET WAITLENGTH

   READ
         WAITTIME = INT(WAITLENGTH * 5.2) && The value 5.2 is system dependent
      CASE ANSWER = 2
         @ 20,0 CLEA
         @ 21,0 SAY "The current PATH is -> " + CPATH + "."+;
                    " The current DEFAULT DRIVE is " + CDRIVE
         @ 22,0 SAY "Which PATH should be the DEFAULT PATH? -> " GET CPATH
         @ 23,0 SAY "Which DRIVE should be the DEFAULT? -> " GET CDRIVE
         READ
         SET DEFA TO &CDRIVE
         SET PATH TO &CPATH
      CASE ANSWER = 3
         @ 20,0 CLEA
         @ 20,0 TO 23,79 DOUB
         @ 21,28 SAY "1. SET DATE TO MM/DD/YY"
         @ 22,28 SAY "2. SET DATE TO DD/MM/YY"
         @ 23,33 SAY " select       "
         @ 23,43 GET SELECTNUM PICT "9" RANG 1,2
         READ
*
** The following variable, DATETYPE, is set in the CLIENT.MEM file by the developer/
** programmer/designer.
*
         DATETYPE = IIF(ANSWER = 1, [AMER], [BRIT])
         SET DATE TO &DATETYPE
      OTHE
         @ 0,0 SAY [That isn't an option.]
         DO POOL
```

Listing 7–18 (cont.)

```
   ENDC
*
ENDD
*
RETU
*
** END OF UTILSYS.PRG
```

As with the main menu, most of this code was discussed in Chapter 6. A new feature is option 3, SETting the DATE TYPE. dBASE III PLUS allows for several DATE formats, but the code here only allows for either MM/DD/YY format or DD/MM/YY format.

Code specifically for the client/personnel tracking system can be found in the next listing, UTILCLNT. This is the client system utilities, but we use the kernel first listed in Chapter 6 as the basis for the code.

Listing 7–19

```
** UTILCLNT UTILITIES
*
STORE NEWDRIVE TO SOURCE,TARGET
*
DO WHILE .T.
   CLEAR
   @ 2, 0 TO 18,79 DOUBLE
   @ 3,12 SAY [C L I E N T   S Y S T E M   U T I L I T I E S   M E N U]
   @ 4,1 TO 4,78 DOUBLE
   @  7,26 SAY [1. Set Source and Target Drives]
   @  8,26 SAY [2. Set Memo Width]
   @  9,26 SAY [3. Set Length of Billing Cycle]
   @ 10,26 SAY [4. Use Historical Files]
   @ 11,26 SAY [5. Archive File System]
   @ 12,26 SAY [6. Add New Users]
   @ 13,26 SAY [7. Delete Old User]
   @ 14,26 SAY [8. Change Passwords]
   @ 16, 26 SAY '0. Exit'
   ANSWER = 0
   @ 18,33 SAY " select     "
   @ 18,42 GET ANSWER PICTURE "9" RANGE 0,8
   @ 21,0 SAY "Current SOURCE drive is -> " + SOURCE
   @ 23,0 SAY "Current TARGET drive is -> " + TARGET
   READ
*
   DO CASE
      CASE ANSWER = 0
         SET DEFA TO &CDRIVE
```

Listing 7–19 (cont.)

```
        RETURN
      CASE ANSWER = 1
        @ 20,0 CLEA
        @ 21,0 SAY "New SOURCE drive is -> " GET SOURCE
        @ 23,0 SAY "New TARGET drive is -> " GET TARGET
        READ
        TARGET = TARGET + ":"
        SOURCE = SOURCE + ":"
        SET DEFA TO &SOURCE
        LOOP
      CASE ANSWER = 2
*
&& The variable used here, WIDEMEMO, is part of the CLIENT.MEM
&& file and originally set by the designer/programmer/developer
*
        @ 20,0 CLEA
        @ 21,0 SAY [How wide do you want the memos? (20 to 79 chars) -> ];
               GET WIDEMEMO PICT '99' RANG 20,79
        READ
        SET MEMO TO &WIDEMEMO
        LOOP
      CASE ANSWER = 3
*
&& The variable used here, BILLCYCLE, is part of the CLIENT.MEM file and originally
&& set by the designer/programmer/developer. You must also set the LOW and HIGH RANG
&& arguments
        @ 20,0 CLEA
        @ 21,0 SAY [How long do you want the billing cycle? -> ];
               GET BILLCYCLE PICT '999' RANG low, high
        READ
        LOOP
      CASE ANSWER = 4
        PAST = IIF(PAST, .F., .T.)
        LOOP
      CASE ANSWER = 5
        DO ARBACRES
        LOOP
      CASE ANSWER = 6
        USE password file INDE password NDX
*
&& The following line hinders illicit changes to the password file
*
        SET FILT TO access level field <= ACCESS
        SET FORM TO password format file       && This line isn't truly necessary
        SET STAT ON
```

Listing 7–19 (cont.)

```
         SET MENU ON
         SET MESS TO [Enter the new user's name, password, and access level.]
         APPE
         SET STAT OFF
         SET MENU OFF
         SET MESS TO
         SET FORM TO
         USE
      CASE ANSWER = 7
         USE password file INDE password NDX
*
&& The following line hinders illicit changes to the password file
*
         SET FILT TO access level field <= ACCESS
         NAME = SPAC(length of name field in password file)
         @ 20,0 CLEA
         @ 21,0 SAY [Whom are we deleting? -> ] GET NAME
         READ
*
         IF .NOT. FOUN()
            WAIT [NOBODY LIKE THAT HERE. PRESS ANY KEY TO CONTINUE...]
            LOOP
         ENDI
*
         DELE
         PACK
         USE
         LOOP
      CASE ANSWER = 8
         USE password file INDE password NDX
*
&& The following line hinders illicit changes to the password file
*
         SET FILT TO access level field <= ACCESS
         SET FORM TO password format file       && This line isn't truly necessary
         NAME = SPAC(length of name field in password file)
         @ 20,0 CLEA
         @ 21,0 SAY [Whose password are we going to change? -> ] GET NAME
         SEEK NAME
*
         IF TRIM(A->NAME) # TRIM(M->NAME)
            LOOP
         ELSE
            SET STAT ON
            SET SCOR ON
```

Listing 7–19 (cont.)

```
            SET MENU ON
            EDIT NEXT 1 FILE password field
            SET STAT OFF
            SET SCOR OFF
            SET MENU OFF
            SET FORM TO
            USE
         ENDI
*
      OTHE
         @ 0,0 SAY [Not a valid choice, sorry. Try again.]
         DO POOL
   ENDC
*
ENDD
*
RETU
*
** END OF UTILCLI.PRG
```

Some readers might think there's a duplicity of function in option 1 of UTILCLNT and option 2 of UTILSYS. Not so. This code sets source and target drives. Option 2 of UTILSYS sets the *default* drive and path. The source and target drive designations are only in effect in this system, as shown by the SET DEFA TO &CDRIVE command under CASE 0. Because this code deals with this system's needs, it SETs MEMOWIDTH, the LENGTH of the BILLING CYCLE, SETs files for use, and works on the password database.

Option 2 uses a variable, WIDEMEMO, that the programmer/designer/developer initializes in the CLIENT.MEM file during setup. The CLIENT.MEM file is similar to the INVENTOR.MEM file in Chapter 6. It holds all system and carryover memory variables from one work session to the next. The main menu also SETs the MEMOWIDTH after it RESTOREs that variable from the CLIENT.MEM file. Option 3 works similarly to option 2.

Option 4 sets the PAST flag that was mentioned earlier. Note that this flag is set by the single IIF() function. We run the risk of confusing users unless we somehow let them know they're using historical files. Code to alert users regarding active files is covered last in this chapter, where the PROCedure file is discussed.

Option 5 makes use of another file, ARBACRES.PRG, and will be discussed later.

Option 6 adds new users to the system. The only line of interest is the SET FILTER command. We SET a FILTER on the access level field in the password database to the current user's access level. This means level-one users can add any users they want, but can only see information on other level-one users. Level-two users can add anyone they want, but can only see information on level-one and -two users, and so on.

At this point let's have a small aside on password files. This code makes use of an FMT file to handle work on the password file. I suggest including code that blanks out the password field so that data in that field is never visible, although it can be edited as necessary. Another suggestion is a double pass through the actual password field. The first pass gets the password; the second pass confirms the password and enters it into the password field. Also note that I don't check passwords with UPPER and LOWER case conversions. This gives the users that many more options for their passwords.

Option 7 lets the user remove records from the password file. Option 8 follows a similar logic to option 6, but here only the password field itself can be EDITed, and only the NEXT record in the password database.

Now we return to option 5's subroutine, ARBACRES.

Listing 7–20

```
** ARBACRES.PRG ARCHIVE BACKUP AND RESTORE FILE
*
&& Archive files are made with the DOS BACKUP and RESTORE utilities. These files must
&& be available to the system in standard DOS file form on the source drive to work
&& properly. The archived database uses a DAC extension.
&& The archived index file uses an NAC extension.
*
STOR [] TO FILENAME, NDXFILE1, NDXFILE2, SAYER, GETTER
*
DO WHIL .T.
   CLEAR
   @ 2, 0 TO 13,79 DOUBLE
   @ 3,19 SAY [A R C H I V E   F I L E   F U N C T I O N S]
   @ 4,1 TO 4,78 DOUBLE
   @  7,30 SAY [1. Create Archive File]
   @  8,30 SAY [2. Get Archive File]
   @  9,30 SAY [3. Edit Archive File]
   @ 11, 30 SAY '0. Exit'
   ANSWER = 0
   @ 13,33 SAY " select     "
   @ 13,42 GET ANSWER PICTURE "9" RANGE 0,3
   READ
*
   DO CASE
      CASE ANSWER = 0
         RETU
      CASE ANSWER = 1
*
** THIS OPTION MAKES USE OF THE DOS BACKUP AND COPY COMMANDS. IT ASSUMES YOU
** HAVE MORE THAN 312K AVAILABLE TO YOUR SYSTEM.
*
         DO ARCHMENU
```

Listing 7–20 (cont.)

```
*
        IF .NOT. FILE('&FILENAME')
*
           DO CASE
              CASE FILENAME = [client database.DAC]
                 MOVETHIS = [client database.OLD]
                 ! COPY &MOVETHIS &FILENAME
                 MOVETHIS = [client identification field.NDO]
                 ! COPY &MOVETHIS &NDXFILE1
                 MOVETHIS = [carrier identification field.NDO]
                 ! COPY &MOVETHIS &NDXFILE2
              CASE FILENAME = [billing database.DAC]
                 MOVETHIS = [billing database.OLD]
                 ! COPY &MOVETHIS &FILENAME
                 MOVETHIS = [client identification field.NDO]
                 ! COPY &MOVETHIS &NDXFILE1
                 MOVETHIS = [carrier identification field.NDO]
                 ! COPY &MOVETHIS &NDXFILE2
              CASE FILENAME = [ar database.DAC]
                 MOVETHIS = [ar database.OLD]
                 ! COPY &MOVETHIS &FILENAME
                 MOVETHIS = [client identification field.NDO]
                 ! COPY &MOVETHIS &NDXFILE1
                 MOVETHIS = [carrier identification field.NDO]
                 ! COPY &MOVETHIS &NDXFILE2
*
&& You'll have as many of the next CASE statements as your environment needs
*
              CASE FILENAME = [first-level memo field database.DAC]
                 MOVETHIS = [first-level memo field database.OLD]
                 ! COPY &MOVETHIS &FILENAME
                 MOVETHIS = [client identification field.NDO]
                 ! COPY &MOVETHIS &NDXFILE1
              CASE FILENAME = [second-level memo field database.DAC]
                 MOVETHIS = [second-level memo field database.OLD]
                 ! COPY &MOVETHIS &FILENAME
                 MOVETHIS = [client identification field.NDO]
                 ! COPY &MOVETHIS &NDXFILE1
           ENDC
*
        ENDI
*
        ! BACKUP *.?AC target drive designation
&& You might want to include BACKUP switches
        ! DEL *.?AC
```

Listing 7–20 (cont.)

```
      CASE ANSWER = 2
*
** THIS OPTION MAKES USE OF THE DOS RESTORE COMMAND AND ASSUMES YOU
** HAVE MORE THAN 312K AVAILABLE TO YOUR SYSTEM.
*
         DO ARCHMENU
         ! RESTORE source drive designation target drive designation:*.?AC
&& You might want to include RESTORE switches
      CASE ANSWER = 3
         NDXFILES = NDXFILE1 + IIF(NDXFILE2 # [], ', ' + NDXFILE2, [])
         USE &FILENAME INDE &NDXFILES
         PLACE = 40-]LEN(DBF())/2
         DO &SAYER
         DO &GETTER
         CLEA GETS
         DO EDIT
         LOCA FOR DELE()
*
         IF FOUN()
            TRUTH = .F.
            CLEA
            @ 10,0 SAY [SOME DELETIONS HAVE BEEN MADE.]+;
                       [DO YOU WANT TO MAKE THEM PERMANENT? (Y/N) -> ];
                       GET TRUTH
            READ
*
            IF TRUTH
               SET TALK ON
               PACK
               SET TALK OFF
            ENDI
*
         ENDI
*
   ENDCASE
*
ENDDO T
*
** END OF ARBACRES.PRG
```

This is the primary, ARchive, BACkup and RESTore program. It has its own subroutine, ARCHMENU. This code includes ARCHMENU as a PROCedure, but whether to include it is your decision.

Listing 7–21

```
PROC ARCHMENU
   CLEAR
```

Listing 7–21 (cont.)

```
   @ 2, 0 TO 15,79 DOUBLE
   @ 3,27 SAY [A R C H I V E   F I L E S ]
   @ 4,1 TO 4,78 DOUBLE
   @  7,27 SAY [1. Use Archive Clients File]
   @  8,27 SAY [2. Use Archive Billing File]
   @  9,27 SAY [3. Use Archive AR File]
*
&& The following two lines can be duplicated according to your environment's needs
*
   @ 10,27 SAY IIF(ACCESS = 3, [4. USE ARCHIVE first-level memo field FILE], [])
   @ 11,27 SAY IIF(ACCESS = 3, [5. USE ARCHIVE second-level memo field FILE], [])
   ANSWER = 1
   @ 15,33 SAY " select     "
*
** YOU CAN INCLUDE THE FOLLOWING RANG QUALIFIER AND DO AWAY
** WITH SOME OF THE CASE BLOCKS.
*
   @ 15,42 GET ANSWER PICTURE "9" RANGE 1, IIF(ACCESS = 3, 5, 3)
   READ
*
   DO CASE
      CASE ANSWER > 3 AND ACCESS < 3
         CLEA
         WAIT [SORRY, YOU'RE NOT ALLOWED TO DO THAT. PRESS ANY KEY TO CONTINUE...]
         LOOP
      CASE ANSWER = 1
         FILENAME = [client database.DAC]
         NDXFILE1 = [client identification field.NAC]
         NDXFILE2 = [carrier identification field.NAC]
         SAYER = [CLIENSAY]
         GETTER = [CLIENGET]
      CASE ANSWER = 2
         FILENAME = [billing database.DAC]
         NDXFILE1 = [client identification field.NAC]
         NDXFILE2 = [carrier identification field.NAC]
         SAYER = [BILLSAY]
         GETTER = [BILLGET]
      CASE ANSWER = 3
         FILENAME = [ar database.DAC]
         NDXFILE1 = [client identification field.NAC]
         NDXFILE2 = [carrier identification field.NAC]
         SAYER = [ACRECSAY]
         GETTER = [ACRECGET]
*
** YOU CAN HAVE AS MANY OF THE FOLLOWING CASEs AS YOU HAVE MEMO FIELD FILES.
```

Listing 7-21 (cont.)

```
*
       CASE ANSWER = 4 .AND. ACCESS = 3
         FILENAME = [first-level memo field database.DAC]
         NDXFILE1 = [client identification field.NAC]
         NDXFILE2 = []
         SAYER = [first-level memo field SAY file]
         GETTER = [first-level memo filed GET file]
       CASE ANSWER = 5 .AND. ACCESS = 3
         FILENAME = [second-level memo field database.DAC]
         NDXFILE1 = [client identification field.NAC]
         NDXFILE2 = []
         SAYER = [second-level memo field SAY file]
         GETTER = [second-level memo filed GET file]
   ENDCASE
*
** END OF ARCHMENU
```

The main archive menu lists three options. The user can create, get, and edit archive files. Working files for this system are chosen with ARCHMENU.

ARBACRES' option 1 first copies the selected historical files to a temporary set of files, all of which have the extension template ?AC. These temporary files are then BACKed UP using the DOS BACKUP utility and DELeted from the system. This ensures that users can make viable backups of the historical data but still keep a set active in the system.

Option 2 is the mirror of option 1, but keeps the files with their ?AC extensions. This negates much of the code necessary in option 2.

Option 3 is the actual editor. Again, this uses files with the ?AC extensions. Note that this is the only place where DELETEd records can be removed from archived files.

The ARCHMENU file tells ARBACRES what files to use. It works simply by storing file and procedure names to the memory variables declared in ARBACRES. It makes use of IIF() to declare menu lines only for users with the proper access level.

A double mcguffin is performed in the code. I limit the input RANG with an IIF() and also limit access with the CASEs. You can choose either method, depending on the needs of your environment.

A REAL-LIFE EXAMPLE OF A CLIENT SERVICE SYSTEM

We now come to the main menu that ties all the subsystems together. It is, of course, a close parallel to the main menu shown in Chapter 6.

Listing 7–22

```
** CLIENT RECORD KEEPING MAIN MENU SYSTEM
*
CLOS ALL
CLEA ALL
*
* FEATURES TURNED ON
SET DELI ON
SET ESCA ON
SET INTE ON
*
* FEATURES TURNED OFF
SET BELL OFF
SET CONF OFF
SET STAT OFF
SET SAFE OFF
SET TALK OFF
*
REST FROM CLIENT
SET PATH TO &CPATH
SET DEFA TO &CDRIVE
SET PROC TO CLIENT.PRC
SET DELI TO '><'
SET MEMO TO WIDEMEMO
SET DATE TO &DATETYPE
*
ON ERROR DO ERRORMSS
*
NEWDRIVE = CDRIVE
NEWPATH = CPATH
PLACE = 0
ACCESS = 0
PAST = .F.
TRUTH = .F.
*
DO WHILE .T.
   CLEAR
   @ 2, 0 TO 16,79 DOUBLE
   @ 3,32 SAY [M A I N   M E N U]
   @ 4,1 TO 4,78 DOUBLE
   @  7,27 SAY [1. Enter Name and Password]
   @  8,27 SAY [2. Client Records System]
   @  9,27 SAY [3. Billing System]
   @ 10,27 SAY [4. Invoice System]
   @ 11,27 SAY [5. Accounts Receivable System]
   @ 12,27 SAY [6. Utilities System]
```

Listing 7–22 (cont.)

```
   @ 14,27 SAY '0. Exit'
   ANSWER = 0
   @ 16,33 SAY " select     "
   @ 16,42 GET ANSWER PICTURE "9" RANGE 0,6
   READ
*
   DO CASE
      CASE ANSWER > 1 .AND. ACCESS = 0
         @ 20,0 SAY [YOU HAVE TO ENTER YOUR NAME AND PASSWORD]+;
                    [BEFORE DOING ANYTHING ELSE.]
         WAIT
         LOOP
      CASE ANSWER = 0
         SAVE TO CLIENT
         RETURN
      CASE ANSWER = 2
         DO CLMAIN
         LOOP
      CASE ANSWER = 3
         DO BILLING
         LOOP
      CASE ANSWER = 4
         DO INVOICE
         LOOP
      CASE ANSWER = 5
         DO ACCREC
         LOOP
      CASE ANSWER = 6
         DO UTILITY
         LOOP
      CASE ANSWER = 1
*
** THIS PASSWORD FILE CONTAINS USER NAMES, THEIR PASSWORDS, AND ACCESS LEVELS.
** IT'S INDEXED ON USER NAMES.
*
         USE passwords file INDE passwords NDX file
*
&& The following code is necessary for installation and should
&& the databases get corrupted
*
         IF RECC() = 0
            CLEA
            SET COLO TO W+
*
            TEXT
```

Listing 7–22 (cont.)

```
              There is no data in the PASSWORD file.
              You must set up the password file be-
              fore doing anything else.
      ENDT
*
            TRUTH = .F.
            SET COLO TO
            @ 10,0 SAY [ARE YOU READY TO SET UP THE PASSWORD FILE? (Y/N) -> ];
                   GET TRUTH
            READ
*
            IF .NOT. TRUTH
               QUIT
            ENDI
*
            SET MENU ON
            SET STAT ON
            SET FORM TO password format file
*
&& The following message depends on the number of file levels in your system
*
            SET MESS TO [Enter each user's name, password, and access level (1-3)]
            APPE
            SET MENU OFF
            SET STAT OFF
            SET FORM TO
            SET MESS TO
            LOOP
         ENDI
*
         N = 1
*
&& This system allows 3 attempts at a correct name and password.
&& You can allow any number of attempts by changing the value of N
*
         DO WHIL N < 4
            ACCE [What is your name, please? -> ] TO NAME
            SEEK M->NAME
*
            IF FOUN()
               TRUTH = .T.
               EXIT
            ENDI
*
            @ ROW() + 1,0 SAY [I can't find that name.]
```

Listing 7–22 (cont.)

```
            N = N + 1
         ENDD
*
         IF .NOT. TRUTH
            CLEA
            @ 1,0 SAY [SORRY, I DON'T KNOW WHO YOU ARE.]
            QUIT
         ENDI
*
         N = 1
         TRUTH = .F.
*
         DO WHIL N < 4
            ACCE M->NAME + [, what is your password? -> ] TO PASSWORD
*
            IF TRIM(password) = M->PASSWORD
               TRUTH = .T.
               EXIT
            ENDI
*
            @ ROW() + 1,0 SAY [That's not exactly what I have.]
            N = N + 1
         ENDD
*
         IF .NOT. TRUTH
            CLEA
            @ 1,0 SAY [SORRY, YOU DON'T KNOW WHO YOU ARE.]
            QUIT
         ELSE
            ACCESS = A->ACCESS
            USE
         ENDI
*
   ENDCASE
*
ENDDO T
*
** END OF CLNTMAIN.PRG
```

The program first CLOSEs any open files and CLEARs the system. It SETs some defaults ON or OFF, then RESTOREs the CLIENT.MEM file and establishes more defaults. A few lines down the PAST and TRUTH flags are initialized.

There isn't much to this code. Note the CASE listings, however. The first CASE is an error loop. You can't do any work unless you've first established yourself as a valid user. CASE 0 exits the system. A QUIT command can replace the RETURN command in this code. CASEs 2 through 6 all call subroutines.

CASE 1 is the largest code segment. The first part of the code is necessary if the system originally runs without information in the password file. If there is no information in the password file, the user is given the option of placing data there or quitting the system. If data exists in the password file, the user has three chances at a correct name and password. Note that this code only serves to set the ACCESS variable for the rest of the system.

We haven't discussed the PACKER module yet. It bears a strong resemblance to those mentioned and listed elsewhere, but includes some code necessary for this system.

Listing 7–23

```
* PACKER.PRG WITH MODIFICATIONS FOR CLIENT/PERSONNEL TRACKING SYSTEM
*
&& You can include as many key field statements as you need. This system uses
&& two NDX files for most databases, so I use two key field statements
*
KEYFIELD1 = FIELD(1)
KEYFIELD2 = FIELD(2)
CLEA
@ 4,0 TO 10,79 DOUBLE
@ 6,20 SAY [0. Quit without Changing Anything]
@ 7,20 SAY [1. Remove Deleted Entries]
@ 8,20 SAY [2. Remove All Entries]
@ 10,33 SAY " select      "
@ 10,42 GET ANSWER PICT "9" RANG 0,2
READ
*
DO CASE
   CASE ANSWER = 0
      RETURN
   CASE ANSWER = 2
      FILENAME = LEFT(DBF(), AT(".", DBF())) + ".OLD"
*
&& You have as many NDXFILE statements as you have key field statements above
*
      NDXFILE1 = LEFT(NDX(1), AT('.', NDX(1))) + "NDO"
      NDXFILE2 = LEFT(NDX(2), AT('.', NDX(2))) + "NDO"
*
      IF FILE('&FILENAME')
         DBF = DBF()
*
&& This next line can be extended as far as necessary for the maximum
&& number of NDX files per DBF in your system
*
         NDXLIST = NDX(1) + IIF(NDX(2) # [], ', ' + NDX(2), []) + IIF(NDX(3)...
         USE &FILENAME INDE &NDXFILE1, &NDXFILE2
```

Listing 7–23 (cont.)

```
            APPE FROM &DBF
            USE &DBF INDE &NDXLIST
         ELSE
            COPY TO &FILENAME
            SELE 2
            USE &FILENAME
            INDE ON &KEYFIELD1 TO &NDXFILE1
            INDE ON &KEYFIELD2 TO &NDXFILE2
            USE
            SELE 1
         ENDI
*
&& Each memo field file in the next command should be separated
&& by a space from the other names.
*
         IF LEFT(FILENAME, AT('.',FILENAME)-]1)$[memo field file list] .AND. ACCESS = 3
            CLEA
            WAIT [Please place a disk in drive (target drive designation).]+;
                 [Press any key to continue...]
            TEXTFILE = FIELD(n)               && All memo field files
                                              && should have the same structure
            CLEA
            SET COLO TO W+*                 && This setting works well on all monitors.
                                            && You can experiment.
            ? [WRITING FILE, PLEASE DO NOT DISTURB]
            SET ALTE TO target drive designation:&TEXTFILE
            SET ALTE ON
            SET CONS OFF
            LIST necessary fields from memo field file     && Note that all memo field
                                                           && files should have the same
                                                           && structure regardless of the
                                                           && information they contain
            CLOS ALTE
            SET COLO TO
            SET CONS ON
            CLEA
            WAIT [Listing complete. Press any key to continue...]
         ENDI
*
         ZAP
      CASE ANSWER = 1
*
         DO CASE
            CASE LEFT(DBF(),AT('.', DBF())-]1)$;
                 [memo field file list, as above] .AND. ACCESS # 3
```

Listing 7-23 (cont.)

```
                @ 20,0 CLEA
                @ 20,0 SAY [Sorry, only ACCESS LEVEL 3 users can delete]+;
                        [records from this file]
                WAIT
                RETU
              CASE LEFT(DBF(),AT('.', DBF())-1)$;
                  [memo field file list, as above] .AND. ACCESS = 3
                FILENAME = SUBSTR(DBF(),AT(":",DBF()) + 1, AT(".",DBF())-1) + ".OLD"
*
&& You have as many NDXFILE statements as you have keyfield statements above
*
                NDXFILE1 = LEFT(NDX(1), AT('.', NDX(1))) + "NDO"
                NDXFILE2 = LEFT(NDX(2), AT('.', NDX(2))) + "NDO"
                SET FILT TO DELE()
*
                IF FILE('&FILENAME')
                  COPY TO TANK
                  SELE 2
                  USE &FILENAME INDE &NDXFILE1, &NDXFILE2
                  APPE FROM TANK
                  ERAS TANK.DBF
                ELSE
                  COPY TO &FILENAME
                  SELE 2
                  USE &FILENAME
                  INDE ON &KEYFIELD1 TO &NDXFILE1
                  INDE ON &KEYFIELD2 TO &NDXFILE2
                ENDI
*
                USE
                SELE 1
            ENDC
*
            SET TALK ON
            ? "PACKING DATABASE TO REMOVE DELETED RECORDS"
            PACK
            SET TALK OFF
ENDC
*
** END OF PACKER
```

Most of the code in PACKER deals with getting the proper filenames. But look at the last IF . . . ENDIF block in option 2. This code creates a word processor editable text file of the confidential information. What a handy feature!

That brings us to the PROCedure file for this system, CLIENT.PRC.

Listing 7–24

```
** CLIENT.PRC CLIENT/PERSONNEL SYSTEM PROCEDURE FILE
*
PROC EDITMENU
@ 20,0 TO 23,79 DOUB
@ 21,1 SAY IIF(EDITFLAG, [  E -> Edit  B -> Back  S -> Skip  G -> Goto]+;
K -> Kill  R -> Rstr  Q -> Quit],;
[  F -> Find  L -> Loca  C -> Cont  D -> Disp]+;
O -> Copy  A -> Add   U -> Upda])
@ 22,1 SAY  [             M -> Memo Search    N -> Next ]
*
PROC MEMO1SAY
CLEA
@ 2,3 SAY IIF(PAST,[HISTORICAL DATA],[])
@  2, PLACE SAY DBF()
*
** SAY STATEMENTS FROM YOUR FIRST MEMO FIELD SAY FILE
*
@  3,  1  TO  3, 78    DOUBLE
@  1,  0  TO 18, 79    DOUBLE
*
PROC NMEMO1GET
*
** GET STATEMENTS FROM YOUR FIRST MEMO FIELD GET FILE
*
@ 24, 50  SAY "Record Number -> " + STR(RECNO(),4,0)
*
PROC MEMO2SAY
CLEA
@ 2,3 SAY IIF(PAST,[HISTORICAL DATA],[])
@  2, PLACE SAY DBF()
*
** SAY STATEMENTS FROM YOUR SECOND MEMO FIELD SAY FILE
*
@  3,  1  TO  3, 78    DOUBLE
@  1,  0  TO 18, 79    DOUBLE
*
PROC MEMO2GET
*
** GET STATEMENTS FROM YOUR SECOND MEMO FIELD GET FILE
*
@ 24, 50  SAY "Record Number -> " + STR(RECNO(),4,0)
*
PROC CLIENSAY
CLEA
@ 2,3 SAY IIF(PAST,[HISTORICAL DATA],[])
```

Listing 7-24 (cont.)

```
@  2, PLACE SAY DBF()
*
** SAY STATEMENTS FROM YOUR SECOND MEMO FIELD SAY FILE
*
@  3,  1  TO  3, 78    DOUBLE
@  1,  0  TO 18, 79    DOUBLE
*
PROC CLIENGET
*
** GET STATEMENTS FROM YOUR CLIENT DATABASE GET FILE
*
@ 24, 50  SAY "Record Number -> " + STR(RECNO(),4,0)
*
PROC BILLSAY
CLEA
@ 2,3 SAY IIF(PAST,[HISTORICAL DATA],[])
@  2, PLACE SAY DBF()
*
** SAY STATEMENTS FROM YOUR ACCOUNTS RECEIVABLE SAY FILE
*
@  3,  1  TO  3, 78    DOUBLE
@  1,  0  TO 18, 79    DOUBLE
*
PROC BILLGET
*
** GET STATEMENTS FROM YOUR ACCOUNTS RECEIVABLE DATABASE GET FILE
*
@ 24, 50  SAY "Record Number -> " + STR(RECNO(),4,0)
*
PROC ACRECSAY
CLEA
@ 2,3 SAY IIF(PAST,[HISTORICAL DATA],[])
@  2, PLACE SAY DBF()
*
** SAY STATEMENTS FROM YOUR ACCOUNTS RECEIVABLE SAY FILE
*
@  3,  1  TO  3, 78    DOUBLE
@  1,  0  TO 18, 79    DOUBLE
*
PROC ACRECGET
*
** GET STATEMENTS FROM YOUR ACCOUNTS RECEIVABLE DATABASE GET FILE
*
@ 24, 50  SAY "Record Number -> " + STR(RECNO(),4,0)
*
```

Listing 7-24 (cont.)

```
PROC INVOISAY
CLEA
@ 2,3 SAY IIF(PAST,[HISTORICAL DATA],[])
@  2, PLACE SAY DBF()
*
** SAY STATEMENTS FROM YOUR BILLING SAY FILE
*
@  3,  1  TO  3, 78    DOUBLE
@  1,  0  TO 18, 79    DOUBLE
*
PROC INVOIGET
*
** GET STATEMENTS FROM YOUR BILLING DATABASE GET FILE
*
@ 24, 50  SAY "Record Number -> " + STR(RECNO(),4,0)
*
PROC ERRORMSS
*
DO CASE
   CASE ERROR() = 1
      @ 0,0 SAY "That file doesn't exist on drive "+NEWDRIVE
      DO POOL
      RETU TO MASTER
   CASE ERROR() = 4
      @ 24,50 say "Record Number ->  END  "
      @ 0,0 SAY "You're at the end of the file now. "
   CASE ERROR() = 5
      @ 24,50 say "Record Number ->  END  "
      @ 0,0 SAY "You can't CONTINUE any further. You're at the end. "
   CASE ERROR() = 38
      @ 24,50 say "Record Number -> 0    "
      @ 0,0 SAY "You can't go any further. You're at the beginning now. "
   CASE ERROR() = 42
      @ 0,0 SAY "You must LOCATE before you can CONTINUE. "
   CASE ERROR() = 114
      CLEAR
      @ 10,10 TO 20,70 DOUBLE
      @ 15,15 SAY "The INDEX file is damaged, excuse me while I REINDEX"
      REIN
   CASE ERROR() = 125
      @ 0,0 SAY "Please turn the PRINTER ON."
   OTHE
      @ 0,0 Say "I've encountered an unknown error. Please try again."
ENDC
*
```

Listing 7–24 (cont.)

```
DO POOL
*
PROC POOL
LAPS = 0
*
DO WHILE LAPS < WAITTIME
   LAPS = LAPS + 1
ENDD
*
PROC ARCHMENU
   CLEAR
   @ 2, 0 TO 15,79 DOUBLE
   @ 3,27 SAY [A R C H I V E   F I L E S  ]
   @ 4,1 TO 4,78 DOUBLE
   @  7,27 SAY [1. Use Archive Clients File]
   @  8,27 SAY [2. Use Archive Billing File]
   @  9,27 SAY [3. Use Archive AR File]
*
&& The following two lines can be duplicated according to your environment's needs
*
   @ 10,27 SAY IIF(ACCESS = 3, [4. USE ARCHIVE first-level memo field FILE], [])
   @ 11,27 SAY IIF(ACCESS = 3, [5. USE ARCHIVE second-level memo field FILE], [])
   ANSWER = 1
   @ 15,33 SAY " select     "
*
** YOU CAN INCLUDE THE FOLLOWING RANG QUALIFIER AND DO AWAY
** WITH SOME OF THE CASE BLOCKS.
*
   @ 15,42 GET ANSWER PICTURE "9" RANGE 1, IIF(ACCESS = 3, 5, 3)
   READ
*
   DO CASE
      CASE ANSWER > 3 AND ACCESS < 3
         CLEA
         WAIT [SORRY, YOU'RE NOT ALLOWED TO DO THAT. PRESS ANY KEY TO CONTINUE...]
         LOOP
      CASE ANSWER = 1
         FILENAME = [client database.DAC]
         NDXFILE1 = [client identification field.NAC]
         NDXFILE2 = [carrier identification field.NAC]
         SAYER = [CLIENSAY]
         GETTER = [CLIENGET]
      CASE ANSWER = 2
         FILENAME = [billing database.DAC]
         NDXFILE1 = [client identification field.NAC]
```

Listing 7–24 (cont.)

```
         NDXFILE2 = [carrier identification field.NAC]
         SAYER = [BILLSAY]
         GETTER = [BILLGET]
      CASE ANSWER = 3
         FILENAME = [ar database.DAC]
         NDXFILE1 = [client identification field.NAC]
         NDXFILE2 = [carrier identification field.NAC]
         SAYER = [ACRECSAY]
         GETTER = [ACRECGET]
*
** YOU CAN HAVE AS MANY OF THE FOLLOWING CASEs AS YOU HAVE MEMO FIELD FILES.
*
      CASE ANSWER = 4 .AND. ACCESS = 3
         FILENAME = [first-level memo field database.DAC]
         NDXFILE1 = [client identification field.NAC]
         NDXFILE2 = []
         SAYER = [first-level memo field SAY file]
         GETTER = [first-level memo filed GET file]
      CASE ANSWER = 5 .AND. ACCESS = 3
         FILENAME = [second-level memo field database.DAC]
         NDXFILE1 = [client identification field.NAC]
         NDXFILE2 = []
         SAYER = [second-level memo field SAY file]
         GETTER = [second-level memo filed GET file]
   ENDCASE
*
** END OF CLIENT.PRC PROCEDURE FILE
```

I mentioned earlier the need to inform users when they're using historical data. Note the IIF(PAST . . .) command at the beginning of each SAY file.

Voilá, our system is complete.

CHAPTER

8

SUBSCRIPTION SYSTEMS

A subscription system can take many forms. All are based on the concept of keeping track of who gets what. Who gets a magazine or magazines? Who gets a newspaper? Who gets to play racquetball? Who gets what cable stations? All these questions are answered by subscription systems.

The Clipper compatible files for this discussion can be found in Appendix A.

THE SPECIAL NEEDS OF HIGH-SPEED SEARCHING SYSTEMS

Most groups that use subscription systems have one great burning desire: to have more subscribers than they need to make ends meet. That's usually a lot of subscribers. You certainly don't think your $11.75 per week pays for all that goes into the *Boston Globe,* do you? Advertisers pay many of the business costs for any magazine or newspaper. That doesn't negate the need for good subscription management, however.

Good subscription management means being able to FIND or SEEK information on a number of fields with little to no difficulty. High-speed searches on more than one field are applicable to many environments, and listings shown in this chapter can be applied to most of them.

Let's take an example of a private cable television company (an earth station system; the code for an existing system is given in Appendix A). They provide subscriber services to homes in various geographic areas. People like to watch TV, and because people usually get more upset when they miss "The Cosby Show" than when they get robbed, they'll complain when something goes wrong with their cable. The cable company's office staff must get information from the database on what services are provided the subscriber, rates, nearest lock box, and so on. The office staff also has to field questions from their repair people and installers regarding these facts.

These needs are met by creating a system with several key fields. Chapter 4 mentions that all key fields should be placed at the top of the database. Obviously, the most important key field should be the first field in the database. The second most important key field should be the second field in the database, and so on.

But what if the searching method must be more elaborate? What if, in addition to having key field searches, you must design an NDX file on a synthesis of different fields, as is the case here? Designing and using such an NDX file isn't difficult. You merely tell III PLUS what fields you want to INDEX ON in the INDEX command. You must make sure that everything is the same data type. Again, this is no problem. dBASE III PLUS has a variety of functions that transfer data from one form to another. You must make sure the entire INDEX field contains fewer than 100 characters. No problem again. An example, taken from a library management system is:

Listing 8–1

```
INDE ON TRIM(TITLE) TO NDXFILE1
INDE ON TRIM(LEFT(AUTHOR,50))+UPPER(TRIM(LEFT(TITLE,50))) TO NDXFILE2
INDE ON TRIM(LEFT(EDITOR,50))+UPPER(TRIM(LEFT(TITLE,50))) TO NDXFILE3
INDE ON TRIM(CATEGORY)+UPPER(TRIM(LEFT(TITLE,50))) TO NDXFILE4
INDE ON TRIM(LEFT(SUBJECT,50))+UPPER(TRIM(LEFT(TITLE,50))) TO NDXFILE5
INDE ON TRIM(LIBRARY)+UPPER(TRIM(LEFT(TITLE,50))) TO NDXFILE6
```

The first-level NDX file is created on TITLE, the second level on AUTHOR and TITLE, the third on EDITOR and TITLE, and so on through the six NDX files. Note that the last five NDX files have a primary and secondary key. The primary keys to the six files are TITLE, AUTHOR, EDITOR, CATEGORY, SUBJECT, and LIBRARY. The last five files have a secondary key of TITLE. You could retrieve a record on a specific SUBJECT-TITLE combination with code like the following:

Listing 8–2

```
ACCE "What is the subject? -> " TO SUBJECT
ACCE "What is the title? -> " TO TITLE
FINDTHIS = TRIM(SUBJECT)+TRIM(TITLE)
SET ORDE TO 5
SEEK FINDTHIS
SET ORDE TO 1
CLEA
DO &SAYER
DO &GETTER
CLEA GETS
```

Notice the flexibility we're designing into this code. We can retrieve information based on TITLE, a specific item, or SUBJECT, a much less specific item. Assume our title is *Day of the Triffids, The,* and the subject is "science fiction" (I don't know if that book is normally considered science fiction, but this is just an example). We can get the record for that one book, or we can retrieve all records for any book under the subject of science fiction by shifting the NDX file ORDER.

Now, with SET EXACT OFF, we can be discriminating in our search. We can declare our subject as science fiction and our title as *Day.* We'll get records on *Day of the Triffids, The* and *Day into Night,* and any other records with titles beginning with *Day.*

The emphasis here is knowing what is going to be looked for before anyone goes looking for it. This involves precognition and places an extra burden on you, the developer/designer/programmer. Usually you're not precognitive and admit it openly, but will still bear the blame when everyone else realizes you're not. The code written and discussed in this chapter attempts to make precognition much easier by designing for hindsight.

Confused? Don't be. We're going to write some code that is what we *think* is necessary, but we're going to code in such a way that more search patterns can be easily added later.

DESIGNING A SUBSCRIPTION SYSTEM

What do we have available from past work? The standard kernels are Recall, Skip, Go To, Back, Edit, Copy, Continue, Display, Locate, and Update.

Three kernels that require modification for this system are Quit, Kill, and Add. The Kill kernel isn't really modified, we just include the DELS flag.

What about Quit and Add? This is a subscription system. There will be a database of addresses and a database of payments. These databases will share the common account number field. There are parallel, INDEXed files present. We must modify the normal Quit and Add kernels accordingly. Much of this was explained in Chapter 5 and is reviewed in this chapter as it applies to this environment.

There is also one gnat in the balm of this system. It has to do with how the data is stored. Specifically, how is the primary key field is stored? Consider what information has to go into these systems.

The first database is merely a list of the subscribers. That information is generic and has a form like:

Account

Name

Address

Telephone

Services/magazine/or other subscription item customer receives

You might add certain accounting items, such as the rate and date started, to that list, but remember that we're primarily interested in the information necessary to contact our subscribers with this database. The second database has more information dealing with actual accounting needs:

Account
Name
Start
Rate
Schedule
Stop
First payment
Last payment
Credit
Limit
Restart

Over time we add more subscribers. Eventually, we realize we didn't design the ACCOUNT field large enough to accommodate all the information we normally place there. We need to increase the field's size. But we want aesthetics, as well. We want to right justify the account numbers in their field. This is most easily handled by getting the account numbers with a PICTURE function that shows the number of available characters in the account number and telling the office staff to right justify during data entry. The other part of the problem is that we must now modify our Find and Add options accordingly.

The Find option uses SEEK to search for information in the key field. But now we must tell III PLUS that certain account numbers aren't '12345' but are ' 12345'. That code is handled with the IIF() function and a knowledge of how the account numbers look. The code in this chapter makes use of account numbers with the form of "two characters in location code-last four digits of the phone number." The key to the problem is the hyphen (-) located at the third character in the account number.

We can get our office staff to enter data according to that template with a command like:

```
@ x,y GET account field PICT "!!-!!!!"
```

This provides a visual cue that data should be entered according to a certain format, as shown in Figure 8–1.

We must also modify the Add kernel to handle parallel data entry checks with the same constraint. We need to check for identical account numbers and must code the Add kernel to check for right-justified data.

What else? This is also the system that checks whether everyone in the subscriber database is in the payments file. That can be handled by a new routine, ACCTCK (ACCounT ChecK). Everything else is straightforward and coded on past modules.

USING THE KERNELS TO BUILD THE SYSTEM

We start by creating the central editor from the needs listed in the design just described:

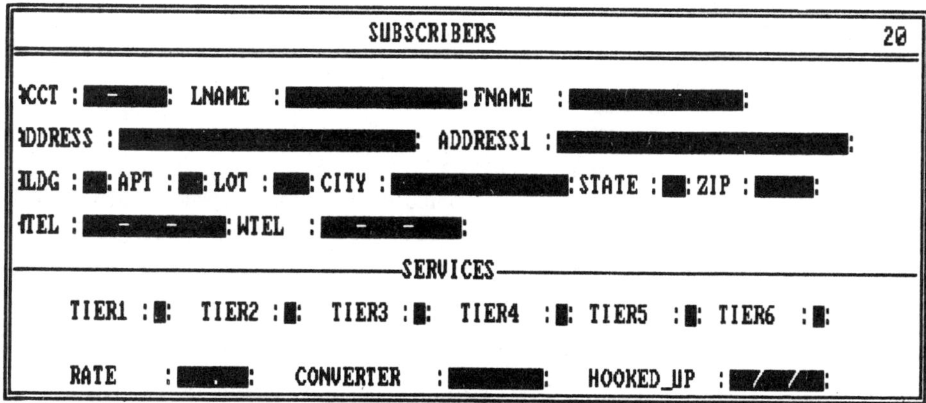

Figure 8–1 Set up a visual cue to show users how to enter data according to a format.

Listing 8–3

```
** EDIT.PRG
*
DO &FRAMER
DO &GETTER
CLEA GETS
DO EDITMENU
ANSWER = 'X'
DELS = .F.
*
DO WHIL .T.
   @ 0,0 SAY SPACE(80)
   @ 24,0 SAY SPACE(80)
   @  2,60 SAY IIF(DELETED(),"DELETED",SPACE(7))
   @ 23,34 SAY " select   "
   @ 23,43 GET ANSWER PICT '!'
   READ
*
   DO CASE
      CASE ANSWER = 'Q'
*
         IF DELS
            @ 20,0 CLEA
            @ 21,0 SAY [SOME RECORDS HAVE BEEN DELETED FROM THIS FILE.]
            @ 23,0 SAY [DO YOU WISH TO REMOVE THEM PERMANENTLY (Y/N)?  ] GET DELS
            READ
```

Listing 8–3 (cont.)

```
*
            DO CASE
               CASE DELS .AND. [payments database]$DBF()
                  @ 21,0 CLEA
                  @ 21,0 SAY [DO YOU WISH TO DELETE CORRESPONDING DATA IN THE]+;
                             [SUBSCRIPTION FILE (Y/N)?  ] GET DELS
                  READ
*
                  IF DELS
                     SELE 1
                     SET RELA TO account number field INTO B
                     LOCA FOR DELETED()
*
                     DO WHIL .NOT. EOF()
                        SELE 2
                        DELE
                        SELE 1
                        CONT
                     ENDD
*
                     SELE 2
                     PACK
                  ENDI
*
                  SELE 1
                  PACK
               CASE DELS
                  PACK
            ENDC
*
         ENDI
*
         RETU
      CASE ANSWER = 'K'
         DELE
         DELS = .T.
         LOOP
      CASE ANSWER = 'R'
         RECA
         LOOP
      CASE ANSWER = 'S'
         SKIP
         DO &GETTER
         CLEA GETS
         LOOP
```

Listing 8–3 (cont.)

```
      CASE ANSWER = 'B'
         SKIP -1
         DO &GETTER
         CLEA GETS
         LOOP
      CASE ANSWER = 'E'
         @ 20,0 CLEA
         @ 22,0 SAY "Press CTRL-W to save edit, CTRL-Q to exit"
         DO &GETTER
         READ
         DO EDITMENU
         LOOP
      CASE ANSWER = 'O'
         COPY NEXT 1 TO TANK
         APPE FROM TANK
         DO &GETTER
         CLEA GETS
         LOOP
      CASE ANSWER = 'C'
         CONT
         DO &GETTER
         CLEA GETS
         LOOP
      CASE ANSWER = 'G'
         ACCE "Record Number -> " TO RECNUM
         GOTO VAL(RECNUM)
         DO &GETTER
         CLEA GETS
         @ 24,0 SAY SPACE(40)
         LOOP
      CASE ANSWER = 'D'
         @ 20,0 CLEA
         ACCE "Display What -> " TO DISPLAYWHAT
*
         IF LEN(TRIM(DISPLAYWHAT)) = 0
            @ 20,0 CLEA
            LOOP
         ENDI
*
         TRUTH = .T.
         @ 21,0 CLEA
         ACCE "DISP FOR -> " TO DISPLAYFOR
         READ
*
         IF LEN(TRIM(DISPLAYFOR)) # 0
```

Listing 8-3 (cont.)

```
            SET FILT TO &DISPLAYFOR
            DISPLAYFOR = 'FOR' + DISPLAYFOR
         ENDI
*
         @ 21,0 CLEA
         @ 21,0 SAY [DO YOU WANT THIS PRINTED (Y/N)?  ] GET TRUTH
         READ
*
         IF TRUTH
            TOPRINT = 'TO PRINT'
            EJECT
         ELSE
            TOPRINT = []
            CLEA
         ENDI
*
         DISP &DISPLAYWHAT &DISPLAYFOR &TOPRINT
*
         IF TRUTH
            EJECT
         ENDI
*
         CLEA
         DO &FRAMER
         DO &GETTER
         CLEA GETS
*
         @ 21,0 CLEA
         SET FILT TO
         DO EDITMENU
         LOOP
      CASE ANSWER = 'F'
         @ 20,0 CLEAR
         ACCE "Find &KEYFIELD  " TO TOFIND
*
         IF [subscriber database]$DBF() .OR. [payments database]$DBF()
            SEEK IIF(SUBSTR(TOFIND,2,1) = '-', ' ' + TOFIND, TOFIND)
         ELSE
            SEEK TOFIND
         ENDI
*
         IF .NOT. FOUND()
           @ 24,50 SAY "Record Number ->  END  "
           @ 0,0 SAY "I can't FIND that entry. Perhaps you should LOCATE it."
                                    && could use WAIT command
```

Listing 8–3 (cont.)

```
            CALL DELAY WITH CHR(1)
         ENDI
*
         DO &GETTER
         CLEA GETS
         DO EDITMENU
         LOOP
      CASE ANSWER = 'L'
         @ 20,0 CLEA
         ACCE "Locate what? -> " TO LOCATEWHAT
         ACCE "Locate where? -> " TO LOCATEWHERE
*
         IF LEN(TRIM(LOCATEWHAT)) # 0 .AND. LEN(TRIM(LOCATEWHERE)) # 0
            LOCA ALL FOR "&LOCATEWHAT"$&LOCATEWHERE
         ENDI
*
         DO &GETTER
         CLEA GETS
         DO EDITMENU
         LOOP
      CASE ANSWER = 'A'
         COPY STRUC TO TANK
         SELE 6
         USE TANK
         @ 20,0 CLEA
         @ 22,0 SAY "Press CTRL-W to save information, CTRL-Q to exit"
*
         IF [subscriber database]$DBF()
            SELE 2
            USE payments database INDE subscriber account NDX file,;
                                       built index field NDX file
            COPY STRUC TO TANK2
            SELE 7
            USE TANK2
            TRUTH = .T.
            GETTER = [SUBGETNA]
*
            DO WHIL .T.
               SELE 6
               APPE BLAN
*
               DO WHIL .T.
                  DO SUBGET
                  CLEA GETS
                  @ 5,7 GET account number field PICT '!!-!!!!'
```

Listing 8–3 (cont.)

```
            READ
*
            IF LEN(TRIM(account number field)) = 0
               EXIT
            ENDI
*
            SELE 1
            SEEK IIF(SUBSTR(F->account number field,2,1) = '-',;
                 ' ' + F->account number field, F->account number field)
*
            IF FOUND()
               DO SUBGET
               CLEA GETS
               @ 20,0 CLEA
               @ 20,0 SAY [SORRY, WE'VE ALREADY GOT ONE OF THOSE.]
               CALL DELAY WITH CHR(1)
               @ 20,0 CLEA
               @ 22,0 SAY "Press CTRL-W to save information, CTRL-Q to exit"
            ELSE
               SELE F
               EXIT
            ENDI
*
            SELE F
         ENDD
*
         IF LEN(TRIM(account number field)) = 0
            DELE
            EXIT
         ENDI
*
         DO &GETTER
         READ
         @ 20,0 CLEA
         @ 22,0 SAY [ADD A NEW PAYMENT RECORD (Y/N)?  ] GET TRUTH
         READ
*
         IF TRUTH
            SELE 7
            CLEA
            APPE BLANK
            REPL account number field WITH F->account number field,;
                 LNAME WITH F->LNAME,FNAME WITH F->FNAME
            DO PAYSAY
            DO PAYGET2
```

Listing 8–3 (cont.)

```
                @ 20,0 CLEA
                @ 22,0 SAY [Press CTRL-W to save information, CTRL-Q to exit]
                READ
                SELE 6
                CLEA
                DO SUBSAY
             ENDI
*
             @ 20,0 CLEA
             @ 22,0 SAY [Press CTRL-W to save information, CTRL-Q to exit]
          ENDD
*
          SELE 7
          USE
          SELE 6
          USE
          SELE 2
          APPE FROM TANK2
          ERAS TANK2.DBF
          GETTER = [SUBGET]
       ELSE * DBF() # SUBSCRIPTIONS
          REPEATER = FIELD(1)
*
          DO WHIL .T.
             APPE BLANK
             DO &GETTER
             READ
*
             IF LEN(TRIM(&REPEATER)) = 0
                DELE
                EXIT
             ENDI
*
          ENDD
*
       ENDI
*
       USE
       SELE 6
       USE
       SELE 1
       SET DELE ON
       APPE FROM TANK
       SET DELE OFF
       DO &GETTER
```

Listing 8-3 (cont.)

```
          CLEA GETS
          DO EDITMENU
          ERAS TANK.DBF
       CASE ANSWER = 'U'
          @ 20,0 CLEA
          ACCE [REPLACE WHAT FIELD?  ] TO REPLACER
*
          IF LEN(TRIM(REPLACER)) = 0
             @ 20,0 CLEA
             LOOP
          ENDI
*
          ACCE [REPLACE WITH  ] TO REPLACEWITH
*
          IF LEN(TRIM(REPLACEWITH)) = 0
             @ 20,0 CLEA
             LOOP
          ENDI
*
          ACCE "CONDITION  " TO CONDITION
*
          IF LEN(TRIM(CONDITION)) # 0
             LOCA FOR &CONDITION
*
             IF .NOT. FOUND()
                @ 20,0 CLEA
                LOOP
             ELSE
                SET FILT TO &CONDITION
             ENDI
*
             REPL &REPLACER WITH &REPLACEWITH
          ENDI
*
          @ 20,0 CLEA
          DO EDITMENU
*
    ENDC
*
ENDD
*
** END OF EDIT.PRG
```

Most of this editor is described adequately elsewhere in the book. Here we'll concentrate on the unique aspects of the Quit, Find, and Add options.

The Quit option is coded to determine parallel records, DELETE them as necessary, and PACK the database. Remembering our logic from earlier discussions on parallel records, we want to DELETE in one direction. Here we're concerned with two conditions. The first condition is deleting from parallel records. The direction of parallel deletion is from payments to subscribers. The databases themselves are declared in the calling program. We use a DO WHILE . . . ENDD loop to CONTinuously LOCATE DELETEd records in work area 1. The databases are linked by RELATEd account numbers. If an account number in work area A doesn't have a corresponding account number in work area B, that work area's record pointer goes to EOF; hence, no valid data is accidentally DELETEd.

The other condition is to DELETE to other files, signified by CASE DELS. That is a straightforward PACK of the database.

I've mentioned the need to SEEK on a specific account number format. That is shown in the Find kernel. The two databases that make use of the account number are those for subscribers and payments. If we're working with either of those databases, then we must modify the ACCEPTed account number. We modify it with IIF(), as in:

```
IIF(SUBS(search string,2,1)='-',' '+search string,search string)
```

Remember that our account numbers have the template !!-!!!!. If the second character of the ACCEPTed search string is a hyphen (-), we need to right justify the search string by adding a blank space. Otherwise, we can use the search string as is. dBASE III PLUS can include all this in the one line command:

```
SEEK IIF(condition, true argument, false argument)
```

The Add kernel also makes use of this SEEK IIF() command, necessary because we're checking new account numbers against account numbers currently in use. Code was shown in Chapter 5 for having dBASE III PLUS automatically build the key field. That isn't used here, because special considerations may prevent it. You can include necessary code to build key field data in the Add kernel shown, but make sure the user has the option of okaying the data before continuing with the rest of the code.

The EDITMENU doesn't require any special coding and is included in the procedure file later in the chapter.

MODIFYING THE SYSTEM

We'll need a main menu to link everything together. The naked subscription system needs the ability to work with subscriber records and payment records, and it must perform some utility functions. It also needs to generate mailing labels on a regular basis. We may or may not use boilerplate letters. If we do, there is no problem, and that's shown in this chapter. But it's also nice to customize letters when the need arises. That means incorporating a word processor directly into the system. Last, we include the ability to RUN/! DOS-level commands directly from the system.

We've already mentioned the strong need to check present subscribers against present payment records. This is an area where high-speed searches are brought to the fore. What happens if we can't find the account number but there is a match on a built key field, such as location code + last name + first name? Records exist, but not as subscribers and payments. Those records should be modified.

The system is designed for companies that base their income on regular, fixed payments. The AR module, originally designed in the last section, can be easily modified to handle the same tasks in this application. But that brings us back to the design of the payments database. Our AR module still needs to determine past due accounts (past due accounts are handled in this code with the payments subsystem). We can include fields in our database that bear the names of months. Each of these fields contains NUMERIC data. We can test for past due accounts by coding in one of two ways. The first option uses fields with the names of months. Our test takes the following form:

Listing 8–4

```
MONTH = CMONTH(DATE()-30)
*
IF &MONTH = 0
   DO LATENOTE
ENDI
```

An alternative that makes use of the FIELD() function and doesn't need months as field names uses our knowledge of the database design to get information. For example, we design a database so that the third field contains January's data, but doesn't have January as a field name. The fourth field contains February's data, but doesn't use February as a field name. The fifth field is March's data, and so on. We can provide a functionally identical yet alternate code to Listing 8–4 with the following:

Listing 8–5

```
DATAFIELD = FIELD(MONTH(DATE()) + 2)
*
IF &DATAFIELD = 0
   DO LATENOTE
ENDI
```

All is laid out, and as you can see, design and modification are easy because we make use of what we've done before. Now to the coding.

SUBSCRIBER RECORDS

Our first concern for coding is handling subscriber records. This code isn't involved and is easily followed:

Listing 8–6

```
** SUBSMENU SUBSCRIBER MENU GENERATOR
*
DO WHILE .T.
   ANSWER = 'Q'
   CLEA
   @ 1,0 TO 20,79 DOUB
   @ 2,23 SAY [ S U B S C R I B E R    M E N U ]
   @ 3,1 TO 3,78 DOUB
   @ 6,21 SAY [E  Edit Subscriber Records]
   @ 7,21 SAY [R  Print a Report]
   @ 8,21 SAY [T  Print Special Purpose Labels]
   @ 9,21 SAY [C  Check Payments & Subs Files]
   @ 18,21 SAY [Q  Quit]
   @ 20,34 SAY [ select   ]
   @ 20,43 GET ANSWER PICTURE '!'
   READ
   CLEA
*
   DO CASE
      CASE .NOT. ANSWER $ [ERTCQ]
         @ 22,0 SAY [GOOD CHOICE, BUT NOT ONE I CAN USE]
         CALL DELAY WITH CHR(1)
         @ 22,0 CLEA
      CASE ANSWER = 'Q'
         CLOSE DATA
         RETU
      CASE ANSWER = 'E'
         KEYFIELD = "ACCOUNT"
         FRAMER = "SUBSAY"
         GETTER = "SUBGET"
         USE subscribers database INDE subscriber account NDX file,;
                                  built index field NDX file
         DO EDIT
      CASE ANSWER = 'R'
         DO REPORTER
      CASE ANSWER = 'C'
         DO ACCTCK
      CASE ANSWER = 'T'
         CLEA
         @  1,10 TO 9,69 DOUB
         @  3,11 TO 3,68 DOUB
         @  2, 32  SAY "form LABELS"
         @  5, 19  SAY "S  START WITH SAMPLES TO ALIGN PRINTER"
         @  6, 19  SAY "P  START WITHOUT SAMPLES"
         @ 7,19 SAY [Q  QUIT]
```

Listing 8–6 (cont.)

```
        @ 9, 32  SAY " select   "
*
        ANSWER = "Q"
        @ 9,41 GET ANSWER PICT '!'
        READ
        SAMPLES = []
*
        DO CASE
           CASE .NOT. ANSWER $ [SPQ]
              @ 22,0 SAY [GOOD CHOICE, BUT NOT ONE I CAN USE]
              CALL DELAY WITH CHR(1)
              @ 22,0 CLEA
              LOOP
           CASE ANSWER = 'Q'
              EXIT
           CASE ANSWER = "S"
              SAMPLES = [SAMP]
        ENDC
*
        SET CONS OFF
        LABEL FORM lbl form name FOR conditions for this special labeling need;
                 &SAMP TO PRINT
        SET CONS ON
*
   ENDC
*
ENDD
*
** END OF SUBSMENU
```

The first level of the subscriber subsystem is the subscriber menu, SUBSMENU. The options are standard menu items. The user can edit records, print reports, print special labels, and—the heavily emphasized option—check payments against the subscribers file. We include an option to print special labels because subscriber systems generally have two mailing needs. One need is to get information to the established subscriber base. That means sending out labels, letters, and so on, according to some pre-established criteria. The other mailing need is general-purpose mailings, canvassings, and the like. The menu option here prints the special labels.

This code does include a different kind of error check than was used previously. Note that we don't number our options as we did in previous listings. Here the options are lettered E, R, T, C, and Q. We check for valid responses with:

```
CASE .NOT. ANSWER $ [ERTCQ]
```

and ensure uppercase input with:

```
GET ANSWER "!"
```

This code also uses the DELAY.BIN file available from Ashton-Tate as part of the dBASE PROGRAMMER'S UTILITIES package. The DELAY.BIN file is LOADed in the main menu described earlier. You can substitute the DO POOL command and include the POOL procedure in the PRC file if you don't want to use DELAY.BIN.

Skip down to:

```
CASE ANSWER = 'E'
```

The KEYFIELD is declared here as ACCOUNT. This means the user is only allowed access through a single NDX file. Other key field access is reserved for the system itself. Why is this? This particular system builds the secondary key field from different fields in the database. We can't trust the user to properly enter that information, and we use the secondary NDX file to perform parallel file checks, so there is no need to grant the user that privilege.

Options R and C call subroutines that we'll cover momentarily. Option T prints out our special case labels with its own menu. Note that this menu doesn't offer the user a chance to place restrictions on the labels being generated. Those conditions are already set when the system is installed. The only options are to quit, start printing with samples, or print without first sending samples. This menu isn't even enclosed in a DO WHILE . . . ENDDO loop, as most subscriber systems don't care to repeatedly send out more than a single label list at a time.

The actual label menu options are handled with a DO CASE . . . ENDCASE block. As in the previous listing, our options are letters, not numbers. We test for valid input with:

```
CASE .NOT. ANSWER $ [SPQ]
```

We initialize a variable, SAMPLES, before evaluating our ANSWER. The Q option quits back to the top of SUBSMENU. The option lettered S changes the value of SAMPLES to [SAMP]. The only other menu option is P for print. If the user has entered a valid response and hasn't selected Quit, there is no need for a separate P CASE. The option P tells III PLUS to begin printing the labels, but without first sending SAMPLEs to the printer. So be it. The last part of the label generator code is that necessary to PRINT the labels. Note the macroized use of SAMPLES to tell III PLUS whether or not to send SAMPLES to the printer.

Two SUBSMENU options call their own subroutines. The first subroutine listed is REPORTER:

Listing 8–7

```
** REPORTER.PRG
*
USE subscribers database INDE built index field NDX file, subscriber account NDX file
YESCON = .F.
```

Listing 8-7 (cont.)

```
*
DO WHIL .T.
   CLEA
   @  1,0 TO 15,79 DOUB
   @ 3,1 TO 3,78 DOUB
   @  2, 24  SAY "SUBSCRIBERS REPORT MENU"
   @  5, 24  SAY "P  Print Reports"
   @  7, 24  SAY "C  Create Condition"
   @  9, 24  SAY "D  Determine Area Totals"
   @ 11, 24  SAY "Q  Quit"
   @ 2,60 SAY IIF(YESCON,[CONDITION EXITS],SPACE(16))
   ANSWER = 'Q'
   @ 15,31 SAY [ select    ]
   @ 15,40 GET ANSWER PICT '!'
   READ
*
   DO CASE
      CASE .NOT. ANSWER $ 'PCDQ'
         @ 22,0 SAY [GOOD CHOICE, BUT NOT ONE I CAN USE]
         CALL DELAY WITH CHR(1)
         @ 22,0 CLEA
         LOOP
      CASE ANSWER = 'Q'
         RETU
      CASE ANSWER = 'D'
         S7 = '       '  && this variable is just a spacer for printing
         CLEA
         ? [PLEASE WAIT WHILE I REINDEX THE FILE]
         INDEX ON LEFT(account number field,2) TO TEMPSUB
         CLEA
         @ 1,0  SAY [AREA service COUNTS FOR -> ] + STR(DAY(DATE()),2) + ', ' +;
                    CMONTH(DATE()) + ' ' + STR(YEAR(DATE()),4)
         @ 3,0 SAY [AREA      service1   service2   service3   service4   ]+;
                   [service5   service6    ]
         SET DEVI TO PRIN
         @ 1,10  SAY [AREA service COUNTS FOR -> ] + STR(DAY(DATE()),2) + ', ' +;
                    CMONTH(DATE()) + ' ' + STR(YEAR(DATE()),4)
         @ 3,10 SAY [AREA      service1        service2        service3        ]+;
                    [service4        service5        service6        ]
         SET DEVI TO SCREEN
         GOTO TOP
*
         DO WHIL .NOT. EOF()
            AREA = LEFT(account number field,2)
            STARTHERE = RECNO()
```

Listing 8-7 (cont.)

```
            COUNT TO T1 FOR service1 WHILE AREA = LEFT(account number field,2)
            GOTO STARTHERE
            COUNT TO T2 FOR service2 WHILE AREA = LEFT(account number field,2)
            GOTO STARTHERE
            COUNT TO T3 FOR service3 WHILE AREA = LEFT(account number field,2)
            GOTO STARTHERE
            COUNT TO T4 FOR service4 WHILE AREA = LEFT(account number field,2)
            GOTO STARTHERE
            COUNT TO T5 FOR service5 WHILE AREA = LEFT(account number field,2)
            GOTO STARTHERE
            COUNT TO T6 FOR service6 WHILE AREA = LEFT(account number field,2)
            @ ROW()+2,0 SAY AREA + '       ' + STR(T1,5) + S7 + STR(T2,5) +;
                 S7 + STR(T3,5) + S7 + STR(T4,5) + S7 + STR(T5,5) + S7 +;
                 STR(T6,5)
            SET DEVI TO PRIN
            @ PROW()+2,10 SAY AREA + S7 + STR(T1,5) + S7 + STR(T2,5) + S7 +;
                 STR(T3,5) + S7 + STR(T4,5) + S7 + STR(T5,5) + S7 +;
                 STR(T6,5)
            SET DEVI TO SCREEN
         ENDD
*
         EJECT
         WAIT
         SET INDE TO built index field NDX file, subscriber account NDX file
         ERAS TEMPSUB.NDX
      CASE ANSWER = 'C'
*
         IF YESCON
            CONDITION = []
            SET FILT TO
            YESCON = .F.
         ELSE
            CLEA
            DO SUBSAY
            DO SUBGET
            CLEA GETS
            CONDITION = SPACE(60)
            @ 21,0 SAY [CONDITION  ] GET CONDITION
            READ
*
            IF TRIM(CONDITION) = []
               LOOP
            ELSE
               SET FILT TO &CONDITION
               YESCON = .T.
```

Listing 8–7 (cont.)

```
                ENDI
*
            ENDI
*
            LOOP
        OTHE
            SET PRIN ON
            SET CONS OFF
            ? CHR(control codes for special printing features, if necessary)
            REPORT FORM SUBS
            ? CHR(control codes to return to normal printing features, if necessary)
            SET PRIN OFF
            SET CONS ON
    ENDC
*
ENDD
*
** END OF REPORTER.PRG
```

This report generator is accessed from the SUBSMENU file, hence we only want it to work with the subscribers database. That database is declared before doing anything else. The actual module works slightly differently than Listing 8–7. In modular form, the database is declared before this code is called, and the normal options are P, C, and Q. The code starts with an error check similar to that used in code previously shown. Option D is one normally found in subscription systems; it informs the company how successful its marketing is. Option D generates area totals. This information answers the question of how many subscribers are in each location. The code here shows six different totals, but you can increase that to any number allowed by your database structure.

The first item is S7. S7 is a mnemonic for "seven spaces." Look at the string value of S7—it is a text string seven spaces wide. Looking further, we see that S7 only serves as a space marker during certain printouts.

In this code we need to INDEX the subscriber file on the location code of the account number. Remember that this system uses the first two characters in the account number field to determine subscriber location and the last four characters after the hyphen for the actual account. We need these particular listings by location. But we don't want this large an NDX file permanently in the system. We only use it once in a great while (some environments have absolutely no need for this capability and can use the more generic report generator) and there is no need to place the file on disk, except when needed. Now we need it.

At this point we should discuss database design once more. There are two ways to code a count of subscribers/services per location. Each method assumes a different means of recording subscriber/service data. The first method is to create each service field as a LOGICAL field. This allows us to perform tests such as:

```
IF service
```

instead of an alternate

```
IF service = (a numeric expression or text string)
```

If we design the databases so that each service field is nonLOGICAL data we can use a REPORT form for the rest of the code. That REPORT would be grouped on:

```
LEFT(account field,2)
```

and would still use the temporary NDX file mentioned earlier and total the number of services in each area. To properly use a REPORT form, the data would have to be NUMERIC. This would allow III PLUS's REPORT writer to automatically total the fields at the end of the report.

Note that Listing 8–7 makes use of LOGICAL service fields, as several of the former logical tests are performed in other REPORT forms. So saying, the next six lines place some information on the screen and at the printer. Basically, we're creating a header for this particular "longhand" report.

We GOTO the TOP of the database and then perform COUNTs until we've gone completely through the database, as defined by the EOF() function in the DO WHILE . . . ENDDO loop. We do this in a clever way, however. The TOP of the database has the lowest character value for LEFT(account field, 2). We store that character data to a local variable, AREA, and store the database record pointer location, given by RECNO(), to another local variable, STARTHERE.

Now we begin COUNTing. But we COUNT to a variable, T1, WHILE the local variable AREA is identical to:

```
LEFT(account number field, 2)
```

Once the first service COUNT is completed, we GOTO STARTHERE, the original record we started COUNTing from. We COUNT the second service just as we COUNTed the first service. When we've completed that COUNT we GOTO STARTHERE again and COUNT the third service. This code can be expanded to include as many services as your environment provides.

Eventually, we've counted all the services this subscription system provides. It would be nice to share that information. That is done with the next four lines.

Immediately following those four lines is the ENDD. We've made only one pass (assuming your environment requires more than one location code, hence more than one pass). The active NDX file is INDEXed on:

```
LEFT(account number field, 2)
```

We can't be at EOF(), but we can be at the first record that doesn't satisfy the condition:

```
AREA = LEFT(account number field, 2)
```

Back to the top of the DO WHILE . . . ENDDO loop. Once again, we store the new location code to AREA and the new starting record pointer location to STARTHERE. Now we COUNT again.

Eventually, we'll have gone through all the location codes and actually arrive at EOF() when we hit ENDD. At that point the program exits the loop, EJECTs the printout, WAITs for the user to study the screen (which has echoed the printout), reSETs the INDEX files to our standards, and ERASEs the temporary NDX file. Slick, isn't it?

Option C sets any conditions we want on our reports. This is done as a toggle and uses the logical YESCON (YES, there is a CONdition) variable initialized at the start of REPORTER.PRG. Because this variable acts as a toggle, we can turn it on and off by merely entering C at the ANSWER prompt on the menu. IF a condition exists (as indicated with @ 2,60 by the IIF() function in the menu itself), then we want to turn the condition off. We store [] to the condition, shut any FILTERs off, and declare YESCON as .F.

But what if there is no condition? That means we want to establish a condition on the reports. How does the user know what conditions are available? We explain the conditions by CLEARing the screen and displaying our subscriber SAY and GET files. We don't want the user to edit any data in the current record, so we CLEAR GETS. The user then enters the condition at the prompt. We also provide a bailout. IF the user presses RETURN—enters no condition—we leave YESCON as .F. and leave all FILTERs off. Entering anything SETs a FILTER to the condition by macroizing the CONDITION variable and toggling YESCON to .T.

It might be worthwhile to test the validity of the entered condition with:

```
IF TYPE('&CONDITION') = 'U'
```

Listing 8–7 doesn't equal 'U', as invalid FILTERs are ignored by III PLUS.

The last option is handled by the OTHE condition. Reports are sent to the printer by SETting PRINT ON. Why not simply use the TO PRINT qualifier on the REPORT command? The REPORT command doesn't pass control codes to the printer, but combining SET PRIN ON and ? CHR (control codes for special printing options) does. We might be printing an extra-wide report, and with these codes we can do it on a narrow-carriage printer. We set the printer to normal print mode with another ? CHR() command when we're through REPORTing.

The last option on the SUBSMENU to discuss is the ACCTCK file.

Listing 8–8

```
** ACCTCK.PRG
*
SELE 2
USE payments database INDEX subscriber account NDX file, built index field NDX file
SELE 1
USE subscribers database INDEX subscriber account NDX file,;
                              built index field NDX file
SET RELA TO account number field INTO B
```

Listing 8–8 (cont.)

```
N = 0
THEREST = RECCOUNT()
CLEA
@ 3,0 TO 10,30 DOUB
@ 4,3 SAY [CHECKING ACCOUNT NUMBERS]
@ 5,1 TO 5,29
@ 6,4 SAY [RECORDS LEFT  ]
@ 7,4 SAY [RECORD        ]
@ 8,4 SAY [SUBSCRIBER #  ]
CALL CURSOR2 WITH '0'
*
DO WHILE .NOT. EOF()
   N = N + 1
*
   DO CASE
      CASE LEN(TRIM(account number field)) = 0
         DELE
         @ 8,21 SAY [DELETED]
         SKIP
         LOOP
      CASE DELETED()
         SKIP
         LOOP
      OTHE
         @ 6,21 SAY STR(THEREST-N, 6, 0)
         @ 7,21 SAY STR(RECNO(), 6, 0)
         @ 8,21 SAY account number field
         AREC = RECNO()
*
         IF account number field = B->account number field
            SKIP
            LOOP
         ELSE
            @ 16,10 TO 21,50 DOUB
            @ 18,15 SAY [NAME      ] + A->name information
            @ 19,15 SAY [ADDRESS   ] + A->address information
            @ 3,40 TO 14,79 DOUB
            @ 7,45 SAY [SUBSCRIBER NOT IN PAYMENTS FILE]
            @ 10,44 SAY [CHECKING BY ACCOUNT AND LAST NAME]
            SELE 2
            SET ORDE TO 2
            SELE 1
            SET ORDE TO 2
            SET RELA TO built index file index key INTO B
*
```

Listing 8–8 (cont.)

```
            IF account number field # B->account number field .AND.;
               name information # B->name information .AND.;
               some other field # B->identical field in payments database
               CALL CURSOR2 WITH 'B'
               @ 4,43 SAY [NO PAYMENT RECORD FOR SUBSCRIBER ]
               @ 5,41 TO 5,78
               @ 6,41 CLEA TO 13,78
               @ 7,45 SAY [E  Edit This Record]
               @ 8,45 SAY [A  Add This to Payments]
               @ 9,45 SAY [P  Print This Record]
               @ 10,45 SAY [D  Delete This Record]
               @ 11,45 SAY [C  Continue Checking]
               @ 12,45 SAY [Q  Quit to Subscriber Menu]
               @ 14,51 SAY [ select    ]
*
               DO WHILE .T.
                  SELE 1
                  @ 2,31 SAY IIF(DELETED(), [SUBSCRIBER DELETED], SPACE(20))
                  SELE 2
                  ANSWER = 'Q'
                  @ 14,60 GET ANSWER PICT '!'
                  READ
*
                  DO CASE
                     CASE .NOT. ANSWER $ [EAPDCQ]
                        @ 23,0 CLEA
                        @ 23,0 SAY [GOOD CHOICE, BUT NOT ONE I CAN USE]
                        CALL DELAY WITH CHR(1)
                        @ 23,0 CLEA
                        LOOP
                     CASE ANSWER = 'Q'
                        CALL CURSOR2 WITH 'N'
                        CLOSE DATA
                        RETURN
                     CASE ANSWER = 'C'
                        @ 2,31 SAY SPACE(20)
                        CALL CURSOR2 WITH 'O'
                        @ 3,40 CLEA TO 14,79
                        @ 16,10 CLEA TO 21,50
                        SELE 2
                        SET ORDE TO 1
                        SELE 1
                        SET ORDE TO 1
                        SET RELA TO account number field INTO B
                        EXIT
```

Listing 8–8 (cont.)

```
          CASE ANSWER = 'A'
             CLEA
             APPE BLANK
             REPL account number field WITH A->account number field,;
                  name information WITH A->name information,;
                  FNAME WITH A->FNAME
             DO PAYSAY
             @ 22,0 SAY [PRESS CTRL-W TO CONTINUE]
             DO PAYGET2
             READ
             @ 4,43 SAY [NEW PAYMENT RECORD FOR SUBSCRIBER]
             CLEA
          CASE ANSWER = 'E'
             CLEA
             SELE 1
             DO SUBSAY
             @ 22,0 SAY [PRESS CTRL-W TO CONTINUE]
             DO SUBGET
             READ
             SELE 2
             CLEA
          CASE ANSWER = 'P'
             SET DEVI TO PRIN
             DO PRINTSUB
             SET DEVI TO SCREEN
          CASE ANSWER = 'D'
             SELE 1
             DELE
             SELE 2
       ENDC
*
       IF ANSWER $ [AE]
          @ 3,0 TO 10,30 DOUB
          @ 4,3 SAY [CHECKING ACCOUNT NUMBERS]
          @ 5,1 TO 5,29
          @ 6,4 SAY [RECORDS LEFT  ]
          @ 7,4 SAY [RECORD        ]
          @ 8,4 SAY [SUBSCRIBER #  ]
          @ 6,21 SAY STR(THEREST-N, 6, 0)
          @ 7,21 SAY STR(AREC,6,0)
          @ 8,21 SAY A->account number field
          @ 16,10 TO 21,50 DOUB
          @ 18,15 SAY [NAME      ] + A->name information
          @ 19,15 SAY [ADDRESS   ] + A->address information
          @ 3,40 TO 14,79 DOUB
```

Listing 8-8 (cont.)

```
                @ 4,43 SAY IIF(ANSWER = 'A',[NEW],[NO]) +;
                         [ PAYMENT RECORD FOR SUBSCRIBER]
                @ 5,41 TO 5,78
                @ 7,45 SAY [E  Edit This Record]
                @ 8,45 SAY [A  Add This to Payments]
                @ 9,45 SAY [P  Print This Record]
                @ 10,45 SAY [D  Delete This Record]
                @ 11,45 SAY [C  Continue Checking]
                @ 12,45 SAY [Q  Quit to Subscriber Menu]
                @ 14,51 SAY [ select   ]
             ENDI
*
          ENDD
*
       ELSE
          CALL CURSOR2 WITH 'B'
          CLEA
          @ 5,0 TO 14,38 DOUB
          @ 5,40 TO 14,78 DOUB
          @ 2,3 SAY [THE SUBSCRIBER ACCOUNT NUMBER DOESN'T MATCH THE ] +;
                    [PAYMENT ACCOUNT NUMBER]
          @ 4,6 SAY [SUBSCRIBER INFORMATION]
          @ 4,48 SAY [PAYMENT INFORMATION]
          @ 6,2 SAY [ACCT        ] + subscribers database->account number field
          @ 6,42 SAY [ACCT       ] + payments database->account number field
          @ 7,2 SAY [NAME        ] + subscribers database->name information
          @ 7,42 SAY [NAME       ] + payments database->name information
          @ 8,2 SAY [other field ] + subscribers database->other field
          @ 8,42 SAY [other field] + payments database->other field
          @ 9,2 SAY [address    ] + subscribers database->address information
          @ 10,2 SAY [city       ] + subscribers database->city
          @ 10,42 SAY [service on?] +;
                     IIF(payments database->service on flag,'Y','N')
          @ 11,2 SAY [state      ] + subscribers database->state
          @ 12,2 SAY [zip        ] + subscribers database->zip
          @ 13,2 SAY [date started] +;
                    DTOC(subscribers database->date started field)
          @ 13,42 SAY [date paid  ] +;
                     DTOC(payments database->date of first payment field)
          @ 16,1 TO 23,72 DOUB
          @ 18,10 SAY [L  REPLACE PAYMENT ACCOUNT WITH SUBSCRIBER ACCOUNT]
          @ 19,10 SAY [R  REPLACE SUBSCRIBER ACCOUNT WITH PAYMENT ACCOUNT]
          @ 20,10 SAY [D  DELETE BOTH RECORDS]
          @ 21,10 SAY [Q  QUIT ]
          ANSWER = 'Q'
```

Listing 8–8 (cont.)

```
*
          DO WHIL .T.
             @ 23,28 SAY IIF(.NOT. ANSWER $ [LRDQ],[TRY AGAIN],[ select   ])
             @ 23,28 SAY [ select   ]
             @ 23,37 GET ANSWER PICT '!'
             READ
*
             DO CASE
                CASE ANSWER = 'Q'
                   CLEA
                   @ 3,0 TO 10,30 DOUB
                   @ 4,3 SAY [CHECKING ACCOUNT NUMBERS]
                   @ 5,1 TO 5,29
                   @ 6,4 SAY [RECORDS LEFT  ]
                   @ 7,4 SAY [RECORD        ]
                   @ 8,4 SAY [SUBSCRIBER #  ]
                   CALL CURSOR2 WITH '0'
                   SELE 2
                   SET ORDE TO 1
                   SELE 1
                   SET ORDE TO 1
                   SET RELA TO account number field INTO B
                   CALL CURSOR2 WITH '0'
                   EXIT
                CASE ANSWER = 'L'
                   SELE 2
                   REPL account number field WITH A->account number field
                   @ 5,0 SAY []
*
                   DO WHIL ROW() < 13
                      @ ROW() + 1, 39 SAY []
                   ENDD
*
                   @ 6,53 SAY account number field
                CASE ANSWER = 'R'
                   SELE 1
                   REPL account number field WITH B->account number field
                   @ 5,0 SAY []
*
                   DO WHIL ROW() < 13
                      @ ROW() + 1,39 SAY []
                   ENDD
*
                   @ 6,12 SAY account number field
                CASE ANSWER = 'D'
```

Listing 8–8 (cont.)

```
                    SELE 1
                    DELE
                    SELE 2
                    DELE
                    @ 15,27 SAY [BOTH RECORDS DELETED]
                ENDC
*
              ENDD
*
            ENDI
*
            SELE 1
            SKIP
          ENDI
*
   ENDC
*
ENDD
*
CLOSE DATA
CALL CURSOR2 WITH 'N'
*
** END OF ACCTCK.PRG
```

This file determines if all subscribers are getting billed. The heart of the code was shown earlier. This portion of the code is fully realized for a working environment.

We place our two main use databases in the first two work areas. Then the code SETs a RELATION on the account number field, common to both databases, from the first work area INTO the second work area. A few variables are declared, and the screen is CLEARed for the first information screen, shown in Figure 8–2.

The screen in the figure is merely a box that shows which work area 1 database record is being scanned, how many work area 1 database records are left to scan, and what the current record's subscriber account number is.

This code also makes use of another BIN file included in the Ashton-Tate dBASE PROGRAMMER'S UTILITIES package, CURSOR2.BIN. This BIN file basically turns the cursor off and on, something useful for this screen. You don't need CURSOR2.BIN; it simply adds some aesthetics by keeping the cursor from jumping all over the screen. The dBASE III PLUS package has two files that perform much the same function, CURSOFF.BIN and CURSON.BIN. You can use those files in place of CURSOR2.BIN. Remember to include the lines LOAD CURSOFF and LOAD CURSON in your main menu or start-up file. Whenever the Listing 8–8 has the following:

```
CALL CURSOR2 WITH 'O'
```

```
CHECKING ACCOUNT NUMBERS

RECORDS LEFT »
RECORD       »
SUBSCRIBER # »
```

```
->
```

Figure 8–2 This is the first information screen for the ACCTCK.PRG file.

you'll use:

```
CALL CURSOFF
```

Similarly, wherever Listing 8–8 has either of the following:

Listing 8–9

```
CALL CURSOR2 WITH 'B'
CALL CURSOR2 WITH 'N'
```

you'll include the line:

```
CALL CURSON
```

The rest of the code is a large DO WHILE . . . ENDDO block. The block is terminated primarily through an EOF() condition. Remember that this code is supposed to match all subscriber records with their payment counterparts. This means you normally want to scan until EOF().

We increase our counter, N, by 1. Each time we come to the top of the DO WHILE . . . ENDDO loop, we're scanning another record. N keeps count of that.

There are three CASEs (actually two CASEs and an OTHERWISE) that do the work in the DO WHILE . . . ENDDO loop. The first CASE is included for blank or incomplete records. There shouldn't be any in the database, but it's a good idea to make sure. If there are any blank records (blank as determined by a lack of an account number), DELETE the record, SKIP to the next one, and LOOP to the top of the DO WHILE . . . ENDDO loop. This code includes a message in this CASE's block as follows:

```
@ 8,21 SAY [DELETED]
```

```
CHECKING ACCOUNT NUMBERS
RECORDS LEFT »
RECORD       »
SUBSCRIBER # »
```

```
SUBSCRIBER NOT IN PAYMENTS FILE

CHECKING BY ACCOUNT AND LAST NAME
```

```
NAME    »
ADDRESS »
```

```
->
```

Figure 8–3 This is the second information screen for the ACCTCK.PRG file.

This is displayed on the screen in an area that normally holds the account number field and is the same length as that field. It flashes when a record is DELETEd and written over if the next record isn't. Pretty slick! You may want to include the lines that rewrite the record pointer location to the screen in this block. Few records are DELETEd here, and most times there is no need to include such code.

The next CASE detects DELETED()—but not physically removed—records and SKIPs over them.

The OTHERWISE block is the workhorse of the code. The two possible invalid record CASEs have stopped bogus records from being processed. Now we scan valid information. This block starts by listing the number of records left to scan, the record number of the current record, and the account number field. Remember that we've previously SET a RELATION from subscribers to payments. We now test that there is a one-to-one correspondence from subscriber record to payment record (there is a record in work area B that has an account number identical to the account number of the current record in work area A) with:

```
IF account number field = B->account number field
```

If this condition is met, then a one-to-one correspondence exists for this account number. Therefore, SKIP and LOOP back to the top of the DO WHILE . . . ENDDO block.

But what if no record in work area B has an account number that matches the account number in work area A? We start by creating another information screen, as shown in Figure 8–3.

This box says we're checking by account and last name, and the code SETs both work areas' NDX file ORDERs to 2, which means we've started to use our secondary NDX files for searching purposes. We looked at this use of the secondary NDX files earlier in this chapter. We also SET a new RELATION between

```
CHECKING ACCOUNT NUMBERS
RECORDS LEFT »
RECORD       »
SUBSCRIBER # »
```

```
NO PAYMENT RECORD FOR SUBSCRIBER

E » EDIT THIS RECORD
A » ADD THIS TO PAYMENTS
P » PRINT THIS RECORD
D » DELETE THIS RECORD
C » CONTINUE CHECKING
Q » QUIT TO SUBSCRIBER MENU
select » «
```

```
NAME    »
ADDRESS »
```

```
->
```

Figure 8–4 When ACCTCK can't find any matches between subscriber records and payment records, it offers this menu.

our files. This new RELATION is based on the secondary, built index file key. This particular system uses account number and last name for the secondary NDX file's built key field. You can create any field combination that's appropriate for your environment.

The fact that we've juggled NDX files won't alter the record pointer locations in either work area. However, establishing a new RELATIONship between our databases will move the record pointer in work area 2. Work area 1's record pointer won't move because that is the currently SELECTed work area.

As always, when we SET a RELATION, dBASE III PLUS either matches the primary work area key to the secondary work area key *or* matches the primary work area key to the end of the secondary file when no matching key data exists. We test that with:

Listing 8–10

```
IF account number field # B->account number field .AND.;
   name information # B->name information .AND.;
   some other field # B->identical field in payments database
```

The code is written to assume the match isn't found. That forces the menu shown in Figure 8–4. This menu has much information, as the figure and code that generates the menu shown. We are told there's:

```
NO PAYMENT RECORD FOR SUBSCRIBER
```

We're also told @ 2,31 IIF the subscriber's record is DELETED() or not. At this point the user enters an option, and processing continues through a DO CASE . . . ENDCASE block.

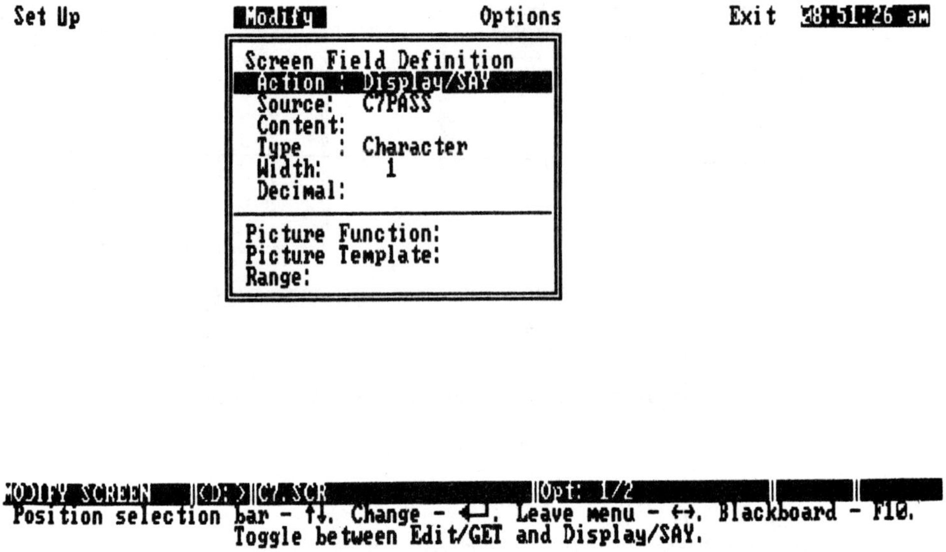

```
Set Up            Modify            Options            Exit  08:51:26 am
              Screen Field Definition
               Action : Display/SAY
               Source:  C7PASS
               Content:
               Type    : Character
               Width:       1
               Decimal:

              Picture Function:
              Picture Template:
              Range:

MODIFY SCREEN  ||<D:>||C7.SCR             ||Opt: 1/2
Position selection bar - ↑↓.  Change - ←┘.  Leave menu - ←→.  Blackboard - F10.
              Toggle between Edit/GET and Display/SAY.
```

Figure 8–5   The MODI SCRE menu system lets you change GETs to SAYs, provided the cursor is currently on a database field in the SCREEN image.

The first CASE is an error check. The second CASE Quits the entire ACCTCK program. The third CASE continues checking subscriber records against payment records. It doesn't edit the information in either database in any way; it simply continues scanning. Note that this means CLEARing the right and bottom windows from the screen, reSETting NDX file ORDERs and RELATIONs between the databases.

The next CASE tells dBASE III PLUS to Add the subscriber information to the payments database. Remember that this system checks two different ways before it determines that no records match. It performs a standard account number cross check and, failing that, a built key field cross check. This is done because we might enter the subscriber account as 1–0001 and later edit the payment account to 1–1. We APPEND a BLANK record to the payments database, REPLACE information in the BLANK record with data from work area 1, then put up the payments' SAY and GET files. This is necessary for any data addition or editing that you want to do at this time. Once the new payments record has been READ, the message @ 4,43 changes to:

```
NEW PAYMENT RECORD FOR SUBSCRIBER
```

With CASE ANSWER = 'E', the user can edit the subscriber record. Option P prints the subscriber record. This is useful when you want to take the information in hand to some other area, say perhaps an archive office. The PRINTSUB file, shown in Listing 8–11, is a special collection of @ SAY statements. We can create it most easily by generating an FMT file and either using the MODI SCRE menus (see Figure 8–5) to change all GETs to SAYs or using a word processor to globally change the GETs to SAYs.

THE SUBSCRIBER ACCOUNT NUMBER DOESN'T MATCH THE PAYMENT ACCOUNT NUMBER

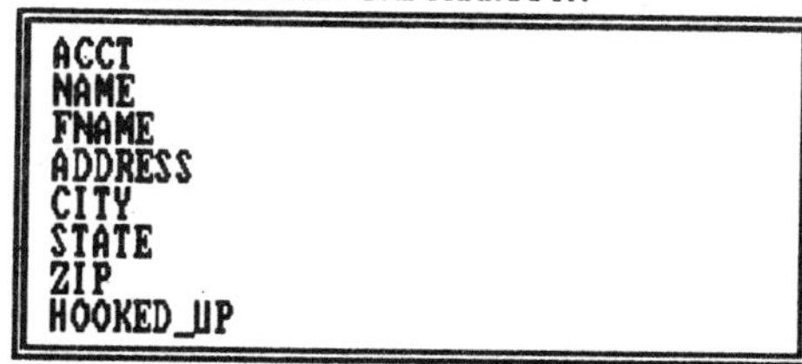

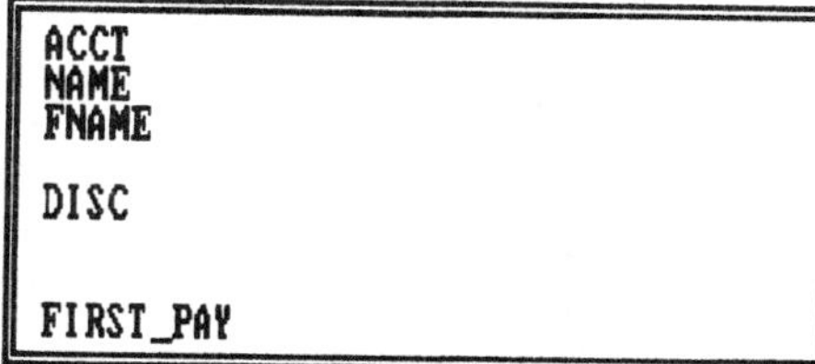


```
L » REPLACE PAYMENT ACCOUNT WITH SUBSCRIBER ACCOUNT
R » REPLACE SUBSCRIBER ACCOUNT WITH PAYMENT ACCOUNT
D » DELETE BOTH RECORDS
Q » QUIT
-)
```

Figure 8–6 This is an example of a screen showing mismatched account numbers.

Listing 8–11

```
** PRINTSUB
*
@  2, PLACE  SAY DBF()
@  2, 50 SAY IIF(DELETED(),[DELETED],[])
@ 2,65 SAY STR(RECNO(),6)
*
** All SAY STATEMENTS WILL COVER NECESSARY INFORMATION IN THIS RECORD.
*
** END OF PAYMENU.PRG
```

CASE ANSWER = 'D' merely DELETEs the subscriber record.

This menu section has done a lot of work. Both adding and editing information paint new screens, so now we need to get our old screens back:

```
IF ANSWER $ [AE]
```

This redisplays the screen shown in Figure 8–4. Note that we determine IIF() a NEW or NO payment record exists for the subscriber @ 4,43.

All of that code offers options IF there is absolutely no payment record for the subscriber. What about mismatched account numbers? This means a payment record does exist for the subscriber, but the two records have different account numbers as determined by the secondary NDX file. That is handled by the ELSE code. We start with a new information screen, as shown in Figure 8–6.

This screen is a side-by-side listing of parallel information. Remember, however, that they are parallel on a secondary search pattern, not a primary search pattern. It is possible that our secondary search will make mistakes. We offer four options to cover that.

The first option is Quit. This CLEARs the screen and returns us to the

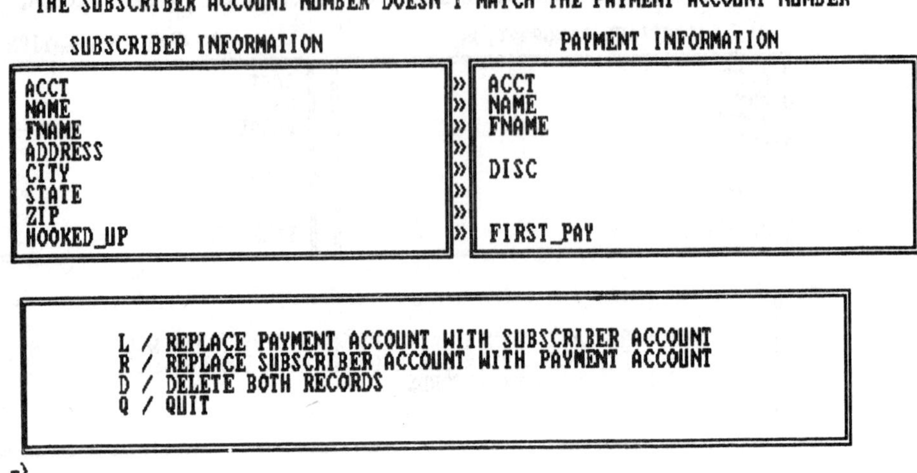

Figure 8–7 Options L and R provide visual cues to the user about the selected choice to transfer information.

display in Figure 8–2. Scanning continues with the next record in the subscribers database. Option L transfers information from the Figure 8–6's left box to the right box. The user is given a visual cue that this has happened with a series of graphic arrows, as shown in Figure 8–7.

This code only REPLACEs the account number field. You may wish to REPLACE other fields, as well. Option R is the right to left image of option L. Option D DELETEs the current records in both databases and alerts the user with:

```
@ 15,27 SAY [BOTH RECORDS DELETED]
```

That brings us to the close of the DO WHILE . . . ENDDO loop originated at the start of ACCTCK.PRG. If the user hasn't Quit the ACCTCK program, we CLOSE the DATAbases and return the CURSOR to Normal, and we're done.

PAYMENT RECORDS

The payments subsystem is not as elaborate as the subscriber subsystem.

Listing 8–12

```
** PAYMENU.PRG
*
GETTER = "PAYGET"
FRAMER = "PAYSAY"
KEYFIELD = "ACCOUNT"
YESCON = .F.
```

Listing 8–12 (cont.)

```
SELE 2
USE subscribers database INDE subscriber account NDX file, built index field NDX file
SELE 1
USE payments database INDE subscriber account NDX file, built index field NDX file
*
DO WHILE .T.
   ANSWER = 'Q'
   CLEAR
   @  1,0 TO 17,79 DOUB
   @ 3,1 TO 3,78 DOUB
   @  2, 31  SAY "PAYMENT MENU"
   @ 2,60 SAY IIF(YESCON,'CONDITION EXITS',SPACE(17))
   @  5, 23  SAY "E  Edit Payments"
   @  8, 23  SAY "P  Print Payments Report"
   @ 10, 23  SAY "L  Print Late Payments Report"
   @ 13, 23  SAY "F  Print Late Payment Letters"
   @ 15, 23  SAY "Q  Quit"
   @ 17, 32  SAY " select    "
   @ 17,41 GET ANSWER PICT '!'
   READ
*
   DO CASE
      CASE .NOT. ANSWER $ 'EPLFQ'
         @ 22,0 CLEA
         @ 22,0 SAY [GOOD CHOICE, BUT NOT ONE I CAN USE]
         CALL DELAY WITH CHR(1)
         @ 22,0 CLEA
         LOOP
      CASE ANSWER='Q'
         CLOSE DATA
         RETU
      CASE ANSWER='E'
         CLEAR
         DO EDIT
         LOOP
      CASE ANSWER='F'
         DO LETTER
   ENDC
*
   TRUTH = .T.
   @ 20,0 SAY "DO YOU WANT A CONDITION ON THE REPORTS (Y/N)? -> " GET TRUTH
   READ
   CLEAR
*
   IF TRUTH
      DO PAYSAY
```

Listing 8–12 (cont.)

```
         DO PAYGET
         CLEA GETS
         CONDITION = SPACE(60)
         @ 23,0 SAY "CONDITION -> " GET CONDITION
         READ
      ELSE
         CONDITION = []
      ENDI
*
      IF LEN(TRIM(CONDITION)) # 0
         YESCON = .T.
         SET FILT TO &CONDITION
         HEADER = [HEAD "&CONDITION"]
      ELSE
         YESCON = .F.
         SET FILT TO
         HEADER = []
      ENDI
*
      SET CONS OFF
      SET PRIN ON
      ? CHR(control codes for special printing features, if necessary)
*
      DO CASE
         CASE ANSWER = 'P'
            REPO FORM payment report form &HEADER TO PRINT
         CASE ANSWER = 'L'
            REPO FORM payment report form &HEADER FOR CMONTH(DATE()) = 0 TO PRINT
      ENDC
*
      ? CHR(control codes for normal printing features, if necessary)
      SET PRIN OFF
      SET CONS ON
ENDD
*
** END OF PAYMENU.PRG
```

We start by declaring our SAY and GET files, naming our key field, establishing a condition flag, and SELECTing our databases. The first CASE is an error condition. Option Q handles normal exiting of the module. Option E engages the editor. Option F generates late payment letters through a subroutine, LETTER, which will be described later.

Note that the PAYMENU subsystem is broken into two DO CASE . . . ENDCASE blocks. The first block handles the normal, more mundane CASEs of quitting, editing, processing error conditions, and calling subroutines.

The second DO CASE . . . ENDCASE block handles the slightly more exotic functions of generating reports. In truth there is no need to separate the two blocks. This subsystem keeps them separate due to the condition setting code between the first and second DO CASE . . . ENDCASE blocks. An alternate coding would include:

```
CASE ANSWER $ [PL]
```

in the first DO CASE . . . ENDCASE block. This CASE would then start with the condition setting code and end with the present second DO CASE . . . ENDCASE block at the end of the PAYMENU subsystem. This alternative code is shown in Listing 8–13.

Listing 8–13

```
** PAYMENU.PRG, 2ND VERSION
*
GETTER = "PAYGET"
FRAMER = "PAYSAY"
KEYFIELD = "ACCOUNT"
YESCON = .F.
SELE 2
USE subscribers database INDE subscriber account NDX file, built index field NDX file
SELE 1
USE payments database INDE subscriber account NDX file, built index field NDX file
*
DO WHILE .T.
   ANSWER = 'Q'
   CLEAR
   @  1,0 TO 17,79 DOUB
   @ 3,1 TO 3,78 DOUB
   @  2, 31  SAY "PAYMENT MENU"
   @ 2,60 SAY IIF(YESCON,'CONDITION EXITS',SPACE(17))
   @  5, 23  SAY "E  Edit Payments"
   @  8, 23  SAY "P  Print Payments Report"
   @ 10, 23  SAY "L  Print Late Payments Report"
   @ 13, 23  SAY "F  Print Late Payment Letters"
   @ 15, 23  SAY "Q  Quit"
   @ 17, 32  SAY " select   "
   @ 17,41 GET ANSWER PICT '!'
   READ
*
   DO CASE
      CASE .NOT. ANSWER $ 'EPLFQ'
         @ 22,0 CLEA
         @ 22,0 SAY [GOOD CHOICE, BUT NOT ONE I CAN USE]
         CALL DELAY WITH CHR(1)
         @ 22,0 CLEA
```

Listing 8–13 (cont.)

```
      LOOP
   CASE ANSWER='Q'
      CLOSE DATA
      RETU
   CASE ANSWER='E'
      CLEAR
      DO EDIT
      LOOP
   CASE ANSWER='F'
      DO LETTER
   CASE ANSWER $ [PL]
      TRUTH = .T.
      @ 20,0 SAY "DO YOU WANT A CONDITION ON THE REPORTS (Y/N)? -> " GET TRUTH
      READ
      CLEAR
*
      IF TRUTH
         DO PAYSAY
         DO PAYGET
         CLEA GETS
         CONDITION = SPACE(60)
         @ 23,0 SAY "CONDITION -> " GET CONDITION
         READ
      ELSE
         CONDITION = []
      ENDI
*
      IF LEN(TRIM(CONDITION)) # 0
         YESCON = .T.
         SET FILT TO &CONDITION
         HEADER = [HEAD "&CONDITION"]
      ELSE
         YESCON = .F.
         SET FILT TO
         HEADER = []
      ENDI
*
      SET CONS OFF
      SET PRIN ON
      ? CHR(control codes for special printing features, if necessary)
*
      DO CASE
         CASE ANSWER = 'P'
            REPO FORM payment report form &HEADER TO PRINT
         CASE ANSWER = 'L'
```

Listing 8–13 (cont.)

```
                REPO FORM payment report form &HEADER FOR CMONTH(DATE()) = 0 TO PRINT
          ENDC
*
          ? CHR(control codes for normal printing features, if necessary)
          SET PRIN OFF
          SET CONS ON
    ENDC
*
ENDD
*
** END OF PAYMENU.PRG
```

Using either listing, we need to find out if there is any condition on the REPORTs. If there is, we put up the SAY and GET files so the user knows what there is to work with. If no condition applies, we declare the CONDITION as [].

Once the CONDITION is entered, we check to make sure the user didn't simply press RETURN with:

```
IF LEN(TRIM(CONDITION)) # 0
```

and set the YESCON flag and FILTERs accordingly. We also make use of another macro expression with:

```
HEADER = [HEAD "&CONDITION"]
```

An interesting point arises here. The user could generate the late payment reports by entering:

```
CMONTH(DATE()) = 0
```

as the CONDITION (remember that we're using database fields named after months). That may or may not be too sophisticated for the users in your environment. You decide.

As before, we include:

```
? CHR(control codes)
```

to alert the printer to special printing considerations, if any.

This brings us to the LETTER subroutine we mentioned earlier.

Listing 8–14

```
** LETTER.PRG FORM LETTER GENERATOR
*
CLEA
SET RELATION TO account field INTO B
ACCEPT [WHAT MONTH ARE WE SENDING NOTICES FOR? -> ] TO MONTH
```

Listing 8–14 (cont.)

```
SET FILTER TO &MONTH=0.00
SET DEVI TO PRINT
*
DO WHILE .NOT. EOF()
*
&& The following four lines may or may not be necessary. If you use letterhead,
&& you probably don't want to use them
*
   @ 8,50 SAY [company name]
   @ 9,50 SAY [company address]
   @ 10,50 SAY [city, state, and zip code information]
   @ 11,50 SAY [company phone number]
*
&& The following code prints a standard example of a late notice
*
   @ 12,50 SAY STR(DAY(DATE()),2,0) + ', ' + CMONTH(DATE()) + ' '
 + STR(YEAR(DATE()),4,0)
   @ 16,5 SAY TRIM(name information)
   @ 17,5 SAY B->address information
   @ 18,5 SAY TRIM(B->city) + ', ' + state + '    ' + zip code
   @ 23,5 SAY [Dear Subscriber:]
   @ 26,5 SAY 'In checking our records we have not received your ' + UPPE(month) +;
              ' payment for ' + STR(B->rate,5,2) + '.'
   @ 27,5 SAY 'Please remit as soon as possible so you can avoid having your service'
   @ 28,5 SAY 'disconnected.  If you have already submitted your payment, disregard'
   @ 29,5 SAY 'this letter.  If you have any questions about your billing contact our'
   @ 30,5 SAY 'office between the hours of 9:00 and 5:00, Monday through Friday.'
   @ 33,5 SAY 'Please return the coupons from your payment book so we can properly'
   @ 34,5 SAY 'credit your account.  Thank you for your payment.'
   @ 37,50 SAY 'Best Regards,'
   @ 40,50 SAY [company name or officer and title]
   SKIP
ENDDO
*
SET FILT TO
SET DEVI TO SCREEN
*
** END OF LETTER.PRG
```

Note the apparent incongruity between the late payments report CASE and this CASE. Here we asked what month to send notices for, while there we determined the month from the system date. This code is designed for payments more than 30 days late, and the code in the late payments report is for use immediately after data has been entered.

We SET a FILTER based on the month field having a value of 0. From there we print out letters. This code can be easily modified to print any letters for any conditions:

Listing 8–15

```
** LETTER.PRG SECOND VERSION, MODIFIED LETTER GENERATOR
*
CLEA
FILENAME = SPAC(12)
*
DO CASE
   CASE [subscriber database]$DBF()
      SELE 2
*
&& This code assumes all subscriber based letters have an 'SUB' extension
*
      DIR *.SUB
   CASE [payments database]$DBF()
      SELE 1
*
&& This code assumes all payment based letters have an 'PMT' extension
*
      DIR *.PMT
ENDC
*
@ 22,0 SAY [Which letter do you want to use (8 CHAR MAX)? -> ] ;
       GET FILENAME PICT IIF([payments database]$DBF(),"XXXXXXXX.PMT","XXXXXXXX.SUB")
READ
*
DO CASE
   CASE .NOT. FILE('&FILENAME')
      WAIT [THAT FILE DOESN'T EXIST. PRESS ANY KEY TO CONTINUE...]
      RETU
   CASE [payments database]$DBF()
      SET RELA TO account field INTO B
   OTHE
      SET RELA TO account field INTO A
ENDC
*
TRUTH = .T.
@ 22,0 CLEA
@ 22,0 [Do you want a condition on these letters? (Y/N) -> ] GET TRUTH
READ
*
IF TRUTH
   CLEA
   CONDITION = SPACE(60)
*
   DO CASE
      CASE [payments database]$DBF()
```

Listing 8–15 (cont.)

```
        DO PAYSAY
        DO PAYGET
      CASE [subscriber database]$DBF()
        DO SUBSAY
        DO SUBGET
  ENDC
*
  CLEA GETS
  @ 23,0 SAY "CONDITION -> " GET CONDITION
  READ
  SET FILTER TO &CONDITION
ENDI
*
SET DEVI TO PRINT
*
DO WHILE .NOT. EOF()
  DO &FILENAME
  SKIP
ENDDO
*
SET FILT TO
SET DEVI TO SCREEN
SET RELA TO
SELE 1
SET RELA TO account field INTO B
*
** END OF LETTER.PRG
```

As you might guess, this file is a kernel that can be used in several applications. That also explains the DO CASE . . . ENDCASE blocks when only two databases are used. The code is easily understood, but note the use of IIF() to determine the PICTURE argument when the program GETs the filename.

The letter generator in Listing 8–15 also places some extra responsibility on the programmer/developer/designer. You must somehow let your users know what fields are available and how they should be inserted in the letters being written.

A REAL-LIFE EXAMPLE OF A SUBSCRIPTION SYSTEM

Now we come to the final part of this chapter, where we tie the complete system together. We start with a main menu generator.

Listing 8–16

```
** SUBMAIN.PRG FOR WORKING WITH SUBSCRIBER AND PAYMENT RECORDS
*
CLOS ALL
CLEA ALL
*
* THINGS TURNED ON
SET DELI ON
SET ESCA ON
SET INTE ON
*
* THINGS TURNED OFF
SET BELL OFF
SET CONF OFF
SET STAT OFF
SET SAFE OFF
SET TALK OFF
*
REST FROM SUBS
SET PROC TO SUBS.PRC
SET PATH TO &CPATH
SET DEFA TO &CDRIVE
SET DELI TO '><'
SET DATE TO &DATETYPE
*
ON ERROR DO ERRORMSS
*
PLACE = 0
TRUTH = .F.
*
* LOAD BIN FILES INTO MEMORY
LOAD CURSOR2
LOAD DELAY
LOAD SAVESCR
*
CLEA
@  1,0 TO 20,79 DOUB
@ 3,1 TO 3,78 DOUB
@  2, 24  SAY "SUBSCRIBER SYSTEM CABLE MAIN MENU"
@  5, 22  SAY "S  Subscription System"
@  6, 22  SAY [P  Payments System]
@ 9,22 SAY [U  Utility Menu]
@ 10,22 SAY [L  Label Generator]
@ 11,22 SAY [W  Use Word Processor]
@ 12,22 SAY [D  Execute DOS Command]
@ 18, 22  SAY "Q  Quit to System"
```

Listing 8–16 (cont.)

```
@ 20, 34  SAY " select   "
*
DO WHILE .T.
   @ 21,0 CLEA
   ANSWER = 'Q'
   @ 20, 43 GET ANSWER PICT '!'
   READ
*
   IF ANSWER $ [SPLUWDQ]
      CALL SAVESCR WITH 'S1'
   ELSE
      @ 22,0 SAY [GOOD ANSWER, BUT NOT ONE I CAN USE]
      CALL DELAY WITH CHR(1)
      @ 22,0 CLEA
      LOOP
   ENDI
*
   DO CASE
      CASE ANSWER = 'Q'
         SAVE TO SUBS
         QUIT
      CASE ANSWER = 'S'
         DO SUBSMENU
      CASE ANSWER = 'P'
         DO PAYMENU
      CASE ANSWER = 'L'
         DO LABELS
      CASE ANSWER = 'U'
         DO UTILMENU
      CASE ANSWER = 'W'
         ! &WORDPROC
      CASE ANSWER = 'D'
         @ 22,0
         ACCE [EXECUTE WHAT DOS COMMAND? -> ] TO DOSCOMM
         CLEA
         ! &DOSCOMM
         WAIT
  ENDC
*
  CLEA
  CALL SAVESCR WITH 'R1'
*
ENDD
*
** END OF SUBMAIN.PRG
```

This main module is similar to our other standard modules. We CLOSE and CLEAR everything, turn some dBASE III PLUS defaults ON, turn others OFF, RESTORE variables from SUBS.MEM, establish a PROCedure file, SET some system defaults (PATH, DEFAULT drive, DELIMITERS, and DATE type), declare an error trapping routine, and declare some system variables for the work session.

Earlier I mentioned some BIN files that should be LOADed into memory. That is done with the next three lines. The SAVESCR.BIN file is available in Ashton-Tate's dBASE PROGRAMMER'S UTILITIES package. The purpose of SAVESCR is to SAVE the current SCREEN to a buffer. Instead of painting the screen each time we need only to use:

```
CALL SAVESCR WITH 'Sn'
```

to store the current screen and:

```
CALL SAVESCR WITH 'Rn'
```

to restore the stored screen. In both cases, *n* represents one of the five buffers available to SAVESCR. The major advantage in the main menu generator is not having to perform the declaration lines each time you go through the DO WHILE ... ENDDO loop. This file is CALLed only from this menu and in the UTILMENU subroutine. It can be done without. All you need do is remove all lines of the form:

```
CALL SAVESCR WITH 'An'
```

where *A* is either S or R and *n* is defined again as one of the buffers. Then you include the declaration lines in the DO WHILE ... ENDDO loop.

Similarly, you can replace:

```
LOAD CURSOR2
```

with code shown earlier.

The actual options are evaluated beginning with the IF ... ELSE ... ENDIF block immediately following the READ command. This block tests for valid options. Valid options cause III PLUS to SAVE the SCReen and continue. Invalid options put up an error message and loop back to the top of the DO WHILE ... ENDDO loop.

Option Q is the standard quit to system option. Options S and P also call their previously listed subsystems. We haven't yet talked about the LABELS and UTILMENU subsystems, but you can call them up the same way you do PAYMENU and SUBSMENU.

Option W activates the declared word processor. This word processor is declared in the utilities menu, shown later in this section. Both options W and D make use of III PLUS's RUN/! command and require systems with more than 256K memory. Again, you'll be much better off if your system has as much memory as possible.

Option D is a new one in this listing. It prompts the user for a DOS-level command. This could be an alternate word processor, a spreadsheet system, a telecommunications package, or whatever.

The last two lines before the ENDDO are based on this code using SAVE-SCR and can be removed as described earlier.

The next code to investigate is the LABELS.PRG file, a label-generating kernel that can be used in several applications with few modifications.

Listing 8–17

```
** LABELS.PRG LABEL GENERATOR
*
USE subscribers database INDEX built index field NDX file
CONDITION = SPACE(65)
YESCON = .F.
FILENAME = [standard label form]
*
DO WHIL .T.
   ANSWER = 'Q'
   CLEAR
   @  5, 24  SAY "S  Select Label Form"
   @  6, 24  SAY "C  Create Condition"
   @  7, 24  SAY "P  Print Labels"
   @ 11, 24  SAY "Q  Quit"
   @  1,0 TO 15,79 DOUB
   @ 3,1 TO 3,78 DOUB
   @ 2,3 SAY [CURRENT LABEL -> ] + FILENAME
   @ 2,33 SAY [LABEL GENERATOR]
   @ 2,55 SAY IIF(YESCON,[CONDITION EXITS],SPACE(16))
   @ 15, 31 SAY [ select    ]
   @ 15,40 GET ANSWER PICT '!'
   READ
*
   DO CASE
      CASE .NOT. ANSWER $ [SCPQ]
         @ 22,0 SAY [GOOD CHOICE, BUT NOT ONE I CAN USE]
         CALL DELAY WITH CHR(1)
         @ 22,0 CLEA
         LOOP
      CASE ANSWER = 'Q'
         CLOS DATA
         RETU
      CASE ANSWER = 'S'
         CLEA
         DIR *.LBL
              && all standard III PLUS LABEL files use an 'LBL' extension
         @ 22,0 SAY [Which letter do you want to use (8 CHAR MAX)? -> ];
```

Listing 8–17 (cont.)

```
                GET FILENAME PICT "XXXXXXXX"
          READ
*
          IF .NOT. FILE('&FILENAME')
             WAIT [THAT FILE DOESN'T EXIST. PRESS ANY KEY TO CONTINUE...]
             CLEA
             LOOP
          ENDI
*
       CASE ANSWER = 'C'
*
          IF YESCON
             SET FILT TO
             CONDITION = SPACE(65)
             YESCON = .F.
          ELSE
             YESCON = .T.
             CLEA
             DO SUBSAY
             DO SUBGET
             CLEA GETS
             @ 23,0 SAY [CONDITION  ] GET CONDITION
             READ
             SET FILT TO &CONDITION
          ENDI
*
          LOOP
       CASE ANSWER = 'P'
          @ 24,0 SAY [DO YOU WANT TO START WITH SAMPLES? (Y/N)  ] GET TRUTH
          READ
          SAMPLES = IIF(TRUTH, [SAMP], [])
          CLEA
          SET CONS OFF
          LABEL FORM &FILENAME &SAMPLES TO PRINT
          SET CONS ON
    ENDCASE
*
ENDD
*
** END OF LABELS.PRG
```

We declare three local variables, CONDITION, YESCON, and FILENAME, which you've seen before. The generator is enclosed in a DO WHILE . . . ENDDO loop. Normally, such generators are one-shot deals. We generate a set of labels and return to our main task. This generator is designed to work with several LBL files, not just one. This allows you to create a variety of labels, based on available LBL files. The logic of the module is shown in the menu listing.

We start by selecting a LBL form. A "standard label form" is declared in FILENAME and shown on the menu @ 2,3. Once we've selected a label form, we might want to create a condition on the labels. Next we print them, and last we quit.

The options are coded into a DO CASE . . . ENDCASE block. The first CASE is an error trap. The second CASE RETURNs to the calling program. The third CASE is where selection of LBL files is made. Note how similar this code is to that in Listing 8–15. Here we include the LOOP command should the user enter an unavailable filename.

Option C operates the YESCON toggle. If a condition exists (YESCON = .T.), it removes the existing condition, sets YESCON to .F., and shuts off any FILTERs on the database. If no conditions exist (YESCON = .F.), then it displays the SAY and GET files so the user can establish a condition on the LBL file, READs the condition, and SETs a FILTER TO that condition, now macroized with &CONDITION.

Option P is where label printing actually occurs. Before printing starts, the program asks if the user wants any SAMPLES to align the labels in the printer. The response goes into the macro SAMPLES and gets included in the command line:

```
LABEL FORM &FILENAME &SAMPLES TO PRINT
```

The subscriber system also uses a utility file, UTILMENU. The routine showed here contains the necessities for this system, but isn't necessarily all the functions you might want to include in your own utility file. UTILMENU is a composite of utilities listed elsewhere in the book and can be modified by using code from previously listed modules as needed.

Listing 8–18

```
** UTILMENU.PRG SUBSCRIBER SYSTEM UTILITIES
*
   CLEAR
   @ 2, 0 TO 19,79 DOUB
   @ 3,21 SAY [S U B S C R I B E R   U T I L I T I E S]
   @ 4,1 TO 4,78 DOUB
   @  7,28 SAY [D  Set Date Type]
   @  9,28 SAY [S  Set Default Drive]
   @ 10,28 SAY [P  Set Default Path]
   @ 11,28 SAY [R  Reindex Files]
   @ 12,28 SAY [W  Select Word Processor]
   @ 15,28 SAY [Q  Quit]
   @ 19,33 SAY " select   "
*
DO WHILE .T.
   ANSWER = 'Q'
```

Listing 8–18 (cont.)

```
   @ 19,42 GET ANSWER PICT "!"
   READ
*
   DO CASE
      CASE .NOT. ANSWER $ [DSPRWQ]
         @ 22,0 SAY [GOOD CHOICE, BUT NOT ONE I CAN USE]
         CALL DELAY WITH CHR(1)
         LOOP
      CASE ANSWER = 'Q'
         RETURN
      CASE ANSWER = 'S'
         @ 20,0 CLEA
         @ 21,0 SAY "Current default drive is " + CDRIVE
         @ 22,0 SAY "New default drive is -> " GET CDRIVE PICT "A"
         READ
         SET DEFA TO &CDRIVE
      CASE ANSWER = 'P'
         @ 20,0 CLEA
         @ 21,0 SAY "Current default path is " + CPATH
         CPATH = CPATH + SPACE(30)
         @ 22,0 SAY "New default path is -> " GET CPATH
         READ
         CPATH = TRIM(CPATH)
         SET PATH TO &CPATH
      CASE ANSWER = 'W'
         @ 20,0 CLEA
         ACCE "What is the DOS command to start the word processor? -> ";
              TO WORDPROC
      CASE ANSWER = 'D'
         @ 20,0 CLEA
         @ 20,0 TO 23,79 DOUB
         @ 21,28 SAY "M  Set Date to MM/DD/YY"
         @ 22,28 SAY "D  Set Date to DD/MM/YY"
         @ 23,33 SAY " select   "
         @ 23,42 GET ANSWER PICT "!"
         READ
         DATETYPE = IIF(ANSWER = 'M',[AMER],[BRIT])
         LOOP
      CASE ANSWER = 'R'
         CALL SAVESCR WITH 'S2'
         DO INDEXER
         CLEA
         CALL SAVESCR WITH 'R2'
   ENDCASE
*
```

Listing 8–18 (cont.)

```
   @ 20,0 CLEA
ENDDO T
*
** END OF UTILMENU.PRG
```

The options are standards until we get to R. This is the part of UTILMENU that CALLs SAVESCR. It also calls its own subroutine, INDEXER. As with so much of the code in this book, INDEXER is a module that can be used in several systems. It provides a quick means of INDEXing files that have problems. Note that this is different from the CASE ERROR() = 114 line included in the ERRORMSS PROCedure. That REINDEXes the current file. INDEXER INDEXes any or all files should the need arise.

Listing 8–19

```
** INDEXER.PRG
*
CLEA
@ 1,0 TO 15,79 DOUB
@ 2,25 SAY [SELECT A DATABASE TO REINDEX]
@ 3,1 TO 3,78
@ 5,30 SAY [S  Subscribers File]
@ 6,30 SAY [P  Payments File]
@ 12,30 SAY [A  All]
@ 13,30 SAY [Q  Quit]
@ 15,34 SAY [ select   ]
*
DO WHIL .T.
   ANSWER = 'Q'
   @ 15,43 GET ANSWER PICT "!"
   @ 21,0 CLEA
   READ
*
   DO CASE
      CASE ANSWER = 'Q'
         EXIT
      CASE ANSWER = 'P'
         @ 21,0 SAY [USE PAYMENTS FILE: TWO INDEX FILES]
         USE payments database
         @ 22,0 SAY [REBUILDING FIRST INDEX FILE]
         INDEX ON account number field TO subscriber account NDX file
         @ 23,0 SAY [REBUILDING SECOND INDEX FILE]
         INDEX ON built index key TO built index field NDX file
      CASE ANSWER = 'S'
         @ 21,0 SAY [USE SUBSCRIBER FILE: TWO INDEX FILES]
         USE subscribers database
```

Listing 8–19 (cont.)

```
        @ 22,0 SAY [REBUILDING FIRST INDEX FILE]
        INDEX ON account number field TO subscriber account NDX file
        @ 23,0 SAY [REBUILDING SECOND INDEX FILE]
        INDEX ON built index key TO built index field NDX file
      CASE ANSWER = 'A'
        @ 21,0 SAY [USE PAYMENTS FILE: TWO INDEX FILES]
        USE payments database
        @ 22,0 SAY [REBUILDING FIRST INDEX FILE]
        INDEX ON account number field TO subscriber account NDX file
        @ 23,0 SAY [REBUILDING SECOND INDEX FILE]
        INDEX ON built index key TO built index field NDX file
        @ 21,0 CLEA
        @ 21,0 SAY [USE SUBSCRIBER FILE: TWO INDEX FILES]
        USE subscribers database
        @ 22,0 SAY [REBUILDING FIRST INDEX FILE]
        INDEX ON account number field TO subscriber account NDX file
        @ 23,0 SAY [REBUILDING SECOND INDEX FILE]
        INDEX ON built index key TO built index field NDX file
   ENDCASE
*
ENDD
*
** END OF INDEXER.PRG
```

The only file not yet shown is the SUBS.PRC procedure file. This file follows the logic of procedure files as described in Part 1 of this book, and in earlier chapters in Part 2.

Listing 8–20

```
* SUBS.PRC PROCEDURE FILE
*
PROC EDITMENU
@ 20,0 TO 23,79 DOUB
@ 21,1 SAY [  E -> Edit  B -> Back  S -> Skip  G -> Goto  K -> Kill  R -> Rstr]+;
           [Q -> Quit]
@ 22,1 SAY [  F -> Find  L -> Loca  C -> Cont  D -> Disp  O -> Copy  A -> Add]+;
           [U -> Upda]
*
PROC SUBSAY
@  2, PLACE SAY DBF()
*
** SAY STATEMENTS HERE ARE FROM YOUR SUBSCRIBER SAY FILE.
*
@  3,  1  TO  3, 78    DOUBLE
@  1,  0  TO 18, 79    DOUBLE
```

Listing 8–20 (cont.)

```
*
PROC SUBGET
@ 2,73 SAY STR(RECNO(),5,0)
*
** GET STATEMENTS HERE ARE FROM YOUR BILLING DATABASE GET FILE.
*
PROC SUBGETNA
*
&& This file is identical to SUBGET but lacks the GET account field command.
* PROC PAYSAY
@  2, PLACE SAY DBF()
*
** SAY STATEMENTS HERE ARE FROM YOUR PAYABLES DATABASE SAY FILE.
*
@  3,  1  TO  3, 78    DOUBLE
@  1,  0  TO 18, 79    DOUBLE
*
PROC PAYGET
@ 2,73 SAY STR(RECNO(),5,0)
*
** THIS FILE CONTAINS THE PAYMENTS DATABASE GET COMMANDS.
*
PROC PAYGET2
@ 2,73 SAY STR(RECNO(),5,0)
*
&& This PROCedure SAYs the information REPLACEd from the subscriber
&& databases in the ACCTCK.PRG file. The rest of the file contains
&& the GET statements from your normal PAYGET file
*
PROC ERRORMSS
*
DO CASE
   CASE ERROR() = 1
      @ 0,0 SAY "That file doesn't exist on drive " + CDRIVE
      CALL DELAY WITH CHR(1)
      RETU TO MASTER
   CASE ERROR() = 4
      @ 24,50 say "Record Number ->  END  "
      @ 0,0 SAY "You're at the end of the file now. "
   CASE ERROR() = 5
      @ 24,50 say "Record Number ->  END  "
      @ 0,0 SAY "You can't CONTINUE any further. You're at the end. "
   CASE ERROR() = 38
      @ 24,50 say "Record Number -> 0   "
      @ 0,0 SAY "You can't go any further. You're at the beginning now. "
```

Listing 8–20 (cont.)

```
   CASE ERROR() = 42
      @ 0,0 SAY "You must LOCATE before you can CONTINUE. "
   CASE ERROR() = 114
      CLEAR
      @ 10,10 TO 20,70 DOUBLE
      @ 15,15 SAY "The INDEX file is damaged, excuse me while I REINDEX"
      REIN
   CASE ERROR() = 125
      @ 0,0 SAY "Please turn the PRINTER ON."
   OTHE
      @ 0,0 SAY "I'VE ENCOUNTERED AN UNKNOWN ERROR. PLEASE TRY AGAIN"
ENDC
*
** END OF SUBS.PRC
```

This is much simpler than previous PROCedure files shown in the book, but necessarily so. Much of what we coded into other PROCedure files is done less frequently in this system and, when it is done, is handled by the code itself. As a final note, you can include the AR module from Chapter 7 into this system with a few minor modifications.

CHAPTER

9

GENERAL ACCOUNTING SYSTEM

What is a generalized accounting system? That is a question with more answers than people to answer it. For the purposes of this book, we'll consider the system to be programming that keeps a business's finances running smoothly. This definition may not please an accountant, but it will provide the information you or your client needs to pay taxes, fill out official forms, and generally keep heads above water.

THE SPECIAL NEEDS OF AN ACCOUNTING SYSTEM

There are two needs to emphasize about accounting systems. One is multiple field indexing, the other is a heavy need for masterbases and databases. Both of these topics have been discussed in Chapter 4 and other chapters of this book. An overview of these concepts follows.

Multiple Field Indexing

Any accounting system needs to find data fast. This isn't necessary only for answering questions from clients. The great need is keeping several NDX files active and switching from one key field sort to another key field sort. A user needs to find an invoice number, then a client number, then an item name, and on and on. Methods for keeping several NDX files active and accessible to the system were introduced in Chapter 6. Those techniques are used again here. Some modifications are added, but nothing to throw you off.

When you keep several NDX files active, other parts of the system are affected. You'll probably want REPORTs written from the NDX files. You may also want to create subsets of the database according to the NDX file lines. That brings us to the next topic, masterbases and databases.

Masterbases and Databases

The concepts of masterbases and databases were covered in Chapter 4. What are they? A *masterbase* is all the information necessary for a system. A system might have more than one masterbase, but these different masterbases are usually broken down along specialized lines. One masterbase might hold all client information (address, billing, histories, and so on); another masterbase might hold all inventory information (warehouse number, part number, activity, and so on); and another masterbase might hold all personnel information.

Databases are the parts of masterbases that are used for specific applications. You create a masterbase of all client information. You create databases of address information, billing information, and client history. Each of the separate databases are used for different parts of the system. They all update the masterbase. This updating can be initiated by the user or done on a "clock." The system can detect the need to update based on day of week or date of last update using the dBASE III PLUS UPDATE() function. The actual updating algorithm can be pseudocoded as follows:

```
USE masterbase INDEX NDX file list
UPDATE ON MASTER KEY FIELD FROM database
SET RELATION ON MASTER KEY FIELD FROM masterbase TO
database
DO WHILE NOT EOF()
APPEND masterbase WITH database records NOT INCLUDED IN
UPDATE
ENDDO
```

DESIGNING A GENERAL ACCOUNTING SYSTEM

An accounting system is the most complex and challenging programming exercise covered in this book. Fortunately, we've coded most of it before. A general accounting system flowchart can be likened to an outline. The outline provides the template around which we'll code. We start with the needs outline shown in Figure 9–1.

We know from past work that the needs outline is based on the user's needs, not programming needs. This is a fairly complete system, and you'll notice we've coded much of the system in earlier chapters. All the databases require an editor. There is a lot of printing that the system requires, and all those needs can be driven by the same module. (Note: We may not send all the printing tasks through one module, but the one module may be the model for all our printing tasks.)

We've designed an accounts receivable (AR) system. We want to expand that system to keep track of finances using a general ledger chart of accounts. This also means we need some kind of posting mechanism. This posting mechanism needs to show individual transactions on an account and show the total amount of transactions on an account. The other side of AR is accounts payable (AP). Like the AR, the AP must show individual transactions on an account and the total transaction amount on an account.

MAIN MENU

- ACCOUNTS MENU
  - Receivables
    - Edit Accounts
    - List Past Due Accounts
    - Print Invoices
  - Payables
    - Edit Accounts
    - Cut Checks
      - Manual Checks
      - Computer Checks
  - Charts of Accounts
    - Edit Chart of Accounts
    - Print Chart of Accounts
    - Print Active/Inactive Accounts
    - Print Accounts Activity
  - End-of-Term Reports
    - Monthly Reports
    - Daily Disbursements
    - Quarterly Reports
    - Check Register Report
    - Yearly Reports
- CLIENT MENU
  - Edit Records
  - Update Receivables Database
- PERSONNEL MENU
  - Edit Records
- PAYCHECK MENU
    - Edit Paycheck Database
    - Print Checks
    - Update Payables Database
- INVENTORY MENU (if necessary)
  - Edit Inventory
  - Order Tracking
    - Generate Invoices
    - Update Receivables Database
  - Inventory Reports
    - Reorder Information
    - Inventory Status
- UTILITIES MENU
  - SYSTEM UTILITIES MENU
    - Set Date Type
    - Set Memo Width

Figure 9–1 This flowchart shows an outline of the accounting system.

Set Default Drive and Path
Set Error Message Wait Time
Set Past Due Period
Set Billing Period
Set Check Number
Set Default Printer Destination
Set Word Processor
Set Spreadsheet (if necessary)
Program Utilities
Set Source and Target Drives
Create New Files
Copy File
Create Backups
Close Month
Close Quarter
Use Word Processor
Create Mailmerge File
Use Spreadsheet
Create Spreadsheet File
Execute DOS-Level Command

Figure 9–1 (cont.)

If you're getting the impression the AR in this application is more sophisticated than the previous AR module, you're right. You can use the previous module, but I'll offer some suggestions here.

The AR database structure has a basic form. One field that takes on a much greater import in this module is the account number. Why so? Accounting systems make use of account numbers in much the same way inventory systems track orders. We need to create a historical database of account numbers, descriptions of the separate accounts, and perhaps the account totals. Each entry into both AR and AP databases should check the account numbers entered by the user against the account numbers in the historical database. There's no need to constantly update the historical database's totals, although you could do so by placing a REPLACE command in the code.

Along the lines of this historical database, a need arises to list the accounts. This is usually called a *chart of accounts.* This chart of accounts has a simple structure, shown in Figure 9–2.

The account number ranges are fairly standard. You don't necessarily have to use them (they go from 1000 for Current Assets to 9999 for Temporary Distribution), but they do make later tranactions easier and less worrisome.

We can also look at our needs outline and see every kernel we've developed being used in the editor. The other parts of the system already exist in our toolkit. We use the client system previously coded. The personnel menu is identical to the client system. The difference between the two is billing clients for time and

```
<DATE>               <COMPANY NAME>                <PAGE>
                     CHART OF ACCOUNTS

Account Range        Account Number and Title

1000 - 1299          Current Assets:               (1040 Checking Account)
                                                   (1190 Bad Debt Allowance)

1300 - 1349          Refundable Taxes

1500 - 1699          Property and Equipment:
                                                   (1500 Land)
                                                   (1650 Vehicles)

2000                 Accounts Payable
```

Figure 9–2 This display is a sample chart of accounts listing.

tracking our personnel's hours for payment purposes. The project system is a variation of the inventory tracking system and shouldn't be confused with the client billing system. The inventory system has been coded, as well as many of the utilities. We've also shown how to incorporate a word processor into the main menu system. That same methodology can be used for a spreadsheet program. Executing a DOS-level command was also developed in a previous system. We bring all our past work together in this final system.

USING THE KERNELS TO BUILD THE SYSTEM

We're going to use all our previously coded kernels here. That means there'll be more menu options on the editor than there's room on the screen, if we continue with a two-line menu system. All the kernels have been described previously and are only briefly referenced here.

Listing 9–1

```
* EDIT.PRG
* CALLS EDITMENU FROM PROCEDURE FILE
*
DO &SAYER
DO &GETTER
CLEA GETS
EDITFLAG = .T.
DO EDITMENU
ANSWER = 'X'
```

Listing 9–1 (cont.)

```
*
DO WHIL .T.
   @ 0,0 SAY SPACE(80)
   @ 24,0 SAY SPACE(80)
   @  2,60 SAY IIF(DELETED(),"DELETED",SPACE(7))
   @ 23,34 SAY " select / . "
   @ 23,43 GET ANSWER PICT '!'
   READ
*
   DO CASE
      CASE .NOT. ANSWER $ 'XQKRSBEOCGDFLAUTMN'
         @ 20,0 CLEA
         WAIT [NOT ONE OF THE OPTIONS. PRESS ANY KEY TO CONTINUE.]
         @ 20,0 CLEA
         DO EDITMENU
         LOOP
      CASE ANSWER = 'X'
         CANC           && programmer's bailout
      CASE ANSWER = 'N'
         EDITFLAG = IIF(EDITFLAG, .F., .T.)
         DO EDITMENU
         LOOP
      CASE ANSWER = 'Q'
         RETU
      CASE ANSWER = 'K'
         DELE
         LOOP
      CASE ANSWER = 'R'
         RECA
         LOOP
      CASE ANSWER = 'S'
         SKIP
         DO &GETTER
         CLEA GETS
         LOOP
      CASE ANSWER = 'B'
         SKIP -1
         DO &GETTER
         CLEA GETS
         LOOP
      CASE ANSWER = 'E'
         @ 20,0 CLEA
         @ 22,0 SAY "Press CTRL-W to save edit, ESC to exit"
         DO &GETTER
         READ
```

Listing 9–1 (cont.)

```
      DO EDITMENU
      LOOP
   CASE ANSWER = 'O'
      COPY NEXT 1 TO TANK
      APPE FROM TANK
      DO &GETTER
      CLEA GETS
      LOOP
   CASE ANSWER = 'C'
      SET ORDER TO 0
      CONT
      DO &GETTER
      CLEA GETS
      SET ORDER TO 1
      LOOP
   CASE ANSWER = 'G'
      ACCE "Record Number -> " TO RECNUM
      GOTO VAL(RECNUM)
      DO &GETTER
      CLEA GETS
      @ 24,0 SAY SPACE(40)
      LOOP
   CASE ANSWER = 'D'
      @ 20,0 CLEA
      ACCE "Display What -> " TO DISPLAYWHAT
*
      IF LEN(TRIM(DISPLAYWHAT)) = 0
         @ 20,0 CLEA
         DO EDITMENU
         LOOP
      ENDI
*
      TRUTH = .T.
      @ 21,0 CLEA
      ACCE "DISP FOR -> " TO DISPLAYFOR
      READ
*
      IF LEN(TRIM(DISPLAYFOR)) # 0
         SET FILT TO &DISPLAYFOR
         DISPLAYFOR = 'FOR' + DISPLAYFOR
      ENDI
*
      @ 21,0 CLEA
      @ 21,0 SAY [DO YOU WANT THIS PRINTED (Y/N)? ] GET TRUTH
      READ
```

Listing 9–1 (cont.)

```
*
         IF TRUTH
            TOPRINT = 'TO PRINT'
            EJECT
         ELSE
            TOPRINT = []
            CLEA
         ENDI
*
         DISP &DISPLAYWHAT &DISPLAYFOR &TOPRINT
*
         IF TRUTH
            EJECT
         ENDI
*
         CLEA
         DO &SAYER
         DO &GETTER
         CLEA GETS
         SET FILT TO
         DO EDITMENU
         LOOP
      CASE ANSWER = 'F'
         @ 20,0 CLEAR
         ACCE "Find &KEYFIELD / " TO TOFIND
         SEEK TOFIND
         DO &GETTER
         CLEA GETS
         DO EDITMENU
         LOOP
      CASE ANSWER = 'L'
         SET ORDER TO 0
         @ 20,0 CLEA
         ACCE "Locate what? -> " TO LOCATEWHAT
         ACCE "Locate where? -> " TO LOCATEWHERE
         LOCA FOR "&LOCATEWHAT"$&LOCATEWHERE
         SET ORDER TO 1
         DO &GETTER
         CLEA GETS
         DO EDITMENU
         LOOP
      CASE ANSWER = 'A'
         COPY STRUC TO TANK
         SELE 6
         USE TANK
```

Listing 9-1 (cont.)

```
        @ 20,0 CLEA
        @ 22,0 SAY "Press CTRL-W to save information, ESC to exit"
*
        IF [primary database file list]$DBFILE
           SELE 2
*
** THIS DO CASE...ENDCASE BLOCK MUST DECLARE THE PRIMARY FILE'S SECONDARY DATABASE
** AND THE SECONDARY FILE'S SAY AND GET FILES.
*
           DO CASE
              CASE DBF() = primary database 1
                 USE secondary database 1 INDE index file list
                 GETTER2 = [secondary database 1's GET file]
                 SAYER2 = [secondary database 1's SAY file]
              CASE DBF() = primary database 2
                 USE secondary database 2 INDE index file list
                 GETTER2 = [secondary database 2's GET file]
                 SAYER2 = [secondary database 2's SAY file]
              CASE DBF() = primary database 3
                 USE secondary database 3 INDE index file list
                 GETTER2 = [secondary database 3's GET file]
                 SAYER2 = [secondary database 3's SAY file]
*
** THESE CASES CAN BE CARRIED OUT FOR AS MANY PARALLEL SYSTEMS AS YOUR ENVIRONMENT
** REQUIRES.
*
           ENDC
*
           COPY STRUC TO TANK2
           SELE 7
           USE TANK2
           TRUTH = .T.
           GETTER = [edited primary GETTER file]
*
           DO WHIL .T.
              SELE 6
              APPE BLAN
*
              DO WHIL .T.
                 DO primary GETTER file
                 CLEA GETS
                 @ 5,7 GET key field
                 READ
*
                 IF LEN(TRIM(key field)) = 0
```

Listing 9–1 (cont.)

```
                    EXIT
                 ENDI
*
                 SELE 1
                 SEEK  F->key field
*
                 IF FOUND()
                    DO primary GETTER file
                    CLEA GETS
                    @ 20,0 CLEA
                    @ 20,0 SAY [SORRY, WE'VE ALREADY GOT ONE OF THOSE.]
                    DO POOL
                    @ 20,0 CLEA
                    @ 22,0 SAY "Press CTRL-W to save information, ESC to exit"
                 ELSE
                    SELE F
                    EXIT
                 ENDI
*
                 SELE F
              ENDD
*
              IF LEN(TRIM(key field)) = 0
                 DELE
                 EXIT
              ENDI
*
              DO &GETTER
              READ
              @ 20,0 CLEA
              @ 22,0 SAY [ADD A NEW RECORD TO secondary database+;
                       (Y/N)? ] GET TRUTH
              READ
*
              IF TRUTH
                 SELE 7
                 CLEA
                 APPE BLANK
                 REPL key field WITH F->key field,;
                      other field WITH F->other field, etc.
                 DO &SAYER2
                 DO &GETTER2
                 @ 20,0 CLEA
                 @ 22,0 SAY [Press CTRL-W to save information, ESC to exit]
                 READ
```

Listing 9–1 (cont.)

```
              SELE 6
              CLEA
              DO primary SAY file
           ENDI
*
           @ 20,0 CLEA
           @ 22,0 SAY [Press CTRL-W to save information, ESC to exit]
        ENDD
*
        SELE 7
        USE
        SELE 6
        USE
        SELE 2
        APPE FROM TANK2
        ERAS TANK2.DBF
        GETTER = [primary GETTER file]
     ELSE * DBFILE # primary database
        REPEATER = FIELD(1)
*
        DO WHIL .T.
           APPE BLANK
           DO &GETTER
           READ
*
           IF LEN(TRIM(&REPEATER)) = 0
              DELE
              EXIT
           ENDI
*
        ENDD
*
     ENDI
*
     USE
     SELE 6
     USE
     SELE 1
     SET DELE ON
     APPE FROM TANK
     SET DELE OFF
     DO &GETTER
     CLEA GETS
     DO EDITMENU
     ERAS TANK.DBF
```

Listing 9–1 (cont.)

```
      CASE ANSWER = 'U'
         @ 20,0 CLEA
         ACCE [REPLACE WHAT FIELD? ] TO REPLACER
*
         IF LEN(TRIM(REPLACER)) = 0
            @ 20,0 CLEA
            DO EDITMENU
            LOOP
         ENDI
*
         ACCE [REPLACE WITH ] TO REPLACEWITH
*
         IF LEN(TRIM(REPLACEWITH)) = 0
            @ 20,0 CLEA
            DO EDITMENU
            LOOP
         ENDI
*
         ACCE "CONDITION " TO CONDITION
*
         IF LEN(TRIM(CONDITION)) # 0
            LOCA FOR &CONDITION
*
            IF .NOT. FOUND()
               @ 20,0 CLEA
               WAIT "NOTHING MATCHES THAT CONDITION. PRESS ANY KEY TO CONTINUE"
               @ 20,0 CLEA
               DO EDITMENU
               LOOP
            ELSE
               SET FILT TO &CONDITION
            ENDI
*
            REPL &REPLACER WITH &REPLACEWITH

         ENDI
*
         @ 20,0 CLEA
         DO EDITMENU
      CASE ANSWER = 'T'
*
         IF DBFILE # "order database"
            @ 0,0 SAY "That isn't one of the options. Try again"
            DO POOL
            @ 20,0 CLEA
```

Listing 9–1 (cont.)

```
            DO EDITMENU
            LOOP
         ELSE
            DO TRACK
         ENDI
*
       CASE ANSWER = 'M'
*
         IF .NOT. [memo field file list]$DBF()
         @ 0,0 SAY "This option only works on Memo field files. Try again"
            DO POOL
            LOOP
         ELSE
            RELE LOCATEWHERE, LOCATEWHAT
            TRUTH = .F.
         ENDI
*
            DO WHIL TYPE('&LOCATEWHERE') # 'M' .AND. .NOT. TRUTH
            @ 20,0 CLEA
            @ 20,0 SAY [I NEED A MEMO FIELD NAME]
            ACCE "Use which memo field -> " TO LOCATEWHERE
*
            IF LEN(TRIM(&LOCATEWHERE)) = 0
               TRUTH = .T.
            ENDI
*
         ENDD
*
&& The following block is used if there is more than one memo field in the database
&& and makes use of the FIELD() function, which allows for more than one memo field
&& file to be used. Note that the memo fields and their associated key word fields
&& must share the same position in all memo field databases
*
         DO CASE
            CASE LOCATEWHERE = FIELD(first memo field)
               LOCATEWHERE = FIELD(first memo field's key word field number)
            CASE LOCATEWHERE = FIELD(second memo field)
               LOCATEWHERE = FIELD(second memo field's key word field number)
*
** YOU CAN INCLUDE AS MANY CASE STATEMENTS AS ARE NECESSARY.
*
         ENDC
**
         DO WHIL TYPE("LOCATEWHAT$LOCATEWHERE") = 'U' .AND. .NOT. TRUTH
            @ 22,0 CLEA
```

Listing 9–1 (cont.)

```
            @ 22,0 SAY [I NEED A VALID EXPRESSION]
            ACCE "Key word? -> " TO LOCATEWHAT
*
            IF LEN(TRIM(LOCATEWHAT)) = 0
               TRUTH = .T.
            ENDI
*
         ENDD
*
         IF .NOT. TRUTH
            LOCA FOR "&LOCATEWHAT"$&LOCATEWHERE
*
            DO WHIL FOUN()
               DO &GETTER
               @ 20,0 CLEA
               @ 20,0 SAY [RECORD MATCHES SEARCH STRING.]+;
                          [DO YOU WISH TO EDIT? (Y/N) -> ] GET TRUTH
               READ
*
               IF TRUTH
                  DO memo format file
                  @ 20,0 SAY [CONTINUE TO NEXT MATCHING RECORD? (Y/N) -> ] GET TRUTH
                  READ
*
                  IF .NOT. TRUTH
                     EXIT
                  ENDI
*
                  CONT
               ENDI
*
            ENDD
*
         ENDI
*
         DO &GETTER
         CLEA GETS
   ENDC
*
ENDD
*
** END OF EDIT.PRG
```

The first CASE is an error trap. Other editors have used the OTHERWISE clause of the DO CASE . . . ENDCASE block. CASE ANSWER = 'X' is the programmer's bailout and nothing new. The Quit option is rewritten so that no permanent deletions are made from this menu. This means all deletions are handled by a PACKER routine that is called from the other menus. Because Quit is a simple RETURN to the calling program, Kill doesn't activate any DELS flag.

The Recall, Skip, Back, Edit, Copy, Continue, and Go To options are identical to their previous counterparts. The Display option builds the final DISPLAY command line through a series of macro substitutions. We place the fields to display in the DISPLAYWHAT variable, the conditions for the display in DISPLAYFOR, and whether we're generating hard copy with TOPRINT.

The Find option is similar to those in previous chapters. The .NOT. FOUND() error condition has been transferred from the editor to the ERRORMSS PROCedure block. You could leave the code in the editor with:

Listing 9–2

```
*
        IF .NOT. FOUND()
           @ 24,50 SAY "Record Number ->  END  "
           @ 0,0 SAY "I can't FIND that entry. Perhaps you should LOCATE it."
           DO POOL
         ENDI
*
```

The Add kernel must also be modified to handle the variety of separate parallel database systems that exist in this system. Note that a DO CASE . . . ENDCASE block is included here. This block can be extended for as many parallel systems or as large a single parallel system as your work requires.

The Update kernel hasn't been changed, nor has the Track kernel. The Memo searching kernel is expanded to handle the entire memo field file list. The EDITMENU routine is also updated to include all the options on a "rotating" scheme.

Listing 9–3

```
PROC EDITMENU
@ 20,0 TO 23,79 DOUB
@ 21,1 SAY IIF(EDITFLAG, [  E -> Edit  B -> Back  S -> Skip  G -> Goto]+;
                         [K -> Kill  R -> Rstr  Q -> Quit],;
                         [  F -> Find  L -> Loca  C -> Cont  D -> Disp]+;
                         [O -> Copy  A -> Add  U -> Upda])
@ 22,1 SAY [  M -> Memo Search     T -> Trck               N -> Next ]
*
```

Depending on the complexity of your system, you may want to recode the Add kernel to include a hunt for valid ledger account numbers. These are the numbers running from 1000 to 9999 and shouldn't be confused with your client account numbers. This means segregating one work area for the chart of accounts database. This database was mentioned earlier and has the following basic structure:

Account Number
Account Description
Account Balance

As always, you can include other fields that you feel are necessary. The recoding isn't complex:

Listing 9–4

```
      CASE ANSWER = 'A'
         COPY STRUC TO TANK
         SELE 6
         USE TANK
         @ 20,0 CLEA
         @ 22,0 SAY "Press CTRL-W to save information, ESC to exit"
*
         IF [primary database file list]$DBFILE
            SELE 2
*
** THIS DO CASE...ENDCASE BLOCK MUST DECLARE THE PRIMARY FILE'S SECONDARY DATABASE
** AND THE SECONDARY FILE'S SAY AND GET FILES.
*
            DO CASE
               CASE DBF() = primary database 1
                  USE secondary database 1 INDE index file list
                  GETTER2 = [secondary database 1's GET file]
                  SAYER2 = [secondary database 1's SAY file]
               CASE DBF() = primary database 2
                  USE secondary database 2 INDE index file list
                  GETTER2 = [secondary database 2's GET file]
                  SAYER2 = [secondary database 2's SAY file]
               CASE DBF() = primary database 3
                  USE secondary database 3 INDE index file list
                  GETTER2 = [secondary database 3's GET file]
                  SAYER2 = [secondary database 3's SAY file]
*
** THESE CASES CAN BE CARRIED OUT FOR AS MANY PARALLEL SYSTEMS AS YOUR ENVIRONMENT
** REQUIRES.
*
            ENDC
*
            COPY STRUC TO TANK2
            SELE 7
            USE TANK2
            TRUTH = .T.
            GETTER = [edited primary GETTER file]
*
```

Listing 9–4 (cont.)

```
** THE FOLLOWING IF...ENDIF BLOCK PLACES THE CHART OF ACCOUNTS DATABASE IN WORK
** AREA 10.
*
            IF [receivables database payables database]$DBFILE
               SELE 10
               USE chart of accounts database INDE account number field
            ENDI
*
            DO WHIL .T.
               SELE 6
               APPE BLAN
*
               DO WHIL .T.
                  DO primary GETTER file
                  CLEA GETS
                  @ 5,7 GET key field
                  READ
*
                  IF LEN(TRIM(key field)) = 0
                     EXIT
                  ENDI
*
** THE NEXT THREE LINES REPLACE THE ORIGINAL SELE 1/SEEK F->KEY FIELD LINES.
*
                  WORKAREA = IIF([receivables database payables database];
                                 $DBFILE,'J','A')
                  SELE &WORKAREA
                  SEEK  IIF([receivables database payables database];
                             $DBFILE,F->ledger account number,F->key field)
*
                  IF WORKAREA = 'J' .AND. .NOT. FOUND()
                     @ 20,0 CLEA
                     @ 21,0 SAY [WE DON'T HAVE THAT ACCOUNT IN THE LEDGER.]+;
                                [WANT TO ENTER IT? (Y/N) -> ] GET TRUTH
                     READ
*
                     IF TRUTH
                        @ 20,0 CLEA
                        @ x,y GET ledger account title field
                        READ
                     ENDI
*
                  ENDI
*
                  IF WORKAREA = 'A' .AND. FOUND()
```

Listing 9–4 (cont.)

```
                DO primary GETTER file
                CLEA GETS
                @ 20,0 CLEA
                @ 20,0 SAY [SORRY, WE'VE ALREADY GOT ONE OF THOSE.]
                DO POOL
                @ 20,0 CLEA
                @ 22,0 SAY "Press CTRL-W to save information, ESC to exit"
             ELSE
                SELE F
                EXIT
             ENDI
*
             SELE F
          ENDD
*
          IF LEN(TRIM(key field)) = 0
             DELE
             EXIT
          ENDI
*
          DO &GETTER
          READ
          @ 20,0 CLEA
          @ 22,0 SAY [ADD A NEW RECORD TO secondary database]
                  [(Y/N)? ] GET TRUTH
          READ
*
          IF TRUTH
             SELE 7
             CLEA
             APPE BLANK
             REPL key field WITH F->key field,;
             other field WITH F->other field, etc.
             DO &SAYER2
             DO &GETTER2
             @ 20,0 CLEA
             @ 22,0 SAY [Press CTRL-W to save information, ESC to exit]
             READ
             SELE 6
             CLEA
             DO primary SAY file
          ENDI
*
          @ 20,0 CLEA
          @ 22,0 SAY [Press CTRL-W to save information, ESC to exit]
```

Listing 9-4 (cont.)

```
          ENDD
*
          SELE 7
          USE
          SELE 6
          USE
          SELE 2
          APPE FROM TANK2
          ERAS TANK2.DBF
          GETTER = [primary GETTER file]
       ELSE * DBFILE # primary database
          REPEATER = FIELD(1)
*
          DO WHIL .T.
             APPE BLANK
             DO &GETTER
             READ
*
             IF LEN(TRIM(&REPEATER)) = 0
                DELE
                EXIT
             ENDI
*
          ENDD
*
       ENDI
*
** THE FOLLOWING IF...ENDIF BLOCK CLOSES THE CHART OF ACCOUNTS DATABASE OPENED IN
** WORK AREA 10.
*
       IF [receivables database payables database]$DBFILE
          SELE 10
          USE
       ENDI
*
       USE
       SELE 6
       USE
       SELE 1
       SET DELE ON
       APPE FROM TANK
       SET DELE OFF
       DO &GETTER
       CLEA GETS
       DO EDITMENU
       ERAS TANK.DBF
```

Note that this is where you build the original chart of accounts database, but not where you necessarily perform any editing on that database.

MODIFYING THE SYSTEM

Here we begin modifying previously written code for use with this particular system. We're going to heavily rewrite the AR module for this more sophisticated application. The previous AR main module should be recoded to include the options shown in Listings 9–5 to 9–8. The code is:

Listing 9–5

```
** ACCounTs RECeivables PROGRAM
** USES EDIT.PRG
*
&& The receivables file list should be INDEXed on fields that show
&& when payments are due, whom they are from, what they are for, when
&& they're received, and the amount received
*
DBFILE = [RECEIVABLES]
USE receivables database INDE NDX file list
TRUTH = .T.
*
&& The following IF...ENDIF block determines if a historical file is in use.
&& The REUSEREC flag is a PUBLIC variable that is SAVEd and RESTOREd with the
&& ACCOUNT.MEM file
*
IF REUSEREC
   CLEA
   @ 2,0 SAY [You're using a past database in this system.
   @ 4,0 SAY [Okay to continue? (Y/N) -> ] GET TRUTH
   READ
*
   IF .NOT. TRUTH
      RETU
   ENDI
*
   @ 8,0 SAY [Do you want to change back to the current file? (Y/N) -> ] GET TRUTH
   READ
*
   IF TRUTH
      USE
      RENA receivables database TO &REUSERF
      RENA REUSEREC.DBF TO receivables database
      USE receivables database INDE NDX file list
      REIN
      WAIT "READY. PRESS ANY KEY TO CONTINUE"
```

Listing 9–5 (cont.)

```
      REUSEREC = .F.
   ENDI
*
ENDI             && end of historical database checking algorithm
*
DO WHILE .T.
   CLEA
   @ 2, 0 TO 19,79 DOUB
   @ 3,25 SAY [R E C E I V A B L E S   M E N U]
   @ 4,1 TO 4,78 DOUB
   @  7,28 SAY [1. Edit Record]
   @  8,28 SAY [2. Remove Deleted Records]
   @  9,28 SAY [3. Report Menu]
   @ 10,28 SAY [4. Use Another File's Data]
   @ 11,28 SAY [5. List Past Due Accounts]
   @ 12,28 SAY [6. Print Invoices]
   @ 17, 28 SAY '0. Exit'
   ANSWER = 0
   @ 19,33 SAY " select      "
   @ 19,42 GET ANSWER PICT "9" RANGE 0,6
   READ
*
   DO CASE
      CASE ANSWER = 0
*
         IF REUSEREC
            CLEA
            @ 10,0 SAY "The file you're using isn't the file you started with."
            @ 12,0 SAY "Do you want to change the file back to your original"
            @ 14,0 SAY "working file? (Y/N) -> " GET REUSEREC
            READ
*
            IF REUSEREC
               USE
               RENA receivables database TO &REUSERF
               RENA REUSEREC.DBF TO receivables database
               USE receivables database INDE NDX file list
               REIN
               WAIT "READY. PRESS ANY KEY TO CONTINUE"
            ENDIF * SWITCH FILES BACK
*
         ENDIF * DO YOU WANT TO SWITCH FILES BACK
*
         RETU
      CASE ANSWER = 1
```

Listing 9–5 (cont.)

```
         DO RECSAY
         DO RECGET
         CLEA GETS
         DO EDIT
      CASE ANSWER = 2
         DO PACKER
      CASE ANSWER = 3
         TOPRINT = [TO PRINT]
*
&& These report menu options should be an indication of why you want to INDEX the
&& receivables database as suggested at the start of this listing
*
         DO WHILE .T.
            CLEA
            @ 2, 0 TO 19,79 DOUB
            @ 3,28 SAY [R E P O R T S   M E N U]
            @ 4,1 TO 4,78 DOUB
            @  7,28 SAY [1. Report by Date Due]
            @  8,28 SAY [2. Report by From]
            @  9,28 SAY [3. Report by For]
            @ 10,28 SAY [4. Report by Date Received]
            @ 11,28 SAY [5. Report by Amount]
            @ 12,28 SAY [6. Report to ] + IIF(TOPRINT = "TO PRINT",;
                        "screen/PRINTER", "SCREEN/printer")
            @ 17, 28 SAY '0. Exit'
            ANSWER = 0
            @ 19,33 SAY " select       "
            @ 19,42 GET ANSWER PICT "9" RANG 0,6
            READ
*
            IF TOPRINT = "TO PRINT"
               SET CONS OFF
            ENDI
*
            DO CASE
               CASE ANSWER = 0
                  SET ORDE TO 1
                  EXIT
               CASE ANSWER = 6
                  TOPRINT = IIF(TOPRINT = [TO PRINT], [PLAIN], [TO PRINT])
                  LOOP
               OTHE
                  SET ORDE TO ANSWER
                  REPOFORM = 'R' + STR(ANSWER,1)
                  REPO FORM &REPOFORM &TOPRINT
```

Listing 9-5 (cont.)

```
            ENDC
*
            SET CONS ON
*
            IF TOPRINT = [PLAIN]
               WAIT
            ENDI
*
         ENDDO  INNER T
*
      CASE ANSWER = 4
         CLEA
         ? "LISTING AVAILABLE FILES"
         ?
         DIR *.REC
         ACCE "WHICH FILE [RETURN TO QUIT]? " TO REUSERF
*
         IF .NOT. FILE("&REUSERF")
            CLEA
            ? "You entered '" + REUSERF + "', which doesn't exist."
            WAIT
            LOOP
         ENDIF
*
         IF LEN(REUSERF) # 0
            USE
            RENA receivables database TO REUSEREC.DBF
            RENA &REUSERF TO receivables database
            USE receivables database INDE NDX file list
            REIN
            REUSEREC = .T.
            WAIT "READY. PRESS ANY KEY TO CONTINUE"
         ENDI
*
      CASE ANSWER = 5
         @ 20,0 CLEA
         @ 22,0 SAY [DO YOU WANT THIS PRINTED? (Y/N) -> ] GET TRUTH
         READ
*
         IF TRUTH
            SET CONS OFF
            TOPRINT = [TO PRINT]
         ELSE
            TOPRINT = [PLAIN]
            CLEA
```

Listing 9–5 (cont.)

```
         ENDI
*
         SET ORDE TO 2
*
&& The past due period is a variable initialized by the developer but adjustable
&& through the utilities menu system
*
         REPO FORM RECFROM FOR date due field < DATE()-past due period &TOPRINT
*
         IF TOPRINT = [PLAIN]
            WAIT
         ENDI
*
         SET ORDE TO 1
         SET CONS ON
      CASE ANSWER = 6
         WAIT [PLEASE MAKE SURE THE INVOICES ARE IN THE PRINTER.]+;
              [PRESS ANY KEY WHEN READY...]
*
&& The billing period is a variable initialized by the developer but adjustable
&& through the utilities menu system. Note that this code assumes records are deleted
&& when payment is received
*
         SET FILT TO date due field < DATE() + billing period .AND. .NOT. DELE()
         GOTO TOP
         SET CONS OFF
*
&& The INVOICE report form makes use of the REPORT command's ability to automatically
&& total numeric fields according to selected groupings. This report form's groupings
&& are the individual client accounts
*
         REPO FORM INVOICE TO PRINT
         SET CONS ON
   ENDCASE
*
ENDDO  OUTER T
*
** END OF ACCTREC.PRG
```

What does the receivables database look like? It must include the following fields:

Client Account Number
Ledger Account Number
Received for

Received from
Date Due
Date Received
Amount Received

You can include any other fields you wish, but these are a good start. You must include the client's account number to track who paid for what or when bills were paid. The ledger account number is based on an accounting system that uses a chart of accounts. The code in this section makes use of the chart of accounts quite heavily, but that database and code can be removed if necessary.

The next code to work on is the payables system. That is actually a mirror of the receivables system.

Listing 9–6

```
** ACCounT PAYment.PRG
** USES EDIT.PRG
*
&& The payables database should be INDEXed on fields that show
&& their check number, when payments are sent out, whom they are for,
&& what they are for, and the amount sent
**
DBFILE = [PAYABLES]
USE payables database INDE NDX file list
TRUTH = .T.
*
&& The following IF...ENDIF block determines if a historical file is in use.
&& The REUSEPAY flag is a PUBLIC variable that is SAVEd and RESTOREd with the
&& ACCOUNT.MEM file
*
IF REUSEPAY
   CLEA
   @ 2,0 SAY [You're using a past database in this system.
   @ 4,0 SAY [Okay to continue? (Y/N) -> ] GET TRUTH
   READ
*
   IF .NOT. TRUTH
      RETU
   ENDI
*
   @ 8,0 SAY [Do you want to change back to the current file? (Y/N) -> ] GET TRUTH
   READ
*
   IF TRUTH
      USE
      RENA payables database TO &REUSEPF
      RENA REUSEPAY.DBF TO payables database
```

Listing 9–6 (cont.)

```
        USE payables database INDE NDX file list
        REIN
        WAIT "READY. PRESS ANY KEY TO CONTINUE"
        REUSEPAY = .F.
    ENDI
*
ENDI            && end of historical database checking algorithm
*
DO WHILE .T.
   CLEA
   @ 2,0 TO 19,79 DOUB
   @ 3,28 SAY [P A Y A B L E S   M E N U]
   @ 4,1 TO 4,78 DOUB
   @  7,28 SAY [1. Edit Expenses]
   @  8,28 SAY [2. Remove Deleted Entries]
   @  9,28 SAY [3. Report Menu]
   @ 10,28 SAY [4. Use Another File's Data]
   @ 11,28 SAY [5. Print Manual Checks]
   @ 12,28 SAY [6. Print Computer Checks]
   @ 17,28 SAY '0. Exit'
   ANSWER = 0
   @ 19,33 SAY " select      "
   @ 19,42 GET ANSWER PICT "9" RANG 0,6
   READ
*
   DO CASE
      CASE ANSWER = 0
*
         IF REUSEPAY
            CLEA
            @ 10,0 SAY "The file you're using isn't the file you started with."
            @ 12,0 SAY "Do you want to change the file back to your original"
            @ 14,0 SAY "working file? (Y/N) -> " GET REUSEPAY
            READ
*
            IF REUSEPAY
               USE
               RENA payables database TO &REUSEPF
               RENA REUSEPAY.DBF TO payables database
               USE payables database INDE NDX file list
               REIN
               WAIT "READY. PRESS ANY KEY TO CONTINUE"
            ENDIF * SWITCH FILES BACK
*
         ENDIF * DO YOU WANT TO SWITCH FILES BACK
```

Listing 9–6 (cont.)

```
*
        RETU
      CASE ANSWER = 1
        DO PAYSAY
        DO PAYGET
        CLEA GETS
        DO EDIT
      CASE ANSWER = 2
        DO PACKER
      CASE ANSWER = 3
        TOPRINT = [TO PRINT]
*
        DO WHILE .T.
          CLEA
          @ 2, 0 TO 19,79 DOUB
          @ 3,18 SAY [P A Y A B L E S   R E P O R T S   M E N U]
          @ 4,1 TO 4,78 DOUB
          @  7,28 SAY [1. Report by Check Number]
          @  8,28 SAY [2. Report by To]
          @  9,28 SAY [3. Report by For]
          @ 10,28 SAY [4. Report by Date]
          @ 11,28 SAY [5. Report to ] + IIF(TOPRINT = "TO PRINT",;
                      "screen/PRINTER", "SCREEN/printer")
          @ 17, 28 SAY 'Exit'
          ANSWER = 0
          @ 19,33 SAY " select      "
          @ 19,42 GET ANSWER PICT "9" RANG 0,5
          READ
*
          IF TOPRINT = "TO PRINT"
            SET CONS OFF
          ENDI
*
          DO CASE
            CASE ANSWER = 0
              SET ORDE TO 1
              EXIT
            CASE ANSWER = 6
              TOPRINT = IIF(TOPRINT = [TO PRINT], [PLAIN], [TO PRINT])
              LOOP
            OTHE
              SET ORDE TO ANSWER
              REPOFORM = 'P' + STR(ANSWER,1)
              REPO FORM &REPOFORM &TOPRINT
          ENDC
```

Listing 9–6 (cont.)

```
*
            SET CONS ON
*
            IF TOPRINT = [PLAIN]
               WAIT
            ENDI
*
         ENDDO  INNER T
*
      CASE ANSWER = 4
         CLEA
         ? "LISTING AVAILABLE FILES"
         DIR *.PAY
         ACCE "WHICH FILE [RETURN TO QUIT]? " TO REUSEPF
*
         IF .NOT. FILE("&REUSEPF")
            CLEA
            ? "You entered '" + REUSEPF + "', which doesn't exist."
            WAIT
            LOOP
         ENDIF
*
         IF LEN(REUSEPF) # 0
            USE
            RENA payables database TO REUSEPAY.DBF
            RENA &REUSEPF TO expenses database
            USE payables database INDE NDX file list
            REIN
            REUSEPAY = .T.
            WAIT "READY. PRESS ANY KEY TO CONTINUE"
         ENDI
*
      CASE ANSWER = 5
*
&& Even though this CASE cuts manual checks, the data is still entered into the
&& database. The records are deleted now because the checks are printed. The database
&& isn't PACKed, however. This loop enables several manual checks, not just one. Note
&& that the computer should determine the check number, as from a memory variable.
&& The check number shouldn't be entered by hand unless necessary. Doing so might
&& produce nonsequential check numbers
*
         COPY STRUC TO TANK
         SELE 2
         USE TANK
*
```

Listing 9–6 (cont.)

```
** TANK'S NDX FILE MUST BE INDEXED ON THE SAME FIELD AS THE PAYABLES
** DATABASE'S FIRST ORDER NDX FILE.
*
        INDE ON master index file key field TO TANK
        CLEA
        DO PAYSAY
        @ 22,0 SAY [PRESS CTRL-W TO SAVE A RECORD, CTRL-Q TO EXIT WITHOUT SAVING]
*
        DO WHIL .T.
           APPE BLANK
           DO PAYGET
           READ
*
           IF LEN(TRIM(key field)) = 0
              DELE
              EXIT
           ENDI
*
        ENDD
*
&& You may be able to define your checks with the CREATE LABEL menu system. If this
&& is the case, you can use the following code
*
        CLEA
        @ 10,0 SAY [DO YOU WANT SAMPLES? (Y/N) -> ] GET TRUTH
        READ
        SAMPLES = IIF(TRUTH, [SAMP], [])
        SET CONS OFF
        LABE FORM check form TO PRINT &SAMPLES
        SET CONS ON
*
&& Use the following code if you can't define your check layout with the CREATE LABEL
&& menu system
*
        WAIT [PLEASE MAKE SURE THE PRINTER IS READY. PRESS ANY KEY TO CONTINUE...]
        SET CONS OFF
        SET PRIN ON
        ? CHR(control codes to change the number of lines per page on the printer,
special printing effects)
        1
*
        DO WHIL .NOT. EOF()
*
** PLACE THE @ SAY STATEMENTS HERE THAT GENERATE YOUR CHECK LAYOUT.
*
```

Listing 9–6 (cont.)

```
            SKIP
         ENDD
*
         ? CHR(control codes to return printer to normal printing)
         SET PRIN OFF
         SET CONS ON
         USE
         SELE 1
         APPE FROM TANK
         SELE 2
         USE TANK INDE TANK
         SELE 1
         SET RELA TO client account number field INTO B
         DELE FOR A->client account number field = B->client account number field
         SELE 2
         USE
         ERAS TANK.DBF
         ERAS TANK.NDX
      CASE ANSWER = 6
*
&& You may be able to define your checks with the CREATE LABEL menu system. If this
&& is the case you can use the following code
*
         CLEA
         @ 10,0 SAY [DO YOU WANT SAMPLES? (Y/N) -> ] GET TRUTH
         READ
         SAMPLES = IIF(TRUTH, [SAMP], [])
         SET CONS OFF
         LABE FORM check form TO PRINT &SAMPLES
         SET CONS ON
*
&& Use the following code if you can't define your check layout with the CREATE LABEL
&& menu system
*
         WAIT [PLEASE MAKE SURE THE PRINTER IS READY. PRESS ANY KEY TO CONTINUE...]
         SET CONS OFF
         SET PRIN ON
         ? CHR(control codes to change the number of lines per page on the printer,
special printing effects)
         1
*
         DO WHIL .NOT. EOF()
*
** PLACE THE @ SAY STATEMENTS HERE THAT GENERATE YOUR CHECK LAYOUT.
*
```

Listing 9–6 (cont.)

```
            SKIP
         ENDD
*
         ? CHR(control codes to return printer to normal printing)
         SET PRIN OFF
         SET CONS ON
         DELE ALL
   ENDCASE
*
ENDDO  OUTER T
*
** END OF ACCTPAY.PRG
```

Listing 9–6 can be understood from reading through the previous material on the ACCTREC module. There are still some things to note, however. The most important thing is the check number reference. Most systems need some way to properly and sequentially order the checks they write. Normally this is done with a memory variable (the name CHECKNUM comes to mind), which is initialized at system setup. Each check written increases the value of CHECKNUM by one. This is true of both manually and computer generated checks. It is also a good idea to create a field in the payables database for the check number value. This helps the system prepare the check register report.

The next module works on the chart of accounts. The first part of the COA.PRG file handles editing the chart of accounts database. The second option runs the PACKER routine. By now you should begin appreciating how much of database work is done by the editing module. The last four options are merely report generators under the guise of separate menu headings.

Listing 9–7

```
&& Chart of Accounts PROGRAM
&& Options 3-5 make use of a REPORT FORM, COA. The last option makes use of
&& another FORM, COA_ACTV. You have to design these forms for your needs.
&& The text gives an idea of what the chart of accounts should look like.
&& Active and inactive accounts are determined by a flag included in
&& the database. This flag can be a separate logical field in each ledger
&& account's record
*
USE chart of accounts file INDE ledger account numbers
SAYER = [COASAY]
GETTER = [COAGET]
DBFILE = [COA]
KEYFIELD = [LEDGER ACCOUNT]
*
DO WHILE .T.
   CLEAR
```

Listing 9–7 (cont.)

```
   @ 2, 0 TO 16,79 DOUBLE
   @ 3,19 SAY [C H A R T   O F   A C C O U N T S   M E N U]
   @ 4,1 TO 4,78 DOUBLE
   @  7,28 SAY [1. Edit Chart of Accounts]
   @  8,28 SAY [2. Remove Deleted Entries]
   @  9,28 SAY [3. Print Chart of Accounts]
   @ 10,28 SAY [4. Print Active Accounts]
   @ 11,28 SAY [5. Print Inactive Accounts]
   @ 12,28 SAY [6. Print Account Activity]
   @ 14, 28 SAY '0. Exit'
   ANSWER = 0
   @ 16,33 SAY " select     "
   @ 16,42 GET ANSWER PICTURE "9" RANGE 0,6
   READ
*
   DO CASE
      CASE ANSWER = 0
         CLOS DATA
         RETURN
      CASE ANSWER = 1
         CLEA
         DO &SAYER
         DO &GETTER
         CLEA GETS
         DO EDIT
      CASE ANSWER = 2
         DO PACKER
      CASE ANSWER = 3
         SET CONS OFF
         REPO FORM COA TO PRINT
         SET CONS ON
      CASE ANSWER = 4
         SET CONS OFF
         REPO COA FOR active TO PRINT
         SET CONS ON
      CASE ANSWER = 5
         SET CONS OFF
         REPO COA FOR .NOT. active TO PRINT
         SET CONS ON
      CASE ANSWER = 6
         SELE 2
         USE payables INDE ledger account number
         SELE 1
         JOIN WITH B TO TANKP FOR A->ledger account number =;
                    B->ledger account number ;
```

Listing 9–7 (cont.)

```
          FIEL all fields in A and amount and paid to fields from B
      SELE 2
      USE receivables INDE ledger account number
      SELE 1
      JOIN WITH B TO TANKR FOR A->ledger account number =;
              B->ledger account number ;
          FIEL all fields in A and amount and received from fields from B
      SELE 2
      USE TANKR
      INDE ON ledger account number TO TANK
      APPE FROM TANKP                && this makes use of similarly structured
                                     && files
      SET CONS OFF
      REPO FORM COA_ACTV TO PRINT
      SET CONS ON
      USE
      SELE 1
      ERAS TANKR.DBF
      ERAS TANKP.DBF
      ERAS TANK.NDX
   ENDCASE
*
ENDDO T
*
** END OF A:COA.PRG
```

The next menu system, EOTREPT.PRG, is another report-based menu system. Its sole function is to generate End-of-Term reports. These reports can be for the end of a day, month, quarter, or year. The one exception is the Check Register Report. This report merely lists by check number what checks have been cut by the system to date.

Listing 9–8

```
** End-of-Term REPorT.PRG
*
SELE 2
USE receivables database INDE date received field, client account number field,;
ledger account number field
SELE 1
USE payables database INDE date paid field, check register field,;
ledger account number field
*
DO WHILE .T.
   CLEAR
   @ 2, 0 TO 15,79 DOUBLE
```

Listing 9–8 (cont.)

```
   @ 3,17 SAY [E N D   O F   T E R M   R E P O R T S   M E N U]
   @ 4,1 TO 4,78 DOUBLE
   @  7,28 SAY [1. Daily Disbursements]
   @  8,28 SAY [2. Check Register Report]
   @  9,28 SAY [3. Monthly Report]
   @ 10,28 SAY [4. Quarterly Report]
   @ 11,28 SAY [5. Yearly Report]
   @ 13, 28 SAY '0. Exit'
   ANSWER = 0
   @ 15,33 SAY " select     "
   @ 15,42 GET ANSWER PICTURE "9" RANGE 0,5
   READ
*
   DO CASE
      CASE ANSWER = 0
         CLOSE DATA
         RETURN
      CASE ANSWER = 1
         SEEK DATE()
         SET CONS OFF
         REPO FORM daily disbursements form FOR date paid field = DATE() TO PRINT
         SET CONS ON
         LOOP
      CASE ANSWER = 2
         SET ORDE TO 2
         SET CONS OFF
         REPO FORM check register report form TO PRIN
         SET CONS ON
         SET ORDE TO 1
         LOOP
*
&& CASEs 3 through 5 use the same REPORT FORMs, but do so with different
&& FILTERs. This can be coded more efficiently as follows.
&& Note that this code may include too many reports for your needs.
&& I generally give as much information as possible in as many forms
&& as possible. This makes cross referencing easy. Note that the FILTERs
&& assume the databases contain only this year's data. If that isn't the
&& case, the FILTERs should be SET FILT TO MONTH(date field) = MONTH(DATE())
&& .AND. YEAR(date field) = YEAR(DATE())
*
*
      CASE ANSWER = 3
         SELE 2
         SET FILT TO MONTH(date received field) = MONTH(DATE())
         SELE 1
```

Listing 9–8 (cont.)

```
         SET FILT TO MONTH(date paid field) = MONTH(DATE())
      CASE ANSWER = 4
         SELE 2
         SET FILT TO MONTH(date received field) <= MONTH(DATE()) .AND.;
                     MONTH(date received field) >= MONTH(DATE()-3)
         SELE 1
         SET FILT TO MONTH(date paid field) <= MONTH(DATE()) .AND.;
                     MONTH(date paid field) >= MONTH(DATE()-3)
*
&& CASE 5, the yearly reports, requires no special FILTERing if data is limited to
&& this year's data.
*
   ENDCASE
*
   SET CONS OFF
   REPO FORM daily disbursements report form TO PRIN
   SET ORDE TO 2
   REPO FORM check register report form TO PRINT
   SET ORDE TO 3
   REPO FORM daily disbursements report form TO PRINT
   REPO FORM check register report form TO PRINT
   SET ORDE TO 1
   SELE 2
   REPO FORM monthly receivables report form TO PRINT
&& This is GROUPed on the date received field
   SET ORDE TO 2
   REPO FORM monthly receivables report form TO PRINT
&& This is GROUPed on the client account number field
   SET ORDE TO 3
   REPO FORM monthly receivables report form TO PRINT
&& This is GROUPed on the ledger account number field
   SET ORDE TO 1
   SET FILT TO
   SELE 1
   SET FILT TO
ENDDO T
*
** END OF A:EOTREPT.PRG
```

Note that reports generated by options 3 through 5 are the same REPORT FORM used with different FILTERs. Option 5 doesn't use any FILTERs and assumes the databases only contain this year's data. This method of coding is more efficient than coding separate REPORT blocks for each option. I tend to include a variety of reports, all of which show the same information but in different formats. This aids the user in cross checking data should the need arise.

Next is the client menu. This has been previously coded and will not be repeated here in its entirety. The new need is to include a way of updating the receivables database in the client menu itself. The code for that was originally written as part of a separate module in Chapter 7. We code in kernels, so we can lift that code and place in the modified client menu system, as shown here:

Listing 9–9

```
** CLIENT MAIN MENU SYSTEM
** This code retains the ACCESS LEVEL routines. You can  include the access-dependent
** code blocks here and save the need for them elsewhere in the code.
*
DO ACCESSOR
*
DO WHILE .T.
   CLEAR
   @ 2, 0 TO 15,79 DOUBLE
   @ 3,21 SAY [C L I E N T   R E C O R D   S Y S T E M]
   @ 4,1 TO 4,78 DOUBLE
   @  7,24 SAY [1. Edit Client Accounts]
   @  8,24 SAY [2. Update Receivables Database]
   @  9,24 SAY [3. Remove Deleted Records from ] + DBF()
*
** YOU CAN HAVE AS MANY LEVELS OF THE NEXT LINE AS YOUR SYSTEM REQUIRES.
*
   @ 10,24 SAY IIF(ACCESS > 1, [4. Edit Client History], [])
   @ 11,24 SAY IIF(ACCESS = 3, [5. Edit Client (next level file)], [])
   @ 13, 24 SAY '0. EXIT'
   ANSWER = 0
   @ 15,33 SAY " select     "
   @ 15,42 GET ANSWER PICTURE "9"
 RANGE 0, ACCESS + 2
&& note the change from the code in Chapter 7
   READ
*
   DO CASE
      CASE ANSWER = 0
         CLOS DATA
         RETURN
      CASE ANSWER = 1
*
&& This part of the code originally tested for historical files. You may wish to
&& include that code here or do away with the PAST test all together
*
         USE clients database INDE clients account NDX file
         PLACE = 40-LEN(DBF())/2
         SAYER = [CLIENSAY]
```

Listing 9–9 (cont.)

```
        GETTER = [CLIENGET]
        DO EDIT
      CASE ANSWER = 2
*
&& This code assumes all invoices are sent out periodically. This means your billing
&& cycle is weekly, biweekly, monthly, or quarterly. This differs from code in
&& Chapter 7, because it assumes there are no carriers. Include carriers by more
&& closely following the code shown in that chapter
*
        SELE 1
        TOTA ON client account field TO TANK
        SELE 4
        USE TANK
        INDE ON client account field TO TANK
        SELE 3
        USE receivables database INDE client account number
*
** REMEMBER TO ADD FIELDS WHEN YOU USE UPDATE.
*
        UPDA ON client account number field FROM D;
            REPL necessary fields WITH data from TANK
        SELE 4
        SET RELA TO client account field INTO C
        GO TOP
*
&& The following DO WHILE...ENDDO loop makes sure everything is copied from TANK to
&& the AR database
*
        DO WHIL .NOT. EOF()
*
          IF client account field # C->client identification field
            SELE 3
            APPE BLAN
            REPL necessary fields in AR database WITH data from TANK
            SELE 4
          ENDI
*
          SKIP
        ENDD
*
        USE
        SELE 3
        SET ORDE TO 1
        ERAS TANK.DBF
```

Listing 9–9 (cont.)

```
         ERAS TANK.NDX
         SELE 1
         USE historical billing file INDE historical billing file NDX
         APPE FROM billing database
         USE billing database INDE client identification NDX file
*
&& The following code places some extra responsibility on the user. You must decide
&& if such is advisable in your application's environment
*
         TRUTH = .F.
         SET COLOR TO W+
         CLEA
         @ 10,0 SAY [AR FILE UPDATED AND BILLING FILE COPIED TO BACKUP FILE.]
         SET COLO TO W*+
         @ 12,0 SAY [ALL ]
         SET COLO TO W+
         @ 12,4 SAY [RECORDS WILL BE ]
         SET COLO TO W+*
         @ 12,20 SAY [DELETED]
         SET COLO TO W+
         @ 12,27 SAY [ UNLESS YOU SPECIFY OTHERWISE.]
         @ 14,0 SAY [OKAY TO DELETE ALL RECORDS? (Y/N) -> ] GET TRUTH
         READ
*
         IF TRUTH
            DELE ALL
            @ 20,0 SAY [YOU MUST USE OPTION 2 FROM THE MENU TO MAKE]+;
                       [THESE DELETIONS PERMANENT]
      WAIT
         ENDI
*
         SET COLO TO

      CASE ANSWER = 3
*
&& This part of the code originally tested for historical files. You may wish to
&& include that code here or do away with the PAST test all together
*
         DO PACKER
      CASE ANSWER = 4 .AND. ACCESS > 1
*
&& This part of the code originally tested for historical files. You may wish to
&& include that code here or do away with the PAST test all together
*
         USE first-level memo field database INDE first-level memo field NDX file
```

Listing 9–9 (cont.)

```
          PLACE = 40-LEN(DBF())/2
          SAYER = [MEMO1SAY]
          GETTER = [MEMO1GET]
          DO EDIT
       CASE ANSWER = 5 .AND. ACCESS = 3
*
&& This part of the code originally tested for historical files. You may wish to
&& include that code here or do away with the PAST test all together
*
          USE second-level memo field database INDE second-level memo field NDX file
          PLACE = 40-LEN(DBF())/2
          SAYER = [MEMO2SAY]
          GETTER = [MEMO2GET]
          DO EDIT
       OTHE
          @ 20,0
          WAIT [SORRY, YOU CAN'T DO THAT. PRESS ANY KEY TO CONTINUE...]
          LOOP
   ENDCASE
*
   DO &SAYER
   DO &GETTER
   CLEA GETS
   DO EDIT
ENDDO T
*
** END OF CLMAIN.PRG
```

The one addition to the client system is the ACCESSOR.PRG file. This file takes the place of the access-dependent code found in Chapter 7's client system. The access levels are determined by code identical to that used in Chapter 7. The difference is that both personnel and client systems call ACCESSOR.PRG. This provides an extra measure of security, because passwords must be entered both times to enter the separate systems.

Listing 9–10

```
** ACCESSOR.PRG
&& This file takes the place of the access-dependent code found in Chapter 7
*
&& This PASSWORD file contains user names, their passwords, and their access levels.
&& It's INDEXed on user names
*
         USE passwords file INDE passwords NDX file
*
** THE FOLLOWING CODE IS NECESSARY FOR INSTALLATION AND SHOULD THE DATABASES GET
```

Listing 9–10 (cont.)

```
** CORRUPTED.
*
         IF RECC() = 0
            CLEA
            SET COLO TO W+
*
            TEXT
               There is no data in the PASSWORD file.
               You must set up the password file be-
               fore doing anything else.
            ENDT
*
            TRUTH = .F.
            SET COLO TO
            @ 10,0 SAY [ARE YOU READY TO SET UP THE PASSWORD FILE? (Y/N) -> ] GET TRUTH
            READ
*
            IF .NOT. TRUTH
               RETU TO MAST
            ENDI
*
            SET MENU ON
            SET STAT ON
            SET FORM TO password format file
*
** THE FOLLOWING MESSAGE DEPENDS ON THE NUMBER OF FILE LEVELS IN YOUR SYSTEM.
*
            SET MESS TO [Enter each user's name,]+;
                        [password and access level (1-3)]
            APPE
            SET MENU OFF
            SET STAT OFF
            SET FORM TO
            SET MESS TO
            LOOP
         ENDI
*
         N = 1
*
** THIS SYSTEM ALLOWS THREE ATTEMPTS AT A CORRECT NAME AND PASSWORD.
** YOU CAN ALLOW ANY NUMBER OF ATTEMPTS BY CHANGING THE VALUE OF N.
*
         DO WHIL N < 4
            ACCE [What is your name, please? -> ] TO NAME
            SEEK M->NAME
```

Listing 9–10 (cont.)

```
*
          IF FOUN()
             TRUTH = .T.
             EXIT
          ENDI
*
          @ ROW() + 1,0 SAY [I can't find that name.]
          N = N + 1
       ENDD
*
       IF .NOT. TRUTH
          CLEA
          @ 1,0 SAY [SORRY, I DON'T KNOW WHO YOU ARE.]
          RETU TO MAST
       ENDI
*
       N = 1
       TRUTH = .F.
*
       DO WHIL N < 4
          ACCE M->NAME + [, what is your password? -> ] TO PASSWORD
*
          IF TRIM(password) = M->PASSWORD
             TRUTH = .T.
             EXIT
          ENDI
*
          @ ROW() + 1,0 SAY [That's not exactly what I have.]
          N = N + 1
       ENDD
*
       IF .NOT. TRUTH
          CLEA
          @ 1,0 SAY [SORRY, YOU DON'T KNOW WHO YOU ARE.]
          RETU TO MAST
       ELSE
          ACCESS = A->ACCESS
          USE
       ENDI
*
** END OF ACCESSOR.PRG
```

The personnel menu works similarly to the client menu system. Instead of updating the receivables database, we update the payables database, because paychecks are cut from this menu.

Listing 9–11

```
** PERSonnel MENU.PRG
*
DO ACCESSOR
SAYER = [PERSSAY]
GETTER = [PERSGET]
USE personnel database INDE personnel id number, social security number
PLACE = 40-LEN(DBF())/2
*
DO WHILE .T.
   CLEAR
   @ 2, 0 TO 15,79 DOUBLE
   @ 3,22 SAY [P E R S O N N E L   M A I N   M E N U]
   @ 4,1 TO 4,78 DOUBLE
   @  7,25 SAY [1. Edit Personnel Records]
   @  8,25 SAY [2. Paycheck Menu]
   @  9,25 SAY [3. Remove Deleted Entries]
*
** YOU CAN HAVE AS MANY LEVELS OF THE NEXT LINE AS YOUR SYSTEM REQUIRES.
*
   @ 10,25 SAY IIF(ACCESS > 1, [4. Edit Personnel History], [])
   @ 11,25 SAY IIF(ACCESS = 3, [5. Edit Personnel (next level file)], [])
   @ 13, 25 SAY '0. EXIT'
   ANSWER = 0
   @ 15,33 SAY " select     "
   @ 15,42 GET ANSWER PICTURE "9" RANGE 0, ACCESS + 2
   READ
*
   DO CASE
      CASE ANSWER = 0
         CLOSE DATA
         RETURN
      CASE ANSWER = 1
         CLEA
         DO &SAYER
         DO &GETTER
         CLEA GETS
         DO EDIT
      CASE ANSWER = 2
         DO PAYCHECK
         SAYER = [PERSSAY]
         GETTER = [PERSGET]
         SET ORDE TO 1
         PLACE = 40-LEN(DBF())/2
      CASE ANSWER = 3
         DO PACKER
```

Listing 9–11 (cont.)

```
      CASE ANSWER = 4 .AND. ACCESS > 1
         USE first-level personnel memo field database;
INDE first level personnel memo field NDX file
         PLACE = 40-LEN(DBF())/2
         SAYER = [PERM1SAY]
         GETTER = [PERM1GET]
         DO EDIT
         SAYER = [PERSSAY]
         GETTER = [PERSGET]
         USE personnel database INDE personnel id number, social security number
         PLACE = 40-LEN(DBF())/2
      CASE ANSWER = 5 .AND. ACCESS = 3
         USE second-level personnel memo field database;
INDE second level personnel memo field NDX file
         PLACE = 40-LEN(DBF())/2
         SAYER = [PERM2SAY]
         GETTER = [PERM2GET]
         DO EDIT
         SAYER = [PERSSAY]
         GETTER = [PERSGET]
         USE personnel database INDE personnel id number, social security number
         PLACE = 40-LEN(DBF())/2
      OTHE
         @ 20,0
         WAIT [SORRY, YOU CAN'T DO THAT. PRESS ANY KEY TO CONTINUE...]
         LOOP
   ENDCASE
*
   DO &SAYER
   DO &GETTER
   CLEA GETS
   DO EDIT
ENDDO T
*
** END OF PERSMENU.PRG
```

Note that the personnel system calls the paycheck subroutine. This subroutine is pulled apart and coded separately, because as it can be used in a variety of applications without much modification. Both personnel and paycheck systems use the same database, but separate fields are used in each system.

Listing 9–12

```
&& PAYCHECK.PRG
&& Although the PAYCHECK and PERSMENU systems use the same database, they use
&& different fields in that database. Hence, the two systems have separate SAYER
```

Listing 9–12 (cont.)

```
&& and GETTER files. All paychecks have the same ledger account number
*
SAYER = [PAYCKSAY]
GETTER = [PAYCKGET]
SET ORDE TO 2
*
DO WHILE .T.
   CLEAR
   @ 2, 0 TO 13,79 DOUBLE
   @ 3,28 SAY [P A Y C H E C K   M E N U]
   @ 4,1 TO 4,78 DOUBLE
   @  7,20 SAY [1. Edit Paychecks]
   @  8,20 SAY [2. Print Paychecks (Updates Other Files)]
   @  9,20 SAY [3. Remove Deleted Entries]
   @ 11, 20 SAY '0. Exit'
   STORE 0 TO ANSWER
   @ 13,33 SAY " select     "
   @ 13,42 GET ANSWER PICTURE "9" RANGE 0,3
   READ
*
   DO CASE
      CASE ANSWER = 0
         RETURN  && no DATAbases are CLOSEd
      CASE ANSWER = 1
         CLEA
         DO &SAYER
         DO &GETTER
         CLEA GETS
         DO EDIT
         LOOP
      CASE ANSWER = 2
*
&& If your system has more than one printer available, you may want to include
&& the command SET PRINT TO printer designation for printing checks here
*
&& You may be able to design your paychecks from the LABEL FORM system.
&& If that's the case the following command will suffice to print your paychecks
*
         LABE FORM paycheck TO PRINT
*
&& The other option is the following code. I prefer the following code because
&& I gang functions in the DO WHILE...ENDDO loop. If you use the LABEL FORM
&& command above you must break all the nonprinting functions out of the DO
&& WHILE...ENDDO loop and code them as separate blocks
*
```

Listing 9–12 (cont.)

```
        SET CONS OFF
        SET PRINT ON
        ? CHR(special printing codes, if necessary)
        GOTO TOP
*
        DO WHIL .NOT. EOF()
*
** YOU'D PLACE YOUR CHECK FORM'S @ SAY STATEMENTS HERE.
*
           REPL year to date gross pay field WITH;
                year to date gross pay field + earnings field, ;
                year to date federal tax field WITH;
                year to date general tax field + federal tax field, ;
                year to date social security field WITH;
                year to date social security field + social security field, ;
                year to date state tax field WITH;
                year to date state tax field + state tax field, ;
                year to date city tax field WITH;
                year to date city tax field + city tax field, etc.
           SKIP
        ENDD
*
        ? CHR(printer codes to return to normal print, if necessary)
        SET PRIN OFF
        SET CONS ON
        SUM earnings field, federal tax field, social security tax field,;
                 state tax field, city tax field, etc.;
            TO THISPAY, FEDTAX, SSTAX, STATETAX, CITYTAX, ETC.
        SELE 2
        USE payables database INDE ledger account number
        SEEK payroll ledger account number
        REPL payroll data WITH payroll data + THISPAY, etc.
        SEEK federal tax ledger account number
        REPL federal tax data WITH federal tax data + FEDTAX
        SEEK social security ledger account number
        REPL social security data WITH social security data + SSTAX
*
** THE ABOVE PATTERN IS REPEATED FOR STATE AND CITY TAXES, IF ANY ARE NECESSARY.
** THIS CAN ALSO BE EXPANDED FOR ANY OTHER DEDUCTIONS IN YOUR SYSTEM.
*
        USE
        SELE 1
*
** THE FOLLOWING TWO LINES AREN'T NECESSARY IF YOUR SYSTEM HAS MORE THAN ONE PRINTER
** AVAILABLE. THEY CAN BE REPLACED WITH SET PRIN TO PRINTER DESIGNATION FOR NORMAL
```

Listing 9–12 (cont.)

```
** PRINTING.
*
        EJECT
        WAIT [PLEASE PLACE REGULAR PAPER IN THE PRINTER]+;
             [AND PRESS ANY KEY TO CONTINUE...]
        SET CONS OFF
        REPO FORM weekly cost analysis TO PRINT
        SET CONS ON
     CASE ANSWER = 3
        DO PACKER
  ENDCASE
*
ENDDO T
*
** END OF PAYCHECK.PRG
```

The inventory system is identical to that coded in Chapter 6 and can be dropped directly into this system. The last part to code is the utilities. We've coded much of this before and can make use of previous work.

The main utilities module is nothing more than a pathing tool. It allows us to move among system and program utilities.

Listing 9–13

```
** UTILity MAIN Menu.PRG
*
DO WHILE .T.
   CLEAR
   @ 2, 0 TO 12,79 DOUBLE
   @ 3,22 SAY [U T I L I T I E S   M A I N   M E N U]
   @ 4,1 TO 4,78 DOUBLE
   @  7,30 SAY [1. System Utilities]
   @  8,30 SAY [2. Program Utilities]
   @ 10, 30 SAY '0. EXIT'
   ANSWER = 0
   @ 12,33 SAY " select     "
   @ 12,42 GET ANSWER PICTURE "9" RANGE 0,2
   READ
*
   DO CASE
      CASE ANSWER = 0
         RETU
      CASE ANSWER = 1
         DO UTILSYS
      CASE ANSWER = 2
         DO UTILPROG
```

Listing 9–13 (cont.)

```
   ENDCASE
*
ENDDO T
*
** END OF UTILMAIN.PRG
```

The two separate utility systems include some options specific to this type of system, however. We start with the system utilities module.

Listing 9–14

```
** UTILity SYStem menu.PRG
*
DO WHILE .T.
   CLEAR
   @ 2, 0 TO 20,79 DOUBLE
   @ 3,25 SAY [S Y S T E M   U T I L I T I E S]
   @ 4,1 TO 4,78 DOUBLE
   @  7,24 SAY [A. Set Date Type]
   @  8,24 SAY [B. Set Memo Width]
   @  9,24 SAY [C. Set Default Drive and Path]
   @ 10,24 SAY [D. Set Message Wait Time (SET AT ] + STR(WAITLENGTH,4) + [ SECONDS)]
   @ 11,24 SAY [E. Set Past Due Period]
   @ 12,24 SAY [F. Set Billing Period]
   @ 13,24 SAY [G. Set Check Number]
   @ 14,24 SAY [H. Set Default Printer]
   @ 15,24 SAY [I. Set Word Processor]
   @ 16,24 SAY [J. Set Spreadsheet]
   @ 187, 24 SAY '0. Exit'
   ANSWER = 0
   @ 20,33 SAY " select     "
   @ 20,42 GET ANSWER PICTURE "!"
   READ
*
   DO CASE
      CASE .NOT. ANSWER $ [ABCDEFGHIJ0]
         @ 22,0 SAY [SORRY, THAT ISN'T ONE OF THE OPTIONS.]
         DO POOL
         LOOP
      CASE ANSWER = 0
         RETURN
      CASE ANSWER = 'A'
         @ 21,0 CLEA
         @ 21,0 TO 24,79 DOUB
         @ 22,28 SAY "1. SET DATE TO MM/DD/YY"
         @ 23,28 SAY "2. SET DATE TO DD/MM/YY"
```

Listing 9–14 (cont.)

```
         @ 24,33 SAY " select        "
         @ 24,43 GET SELECTNUM PICT "9" RANG 1,2
         READ
*
&& The following variable, DATETYPE, is set in the ACCOUNT.MEM file by the developer/
&& programmer/designer.
*
         DATETYPE = IIF(ANSWER = 1, [AMER], [BRIT])
         SET DATE TO &DATETYPE
         LOOP
      CASE ANSWER = 'B'
*
&& The variable used here, WIDEMEMO, is part of the ACCOUNT.MEM file and originally
&& set by the designer/programmer/developer
*
         @ 21,0 CLEA
         @ 21,0 SAY [How wide do you want the memos? (20 to 79 chars) -> ];
                    GET WIDEMEMO PICT '99' RANG 20,79
         READ
         SET MEMO TO &WIDEMEMO
         LOOP
      CASE ANSWER = 'C'
         @ 21,0 CLEA
         @ 21,0 SAY "The current PATH is -> "+CPATH+;
           ". The current DEFAULT DRIVE is "+CDRIVE
         @ 22,0 SAY "Which PATH should be the DEFAULT PATH? -> " GET CPATH
         @ 23,0 SAY "Which DRIVE should be the DEFAULT? -> " GET CDRIVE
         READ
         SET DEFA TO &CDRIVE
         SET PATH TO &CPATH
      CASE ANSWER = 'D'
         @ 21,0 CLEA
         @ 22,0 SAY "The current ERROR MESSAGE wait time is about "+;
                    STR(WAITLENGTH,4)+" seconds."
         @ 23,0 SAY "How long would you like to wait (seconds)? -> " GET WAITLENGTH
         READ
         WAITTIME = INT(WAITLENGTH * 5.2) && The value 5.2 is system dependent
         LOOP
      CASE ANSWER = 'E'
*
&& The variable used here, PASTDUE, is part of the ACCOUNT.MEM file and originally
&& set by the designer/programmer/developer
*
         @ 21,0 CLEA
         @ 21,0 SAY [How long past due should we allow?]+;
```

Listing 9–14 (cont.)

```
                [(in days) -> ] GET PASTDUE PICT '999'
        READ
        LOOP
      CASE ANSWER = 'F'
*
&& The variable used here, BILLCYCLE, is part of the ACCOUNT.MEM file and originally
&& set by the designer/programmer/developer
*
        @ 21,0 CLEA
        @ 21,0 SAY [How long is the billing cycle?]+;
                [(in days) -> ] GET BILLCYCLE PICT '999'
        READ
        LOOP
      CASE ANSWER = 'G'
*
&& The variable used here, CHECKNUM, is part of the ACCOUNT.MEM file and originally
&& set by the designer/programmer/developer
*
        @ 21,0 CLEA
        @ 21,0 SAY [What is the starting check number?  -> ] GET CHECKNUM PICT '9999'
        READ
        LOOP
      CASE ANSWER = 'H'
*
&& The variable used here, PRINTDEF, is part of the ACCOUNT.MEM file and originally
&& set by the designer/programmer/developer. The code should change according to the
&& number of printers available to the system and can be removed all together if
&& there is only one printer available
*
        @ 21,0 CLEA
        @ 21,0 SAY [What is the default printer? (1, 2, 3, 4, 5) -> ];
                GET PRINTDEF PICT '9' RANG 1,5
        READ
        PRINTDEF = IIF(PRINTDEF < 4, 'LPT', 'COM') + STR(PRINTDEF,1)
        SET PRINT TO &PRINTDEF
        LOOP
      CASE ANSWER = 'I'
*
&& The following variable, WORDPROC, is initialized by the developer
*
        @ 21,0 CLEA
        ACCE "What is the DOS command to start the word processor? -> ";
            TO WORDPROC
      CASE ANSWER = 'J'
*
```

Listing 9–14 (cont.)

```
&& The following variable, SSHEET, is initialized by the developer.
*
   @ 20,0 CLEA
         ACCE "What is the DOS command to start the spreadsheet? -> ";
              TO SSHEET
   ENDCASE
*
ENDDO T
*
** END OF UTILSYS.PRG
```

Most of the separate routines in this module have been pulled from past work. Note that the number of menu selections prohibits us from using numbers to indicate menu options. We use characters instead. This forces us to remove the RANGE error trap from the @ GET command and replace it with the first CASE in the DO CASE . . . ENDCASE block.

That leaves us with the UTILPROG module:

Listing 9–15

```
** UTILity PROGram menu.PRG
*
DO WHILE .T.
   CLOS DATA
   CLEAR
   @ 2, 0 TO 18,79 DOUBLE
   @ 3,24 SAY [P R O G R A M   U T I L I T I E S]
   @ 4,1 TO 4,78 DOUBLE
   @  7,25 SAY [1. Set Source and Target Drives]
   @  8,25 SAY [2. Create New File]
   @  9,25 SAY [3. Copy File]
   @ 10,25 SAY [4. Create Backups]
   @ 11,25 SAY [5. Close Month]
   @ 12,25 SAY [6. Close Quarter]
   @ 12,26 SAY [7. Add New Users]
   @ 13,26 SAY [8. Delete Old User]
   @ 14,26 SAY [9. Change Passwords]
   @ 16, 25 SAY '0. Exit'
   ANSWER = 0
   @ 18,33 SAY " select    "
   @ 18,42 GET ANSWER PICTURE "9" RANG 0,9
   @ 21,0 SAY "Current SOURCE drive is -> " + SOURCE
   @ 23,0 SAY "Current TARGET drive is -> " + TARGET
   READ
*
   DO CASE
```

Listing 9–15 (cont.)

```
    CASE ANSWER = 0
       RETURN
    CASE ANSWER = 1
       @ 21,0 CLEA
       @ 21,0 SAY "Current default drive is " + CDRIVE
       @ 22,0 SAY "New default drive is -> " GET CDRIVE PICT "A"
       READ
       SET DEFA TO &CDRIVE
       @ 21,0 CLEA
       @ 21,0 SAY "Current default path is " + CPATH
       CPATH = CPATH + SPACE(30)
       @ 22,0 SAY "New default path is -> " GET CPATH
       READ
       CPATH = TRIM(CPATH)
       SET PATH TO &CPATH
    CASE ANSWER = 2
       CLEA
       STOR SPACE(12) TO OLDFILE, NEWFILE
       @ 10,0 SAY [What is the name of the source file?]+;
                  [(12 character max) -> ] GET OLDFILE
       READ
*
       IF .NOT. FILE("&OLDFILE")
          @ 20,0 SAY [SORRY, THAT FILE DOESN'T EXIST]
          DO POOL
          LOOP
       ENDI
*
       @ 11,0 SAY [What is the name of the target file?]+;
                  [(12 character max) -> ] GET NEWFILE
       READ
       NEWFILE = TARGET+NEWFILE
*
       IF FILE("&NEWFILE")
          @ 20,0 SAY [SORRY, THAT FILE ALREADY EXISTS]
          DO POOL
          LOOP
       ENDI
*
       COPY STRU TO &NEWFILE
       LOOP
    CASE ANSWER = 3
       CLEA
       STOR SPACE(12) TO OLDFILE, NEWFILE
       @ 10,0 SAY [Which file do you want to copy?]+;
```

Listing 9–15 (cont.)

```
                  [(12 character max) -> ] GET OLDFILE
         READ
*
         IF .NOT. FILE("&OLDFILE")
            @ 20,0 SAY [SORRY, THAT FILE DOESN'T EXIST]
            DO POOL
            LOOP
         ENDI
*
         @ 11,0 SAY [What is the name of the target file?]+;
                  [(12 character max) -> ] GET NEWFILE
         READ
         NEWFILE = TARGET+NEWFILE
*
         IF FILE("&NEWFILE")
            @ 20,0 SAY [SORRY, THAT FILE ALREADY EXISTS]
            DO POOL
            LOOP
         ENDI
*
         ! COPY &OLDFILE &NEWFILE
         LOOP
      CASE ANSWER = 4
*
&& This option assumes the target is a floppy drive
*
         ! BACKUP &SOURCE &TARGET
         LOOP
      CASE ANSWER = 5
         USE receivables INDE received for field, received from field
         CLEA
         FILENAME = 'M' + LEFT(CMONTH(DATE()),5) + RIGHT(STR(YEAR(DATE()),4,0),2);
                  + ".REC"
*
&& The date received field is used to determine when income was entered into the
&& system
*
         COPY TO &FILENAME FOR MONTH(DATE()) = MONTH(date received field)
         USE &FILENAME
         WAIT "MAKE SURE THE PRINTER IS READY. PRESS ANY KEY WHEN READY"
         SET CONS OFF
         INDE ON received from field TO TRECFROM
*
&& The RECFROM report form is merely a report listing information about
&& when income was received and from what organization. Likewise, RECFOR lists
```

Listing 9–15 (cont.)

```
&& what the payment was for
*
         REPO FORM RECFROM TO PRINT
         INDE ON received for field TO TRECFOR
         REPO FORM RECFOR TO PRINT
         EJEC
         SET CONS ON
         ERASE TRECFOR.NDX
         ERASE TRECFROM.NDX
         USE payables database INDE NDX file list
         FILENAME = 'M' + LEFT(CMONTH(DATE()),5) + RIGHT(STR(YEAR(DATE()),4,0),2);
                  + ".PAY"
         COPY TO &FILENAME FOR MONTH(date bill paid) = MONTH(DATE())
         USE &FILENAME
         WAIT "MAKE SURE THE PRINTER IS READY. PRESS ANY KEY WHEN READY"
         ? "PRINTING REPORTS"
         SET CONS OFF
*
&& The PAYTO report form lists where checks were sent
*
         INDE ON paid to field TO TPAYTO
         REPO FORM PAYTO TO PRINT
*
&& The PAYFOR report form lists what checks were sent for
*
         INDE ON what payment was for field TO TPAYFOR
         REPO FORM PAYFOR TO PRINT
         SET CONS ON
         ERAS TPAYTO.NDX
         ERA TPAYFOR.NDX
      CASE ANSWER = 6
         USE receivables INDE received for field, received from field
*
&& The code starts by testing the system date to see if the user is closing the
&& quarter in a valid month. This can be changed according to your needs.
*
         IF MONTH(DATE()) = 1 .OR. MONTH(DATE()) = 4;
            .OR. MONTH(DATE()) = 7 .OR. MONTH(DATE()) = 10
            CLEA
            FILENAME = LEFT(CMONTH(DATE()),5) + RIGHT(STR(YEAR(DATE()),4,0),2);
                     + ".REC"
*
&& The date received field is used to determine when income was entered into the
&& system
*
```

Listing 9–15 (cont.)

```
            COPY TO &FILENAME FOR MONTH(DATE()) > MONTH(date received field)
            USE &FILENAME
            WAIT "MAKE SURE THE PRINTER IS READY. PRESS ANY KEY WHEN READY"
            SET CONS OFF
            INDE ON received from field TO TRECFROM
*
&& The RECFROM report form is merely a report listing information regarding
&& when income was received and from what organization. Likewise, RECFOR lists
&& what the payment was for
*
            REPO FORM RECFROM TO PRINT
            INDE ON received for field TO TRECFOR
            REPO FORM RECFOR TO PRINT
            EJEC
            SET CONS ON
            CLEA
            ? "UPDATING INCOME TOTALS"
            @ 5,0 SAY [ACCOUNT -> ]
            @ 7,0 SAY [TITLE   -> ]
            SELE 2
            USE chart of accounts database INDE ledger account number
            SELE 1
            GOTO TOP
*
            DO WHIL .NOT. EOF()
               SELE 2
               @ 5,13 SAY A->ledger account number field
               @ 7,13 SAY A->account title field
               SEEK A->ledger account number field
*
               IF .NOT. FOUND()
                  APPE BLAN
                  REPL ledger account number WITH A->ledger account number
                  SET COLO TO W+*
&& you can SET your COLOR to whatever is best for your monitor
                  @ 6,0 SAY [!!THE ABOVE ACCOUNT NUMBER ISN'T IN THE FILE!!]
                  SET COLO TO
&& you can SET your COLOR to whatever is best for your monitor
                  @ 7,13 GET account title field
                  READ
               ENDI
*
               @ 6,0 CLEA TO 6,78
               SELE 1
               RECEIVEFOR = RECFOR
```

Listing 9–15 (cont.)

```
                SUM RECAMNT TO INCOME WHILE RECFOR = RECEIVEFOR
                SELE 2
                REPL account total field WITH account total field + INCOME
                SELE 1
             ENDD
*
             IF MONTH(DATE()) = 1
                SELE 2
                FILENAME = STR(YEAR(DATE()),4,0) + ".REC"
                COPY TO &FILENAME
*
&& The RECTTLS report form is used to get a yearly listing of income
*
                REPO FORM RECTTLS TO PRINT
*
&& You may wish to zero out numeric fields instead of ZAPping
*
                ZAP
             ENDI
*
             USE receivables database INDE NDX file list
             DELE FOR MONTH(DATE()) > MONTH(date received field)
             PACK
             ERASE TRECFOR.NDX
             ERASE TRECFROM.NDX
             USE payables database INDE NDX file list
*
             FILENAME = LEFT(CMONTH(DATE()),5) + RIGHT(STR(YEAR(DATE()),4,0),2);
                        + ".PAY"
             COPY TO &FILENAME FOR MONTH(date bill paid) < MONTH(DATE())
             USE &FILENAME
             WAIT "MAKE SURE THE PRINTER IS READY. PRESS ANY KEY WHEN READY"
             ? "PRINTING REPORTS"
             SET CONS OFF
*
&& The PAYTO report form lists where checks were sent
*
             INDE ON paid to field TO TPAYTO
             REPO FORM PAYTO TO PRINT
*
&& The PAYFOR report form lists what checks were sent for
*
             INDE ON what payment was for field TO TPAYFOR
             REPO FORM PAYFOR TO PRINT
             SET CONS ON
```

Listing 9–15 (cont.)

```
          ERAS TPAYTO.NDX
          ? "UPDATING EXPENSE RECORDS"
          @ 5,0 SAY [ACCOUNT -> ]
          @ 7,0 SAY [TITLE   -> ]
          SELE 2
          USE chart of accounts database INDE ledger account number
          SELE 1
          GOTO TOP
*
          DO WHIL .NOT. EOF()
             SELE 2
             @ 5,13 SAY A->ledger account number field
             @ 7,13 SAY A->account title field
             SEEK A->ledger account number field
*
             IF .NOT. FOUND()
                APPE BLAN
                REPL ledger account number WITH A->ledger account number
                SET COLO TO W+*
&& You can SET your COLOR to whatever is best for your monitor
                @ 6,0 SAY [!!THE ABOVE ACCOUNT NUMBER ISN'T IN THE FILE!!]
                SET COLO TO
&& You can SET your COLOR to whatever is best for your monitor
                @ 7,13 GET account title field
                READ
             ENDI
*
             SELE 1
             PAYMENTFOR = payment for field
             SUM payment amount field TO EXPENSES WHIL;
                 payment for field = PAYMENTFOR
             SELE 2
             REPL payment amount field WITH EXPENSES + payment amount field
             SELE 1
          ENDD
*
          SELE 2
*
          IF MONTH(DATE()) = 1
             FILENAME = STR(YEAR(DATE()),4,0) + ".PAY"
             COPY TO &FILENAME
             REPO FORM EXPTTLS TO PRINT
*
&& You may wish to zero out numeric fields instead of ZAPping the database
*
```

Listing 9–15 (cont.)

```
               ZAP
            ENDI
*
            USE
            SELE 2
            USE
            ERAS TPAYFOR.NDX
            SELE 1
            DELE ALL FOR MONTH(date bill paid) < MONTH(DATE())
            PACK
         ELSE
            @ 10,0 SAY "YOU CAN'T CLOSE OUT A QUARTER THIS MONTH."
            @ 12,0 SAY "YOU CAN USE THIS OPTION IN JAN, APR, JUL, OR OCT."
            WAIT
         ENDI
*
      CASE ANSWER = 7
         DO ACCESSOR
         USE password file INDE password NDX
*
&& The following line hinders illicit changes to the password file
*
         SET FILT TO access level field <= ACCESS
         SET FORM TO password format file && This line isn't truly necessary
         SET STAT ON
         SET MENU ON
         SET MESS TO [Enter the new user's name, password and access level]
         APPE
         SET STAT OFF
         SET MENU OFF
         SET MESS TO
         SET FORM TO
         USE
      CASE ANSWER = 8
         DO ACCESSOR
         USE password file INDE password NDX
*
&& The following line hinders illicit changes to the password file
*
         SET FILT TO access level field <= ACCESS
         NAME = SPAC(length of name field in password file)
         @ 20,0 CLEA
         @ 21,0 SAY [Whom are we deleting? -> ] GET NAME
         READ
*
```

Listing 9-15 (cont.)

```
         IF .NOT. FOUN()
            WAIT [NOBODY LIKE THAT HERE. PRESS ANY KEY TO CONTINUE...]
            LOOP
         ENDI
*
         DELE
         PACK
         USE
         LOOP
      CASE ANSWER = 9
         DO ACCESSOR
         USE password file INDE password NDX
*
&& The following line hinders illicit changes to the password file
*
         SET FILT TO access level field <= ACCESS
         SET FORM TO password format file && This line isn't truly necessary
         NAME = SPAC(length of name field in password file)
         @ 20,0 CLEA
         @ 21,0 SAY [Whose password are we going to change? -> ] GET NAME
         SEEK NAME
*
         IF TRIM(A->NAME) # TRIM(M->NAME)
            LOOP
         ELSE
            SET STAT ON
            SET SCOR ON
            SET MENU ON
            EDIT NEXT 1 FIEL password field
            SET STAT OFF
            SET SCOR OFF
            SET MENU OFF
            SET FORM TO
            USE
         ENDI
*   ENDCASE
*
ENDDO T
*
** END OF UTILPROG.PRG
```

This is a synthesis of the code shown in earlier chapters as well. The only parts left to assemble now are the PROCedure file, the main menu, and the PACKER module. The PACKER module has been shown in several other places and won't be repeated here. Similarly, you could include the INDEXER module and other blocks from earlier chapters to flesh out this system according to your needs.

A REAL-LIFE EXAMPLE OF GENERAL ACCOUNTING

This is where all the modules come together. And because of our kernel design techniques, all we need to show here is the main menu and the PROCedure file. Everything else has come from earlier chapters in the book. The main menu is similar to previous ones:

Listing 9–16

```
** ACCOUNTING MAIN MENU.PRG
*
CLOS ALL
CLEA ALL
*
* THINGS TURNED ON
SET DELI ON
SET ESCA ON
SET INTE ON
*
* THINGS TURNED OFF
SET BELL OFF
SET CONF OFF
SET STAT OFF
SET SAFE OFF
SET TALK OFF
*
REST FROM ACCOUNT
SET PROC TO ACCOUNT.PRC
SET PATH TO &CPATH
SET DEFA TO &CDRIVE
SET DELI TO '><'
SET DATE TO &DATETYPE
*
ON ERROR DO ERRORMSS
*
PLACE = 0
TRUTH = .F.
ACCESS = 0
*
DO WHILE .T.
   CLEAR
   @ 2, 0 TO 18,79 DOUBLE
   @ 3,21 SAY [A C C O U N T I N G   M A I N   M E N U]
```

Listing 9–16 (cont.)

```
   @ 4,1 TO 4,78 DOUBLE
   @  7,26 SAY [1. Accounts Menu]
   @  8,26 SAY [2. Client Menu]
   @  9,26 SAY [3. Personnel Menu]
   @ 10,26 SAY [4. Inventory Menu]
   @ 11,26 SAY [5. Utilities Menu]
   @ 12,26 SAY [6. Use Word Processor]
   @ 13,26 SAY [7. Use Spreadsheet]
   @ 14,26 SAY [8. Execute DOS-Level Commands]
   @ 16, 26 SAY '0. Exit'
   ANSWER = 0
   @ 18,33 SAY " select     "
   @ 18,42 GET ANSWER PICTURE "9" RANGE 0,8
   READ
*
   DO CASE
      CASE ANSWER = 0
         SAVE TO ACCOUNT
         RETURN
      CASE ANSWER = 1
         DO ACCTMAIN
      CASE ANSWER = 2
         DO CLMAIN
      CASE ANSWER = 3
         DO PERSMAIN
      CASE ANSWER = 4
         DO INVTMAIN
      CASE ANSWER = 5
         DO UTILMAIN
      CASE ANSWER = 6
         ! &WORDPROC
         WAIT
      CASE ANSWER = 7
         ! &SSHEET
         WAIT
      CASE ANSWER = 8
         @ 20,0
         ACCE [What is the DOS command you want to execute? -> ] TO DOSCOMM
         ! &DOSCOMM
         WAIT
   ENDCASE
*
ENDDO T
*
** END OF A:MAINMENU.PRG
```

This leaves us with the PROCedure file for this system. The PROCedure file is necessarily longer than others we've coded, but nothing to be intimidated about.

Listing 9–17

```
* ACCOUNT.PRC PROCEDURE FILE
*
PROC EDITMENU
@ 20,0 TO 23,79 DOUB
@ 21,1 SAY IIF(EDITFLAG, [  E -> Edit  B -> Back  S -> Skip  G -> Goto]+;
                         [  K -> Kill  R -> Rstr  Q -> Quit],;
                         [  F -> Find  L -> Loca  C -> Cont  D -> Disp]+;
                         [  O -> Copy  A -> Add  U -> Upda])
@ 22,1 SAY [  M -> Memo Search      T -> Trck              N -> Next ]
*
PROC RECSAY
@  2, PLACE SAY DBF()
*
&& SAY statements from your subscriber SAY file
*
@  3,  1  TO  3, 78   DOUBLE
@  1,  0  TO 18, 79   DOUBLE
*
PROC RECGET
@ 2,73 SAY STR(RECNO(),5,0)
*
&& GET statements from your billing database GET file
*
PROC PAYSAY
@  2, PLACE SAY DBF()
*
&& SAY statements from your payables database SAY file
*
@  3,  1  TO  3, 78   DOUBLE
@  1,  0  TO 18, 79   DOUBLE
*
PROC PAYGET
@ 2,73 SAY STR(RECNO(),5,0)
*
&& This file contains the payables database GET commands
*
PROC CLIENSAY
@  2, PLACE SAY DBF()
*
&& SAY statements from your clients database SAY file
*
```

Listing 9–17 (cont.)

```
@  3,  1  TO  3, 78    DOUBLE
@  1,  0  TO 18, 79    DOUBLE
*
PROC CLIENGET
@ 2,73 SAY STR(RECNO(),5,0)
*
&& This file contains the clients database GET commands
*
PROC PERSSAY
@  2, PLACE SAY DBF()
*
&& SAY statements from your personnel database SAY file for the personnel system
*
@  3,  1  TO  3, 78    DOUBLE
@  1,  0  TO 18, 79    DOUBLE
*
PROC PERSGET
@ 2,73 SAY STR(RECNO(),5,0)
*
&& This file contains the personnel database GET commands for the personnel system
*
PROC PAYCKSAY
@  2, PLACE SAY DBF()
*
&& SAY statements from your personnel database SAY file for the paycheck system
*
@  3,  1  TO  3, 78    DOUBLE
@  1,  0  TO 18, 79    DOUBLE
*
PROC PAYCKGET
@ 2,73 SAY STR(RECNO(),5,0)
*
&& This file contains the personnel database GET commands for the paycheck system
*
PROC PERM1SAY
*
&& statements here for your first-level personnel memo field file
*
PROC PERM2SAY
*
&& statements here for your second-level personnel memo field file
*
PROC MEMO1SAY
*
&& statements here for your first-level client memo field file
```

Listing 9–17 (cont.)

```
*
PROC MEMO2SAY
*
&& statements here for your second-level client memo field file
*
PROC INVENTORY
*
&& You may wish to include the entire INVENTORY PROCEDURE file from Chapter 6 here
&& or run that module as a separately called PROC file
*
PROC ERRORMSS
*
DO CASE
   CASE ERROR() = 1
      @ 0,0 SAY "That file doesn't exist on drive " + CDRIVE
      CALL DELAY WITH CHR(1)
      RETU TO MASTER
   CASE ERROR() = 4
      @ 24,50 say "Record Number ->  END  "
      @ 0,0 SAY "You're at the end of the file now. "
   CASE ERROR() = 5
      @ 24,50 say "Record Number ->  END  "
      @ 0,0 SAY "You can't CONTINUE any further. You're at the end. ."
   CASE ERROR() = 38
      @ 24,50 say "Record Number -> 0    "
      @ 0,0 SAY "You can't go any further. You're at the beginning now. "
   CASE ERROR() = 42
      @ 0,0 SAY "You must LOCATE before you can CONTINUE. "
   CASE ERROR() = 114
      CLEAR
      @ 10,10 TO 20,70 DOUBLE
      @ 15,15 SAY "The INDEX file is damaged, excuse me while I REINDEX"
      REIN
   CASE ERROR() = 125
      @ 0,0 SAY "Please turn the PRINTER ON."
   OTHE
      @ 0,0 SAY "I'VE ENCOUNTERED AN UNKNOWN ERROR. PLEASE TRY AGAIN"
ENDC
*
** END OF ACCOUNT.PRC
```

And we're done!

CONCLUSION

This book has presented a great deal of code. Some of it may have been confusing when you first opened the book. I hope that now you are more comfortable when you code and can adapt more easily to coding problems.

I have heavily stressed a modular, task-oriented approach to coding in dBASE III PLUS. That has forced you—if you've been using this book as a learning tool—to build a library of small (and sometimes not so small) packages. Each of these packages can be transported from one work situation to another. A testimony to that is the amount of code we used from early chapters to build the applications in later chapters.

One thing you must remember about any coding problem is that it's been solved before. It may not have been solved entirely. There are always a few new things to be accomplished, but most of the job has probably been done before. Use that information to save yourself time and agony when you code new applications.

Now that I've told you everything has been done before, I'll remind you of this: Every job is new. Don't make yourself stale by always looking for the old solutions. When something presents itself and you feel you've never seen it before, think logically, design your flowcharts according to jobs and tasks, and start coding. That's how you build new tools.

Good luck!

APPENDIX

A

Clipper VERSIONS OF dBASE III PLUS LISTINGS

This appendix lists code shown earlier in the book, but rewritten to work with the Nantucket's Clipper compiler (Winter 1986 release). The code shown here follows the parameters I've repeated in the book: I code from kernels. In the case of Clipper compatible files, this means I don't always make use of all Clipper provides, and usually I only modify my dBASE III PLUS code as necessary for aesthetics or to become Clipper compatible. I don't specifically code for the Clipper environment. That would simply be too much work. My goal is to produce good working code, fast. When more of my clients need and demand more Clipper files, I'll recode everything to make total use of all that Nantucket provides. Until then, here is a launching point for your own explorations. Enjoy.

EDIT MODULE FROM Clipper VERSION OF LISTING 5-11

The following code is the Clipper compilable version of the editor shown in Listing 5-11. There are a few but never the less major differences between Listing 5-11 and Listing A-1 that involve the Display and Update kernels. The version of Clipper I work with has trouble with dBASE III PLUS macros and doesn't support the TYPE() function. The only other item worthy of note is the parallel, indexed record deletions and packing routine incorporated in the Quit kernel.

Listing A-1

```
* EDIT.PRG
* CALLS EDITMENU PROCEDURE FILE
*
DO &FRAMER
DO &GETTER
CLEA GETS
DO EDITMENU
ANSWER = 'X'
DELS = .F.
*
```

Listing A–1 (cont.)

```
DO WHIL .T.
   @ 0,0 SAY SPACE(80)
   @ 24,0 SAY SPACE(80)
   @  2,60 SAY IIF(DELETED(),"DELETED",SPACE(7))
   @ 23,34 SAY " select -> "
   @ 23,43 GET ANSWER PICT '!'
   READ
*
   DO CASE
      CASE ANSWER = 'Q'
*
         IF DELS
            @ 20,0 CLEA
            @ 21,0 SAY [SOME RECORDS HAVE BEEN DELETED FROM THIS FILE.]
            @ 23,0 SAY [DO YOU WISH TO REMOVE THEM PERMANENTLY (Y/N)? -> ] GET DELS
            READ
*
            DO CASE
               CASE DELS .AND. [secondary file]$DBFILE
                  @ 21,0 CLEA
                  @ 21,0 SAY [DO YOU WISH TO DELETE CORRESPONDING DATA]+;
                             [IN THE primary FILE (Y/N)? -> ] GET DELS
                  READ
*
                  IF DELS
                     SELE 1
                     SET RELA TO key field INTO B
                     LOCA FOR DELETED()
*
                     DO WHIL .NOT. EOF()
                        SELE 2
                        DELE
                        SELE 1
                        CONT
                     ENDD
*
                     SELE 2
                     PACK
                  ENDI
*
                  SELE 1
                  PACK
               CASE DELS
                  PACK
            ENDC
```

Listing A-1 (cont.)

```
*
        ENDI
*
        RETU
     CASE ANSWER = 'K'
        DELE
        DELS = .T.
        LOOP
     CASE ANSWER = 'R'
        RECA
        LOOP
     CASE ANSWER = 'S'
        SKIP
        DO &GETTER
        CLEA GETS
        LOOP
     CASE ANSWER = 'B'
        SKIP -1
        DO &GETTER
        CLEA GETS
        LOOP
     CASE ANSWER = 'E'
        @ 20,0 CLEA
        @ 22,0 SAY "Press CTRL-W to save edit, ESC to exit"
        DO &GETTER
        READ
        DO EDITMENU
        LOOP
     CASE ANSWER = 'O'
        COPY NEXT 1 TO TANK
        APPE FROM TANK
        DO &GETTER
        CLEA GETS
        LOOP
     CASE ANSWER = 'C'
        CONT
        DO &GETTER
        CLEA GETS
        LOOP
     CASE ANSWER = 'G'
        ACCE "Record Number -> " TO RECNUM
        GOTO VAL(RECNUM)
        DO &GETTER
        CLEA GETS
        @ 24,0 SAY SPACE(40)
```

Listing A–1 (cont.)

```
        LOOP
      CASE ANSWER = 'D'
        STORE SPACE(10) TO W1,W2,W3,W4,W5
        @ 20,0 CLEA
        @ 21,0 SAY "Display What -> "
        @ 21,18 GET W1
        @ 21,30 GET W2
        @ 21,42 GET W3
        @ 21,54 GET W4
        @ 21,66 GET W5
        READ
*
        IF LEN(TRIM(W1)) = 0
          @ 20,0 CLEA
          DO EDITMENU
          LOOP
        ENDI
*
        DISPLAYFOR = SPACE(60)
        TRUTH = .T.
        @ 21,0 CLEA
        @ 21,0 SAY "DISP FOR -> " GET DISPLAYFOR
        READ
*
        IF LEN(TRIM(DISPLAYFOR)) # 0
          SET FILT TO &DISPLAYFOR
        ENDI
*
        @ 21,0 CLEA
        @ 21,0 SAY [DO YOU WANT THIS PRINTED (Y/N)? -> ] GET TRUTH
        READ
*
        IF TRUTH
          SET CONS OFF
          SET PRIN ON
          EJECT
          PUCK = SPACE(10) && useful to get print off perfory
          MOST = 54
        ELSE
          CLEA
          PUCK = []
          MOST = 23
        ENDI
*
        N = 1
```

Listing A–1 (cont.)

```
        GOTO TOP
*
        DO WHIL .NOT. EOF()
*
           DO CASE
              CASE LEN(TRIM(W5)) # 0
                 ? PUCK,RECNO(),&W1,&W2,&W3,&W4,&W5
              CASE LEN(TRIM(W4)) # 0
                 ? PUCK,RECNO(),&W1,&W2,&W3,&W4
              CASE LEN(TRIM(W3)) # 0
                 ? PUCK,RECNO(),&W1,&W2,&W3
              CASE LEN(TRIM(W2)) # 0
                 ? PUCK,RECNO(),&W1,&W2
              OTHE
                 ? PUCK,RECNO(),&W1
           ENDC
*
           N = N + 1
*
           DO CASE
              CASE N = MOST .AND. TRUTH
                 EJECT
                 N = 1
              CASE N = MOST .AND. .NOT. TRUTH
                 WAIT
                 CLEA
                 N = 1
           ENDC
*
           SKIP
        ENDD
*
        IF TRUTH
           SET PRIN OFF
           SET CONS ON
           EJECT
        ELSE
           CLEA
           DO &FRAMER
           DO &GETTER
           CLEA GETS
        ENDI
*
        @ 21,0 CLEA
        SET FILT TO
```

Listing A–1 (cont.)

```
         DO EDITMENU
         LOOP
      CASE ANSWER = 'F'
         @ 20,0 CLEAR
         ACCE "Find &KEYFIELD   " TO TOFIND
         SEEK TOFIND
*
         IF .NOT. FOUND()
           @ 24,50 SAY "Record Number ->  END  "
           @ 0,0 SAY "I can't FIND that entry. Perhaps you should LOCATE it."
           CALL DELAY WITH CHR(1)
         ENDI
*
         DO &GETTER
         CLEA GETS
         DO EDITMENU
         LOOP
      CASE ANSWER = 'L'
         @ 20,0 CLEA
         ACCE "Locate what? -> " TO LOCATEWHAT
         ACCE "Locate where? -> " TO LOCATEWHERE
*
         IF LEN(TRIM(LOCATEWHAT)) # 0 .AND. LEN(TRIM(LOCATEWHERE)) # 0
            LOCA ALL FOR "&LOCATEWHAT"$&LOCATEWHERE
         ENDI
*
         DO &GETTER
         CLEA GETS
         DO EDITMENU
         LOOP
      CASE ANSWER = 'A'
         COPY STRUC TO TANK
         SELE 6
         USE TANK
         @ 20,0 CLEA
         @ 22,0 SAY "Press CTRL-W to save information, ESC to exit"
*
         IF [primary database]$DBFILE
            SELE 2
            USE secondary database INDE index file list
            COPY STRUC TO TANK2
            SELE 7
            USE TANK2
            TRUTH = .T.
            GETTER = [edited primary GETTER file]
```

Listing A-1 (cont.)

```
*
          DO WHIL .T.
             SELE 6
             APPE BLAN
*
             DO WHIL .T.
                DO primary GETTER
                CLEA GETS
                @ 5,7 GET key field PICT '!!-!!!!'
                READ
*
                IF LEN(TRIM(key field)) = 0
                   EXIT
                ENDI
*
                SELE 1
                SEEK F->key field
*
                IF FOUND()
                   DO primary GETTER
                   CLEA GETS
                   @ 20,0 CLEA
                   @ 20,0 SAY [SORRY, WE'VE ALREADY GOT ONE OF THOSE.]
                   CALL DELAY WITH CHR(1)
                   @ 20,0 CLEA
                   @ 22,0 SAY "Press CTRL-W to save information, ESC to exit"
                ELSE
                   SELE F
                   EXIT
                ENDI
*
                SELE F
             ENDD
*
             IF LEN(TRIM(key field)) = 0
                DELE
                EXIT
             ENDI
*
             DO &GETTER
             READ
             @ 20,0 CLEA
             @ 22,0 SAY [ADD A NEW secondary RECORD (Y/N)? -> ] GET TRUTH
             READ
*
```

Listing A–1 (cont.)

```
          IF TRUTH
             SELE 7
             CLEA
             APPE BLANK
             REPL key field WITH F->key field, etc.
             DO secondary SAY file
             DO edited secondary GETTER file
             @ 20,0 CLEA
             @ 22,0 SAY [Press CTRL-W to save information, ESC to exit]
             READ
             SELE 6
             CLEA
             DO SUBSAY
          ENDI
*
    @ 20,0 CLEA
          @ 22,0 SAY [Press CTRL-W to save information, ESC to exit]
       ENDD
*
       SELE 7
       USE
       SELE 6
       USE
       SELE 2
       APPE FROM TANK2
       ERAS TANK2.DBF
       GETTER = [primary GETTER]
    ELSE * DBFILE # primary database
       REPEATER = FIELD(1)
*
       DO WHIL .T.
          APPE BLANK
          DO &GETTER
          READ
*
          IF LEN(TRIM(&REPEATER)) = 0
             DELE
             EXIT
          ENDI
*
       ENDD
*
    ENDI
*
    USE
```

Listing A-1 (cont.)

```
            SELE 6
            USE
            SELE 1
            SET DELE ON
            APPE FROM TANK
            SET DELE OFF
            DO &GETTER
            CLEA GETS
            DO EDITMENU
            ERAS TANK.DBF
         CASE ANSWER = 'U'
            STORE SPACE(10) TO W1,W2,W3,W4,W5,REPLACER
            @ 20,0 CLEA
            @ 21,0 SAY [REPLACE WHAT FIELD? -> ] GET REPLACER
            READ
*
            IF LEN(TRIM(REPLACER)) = 0
               @ 20,0 CLEA
               DO EDITMENU
               LOOP
            ENDI
*
            @ 22,0 SAY [REPLACE WITH -> ]
            @ 22,18 GET W1
            @ 22,30 GET W2
            @ 22,42 GET W3
            @ 22,54 GET W4
            @ 22,66 GET W5
            READ
*
            IF LEN(TRIM(W1)) = 0
               @ 20,0 CLEA
               DO EDITMENU
               LOOP
            ENDI
*
            ACCE "CONDITION -> " TO CONDITION
*
            IF LEN(TRIM(CONDITION)) # 0
               LOCA FOR &CONDITION
*
               IF .NOT. FOUND()
                  @ 20,0 CLEA
                  @ 21,0 SAY [NO RECORDS MATCH ] + TRIM(CONDITION)
                  CALL DELAY WITH CHR(1)
```

Listing A–1 (cont.)

```
            @ 20,0 CLEA
            DO EDITMENU
            LOOP
         ELSE
            SET FILT TO &CONDITION
         ENDI
*
         GO TOP
*
         DO CASE
            CASE LEN(TRIM(W5)) # 0
               REPL ALL &REPLACER WITH TRIM(&W1) + ' ' + TRIM(&W2) + ;
                  ' ' + TRIM(&W3) + ' ' + TRIM(&W4) + ' ' + TRIM(&W5)
            CASE LEN(TRIM(W4)) # 0
               REPL ALL &REPLACER WITH TRIM(&W1) + ' ' + TRIM(&W2) + ;
                  ' ' + TRIM(&W3) + ' ' + TRIM(&W4)
            CASE LEN(TRIM(W3)) # 0
               REPL ALL &REPLACER WITH TRIM(&W1) + ' ' + TRIM(&W2) + ;
                  ' ' + TRIM(&W3)
            CASE LEN(TRIM(W2)) # 0
               REPL ALL &REPLACER WITH TRIM(&W1) + ' ' + TRIM(&W2)
            OTHE
               REPL ALL &REPLACER WITH TRIM(&W1)
         ENDC
*
      ENDI
*
      @ 20,0 CLEA
      DO EDITMENU
*
   ENDC
*
ENDD
*
** END OF EDIT.PRG
```

Listing A–1 calls an EDITMENU file from a previously declared PROCedure file. The EDITMENU commands are:

Listing A–2

```
PROC EDITMENU
@ 20,0 ,23,79 BOX FRAME
@ 21,1 SAY;
[  E -> Edit  B -> Back  S -> Skip  G -> Goto  K -> Kill  R -> Rstr  Q - > Quit]
@ 22,1 SAY;
[  F -> Find  L -> Loca  C -> Cont  D -> Disp  O -> Copy  A -> Add  U - > Upda]
```

Clipper VERSION OF EDIT MODULE FROM LISTING 6–1

This EDIT module is similar in theory and practice to the Clipper version of the editor shown from Chapter 5. Major differences include the ability to shift NDX file priority and the lack of an UPDATE module.

Listing A–3

```
* EDIT.PRG
* CALLS EDITMENU FROM PROCEDURE FILE
*
DO EDITMENU
ANSWER = 'X'
*
DO WHIL .T.
   @ 0,0 SAY SPACE(80)
   @  2,60 SAY IIF(DELETED(),"DELETED",SPACE(7))
   @ 23,34 SAY "select ->      "
   @ 23,44 GET ANSWER
   READ
   ANSWER = UPPER(ANSWER)
*
   DO CASE
      CASE ANSWER = 'X'
         CANC
      CASE ANSWER = 'Q'
         RETU
      CASE ANSWER = 'K'
         DELE
         LOOP
      CASE ANSWER = 'R'
         RECA
         LOOP
      CASE ANSWER = 'S'
         SKIP
         DO &GETTER
         CLEA GETS
         LOOP
      CASE ANSWER = 'B'
         SKIP -1
         DO &GETTER
         CLEA GETS
         LOOP
      CASE ANSWER = 'E'
         @ 20,0 CLEA
         @ 22,0 SAY "Press CTRL-W to save edits,"+;
                    " CTRL-Q to quit without saving edits"
```

Listing A–3 (cont.)

```
         DO &GETTER
         READ
         DO EDITMENU
         LOOP
      CASE ANSWER = 'O'
         COPY NEXT 1 TO TANK
         APPE FROM TANK
         LOOP
      CASE ANSWER = 'C'
         SET ORDER TO
         CONT
         SET ORDER TO 1
         DO &GETTER
         CLEA GETS
         LOOP
      CASE ANSWER = 'G'
         ACCE "Record Number -> " TO RECNUM
         GOTO VAL(RECNUM)
         DO &GETTER
         CLEA GETS
         @ 24,0 SAY SPACE(40)
         LOOP
      CASE ANSWER = 'D'
         STORE SPACE(10) TO W1,W2,W3,W4,W5
         @ 20,0 CLEA
         @ 21,0 SAY "Display What -> "
         @ 21,18 GET W1
         @ 21,30 GET W2
         @ 21,42 GET W3
         @ 21,54 GET W4
         @ 21,66 GET W5
         READ
*
         IF LEN(TRIM(W1)) = 0
            @ 20,0 CLEA
            DO EDITMENU
            LOOP
         ENDI
*
         ACCE "DISP FOR -> " TO DISPLAYFOR
*
         IF LEN(TRIM(DISPLAYFOR)) # 0
*
            DO CASE
               CASE LEN(TRIM(W5)) # 0
```

Listing A-3 (cont.)

```
                DISP &W1,&W2,&W3,&W4,&W5 FOR &DISPLAYFOR
             CASE LEN(TRIM(W4)) # 0
                DISP &W1,&W2,&W3,&W4 FOR &DISPLAYFOR
             CASE LEN(TRIM(W3)) # 0
                DISP &W1,&W2,&W3 FOR &DISPLAYFOR
             CASE LEN(TRIM(W2)) # 0
                DISP &W1,&W2 FOR &DISPLAYFOR
             OTHE
                DISP &W1 FOR &DISPLAYFOR
          ENDC
*
       ELSE
*
          DO CASE
             CASE LEN(TRIM(W5)) # 0
                DISP ALL &W1,&W2,&W3,&W4,&W5
             CASE LEN(TRIM(W4)) # 0
                DISP ALL &W1,&W2,&W3,&W4
             CASE LEN(TRIM(W3)) # 0
                DISP ALL &W1,&W2,&W3
             CASE LEN(TRIM(W2)) # 0
                DISP ALL &W1,&W2
             OTHE
                DISP ALL &W1
          ENDC
*
       ENDI
*
       WAIT
       CLEA
       DO &SAYER
       DO &GETTER
       CLEA GETS
       DO EDITMENU
       LOOP
    CASE ANSWER = 'F'
       @ 20,0 CLEAR
*
       DO CASE
          CASE DBFILE = "inventory database"
             ACCE "Find 1-key field a, 2-key field b, 3-key field c,]+;
                   [4-key field d, or 5-key field e? -> " TO TOFIND
             TOFIND = VAL(TOFIND)
*
             DO CASE
```

Listing A–3 (cont.)

```
                CASE TOFIND = 1
                   SET INDE TO NDX file a
                CASE TOFIND = 2
                   SET INDE TO NDX file b
                CASE TOFIND = 3
                   SET INDE TO NDX file c
                CASE TOFIND = 4
                   SET INDE TO NDX file d
               CASE TOFIND = 5
                   SET INDE TO NDX file e
             ENDC
*
             @ 20,0 CLEA
             ACCE "Find > " TO TOFIND
          CASE DBFILE = "order database"
             ACCE "Find 1-key fidld a, 2-key field b, 3-key field c,]+;
                   [4-key field d, 5-key field e? -> " TO TOFIND
             TOFIND = VAL(TOFIND)
*
             DO CASE
                CASE TOFIND = 1
                   SET INDE TO NDX file a
                CASE TOFIND = 2
                   SET INDE TO NDX file b
                CASE TOFIND = 3
                   SET INDE TO NDX file c
                CASE TOFIND = 4
                   SET INDE TO NDX file d
                CASE TOFIND = 5
                   SET INDE TO NDX file e
             ENDC
*
             @ 20,0 CLEA
             ACCE "Find > " TO TOFIND
         OTHE
            INDEXKEY = FIELD(1)
            ACCE "Find &INDEXKEY > " TO TOFIND
       ENDCASE
*
       SEEK TOFIND
*
       IF .NOT. FOUND()
         @ 24,50 SAY "Record Number ->  END  "
         @ 0,0 SAY "I can't FIND that entry. Perhaps you should LOCATE it."
          DO POOL
```

Listing A–3 (cont.)

```
        ENDI
*
        DO &GETTER
        CLEA GETS
        DO EDITMENU
        LOOP
     CASE ANSWER = 'L'
        SET ORDER TO 0
        @ 20,0 CLEA
        ACCE "Locate what? -> " TO LOCATEWHAT
        ACCE "Locate where? -> " TO LOCATEWHERE
        LOCA FOR "&LOCATEWHAT"$&LOCATEWHERE
        SET ORDER TO 1
        DO &GETTER
        CLEA GETS
        DO EDITMENU
        LOOP
     CASE ANSWER = 'A'
*
        IF DBFILE = "inventory database"
           SELE 3
           USE inventory totals databases INDE inventory totals NDX file
           SELE 1
        ENDI
*
        COPY STRUC TO TANK
        SELE 2
        USE TANK
        @ 20,0 CLEA
        @ 22,0 SAY "Press CTRL-W to save information, CTRL-Q to exit"
        REPEATER = FIELD(1)
*
        DO WHIL .T.
           APPE BLAN
           DO &GETTER
           READ
*
           IF DBFILE = "inventory database"
*
              IF LEN(TRIM(&REPEATER)) = 0 .AND. LEN(TRIM(secondary key field)) = 0
                 DELE
                 EXIT
              ENDI
*
           ELSE
```

Listing A–3 (cont.)

```
*
            IF LEN(TRIM(&REPEATER)) = 0
               DELE
               EXIT
            ENDI
*
         ENDI
*
         IF DBFILE = "inventory database"
            SELE 3
            SEEK B->key field
*
            DO WHIL .NOT. FOUND()
               @ 20,0 CLEA
               ACCE "I CAN'T FIND THAT ITEM."+;
                    "(U)SE IT OR (L)IST CURRENT STOCK (U/L)? -> " TO UORL
*
               IF UPPER(UORL) = 'U'
                  APPE BLANK
                  REPL NEXT 1 key field WITH B->key field
                  SELE 2
                  EXIT
               ELSE
                  CLEA
                  DISP ALL TRIM(key field)
                  WAIT
                  SELE 2
                  DO inventory say
                  DO inventory get
                  @ 20,0 CLEA
                  UORL = SPACE(40)
                  ACCE "TYPE IN THE CORRECTION,"+;
                       "OR JUST RETURN TO QUIT -> " TO UORL
*
                  IF LEN(UORL) # 0
                     REPL NEXT 1 key field WITH UORL
                     @ x,y SAY key field
                  ENDI * UORL # 0
*
               ENDI * UORL = L
*
               SELE 3
               SEEK B->key field
            ENDD * FOUND()
*
```

Listing A-3 (cont.)

```
            SELE 2
            @ 20,0 CLEA
            @ 22,0 SAY "Press CTRL-W to save information, CTRL-Q to exit"
         ENDI * DBFILE = inventory database
*
      ENDD
*
      USE
      SELE 3
      USE
      SELE 1
      SET DELE ON
      APPE FROM TANK
      SET DELE OFF
      DO &GETTER
      CLEA GETS
      DO EDITMENU
      ERAS TANK.DBF
   CASE ANSWER = 'T'
*
      IF DBFILE <> "order database"
         @ 0,0 SAY "That isn't one of the options. Try again"
         DO POOL
         LOOP
      ELSE
         DO TRACK
      ENDI
*
   OTHE
      @ 0,0 SAY "That isn't one of the options. Try again"
      DO POOL
ENDC
*
ENDD
*
** END OF EDIT.PRG
```

The EDITMENU routine for this code is:

Listing A-4

```
PROC EDITMENU
@ 20,0 ,23,79 BOX FRAME
@ 21,1 SAY;
[  E -> Edit  B -> Back  S -> Skip  G -> Goto  K -> Kill  R -> Rstr  Q - > Quit]
```

Listing A–4 (cont.)

```
@ 22,1 SAY;
[  F -> Find  L -> Loca  C -> Cont  D -> Disp  O -> Copy  A -  > Add              ]
*
IF DBFILE = "order database"
   @ 22,69 SAY "T -> TRCK"
ENDI
*
```

Note the optional 'T' argument in the listing. There is no need to give the user the option of tracking orders if the orders database isn't active.

Clipper VERSION OF SUBSCRIBER SYSTEM FROM CHAPTER 8

The following code is part of an actual subscriber system. Database names are straightforward, as are key field names and references. More information about the non-Clipper version of this code can be found in Chapter 8.

Listing A–5

```
** ACCTCHK.PRG
*
SELE 2
USE PAYMENTS INDEX PACCT, PAYMENTS
SELE 1
USE SUBS INDEX SACCT, SUBS
SET RELA TO ACCT INTO B
N = 0
THEREST = RECCOUNT()
CLEA
@ 3,0,10,30 BOX FRAME
@ 4,3 SAY [CHECKING ACCOUNT NUMBERS]
@ 5,1 SAY LEFT(SLINE,29)
@ 6,4 SAY [RECORDS LEFT    ]
@ 7,4 SAY [RECORD          ]
@ 8,4 SAY [SUBSCRIBER #    ]
CALL CURSOR2 WITH '0'
*
DO WHILE .NOT. EOF()
   N = N + 1
*
   DO CASE
      CASE LEN(TRIM(ACCT)) = 0
```

Listing A–5 (cont.)

```
        DELE
        @ 8,21 SAY [DELETED]
        SKIP
        LOOP
     CASE DELETED()
        SKIP
        LOOP
     OTHE
        @ 6,21 SAY STR(THEREST - N, 6, 0)
        @ 7,21 SAY STR(RECNO(), 6, 0)
        @ 8,21 SAY ACCT
        AREC = RECNO()
*
        IF ACCT = B->ACCT
           SKIP
           LOOP
        ELSE
           @ 16,10,21,50 BOX FRAME
           @ 18,15 SAY [LNAME      ] + A->LNAME
           @ 19,15 SAY [ADDRESS    ] + A->ADDRESS
           @ 3,40,14,79 BOX FRAME
           @ 7,45 SAY [SUBSCRIBER NOT IN PAYMENTS FILE]
           @ 10,44 SAY [CHECKING BY ACCOUNT AND LAST NAME]
           THISONE = RECNO()
           SELE 2
           SET INDE TO PAYMENTS,PACCT
           SELE 1
           SET INDE TO SUBS,SACCT
           SET RELA TO LEFT(ACCT,2) + LNAME + FNAME INTO B
           GOTO THISONE
*
           IF ACCT # B->ACCT .AND. LNAME # B->LNAME .AND. FNAME # B->FNAME
              CALL CURSOR2 WITH 'B'
              @ 4,43 SAY [NO PAYMENT RECORD FOR SUBSCRIBER ]
              @ 5,41 SAY LEFT(SLINE,38)
              @ 6,41,13,78 BOX "          "
              @ 7,45 SAY [E -> Edit This Record]
              @ 8,45 SAY [A -> Add This to Payments]
              @ 9,45 SAY [P -> Print This Record]
              @ 10,45 SAY [D -> Delete This Record]
              @ 11,45 SAY [C -> Continue Checking]
              @ 12,45 SAY [Q -> Quit to Subscriber Menu]
              @ 14,51 SAY [ select -> ]
*
              DO WHILE .T.
```

Listing A-5 (cont.)

```
          SELE 1
          @ 2,31 SAY IIF(DELETED(), [SUBSCRIBER DELETED], SPACE(20))
          SELE 2
          SELECTNUM = 'Q'
          @ 14,60 GET SELECTNUM PICT '!'
          READ
*
          DO CASE
             CASE .NOT. SELECTNUM $ [EAPDCQ]
                @ 23,0 CLEA
                @ 23,0 SAY [GOOD CHOICE, BUT NOT ONE I CAN USE]
                CALL DELAY WITH CHR(1)
                @ 23,0 CLEA
                LOOP
             CASE SELECTNUM = 'Q'
                CALL CURSOR2 WITH 'N'
                CLOSE DATA
                RETURN
             CASE SELECTNUM = 'C'
                @ 2,31 SAY SPACE(20)
                CALL CURSOR2 WITH 'O'
                @ 3,40,14,79 BOX "          "
                @ 16,10,21,50 BOX "          "
                SELE 2
                SET INDE TO PACCT,PAYMENTS
                SELE 1
                SET INDE TO SACCT,SUBS
                SET RELA TO ACCT INTO B
                GOTO THISONE
                EXIT
             CASE SELECTNUM = 'A'
                CLEA
                APPE BLANK
                REPL ACCT WITH A->ACCT, LNAME WITH A->LNAME,;
                     FNAME WITH A->FNAME
                DO PAYSAY
                @ 22,0 SAY [PRESS CTRL-W TO CONTINUE]
                DO PAYGET2
                READ
                @ 4,43 SAY [NEW PAYMENT RECORD FOR SUBSCRIBER]
                CLEA
             CASE SELECTNUM = 'E'
                CLEA
                SELE 1
                DO SUBSAY
```

Listing A–5 (cont.)

```
                    @ 22,0 SAY [PRESS CTRL-W TO CONTINUE]
                    DO SUBGET
                    READ
                    SELE 2
                    CLEA
                 CASE SELECTNUM = 'P'
                    SET DEVIC TO PRIN
                    DO PRINTSUB
                    SET DEVI TO SCREEN
                 CASE SELECTNUM = 'D'
                    SELE 1
                    DELE
                    SELE 2
              ENDC
*
              IF SELECTNUM $ [AE]
                 @ 3,0,10,30 BOX FRAME
                 @ 4,3 SAY [CHECKING ACCOUNT NUMBERS]
                 @ 5,1 SAY LEFT(SLINE,29)
                 @ 6,4 SAY [RECORDS LEFT    ]
                 @ 7,4 SAY [RECORD          ]
                 @ 8,4 SAY [SUBSCRIBER #    ]
                 @ 6,21 SAY STR(THEREST - N, 6, 0)
                 @ 7,21 SAY STR(AREC,6,0)
                 @ 8,21 SAY A->ACCT
                 @ 16,10,21,50 BOX FRAME
                 @ 18,15 SAY [LNAME      ] + A->LNAME
                 @ 19,15 SAY [ADDRESS    ] + A->ADDRESS
                 @ 3,40,14,79 BOX FRAME
                 @ 4,43 SAY IIF(SELECTNUM = 'A',[NEW],[NO]) +;
                         [ PAYMENT RECORD FOR SUBSCRIBER]
                 @ 5,41 SAY LEFT(SLINE,38)
                 @ 6,41,13,78 BOX "         "
                 @ 7,45 SAY [E -> Edit This Record]
                 @ 8,45 SAY [A -> Add This to Payments]
                 @ 9,45 SAY [P -> Print This Record]
                 @ 10,45 SAY [D -> Delete This Record]
                 @ 11,45 SAY [C -> Continue Checking]
                 @ 12,45 SAY [Q -> Quit to Subscriber Menu]
                 @ 14,51 SAY [ select -> ]
           ENDI
*
           ENDD
*
        ELSE
```

Listing A-5 (cont.)

```
CALL CURSOR2 WITH 'B'
CLEA
@ 5,0,14,38 BOX FRAME
@ 5,40,14,78 BOX FRAME
@ 2,3 SAY [THE SUBSCRIBER ACCOUNT NUMBER DOESN'T MATCH THE ] +;
          [PAYMENT ACCOUNT NUMBER]
@ 4,6 SAY [SUBSCRIBER INFORMATION]
@ 4,48 SAY [PAYMENT INFORMATION]
@ 6,2 SAY [ACCT        ] + SUBS->ACCT
@ 6,42 SAY [ACCT        ] + PAYMENTS->ACCT
@ 7,2 SAY [LNAME       ] + SUBS->LNAME
@ 7,42 SAY [LNAME       ] + PAYMENTS->LNAME
@ 8,2 SAY [FNAME       ] + SUBS->FNAME
@ 8,42 SAY [FNAME       ] + PAYMENTS->FNAME
@ 9,2 SAY [ADDRESS     ] + SUBS->ADDRESS
@ 10,2 SAY [CITY        ] + SUBS->CITY
@ 10,42 SAY [DISC        ] + IIF(PAYMENTS->DISC,'Y','N')
@ 11,2 SAY [STATE       ] + SUBS->STATE
@ 12,2 SAY [ZIP         ] + SUBS->ZIP
@ 13,2 SAY [HOOKED_UP   ] + DTOC(SUBS->HOOKED_UP)
@ 13,42 SAY [FIRST_PAY   ] + DTOC(PAYMENTS->FIRST_PAY)
@ 16,1,23,72 BOX FRAME
@ 18,10 SAY [L -> REPLACE PAYMENT ACCOUNT WITH SUBSCRIBER ACCOUNT]
@ 19,10 SAY [R -> REPLACE SUBSCRIBER ACCOUNT WITH PAYMENT ACCOUNT]
@ 20,10 SAY [D -> DELETE BOTH RECORDS]
@ 21,10 SAY [Q -> QUIT ]
SELECTNUM = 'Q'
*
DO WHIL .T.
   IIF .NOT. SELECTNUM $ [LRDQ]
   @ 23,28 SAY [TRY AGAIN] CALL DELAY WITH CHR(1)
   ENDI
   *
   @ 23,28 SAY [ select ]
   @ 23,37 GET SELECTNUM PICT '!'
   READ
*
   DO CASE
      CASE SELECTNUM = 'Q'
         CLEA
         @ 3,0,10,30 BOX FRAME
         @ 4,3 SAY [CHECKING ACCOUNT NUMBERS]
         @ 5,1 SAY LEFT(SLINE,29)
         @ 6,4 SAY [RECORDS LEFT    ]
         @ 7,4 SAY [RECORD          ]
```

Listing A-5 (cont.)

```
                    @ 8,4 SAY [SUBSCRIBER #    ]
                    CALL CURSOR2 WITH 'O'
                    SELE 2
                    SET INDE TO PACCT,PAYMENTS
                    SELE 1
                    SET INDE TO SACCT,SUBS
                    SET RELA TO ACCT INTO B
                    GOTO THISONE
                    CALL CURSOR2 WITH 'O'
                    EXIT
                 CASE SELECTNUM = 'L'
                    SELE 2
                    REPL ACCT WITH A->ACCT
                    @ 5,0 SAY [ ]
*
                    DO WHIL ROW() < 13
                       @ ROW() + 1,39 SAY [ ]
                    ENDD
*
                    @ 6,53 SAY ACCT
                 CASE SELECTNUM = 'R'
                    SELE 1
                    REPL ACCT WITH B->ACCT
                    @ 5,0 SAY [ ]
*
                    DO WHIL ROW() < 13
                       @ ROW() + 1,39 SAY [ ]
                    ENDD
*
                    @ 6,12 SAY ACCT
                 CASE SELECTNUM = 'D'
                    SELE 1
                    DELE
                    SELE 2
                    DELE
                    @ 15,27 SAY [BOTH RECORDS DELETED]
              ENDC
*
           ENDD
*
        ENDI
*
        SELE 1
        SKIP
     ENDI
```

Listing A–5 (cont.)

```
*
   ENDC
*
ENDD
*
CLOSE DATA
CALL CURSOR2 WITH 'N'
*
** END OF ACCTCHK.PRG
```

Listing A–6

```
* PROCEDURE FILE FOR DBPC *
PROC EDITMENU
@ 20,0 ,23,79 BOX FRAME
@ 21,1 SAY;
[  E -> Edit  B -> Back  S -> Skip  G -> Goto  K -> Kill  R -> Rstr  Q - > Quit]
@ 22,1 SAY;
[  F -> Find  L -> Loca  C -> Cont  D -> Disp  O -> Copy  A -> Add  U - > Upda]
*
PROC SUBSAY
@  1,0,19,79 BOX FRAME
@  3,1 SAY DLINE
@ 13,1 SAY SLINE
@  2, 32  SAY "SUBSCRIBERS"
@  5,  2  SAY "ACCT"
@  5, 17  SAY "LNAME"
@  5, 41  SAY "FNAME"
@  7,  2  SAY "ADDRESS"
@  7, 38  SAY "ADDRESS1"
@  9,  2  SAY "BLDG"
@  9, 11  SAY "APT"
@  9, 19  SAY "LOT"
@  9, 28  SAY "CITY"
@  9, 50  SAY "STATE"
@  9, 60  SAY "ZIP"
@ 11,  2  SAY "HTEL"
@ 11, 21  SAY "WTEL"
@ 13, 35  SAY "SERVICES"
@ 15,  7  SAY "TIER1"
@ 15, 18  SAY "TIER2"
@ 15, 29  SAY "TIER3"
@ 15, 40  SAY "TIER4"
@ 15, 51  SAY "TIER5"
```

Listing A-6 (cont.)

```
@ 15, 62  SAY "TIER6"
*@ 16,  7  SAY "TIER7"
*@ 16, 18  SAY "TIER8"
*@ 16, 29  SAY "TIER9"
*@ 16, 40  SAY "TIER10"
*@ 16, 51  SAY "TIER11"
*@ 16, 62  SAY "TIER12"
@ 18,  7  SAY "RATE"
@ 18, 26  SAY "CONVERTER"
@ 18, 51  SAY "HOOKED_UP"
*
PROC SUBGET
@ 2,73 SAY STR(RECNO(),5,0)
@  5,  7  GET  ACCT PICT '!!-!!!!'
@  5, 24  GET  LNAME
@  5, 48  GET  FNAME
@  7, 10  GET  ADDRESS
@  7, 47  GET  ADDRESS1  PICTURE "XXXXXXXXXXXXXXXXXXXXXXXXXXXXXX"
@  9,  7  GET  BLDG
@  9, 15  GET  APT
@  9, 23  GET  LOT
@  9, 33  GET  CITY
@  9, 56  GET  STATE
@  9, 64  GET  ZIP
@ 11,  7  GET  HTEL  PICTURE "999-999-9999"
@ 11, 27  GET  WTEL  PICTURE "999-999-9999"
@ 15, 13  GET  TIER1
@ 15, 24  GET  TIER2
@ 15, 35  GET  TIER3
@ 15, 47  GET  TIER4
@ 15, 58  GET  TIER5
@ 15, 69  GET  TIER6
*@ 16, 13  GET  TIER7
*@ 16, 24  GET  TIER8
*@ 16, 35  GET  TIER9
*@ 16, 47  GET  TIER10
*@ 16, 58  GET  TIER11
*@ 16, 69  GET  TIER12
@ 18, 15  GET  RATE  PICTURE "999.99"
@ 18, 38  GET  CONVERTER
@ 18, 62  GET  HOOKED_UP
*
PROC SUBGETNA
@  5, 24  GET  LNAME
@  5, 48  GET  FNAME
```

Listing A–6 (cont.)

```
@  7, 10  GET  ADDRESS
@  7, 47  GET  ADDRESS1  PICTURE "XXXXXXXXXXXXXXXXXXXXXXXXXXXXXX"
@  9,  7  GET  BLDG
@  9, 15  GET  APT
@  9, 23  GET  LOT
@  9, 33  GET  CITY
@  9, 56  GET  STATE
@  9, 64  GET  ZIP
@ 11,  7  GET  HTEL  PICTURE "999-999-9999"
@ 11, 27  GET  WTEL  PICTURE "999-999-9999"
@ 15, 13  GET  TIER1
@ 15, 24  GET  TIER2
@ 15, 35  GET  TIER3
@ 15, 47  GET  TIER4
@ 15, 58  GET  TIER5
@ 15, 69  GET  TIER6
*@ 16, 13  GET  TIER7
*@ 16, 24  GET  TIER8
*@ 16, 35  GET  TIER9
*@ 16, 47  GET  TIER10
*@ 16, 58  GET  TIER11
*@ 16, 69  GET  TIER12
@ 18, 15  GET  RATE  PICTURE "999.99"
@ 18, 38  GET  CONVERTER
@ 18, 62  GET  HOOKED_UP
*
PROC PAYSAY
@  1,0,19,79 BOX FRAME
@  3,1 SAY DLINE
@  2, 34  SAY "PAYMENTS                            #"
@  4,  2  SAY "ACCT"
@  4, 21  SAY "LNAME"
@  4, 45  SAY "FNAME"
@  5,  2  SAY "DISC"
@  5, 21  SAY "FIRST_PAY"
@  6,  2  SAY "JAN"
@  6, 21  SAY "CK1"
@  6, 41  SAY "N1"
@  7,  2  SAY "FEB"
@  7, 21  SAY "CK2"
@  7, 41  SAY "N2"
@  8,  2  SAY "MAR"
@  8, 21  SAY "CK3"
@  8, 41  SAY "N3"
@  9,  2  SAY "APR"
```

Listing A–6 (cont.)

```
@  9, 21  SAY "CK4"
@  9, 41  SAY "N4"
@ 10,  2  SAY "MAY"
@ 10, 21  SAY "CK5"
@ 10, 41  SAY "N5"
@ 11,  2  SAY "JUN"
@ 11, 21  SAY "CK6"
@ 11, 41  SAY "N6"
@ 12,  2  SAY "JUL"
@ 12, 21  SAY "CK7"
@ 12, 41  SAY "N7"
@ 13,  2  SAY "AUG"
@ 13, 21  SAY "CK8"
@ 13, 41  SAY "N8"
@ 14,  2  SAY "SEP"
@ 14, 21  SAY "CK9"
@ 14, 41  SAY "N9"
@ 15,  2  SAY "OCT"
@ 15, 21  SAY "CK10"
@ 15, 41  SAY "N10"
@ 16,  2  SAY "NOV"
@ 16, 21  SAY "CK11"
@ 16, 41  SAY "N11"
@ 17,  2  SAY "DEC"
@ 17, 21  SAY "CK12"
@ 17, 41  SAY "N12"
@ 18,  2  SAY "NEW"
@ 18, 21  SAY "CKNEW"
@ 18, 41  SAY "INFO"
*
PROC PAYGET
@ 2,73 SAY STR(RECNO(),5,0)
@  4,  8  GET  ACCT PICT '!!-!!!!'
@  4, 28  GET  LNAME
@  4, 52  GET  FNAME
@  5,  8  GET  DISC
@  5, 35  GET  FIRST_PAY
@  6,  8  GET  JAN
@  6, 27  GET  CK1
@  6, 46  GET  N1
@  7,  8  GET  FEB
@ 7,27 GET CK2
@  7, 46  GET  N2
@  8,  8  GET  MAR
@  8, 27  GET  CK3
```

Listing A-6 (cont.)

```
@  8, 46  GET  N3
@  9,  8  GET  APR
@  9, 27  GET  CK4
@  9, 46  GET  N4
@ 10,  8  GET  MAY
@ 10, 27  GET  CK5
@ 10, 46  GET  N5
@ 11,  8  GET  JUN
@ 11, 27  GET  CK6
@ 11, 46  GET  N6
@ 12,  8  GET  JUL
@ 12, 27  GET  CK7
@ 12, 46  GET  N7
@ 13,  8  GET  AUG
@ 13, 27  GET  CK8
@ 13, 46  GET  N8
@ 14,  8  GET  SEP
@ 14, 27  GET  CK9
@ 14, 46  GET  N9
@ 15,  8  GET  OCT
@ 15, 27  GET  CK10
@ 15, 46  GET  N10
@ 16,  8  GET  NOV
@ 16, 27  GET  CK11
@ 16, 46  GET  N11
@ 17,  8  GET  DEC
@ 17, 27  GET  CK12
@ 17, 46  GET  N12
@ 18,  8  GET  NEW
@ 18, 27  GET  CKNEW
@ 18,46 GET INFO
*
PROC PAYGET2
@ 2,73 SAY STR(RECNO(),5,0)
@  4,  8  SAY  ACCT PICT '!!-!!!!'
@  4, 28  SAY  LNAME
@  4, 52  SAY  FNAME
@  5,  8  GET  DISC
@  5, 35  GET  FIRST_PAY
@  6,  8  GET  JAN
@  6, 27  GET  CK1
@  6, 46  GET  N1
@  7,  8  GET  FEB
@ 7,27 GET CK2
@  7, 46  GET  N2
```

Listing A–6 (cont.)

```
@  8,  8 GET  MAR
@  8, 27 GET  CK3
@  8, 46 GET  N3
@  9,  8 GET  APR
@  9, 27 GET  CK4
@  9, 46 GET  N4
@ 10,  8 GET  MAY
@ 10, 27 GET  CK5
@ 10, 46 GET  N5
@ 11,  8 GET  JUN
@ 11, 27 GET  CK6
@ 11, 46 GET  N6
@ 12,  8 GET  JUL
@ 12, 27 GET  CK7
@ 12, 46 GET  N7
@ 13,  8 GET  AUG
@ 13, 27 GET  CK8
@ 13, 46 GET  N8
@ 14,  8 GET  SEP
@ 14, 27 GET  CK9
@ 14, 46 GET  N9
@ 15,  8 GET  OCT
@ 15, 27 GET  CK10
@ 15, 46 GET  N10
@ 16,  8 GET  NOV
@ 16, 27 GET  CK11
@ 16, 46 GET  N11
@ 17,  8 GET  DEC
@ 17, 27 GET  CK12
@ 17, 46 GET  N12
@ 18,  8 GET  NEW
@ 18, 27 GET CKNEW
@ 18, 46 GET  INFO
*
** EOF
```

Listing A–7

```
** DBPCFUNCTIONS
*
FUNCTION LEFT
PARAMETERS cl_string, cl_len
RETURN SUBSTR(cl_string, 1, cl_len)
*
FUNCTION RIGHT
PARAMETERS cl_string, cl_len
```

Listing A–7 (cont.)

```
RETURN SUBSTR(cl_string, LEN(cl_string)-cl_len+1)
*
** EOF
```

Listing A–8

```
* EDIT.PRG
* CALLS EDITMENU
*
DO &FRAMER
DO &GETTER
CLEA GETS
DO EDITMENU
ANSWER = 'X'
DELS = .F.
*
DO WHIL .T.
   @ 0,0 SAY SPACE(80)
   @ 24,0 SAY SPACE(80)
   DELEMESS = IIF(DELETED(),"DELETED",SPACE(7))
   @  2,60 SAY "&DELEMESS"
   @ 23,34 SAY " select "
   @ 23,43 GET ANSWER PICT '!'
   READ
*
   DO CASE
      CASE ANSWER = 'Q'
*
         IF DELS
            @ 20,0 CLEA
            @ 21,0 SAY [SOME RECORDS HAVE BEEN DELETED FROM THIS FILE.]
            @ 23,0 SAY [DO YOU WISH TO REMOVE THEM PERMANENTLY (Y/N)? ] GET DELS
            READ
*
            DO CASE
               CASE DELS .AND. [PAY]$DBFILE
                  @ 21,0 CLEA
                  @ 21,0 SAY [DO YOU WISH TO DELETE CORRESPONDING]+;
                             [DATA IN THE SUBSCRIPTION FILE (Y/N)? ] GET DELS
                  READ
*
                  IF DELS
                     SELE 1
                     SET RELA TO ACCT INTO B
                     LOCA FOR DELETED()
*
```

Listing A-8 (cont.)

```
                    DO WHIL .NOT. EOF()
                       SELE 2
                       DELE
                       SELE 1
                       CONT
                    ENDD
*
                    SELE 2
                    PACK
                 ENDI
*
                 SELE 1
                 PACK
              CASE DELS
                 PACK
        ENDC
*
     ENDI
*
     RETU
  CASE ANSWER = 'K'
     DELE
     DELS = .T.
     LOOP
  CASE ANSWER = 'R'
     RECA
     LOOP
  CASE ANSWER = 'S'
     SKIP
     DO &GETTER
     CLEA GETS
     LOOP
  CASE ANSWER = 'B'
     SKIP -1
     DO &GETTER
     CLEA GETS
     LOOP
  CASE ANSWER = 'E'
     @ 20,0 CLEA
     @ 22,0 SAY "Press CTRL-W to save edit, ESC to exit"
     DO &GETTER
     READ
     DO EDITMENU
     LOOP
  CASE ANSWER = 'O'
```

Listing A–8 (cont.)

```
         COPY NEXT 1 TO TANK
         APPE FROM TANK
         DO &GETTER
         CLEA GETS
         LOOP
      CASE ANSWER = 'C'
         CONT
         DO &GETTER
         CLEA GETS
         LOOP
      CASE ANSWER = 'G'
         ACCE "Record Number -> " TO RECNUM
         GOTO VAL(RECNUM)
         DO &GETTER
         CLEA GETS
         @ 24,0 SAY SPACE(40)
         LOOP
      CASE ANSWER = 'D'
         STORE SPACE(10) TO W1,W2,W3,W4,W5
         @ 20,0 CLEA
         @ 21,0 SAY "Display What -> "
         @ 21,18 GET W1
         @ 21,30 GET W2
         @ 21,42 GET W3
         @ 21,54 GET W4
         @ 21,66 GET W5
         READ
*
         IF LEN(TRIM(W1)) = 0
            @ 20,0 CLEA
            DO EDITMENU
            LOOP
         ENDI
*
         DISPLAYFOR = SPACE(60)
         TRUTH = .T.
         @ 21,0 CLEA
         @ 21,0 SAY "DISP FOR -> " GET DISPLAYFOR
         READ
*
         IF LEN(TRIM(DISPLAYFOR)) # 0
            SET FILT TO &DISPLAYFOR
         ENDI
*
         @ 21,0 CLEA
```

Listing A–8 (cont.)

```
        @ 21,0 SAY [DO YOU WANT THIS PRINTED (Y/N)? ] GET TRUTH
        READ
*
        IF TRUTH
           SET CONS OFF
           SET PRIN ON
           EJECT
           PUCK = SPACE(10)
           MOST = 54
        ELSE
           CLEA
           PUCK = [] && used to keep print off perfory
           MOST = 23
        ENDI
*
        N = 1
        GOTO TOP
*
        DO WHIL .NOT. EOF()
*
           DO CASE
              CASE LEN(TRIM(W5)) # 0
                 ? PUCK,RECNO(),&W1,&W2,&W3,&W4,&W5
              CASE LEN(TRIM(W4)) # 0
                 ? PUCK,RECNO(),&W1,&W2,&W3,&W4
              CASE LEN(TRIM(W3)) # 0
                 ? PUCK,RECNO(),&W1,&W2,&W3
              CASE LEN(TRIM(W2)) # 0
                 ? PUCK,RECNO(),&W1,&W2
              OTHE
                 ? PUCK,RECNO(),&W1
           ENDC
*
           N = N + 1
*
           DO CASE
              CASE N = MOST .AND. TRUTH
                 EJECT
                 N = 1
              CASE N = MOST .AND. .NOT. TRUTH
                 WAIT
                 CLEA
                 N = 1
           ENDC
*
```

Listing A–8 (cont.)

```
            SKIP
         ENDD
*
         IF TRUTH
            SET PRIN OFF
            SET CONS ON
            EJECT
         ELSE
            CLEA
            DO &FRAMER
            DO &GETTER
            CLEA GETS
         ENDI
*
         @ 21,0 CLEA
         SET FILT TO
         DO EDITMENU
         LOOP
      CASE ANSWER = 'F'
         @ 20,0 CLEAR
         ACCE "Find &KEYFIELD   " TO TOFIND
*
         IF DBFILE = [SUBS] .OR. DBFILE = [PAY]
            SEEK IIF(SUBSTR(TOFIND,2,1) = '-', ' ' + TOFIND, TOFIND)
         ELSE
            SEEK TOFIND
         ENDI
*
         IF .NOT. FOUND()
           @ 24,50 SAY "Record Number ->  END  "
           @ 0,0 SAY "I can't FIND that entry. Perhaps you should LOCATE it."
           CALL DELAY WITH CHR(1)
         ENDI
*
         DO &GETTER
         CLEA GETS
         DO EDITMENU
         LOOP
      CASE ANSWER = 'L'
         @ 20,0 CLEA
         ACCE "Locate what? -> " TO LOCATEWHAT
         ACCE "Locate where? -> " TO LOCATEWHERE
*
         IF LEN(TRIM(LOCATEWHAT)) # 0 .AND. LEN(TRIM(LOCATEWHERE)) # 0
            LOCA ALL FOR "&LOCATEWHAT"$&LOCATEWHERE
```

Listing A–8 (cont.)

```
         ENDI
*
         DO &GETTER
         CLEA GETS
         DO EDITMENU
         LOOP
      CASE ANSWER = 'A'
         COPY STRUC TO TANK
         SELE 6
         USE TANK
         @ 20,0 CLEA
         @ 22,0 SAY "Press CTRL-W to save information, ESC to exit"
*
         IF [SUBS]$DBFILE
            SELE 2
            USE PAYMENTS INDE PACCT,PAYMENTS
            COPY STRUC TO TANK2
            SELE 7
            USE TANK2
            TRUTH = .T.
            GETTER = [SUBGETNA]
*
            DO WHIL .T.
               SELE 6
               APPE BLAN
*
               DO WHIL .T.
                  DO SUBGET
                  CLEA GETS
                  @ 5,7 GET ACCT PICT '!!-!!!!'
                  READ
*
                  IF LEN(TRIM(ACCT)) = 0
                     EXIT
                  ENDI
*
                  SELE 1
                  SEEK IIF(SUBSTR(F->ACCT,2,1) = '-',' ' + F->ACCT, F->ACCT)
*
                  IF FOUND()
                     DO SUBGET
                     CLEA GETS
                     @ 20,0 CLEA
                     @ 20,0 SAY [SORRY, WE'VE ALREADY GOT ONE OF THOSE.]
                     CALL DELAY WITH CHR(1)
```

Listing A–8 (cont.)

```
                 @ 20,0 CLEA
                 @ 22,0 SAY "Press CTRL-W to save information, ESC to exit"
              ELSE
                 SELE F
                 EXIT
              ENDI
*
              SELE F
           ENDD
*
           IF LEN(TRIM(ACCT)) = 0
              DELE
              EXIT
           ENDI
*
           DO &GETTER
           READ
           @ 20,0 CLEA
           @ 22,0 SAY [ADD A NEW PAYMENT RECORD (Y/N)? ] GET TRUTH
           READ
*
           IF TRUTH
              SELE 7
              CLEA
              APPE BLANK
              REPL ACCT WITH F->ACCT,LNAME WITH F->LNAME,FNAME WITH F->FNAME
              DO PAYSAY
              DO PAYGET2
              @ 20,0 CLEA
              @ 22,0 SAY [Press CTRL-W to save information, ESC to exit]
              READ
              SELE 6
              CLEA
              DO SUBSAY
           ENDI
*
     @ 20,0 CLEA
           @ 22,0 SAY [Press CTRL-W to save information, ESC to exit]
        ENDD
*
        SELE 7
        USE
        SELE 6
        USE
        SELE 2
```

Listing A–8 (cont.)

```
          APPE FROM TANK2
          ERAS TANK2.DBF
          GETTER = [SUBGET]
       ELSE * DBFILE # SUBSCRIPTIONS
          REPEATER = FIELD(1)
*
          DO WHIL .T.
             APPE BLANK
             DO &GETTER
             READ
*
             IF LEN(TRIM(&REPEATER)) = 0
                DELE
                EXIT
             ENDI
*
          ENDD
*
       ENDI
*
       USE
       SELE 6
       USE
       SELE 1
       SET DELE ON
       APPE FROM TANK
       SET DELE OFF
       DO &GETTER
       CLEA GETS
       DO EDITMENU
       ERAS TANK.DBF
    CASE ANSWER = 'U'
       STORE SPACE(10) TO W1,W2,W3,W4,W5,REPLACER
       @ 20,0 CLEA
       @ 21,0 SAY [REPLACE WHAT FIELD? -> ] GET REPLACER
       READ
*
       IF LEN(TRIM(REPLACER)) = 0
          @ 20,0 CLEA
          DO EDITMENU
          LOOP
       ENDI
*
       @ 22,0 SAY [REPLACE WITH -> ]
       @ 22,18 GET W1
```

Listing A–8 (cont.)

```
        @ 22,30 GET W2
        @ 22,42 GET W3
        @ 22,54 GET W4
        @ 22,66 GET W5
        READ
*
        IF LEN(TRIM(W1)) = 0
           @ 20,0 CLEA
           DO EDITMENU
           LOOP
        ENDI
*
        ACCE "CONDITION " TO CONDITION
*
        IF LEN(TRIM(CONDITION)) # 0
           LOCA FOR &CONDITION
*
           IF .NOT. FOUND()
              @ 20,0 CLEA
              @ 21,0 SAY [NO RECORDS MATCH ] + TRIM(CONDITION)
              CALL DELAY WITH CHR(1)
              @ 20,0 CLEA
              DO EDITMENU
              LOOP
           ELSE
              SET FILT TO &CONDITION
           ENDI
*
           GO TOP
 *
           DO CASE
        CASE LEN(TRIM(W5)) # 0
                 REPL ALL &REPLACER WITH TRIM(&W1) + ' ' + TRIM(&W2) + ;
                    ' ' + TRIM(&W3) + ' ' + TRIM(&W4) + ' ' + TRIM(&W5)
              CASE LEN(TRIM(W4)) # 0
                 REPL ALL &REPLACER WITH TRIM(&W1) + ' ' + TRIM(&W2) + ;
                    ' ' + TRIM(&W3) + ' ' + TRIM(&W4)
              CASE LEN(TRIM(W3)) # 0
                 REPL ALL &REPLACER WITH TRIM(&W1) + ' ' + TRIM(&W2) + ;
                    ' ' + TRIM(&W3)
              CASE LEN(TRIM(W2)) # 0
                 REPL ALL &REPLACER WITH TRIM(&W1) + ' ' + TRIM(&W2)
              OTHE
                 REPL ALL &REPLACER WITH TRIM(&W1)
           ENDC
```

Listing A-8 (cont.)

```
*
         ENDI
*
         @ 20,0 CLEA
         DO EDITMENU
*
   ENDC
*
ENDD
*
** END OF EDIT.PRG
```

Listing A-9

```
** INDEXER.PRG FOR DBPC
*
CLEA
@ 1,0,15,79 BOX FRAME
@ 2,25 SAY [SELECT A DATABASE TO REINDEX]
@ 3,1 SAY SLINE
@ 5,30 SAY [S -> SUBSCRIBERS FILE]
@ 6,30 SAY [P -> PAYMENTS FILE]
*         @ 7,30 SAY [ ]
*         @ 8,30 SAY [ ]
*         @ 9,30 SAY [ ]
*         @ 10,30 SAY [ ]
*         @ 11,30 SAY [ ]
@ 12,30 SAY [A -> ALL]
@ 13,30 SAY [Q -> QUIT]
@ 15,34 SAY [ select ]
*
DO WHIL .T.
   SELECTNUM = 'Q'
   @ 15,43 GET SELECTNUM PICT "!"
   @ 21,0 CLEA
   READ
*
   DO CASE
      CASE SELECTNUM = 'Q'
         EXIT
      CASE SELECTNUM = 'P'
         @ 21,0 SAY [USE PAYMENTS FILE: TWO INDEX FILES]
         USE PAYMENTS
         @ 22,0 SAY [REBUILDING FIRST INDEX FILE]
         INDEX ON ACCT TO PACCT
         @ 23,0 SAY [REBUILDING SECOND INDEX FILE]
```

Listing A-9 (cont.)

```
         INDEX ON LEFT(ACCT,2)+LNAME+FNAME TO PAYMENTS
      CASE SELECTNUM = 'S'
         @ 21,0 SAY [USE SUBSCRIBER FILE: TWO INDEX FILES]
         USE SUBS
         @ 22,0 SAY [REBUILDING FIRST INDEX FILE]
         INDEX ON ACCT TO SACCT
         @ 23,0 SAY [REBUILDING SECOND INDEX FILE]
         INDEX ON LEFT(ACCT,2)+LNAME+FNAME TO SUBS
      CASE SELECTNUM = 'A'
         @ 21,0 SAY [USE PAYMENTS FILE: TWO INDEX FILES]
         USE PAYMENTS
         @ 22,0 SAY [REBUILDING FIRST INDEX FILE]
         INDEX ON ACCT TO PACCT
         @ 23,0 SAY [REBUILDING SECOND INDEX FILE]
         INDEX ON LEFT(ACCT,2)+LNAME+FNAME TO PAYMENTS
         @ 21,0 CLEA
         @ 21,0 SAY [USE SUBSCRIBER FILE: TWO INDEX FILES]
         USE SUBS
         @ 22,0 SAY [REBUILDING FIRST INDEX FILE]
         INDEX ON ACCT TO SACCT
         @ 23,0 SAY [REBUILDING SECOND INDEX FILE]
         INDEX ON LEFT(ACCT,2)+LNAME+FNAME TO SUBS
   ENDCASE
*
ENDD
*
** END OF INDEXER.PRG
```

Listing A-10

```
*FILENAME=LABELS
*
USE subscribers database INDEX built index field NDX file
CONDITION = SPACE(65)
YESCON = .F.
FILENAME = [standard label form]
*
DO WHIL .T.
   SELECTNUM = 'Q'
   CLEAR
   @  5, 24  SAY "S -> Select Label Form"
   @  6, 24  SAY "C -> Create Condition"
   @  7, 24  SAY "P -> Print Labels"
   @ 11, 24  SAY "Q -> Quit"
   @  1,0,15,79 BOX FRAME
   @  3,1 SAY DLINE
```

Listing A–10 (cont.)

```
   @ 2,3 SAY [CURRNET LABEL -> ] + FILENAME
   @ 2,33 SAY [LABEL GENERATOR]
   @ 2,55 SAY IIF(YESCON,[CONDITION EXISTS],SPACE(16))
   @ 15, 31 SAY [ select ]
   @ 15,40 GET SELECTNUM PICT '!'
   READ
*
   DO CASE
      CASE .NOT. ANSWER $ [SCPQ]
         @ 22,0 SAY [GOOD CHOICE, BUT NOT ONE I CAN USE]
         CALL DELAY WITH CHR(1)
         @ 22,0 CLEA
         LOOP
      CASE ANSWER = 'Q'
         CLOS DATA
         RETU
      CASE ANSWER = 'S'
         CLEA
         DIR *.LBL
         @ 22,0 SAY [Which letter do you want to use (8 CHAR MAX)? -> ];
                    GET FILENAME PICT "XXXXXXXX"
         READ
*
         IF .NOT. FILE('&FILENAME')
            WAIT [THAT FILE DOESN'T EXIST. PRESS ANY KEY TO CONTINUE...]
            CLEA
            LOOP
         ENDI
*
      CASE SELECTNUM = 'C'
*
         IF YESCON
            SET FILT TO
            CONDITION = SPACE(65)
            YESCON = .F.
         ELSE
            YESCON = .T.
            USE SUBS INDEX SUBS
            CLEA
            DO SUBSAY
            DO SUBGET
            CLEA GETS
            @ 23,0 SAY [CONDITION -> ] GET CONDITION
            READ
            SET FILT TO &CONDITION
```

Listing A–10 (cont.)

```
         ENDI
*
         LOOP
      CASE SELECTNUM = 'P'
         TRUTH = .T.
         @ 24,0 SAY [DO YOU WANT TO START WITH SAMPLES? (Y/N) ] GET TRUTH
         READ
         CLEA
         SAMPLES = IIF(TRUTH, [SAMP], [])
         CLEA
         SET CONS OFF
         LABEL FORM &FILENAME &SAMPLES TO PRINT
         SET CONS ON
   ENDCASE
*
ENDD
*
** EOF
```

Listing A–11

```
** LETTER.PRG
*
CLEA
SET RELATION TO ACCT INTO B
ACCEPT [WHAT MONTH ARE WE SENDING NOTICES FOR (3 CHAR MAX)? -> ]
TO MONTH
SET FILTER TO &MONTH = 0.00
SET DEVI TO PRINT
*
DO WHILE .NOT. EOF()
   @ 8,50 SAY [company name]
   @ 9,50 SAY [address]
   @ 10,50 SAY [city, state, zip]
   @ 11,50 SAY [phone number]
   @ 12,50 SAY STR(DAY(DATE()),2,0) + ', ' + CMONTH(DATE()) +;
' ' + STR(YEAR(DATE()),4,0)
   @ 16,5 SAY TRIM(FNAME) + ' ' + LNAME
   @ 17,5 SAY B->ADDRESS
   @ 18,5 SAY TRIM(B->CITY) + ', ' + STATE + '     ' + ZIP
   @ 23,5 SAY [Dear Subscriber:]
   @ 26,5 SAY 'In checking our records we have not received your ' + upper(month) +;
' payment for ' + str(B->rate,5,2) + '.'
   @ 27,5 SAY 'Please remit as soon as possible so you can avoid having your service'
   @ 28,5 SAY 'disconnected.  If you have already submitted your payment, disregard'
   @ 29,5 SAY 'this letter.  If you have any questions about your billing contact our'
```

Listing A–11 (cont.)

```
   @ 30,5 SAY 'office between the hours of 9:00 to 5:00, Monday through Friday.'
   @ 33,5 SAY 'Please return the coupons from your payment book so we can properly'
   @ 34,5 SAY 'credit your account.  Thank you for your payment.'
   @ 37,50 SAY 'Best Regards,'
   @ 40,50 SAY [company name]
   SKIP
ENDDO
*
SET FILT TO
SET DEVI TO SCREEN
*
** EOF
```

Listing A–12

```
** DBPCMENU.PRG
** THIS IS THE MENU FOR WORKING WITH SUBSCRIBER AND PAYMENT RECORDS.
*
SET PROC TO DBPC
SET EXACT OFF
*
CLEA
REST FROM DBPC
SET PATH TO &CPATH
SET DEFA TO &CDRIVE
CLEA
@  1,0,20,79 BOX FRAME
@  3,1 SAY DLINE
@  2, 28  SAY "CABLE SYSTEM MAIN MENU"
@  5, 22  SAY "S -> Subscription System"
@  6, 22  SAY [P -> Payments System]
@ 9,22 SAY [U -> Utility Menu]
@ 10,22 SAY [L -> Make a Few Labels]
@ 11,22 SAY [W -> Use Word Processor]
@ 12,22 SAY [D -> Execute DOS Command]
@ 18, 22  SAY "Q -> Quit to System"
@ 20, 34  SAY " select "
*
DO WHILE .T.
   @ 21,0 CLEA
   SELECTNUM = 'Q'
   @ 20, 43 GET SELECTNUM PICT '!'
   READ
*
   IF SELECTNUM $ [SPLUWDQ]
      CALL SAVESCR WITH 'S1'
```

Listing A–12 (cont.)

```
   ELSE
      @ 22,0 SAY [GOOD SELECTNUM, BUT NOT ONE I CAN USE]
      CALL DELAY WITH CHR(1)
      @ 22,0 CLEA
      LOOP
   ENDI
*
   DO CASE
      CASE SELECTNUM = 'Q'
         SAVE TO DBPC
         QUIT
      CASE SELECTNUM = 'S'
         DO SUBSMENU
      CASE SELECTNUM = 'P'
         DO PAYMENU
      CASE SELECTNUM = 'L'
         DO LABELS
      CASE SELECTNUM = 'U'
         DO UTILMENU
      CASE SELECTNUM = 'W'
         ! &WORDPROC
      CASE SELECTNUM = 'D'
         @ 22,0
         ACCE [EXECUTE WHAT DOS COMMAND? -> ] TO DOSCOMM
         CLEA
         ! &DOSCOMM
         WAIT
  ENDC
*
  CLEA
  CALL SAVESCR WITH 'R1'
*
ENDD
*
** END OF DBPCMENU.PRG
```

Listing A–13

```
** PAYMENU.PRG
*
GETTER = "PAYGET"
FRAMER = "PAYSAY"
KEYFIELD = "ACCOUNT"
DBFILE = 'PAYMENTS'
YESCON = .F.
SELE 2
```

Listing A–13 (cont.)

```
USE SUBS INDE SACCT,SUBS
SELE 1
USE PAYMENTS INDE PACCT,PAYMENTS
*
DO WHILE .T.
   SELECTNUM = 'Q'
   CLEAR
   @  1,0,17,79 BOX FRAME
   @  3,1 SAY DLINE
   @  2, 31  SAY "PAYMENT MENU"
   @ 2,60 SAY IIF(YESCON,'CONDITION EXISTS',SPACE(17))
   @  5, 23  SAY "E -> Edit Payments"
   @  8, 23  SAY "P -> Print Payments Report"
   @ 10, 23  SAY "L -> Print Late Payments Report"
   @ 13, 23  SAY "F -> Print Late Payment Letters"
   @ 15, 23  SAY "Q -> Quit"
   @ 17, 32  SAY " select "
   @ 17,41 GET SELECTNUM PICT '!'
   READ
*
   DO CASE
      CASE .NOT. SELECTNUM $ 'EPLFQ'
         @ 22,0 CLEA
         @ 22,0 SAY [GOOD CHOICE, BUT NOT ONE I CAN USE]
         CALL DELAY WITH CHR(1)
         @ 22,0 CLEA
         LOOP
      CASE SELECTNUM = 'Q'
         CLOSE DATA
         RETU
      CASE SELECTNUM = 'E'
         CLEAR
         DO EDIT
         LOOP
      CASE SELECTNUM = 'F'
         DO LETTER
   ENDC
*
   TRUTH = .T.
   @ 20,0 SAY "DO YOU WANT A CONDITION ON THE REPORTS (Y/N)? -> "
GET TRUTH
   READ
   CLEAR
*
   IF TRUTH
```

Listing A-13 (cont.)

```
      DO PAYSAY
      DO PAYGET
      CLEA GETS
      CONDITION = SPACE(60)
      @ 23,0 SAY "CONDITION -> " GET CONDITION
      READ
   ELSE
      CONDITION = []
   ENDI
*
   IF LEN(TRIM(CONDITION)) # 0
      YESCON = .T.
      SET FILT TO &CONDITION
   ELSE
      YESCON = .F.
      SET FILT TO
   ENDI
*
   SET CONS OFF
   SET PRIN ON
   ? CHR(15)
*
   IF YESCON
*
      DO CASE
         CASE SELECTNUM = 'P'
            REPO FORM PAYRPT HEAD "&CONDITION"
         CASE SELECTNUM = 'L'
            REPO FORM PAYRPT FOR UPPE(CMONTH(DATE())) = 0 TO PRINT
      ENDC
*
   ELSE
*
      DO CASE
         CASE SELECTNUM = 'P'
            REPO FORM PAYRPT TO PRINT
         CASE SELECTNUM = 'L'
         REPO FORM PAYRPT FOR UPPE(CMONTH(DATE())) = 0 TO PRINT
      ENDC
*
   ENDI
*
   ? CHR(18)
   SET PRIN OFF
   SET CONS ON
```

Listing A–13 (cont.)

```
ENDD
*
** END OF PAYMENU.PRG
```

Listing A–14

```
* PRINTSUB
*
@  2, 32  SAY "SUBSCRIBERS"
@  2, 50 SAY IIF(DELETED(),[DELETED],[])
@ 2,65 SAY STR(RECNO(),6)
@  5,  2  SAY "ACCT"
@  5,  7  SAY  SUBS->ACCT
@  5, 17  SAY "LNAME"
@  5, 24  SAY  SUBS->LNAME
@  5, 41  SAY "FNAME"
@  5, 48  SAY  SUBS->FNAME
@  7,  2  SAY "ADDRESS"
@  7, 10  SAY  SUBS->ADDRESS
@  7, 38  SAY "ADDRESS1"
@  7, 47  SAY  SUBS->ADDRESS1
@  9,  2  SAY "BLDG"
@  9,  7  SAY  SUBS->BLDG
@  9, 11  SAY "APT"
@  9, 15  SAY  SUBS->APT
@  9, 19  SAY "LOT"
@  9, 23  SAY  SUBS->LOT
@  9, 28  SAY "CITY"
@  9, 33  SAY  SUBS->CITY
@  9, 50  SAY "STATE"
@  9, 56  SAY  SUBS->STATE
@  9, 60  SAY "ZIP"
@  9, 64  SAY  SUBS->ZIP
@ 11,  2  SAY "HTEL"
@ 11,  7  SAY  SUBS->HTEL
@ 11, 21  SAY "WTEL"
@ 11, 27  SAY  SUBS->WTEL
@ 13, 32  SAY "SERVICES"
@ 15,  7  SAY "TIER1"
@ 15, 13  SAY  SUBS->TIER1
@ 15, 18  SAY "TIER2"
@ 15, 24  SAY  SUBS->TIER2
@ 15, 29  SAY "TIER3"
@ 15, 35  SAY  SUBS->TIER3
@ 15, 40  SAY "TIER4"
@ 15, 47  SAY  SUBS->TIER4
```

Listing A–14 (cont.)

```
@ 15, 51  SAY "TIER5"
@ 15, 58  SAY  SUBS->TIER5
@ 15, 62  SAY "TIER6"
@ 15, 69  SAY  SUBS->TIER6
@ 18,  7  SAY "RATE"
@ 18, 15  SAY  SUBS->RATE  PICTURE "999.99"
@ 18, 26  SAY "CONVERTER"
@ 18, 38  SAY  SUBS->CONVERTER
@ 18, 51  SAY "HOOKED_UP"
@ 18, 62  SAY  SUBS->HOOKED_UP
*
** EOF
```

Listing A–15

```
** REPORTER FOR DBPC
*
USE SUBS INDE SUBS,SACCT
YESCON = .F.
*
DO WHIL .T.
   CLEA
   @  1,0,15,79 BOX FRAME
   @  3,1 SAY DLINE
   @  2, 24  SAY "SUBSCRIBERS REPORT MENU"
   @  5, 24  SAY "P -> Print Reports"
   @  7, 24  SAY "C -> Create Condition"
   @  9, 24  SAY "D -> Determine Area Totals"
   @ 11, 24  SAY "Q -> Quit"
   @ 2,60 SAY IIF(YESCON,[CONDITION EXITS],SPACE(16))
   SELECTNUM = 'Q'
   @ 15,31 SAY [ select ]
   @ 15,40 GET SELECTNUM PICT '!'
   READ
*
   DO CASE
      CASE .NOT. SELECTNUM $ 'PCDQ'
         @ 22,0 SAY [GOOD CHOICE, BUT NOT ONE I CAN USE]
         CALL DELAY WITH CHR(1)
         @ 22,0 CLEA
         LOOP
      CASE SELECTNUM = 'Q'
         RETU
      CASE SELECTNUM = 'D'
         S3 = '    '
         CLEA
```

Listing A–15 (cont.)

```
        ? [PLEASE WAIT WHILE I REINDEX THE FILE]
        INDEX ON LEFT(ACCT,2) TO TEMPSUB
        CLEA
        @ 1,0  SAY [AREA TIER COUNTS FOR -> ] + STR(DAY(DATE()),2) + ', ' +;
                   CMONTH(DATE()) + ' ' + STR(YEAR(DATE()),4)
        @ 3,0 SAY [AREA       TIER1   TIER2   TIER3   TIER4   TIER5   TIER6   ]
        SET DEVI TO PRIN
        @ 1,10  SAY [AREA TIER COUNTS FOR -> ] + STR(DAY(DATE()),2) + ', ' +;
                   CMONTH(DATE()) + ' ' + STR(YEAR(DATE()),4)
        @ 3,10 SAY [AREA      TIER1   TIER2   TIER3   TIER4   TIER5   TIER6   ]
        SET DEVI TO SCREEN
        GOTO TOP
*
        DO WHIL .NOT. EOF()
          AREA = LEFT(ACCT,2)
          STARTHERE = RECNO()
*
          COUNT TO T1 FOR TIER1 WHILE AREA = LEFT(ACCT,2)
          GOTO STARTHERE
          COUNT TO T2 FOR TIER2 WHILE AREA = LEFT(ACCT,2)
          GOTO STARTHERE
          COUNT TO T3 FOR TIER3 WHILE AREA = LEFT(ACCT,2)
          GOTO STARTHERE
          COUNT TO T4 FOR TIER4 WHILE AREA = LEFT(ACCT,2)
          GOTO STARTHERE
          COUNT TO T5 FOR TIER5 WHILE AREA = LEFT(ACCT,2)
          GOTO STARTHERE
          COUNT TO T6 FOR TIER6 WHILE AREA = LEFT(ACCT,2)
          @ ROW()+2,0 SAY AREA + '        ' + STR(T1,5) + S3 + STR(T2,5) +;
               S3 + STR(T3,5) + S3 + STR(T4,5) + S3 + STR(T5,5) + S3 +;
               STR(T6,5)
          SET DEVI TO PRIN
          @ PROW()+2,10 SAY AREA + S3 + STR(T1,5) + S3 + STR(T2,5) + S3 +;
               STR(T3,5) + S3 + STR(T4,5) + S3 + STR(T5,5) + S3 +;
               STR(T6,5)
          SET DEVI TO SCREEN
        ENDD
*
        EJECT
        WAIT
        SET INDE TO SUBS, SACCT
        ERAS TEMPSUB.NDX
      CASE SELECTNUM = 'C'
*
        IF YESCON
```

Listing A–15 (cont.)

```
            CONDITION = []
            SET FILT TO
            YESCON = .F.
         ELSE
            CLEA
            DO SUBSAY
            DO SUBGET
            CLEA GETS
            CONDITION = SPACE(60)
            @ 21,0 SAY [CONDITION -> ] GET CONDITION
            READ
*
            IF TRIM(CONDITION) = []
               LOOP
            ELSE
               SET FILT TO &CONDITION
               YESCON = .T.
            ENDI
*
         ENDI
*
         LOOP
      OTHE
         SET PRIN ON
         SET CONS OFF
         ? CHR(15)
         REPORT FORM SUBS
         ? CHR(18)
         SET PRIN OFF
         SET CONS ON
   ENDC
*
ENDD
*
** EOF
```

Listing A–16

```
** MENU.PRG
** THIS IS THE MENU FOR WORKING WITH SUBSCRIBER RECORDS
*
DO WHILE .T.
   SELECTNUM = 'Q'
   CLEA
   @ 1,0,20,79 BOX FRAME
   @ 2,23 SAY [ S U B S C R I B E R   M E N U ]
```

Listing A–16 (cont.)

```
   @ 3,1 SAY DLINE
   @ 6,21 SAY [E -> Edit Subscriber Records]
   @ 7,21 SAY [R -> Print a Report]
   @ 8,21 SAY [T -> Print TV Guide Labels]
   @ 9,21 SAY [C -> Check Payments & Subs Files]
   @ 18,21 SAY [Q -> Quit]
   @ 20,34 SAY [ select ]
   @ 20,43 GET SELECTNUM PICTURE '!'
   READ
   CLEA
*
   DO CASE
      CASE .NOT. SELECTNUM $ [ERTCQ]
         @ 22,0 SAY [GOOD CHOICE, BUT NOT ONE I CAN USE]
         CALL DELAY WITH CHR(1)
         @ 22,0 CLEA
      CASE SELECTNUM = 'Q'
         CLOSE DATA
         RETU
      CASE SELECTNUM = 'E'
         DBFILE = "SUBSCRIPTIONS"
         KEYFIELD = "ACCOUNT"
         FRAMER = "SUBSAY"
         GETTER = "SUBGET"
         USE SUBS INDE SACCT,SUBS
         DO EDIT
      CASE SELECTNUM = 'R'
         DO REPORTER
      CASE SELECTNUM = 'C'
         DO ACCTCK
      CASE SELECTNUM = 'T'
         CLEA
         @  1,10,9,69 BOX FRAME
         @  3,11 SAY LEFT(DLINE,58)
         @  2, 32  SAY "GUIDE LABELS"
         @  5, 19  SAY "S -> START WITH SAMPLES TO ALIGN PRINTER"
         @  6, 19  SAY "P -> START WITHOUT SAMPLES"
         @ 7,19 SAY [Q -> QUIT]
         @  9, 32  SAY " select "
*
         DO WHIL .T.
            SELECTNUM = "Q"
            @ 9,41 GET SELECTNUM PICT '!'
            READ
*
```

Listing A–16 (cont.)

```
            DO CASE
               CASE .NOT. SELECTNUM $ [SPQ]
                  @ 22,0 SAY [GOOD CHOICE, BUT NOT ONE I CAN USE]
                  CALL DELAY WITH CHR(1)
                  @ 22,0 CLEA
                  LOOP
               CASE SELECTNUM = 'Q'
                  EXIT
               CASE SELECTNUM = "S"
                  SET CONS OFF
                  LABEL FORM GUIDES FOR TIER2 .OR. TIER5 SAMPLE TO PRINT
                  SET CONS ON
               CASE SELECTNUM = "P"
                  SET CONS OFF
                  LABEL FORM GUIDES FOR TIER2 .OR. TIER5 TO PRINT
                  SET CONS ON
            ENDC
*
         ENDD
*
   ENDC
*
ENDD
*
** END OF MENU.PRG
```

Listing A–17

```
** DBPC UTILITY
*
   CLEAR
   @ 2, 0, 19,79 BOX FRAME
   @ 3,26 SAY [D B P C   U T I L I T I E S]
   @ 4,1 SAY DLINE
   @  7,28 SAY [D -> Set Date Type]
   @  9,28 SAY [S -> Set Default Drive]
   @ 10,28 SAY [P -> Set Default Path]
   @ 11,28 SAY [R -> Reindex Files]
   @ 12,28 SAY [W -> Select Word Processor]
*   @ 13,28 SAY [ ]
*   @ 14,28 SAY [ ]
   @ 15,28 SAY [Q -> Quit]
   @ 19,33 SAY " select "
*
DO WHILE .T.
   SELECTNUM = 'Q'
```

Listing A–17 (cont.)

```
   @ 19,42 GET selectnum PICT "!"
   READ
*
   DO CASE
      CASE .NOT. SELECTNUM $ [DSPRWQ]
         @ 22,0 SAY [GOOD CHOICE, BUT NOT ONE I CAN USE]
         CALL DELAY WITH CHR(1)
         LOOP
      CASE selectnum = 'Q'
         RETURN
      CASE selectnum = 'S'
         @ 20,0 CLEA
         @ 21,0 SAY "Current default drive is " + CDRIVE
         @ 22,0 SAY "New default drive is -> " GET CDRIVE PICT "A"
         READ
         SET DEFA TO &CDRIVE
      CASE selectnum = 'P'
         @ 20,0 CLEA
         @ 21,0 SAY "Current default path is " + CPATH
         CPATH = CPATH + SPACE(30)
         @ 22,0 SAY "New default path is -> " GET CPATH
         READ
         CPATH = TRIM(CPATH)
         SET PATH TO &CPATH
      CASE SELECTNUM = 'W'
         @ 20,0 CLEA
         ACCE "What is the DOS command to start the word processor? ->  ";
              TO WORDPROC
      CASE selectnum = 'D'
         @ 20,0 CLEA
         @ 20,0, 23,79 BOX FRAME
         @ 21,28 SAY "M -> SET DATE TO MM/DD/YY"
         @ 22,28 SAY "D -> SET DATE TO DD/MM/YY"
         @ 23,33 SAY " select "
         @ 23,42 GET SELECTNUM PICT "!"
         READ
*
         IF SELECTNUM = 'M'
            SETDATE = 1
         ELSE
            SETDATE = 2
         ENDIF
*
         LOOP
      CASE selectnum = 'R'
```

Listing A–17 (cont.)

```
            CALL SAVESCR WITH 'S2'
            DO INDEXER
            CLEA
            CALL SAVESCR WITH 'R2'
      ENDCASE
*
      @ 20,0 CLEA
ENDDO T
*
** END OF UTILMENU.PRG
```

APPENDIX

B

dBASE III PLUS COMMANDS, FUNCTIONS, AND THEIR ABBREVIATIONS

dBASE III PLUS, like many programming languages, makes use of abbreviations in both commands and functions. For example, you can determine the last update of a database with either of these:

```
? LUPDATE()
? LUPD()
```

You can design a new database by coding either one of these commands:

```
CREATE database
CREA database
```

Both of these examples show dBASE III PLUS's flexibility in reading commands and functions. This flexibility has been demonstrated in this book, where four-letter abbreviations and full-length words are used interchangeably. The following isn't a comprehensive list of *all* the variations on III PLUS commands and functions, but it does offer an example of how commands and functions can be abbreviated to save disk and memory space.

dBASE III PLUS COMMANDS, FUNCTIONS, AND THEIR FOUR-LETTER EQUIVALENTS

Not all commands are included in this list; it is merely for example purposes.

Full dBASE III PLUS Command or Function	*Four-Letter Version of Command or Function*
!	!
&	&
*	*
=	=
?	?

Full dBASE III PLUS Command or Function	*Four-Letter Version of Command or Function*
??	??
@ x,y CLEAR	@ x,y CLEA
@ x,y CLEAR TO z,t	@ x,y CLEA TO z,t
@ x,y GET variable	@ x,y GET variable
@ x,y GET variable RANGE	@ x,y GET variable RANG
@ x,y SAY something	@ x,y SAY something
@ x,y SAY something GET variable PICTURE RANGE	@ x,y SAY something GET variable PICT RANG
@ x,y SAY something GET variable RANGE	@ x,y SAY something GET variable RANG
@ x,y SAY something PICTURE	@ x,y SAY something PICT
@ x,y SAY something PICTURE '@func'	@ x,y SAY something PICT '@func'
@ x,y TO z,t	@ x,y TO z,t
@ x,y TO z,t DOUBLE	@ x,y TO z,t DOUB
ACCEPT	ACCE
APPEND	APPE
APPEND BLANK	APPE BLAN
APPEND FROM	APPE FROM
APPEND FROM DELIMETED	APPE FROM DELI
APPEND FROM FOR	APPE FROM FOR
APPEND FROM SDF	APPE FROM SDF
APPEND FROM TYPE	APPE FROM TYPE
ASC()	ASC()
ASSIST	ASSI
AT()	AT()
AVERAGE	AVER
BOF()	BOF()
BROWSE	BROWSE
BROWSE FIELDS	BROW FIEL
BROWSE FREEZE	BROW FREE
BROWSE LOCK	BROW LOCK
BROWSE NOFOLLOW	BROW NOFO
BROWSE NOMENU	BROW NOME
BROWSE WIDTH	BROW WIDT
CALL WITH	CALL WITH
CANCEL	CANCEL
CDOW()	CDOW()
CHANGE	CHAN
CHR()	CHR()
CLEAR	CLEA
CLEAR ALL	CLEA ALL
CLEAR GETS	CLEA GETS
CLEAR MEMORY	CLEA MEMO
CLOSE ALTERNATE	CLOS ALTE
CLOSE DATABASE	CLOS DATA

Full dBASE III PLUS Command or Function	*Four-Letter Version of Command or Function*
CLOSE FORMAT	CLOS FORM
CLOSE INDEX	CLOS INDE
CLOSE PROCEDURE	CLOS PROC
CMONTH()	CMON()
COL()	COL()
CONTINUE	CONT
COPY FILE	COPY FILE
COPY STRUCTURE TO	COPY STRU TO
COPY TO	COPY TO
COPY TO TYPE	COPY TO TYPE
COPY TO file DELIMITED	COPY TO file DELI
COPY TO file FIELDS	COPY TO file FIEL
COPY TO file FIELDS FOR cond1 WHILE cond2	COPY TO file FIEL FOR cond1 WHIL cond2
COPY TO file FIELDS FOR condition	COPY TO file FIEL FOR condition
COPY TO file FOR cond1 WHILE cond2	COPY TO file FOR cond1 WHIL cond2
COPY TO file FOR condition	COPY TO file FOR condition
COPY TO file SDF	COPY TO file SDF
COPY TO file WHILE condition	COPY TO file WHIL condition
COPY TO file WITH DELIMITER character	COPY TO file WITH DELI character
COUNT	COUN
CREATE	CREA
CREATE CATALOG	CREA CATA
CREATE COMMAND	CREA COMM
CREATE LABEL	CREA LABE
CREATE QUERY	CREA QUER
CREATE REPORT	CREA REPO
CREATE VIEW	CREA VIEW
CREATE VIEW FROM ENVIRONMENT	CREA VIEW FROM ENVI
CREATE database	CREA database
CTOD()	CTOD()
DATE()	DATE()
DAY()	DAY()
DBF()	DBF()
DELETE FILE	DELE FILE
DELETED()	DELE()
DIR	DIR
DISKSPACE()	DISK()
DISPLAY	DISP
DISPLAY ALL	DISP ALL
DISPLAY ALL FIELDS	DISP ALL FIEL
DISPLAY FILES	DISP FILE
DISPLAY HISTORY	DISP HIST
DISPLAY MEMORY	DISP MEMO
DISPLAY RECORD()	DISP RECO()

Full dBASE III PLUS Command or Function	*Four-Letter Version of Command or Function*
DISPLAY REST	DISP REST
DISPLAY STATUS	DISP STAT
DISPLAY STRUCTURE	DISP STRU
DISPLAY USERS	DISP USER
DO	DO
DO CASE...CASE...OTHERWISE...ENDCASE	DO CASE...CASE...OTHE...ENDC
DO WHILE...LOOP...EXIT...ENDDO	DO WHIL...LOOP...EXIT...ENDD
DO WITH	DO WITH
DOW()	DOW()
DTOC()	DTOC()
EDIT	EDIT
EJECT	EJEC
EOF()	EOF()
ERASE	ERAS
ERROR()	ERRO()
EXIT	EXIT
EXP()	EXP()
EXPORT	EXPO
FIELD()	FIEL()
FILE()	FILE()
FIND	FIND
FKLABEL()	FKLA()
FKMAX()	FKMA()
FLOCK()	FLOC()
FOUND()	FOUN()
GETENV()	GETE()
GO BOTTOM	GO BOTT
GO TOP	GO TOP
GO n	GO n
GOTO BOTTOM	GOTO BOTT
GOTO TOP	GOTO TOP
GOTO n	GOTO n
HELP	HELP
IF...ELSE...ENDIF	IF...ELSE...ENDI
IIF()	IIF()
IMPORT	IMPO
INDEX	INDE
INKEY()	INKE()
INPUT	INPU
INSERT	INSE
INSERT BEFORE	INSE BEFO
INSERT BLANK	INSE BLAN
INT()	INT()
ISALPHA()	ISAL()

Full dBASE III PLUS Command or Function	*Four-Letter Version of Command or Function*
ISCOLOR()	ISCO()
ISLOWER()	ISLO()
ISUPPER()	ISUP()
JOIN	JOIN
LABEL FORM	LABE FORM
LEFT()	LEFT()
LEN()	LEN()
LIST	LIST
LIST FIELDS	LIST FIEL
LIST HISTORY	LIST HIST
LIST MEMORY	LIST MEMO
LIST RECORD()	LIST RECO()
LIST REST	LIST REST
LIST STATUS	LIST STAT
LIST STRUCTURE	LIST STRU
LOAD	LOAD
LOCATE	LOCA
LOCK()	LOCK()
LOG()	LOG()
LOOP	LOOP
LOWER()	LOWE()
LTRIM()	LTRI()
LUPDATE()	LUPD()
MAX()	MAX()
MESSAGE()	MESS()
MIN()	MIN()
MOD()	MOD()
MODIFY COMMAND	MODI COMM
MODIFY FILE	MODI FILE
MODIFY LABEL	MODI LABE
MODIFY QUERY	MODI QUER
MODIFY REPORT	MODI REPO
MODIFY SCREEN	MODI SCRE
MODIFY STRUCTURE	MODI STRU
MODIFY VIEW	MODI VIEW
MONTH()	MONT()
NDX()	NDX()
NOTE	NOTE
ON ERROR	ON ERRO
ON ESCAPE	ON ESCA
ON KEY	ON KEY
PACK	PACK
PARAMETERS	PARA
PCOL()	PCOL()

Full dBASE III PLUS Command or Function	*Four-Letter Version of Command or Function*
PRIVATE	PRIV
PROW()	PROW()
PUBLIC	PUBL
QUIT	QUIT
READ	READ
READKEY()	READ()
RECALL	RECA
RECCOUNT()	RECC()
RECNO()	RECN()
RECSIZE()	RECS()
REINDEX	REIN
RELEASE	RELE
RELEASE MODULE	RELE MODU
RENAME	RENA
REPLACE	REPL
REPLICATE()	REPL()
REPORT	REPO
RESTORE	REST
RETRY	RETR
RETURN	RETU
RETURN TO MASTER	RETU TO MAST
RIGHT()	RIGH()
RLOCK()	RLOC()
ROUND()	ROUN()
ROW()	ROW()
RTRIM()	RTRI()
RUN	RUN
SAVE	SAVE
SEEK	SEEK
SELECT	SELE
SET	SET
SET ALTERNATE ON/OFF	SET ALTE ON/OFF
SET ALTERNATE TO	SET ALTE TO
SET BELL ON/OFF	SET BELL ON/OFF
SET CARRY ON/OFF	SET CARR ON/OFF
SET CATALOG ON/OFF	SET CATA ON/OFF
SET CATALOG TO	SET CATA TO
SET CENTURY ON/OFF	SET CENT ON/OFF
SET COLOR ON/OFF	SET COLO ON/OFF
SET COLOR TO	SET COLO TO
SET CONFIRM ON/OFF	SET CONF ON/OFF
SET CONSOLE ON/OFF	SET CONS ON/OFF
SET DATE	SET DATE
SET DEBUG ON/OFF	SET DEBU ON/OFF

Full dBASE III PLUS Command or Function	*Four-Letter Version of Command or Function*
SET DECIMALS TO	SET DECI TO
SET DELETED ON/OFF	SET DELE ON/OFF
SET DELIMITER ON/OFF	SET DELI ON/OFF
SET DELIMITER TO DEFAULT	SET DELI TO DEFA
SET DELIMITER TO c1,c2	SET DELI TO c1,c2
SET DEVICE TO SCREEN/PRINTER	SET DEVI TO SCRE/PRIN
SET DOHISTORY ON/OFF	SET DOHI ON/OFF
SET ECHO ON/OFF	SET ECHO ON/OFF
SET ENCRYPTION ON/OFF	SET ENCR ON/OFF
SET ESCAPE ON/OFF	SET ESCA ON/OFF
SET EXACT ON/OFF	SET EXAC ON/OFF
SET FIELDS ON/OFF	SET FIEL ON/OFF
SET FIELDS TO	SET FIEL TO
SET FILTER TO FILE	SET FILT TO FILE
SET FILTER TO condition	SET FILT TO condition
SET FIXED ON/OFF	SET FIXE ON/OFF
SET FORMAT TO	SET FORM TO
SET FUNCTION # TO	SET FUNC # TO
SET FUNCTION name TO	SET FUNC name TO
SET HEADING ON/OFF	SET HEAD ON/OFF
SET HELP ON/OFF	SET HELP ON/OFF
SET HISTORY ON/OFF	SET HIST ON/OFF
SET HISTORY TO	SET HIST TO
SET INDEX TO	SET INDE TO
SET INTENSITY ON/OFF	SET INTE ON/OFF
SET MARGIN TO	SET MARG TO
SET MEMOWIDTH TO	SET MEMO TO
SET MENUS ON/OFF	SET MENU ON/OFF
SET MESSAGE TO	SET MESS TO
SET ORDER TO	SET ORDE TO
SET PATH TO	SET PATH TO
SET PRINTER ON/OFF	SET PRIN ON/OFF
SET PRINTER TO	SET PRIN TO
SET PROCEDURE TO	SET PROC TO
SET RELATION TO	SET RELA TO
SET SAFETY ON/OFF	SET SAFE ON/OFF
SET SCOREBOARD ON/OFF	SET SCOR ON/OFF
SET STATUS ON/OFF	SET STAT ON/OFF
SET STEP ON/OFF	SET STEP ON/OFF
SET TALK ON/OFF	SET TALK ON/OFF
SET TITLE ON/OFF	SET TITL ON/OFF
SET TYPEAHEAD TO	SET TYPE TO
SET UNIQUE ON/OFF	SET UNIQ ON/OFF
SET VIEW TO	SET VIEW TO

Full dBASE III PLUS Command or Function	*Four-Letter Version of Command or Function*
SKIP	SKIP
SORT	SORT
SPACE()	SPAC()
SQRT()	SQRT()
STORE	STOR
STUFF()	STUF()
SUBSTR()	SUBS()
SUM	SUM
TEXT...ENDTEXT	TEXT...ENDT
TIME()	TIME()
TOTAL	TOTA
TRANSFORM()	TRAN()
TRIM()	TRIM()
TYPE()	TYPE()
UNLOCK	UNLO
UPDATE	UPDA
UPPER()	UPPE()
USE	USE
USE ENCRYPTION	USE ENCR
VAL()	VAL()
VERSION()	VERS()
WAIT	WAIT
YEAR()	YEAR()
ZAP	ZAP

INDEX

E

F

G

H

I

Use this form to order a set of two companion diskettes containing all the code in *dBASE III PLUS Programmer's Library*. The diskettes are 5-1/4" floppies prepared for IBM-compatible personal computers running under DOS 2.0 or higher.

The set of diskettes sells for $40 (U.S.), including shipping and handling, and may be purchased with a check or money order made out to "Northern Lights, Inc." (No cash, please.)

Send this form with your payment to:

Joseph-David Carrabis
c/o Howard W. Sams & Company
4300 West 62nd Street
Indianapolis, IN 46268

Howard W. Sams & Company assumes no liability with respect to the use or accuracy of the information contained in these diskettes.

- -

Diskette Order Form

Carrabis, *dBASE III PLUS Programmer's Library,* #22579

Name ______________________ Company ______________________

Address ____

City ______________________ State ______________________

Phone ( ) ______________________ Date ______________________

Place of book purchase ______________________________

Number of sets ordered ______ @ $40 Amount enclosed $ ______

☐ Check number ____________ ☐ Money order number ______